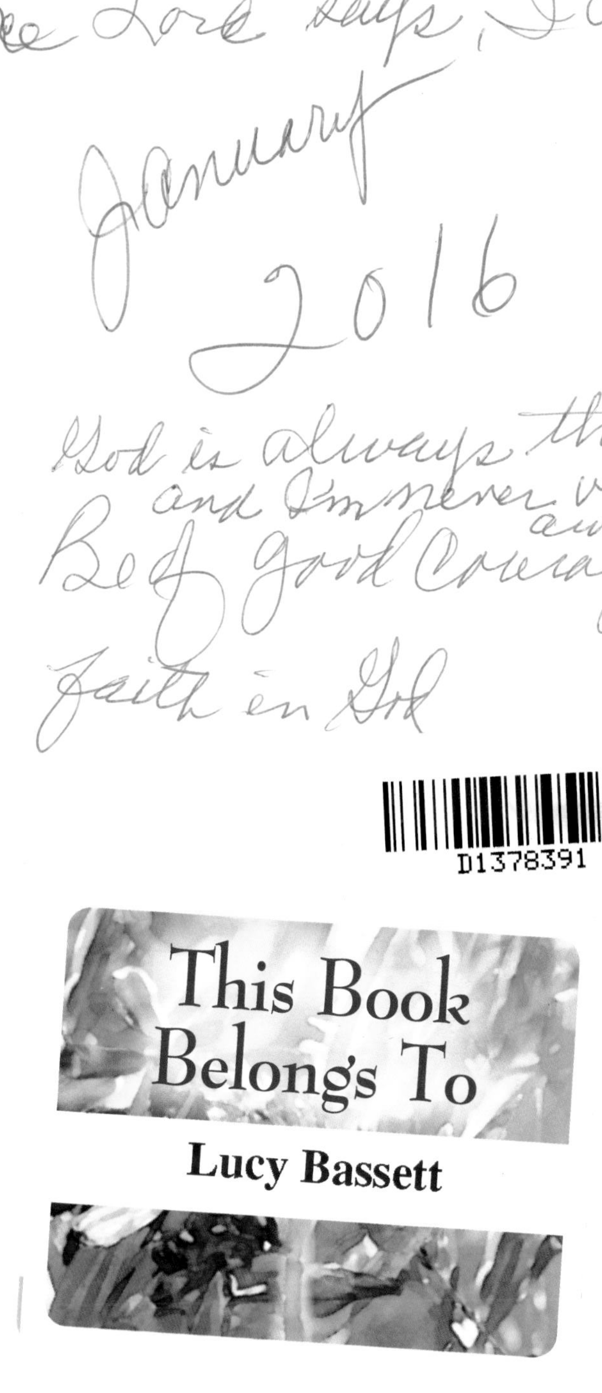
The Lord says, I am c you
January
2016
God is always there for you
and I'm never very far
away either
Be of Good Courage, have
Faith in God
D1378391
This Book
Belongs To
Lucy Bassett

Homeward Bound

Daily Meditations from the Great Themes of Ellen White

ELLEN G. WHITE

REVIEW AND HERALD® PUBLISHING ASSOCIATION
Since 1861 | www.reviewandherald.com

Cover design by Gerald Lee Monks
Cover design resources from iStockphoto
Inside design by Aaron Troia

Printed by Pacific Press® Publishing Association, Nampa, ID
Printed in the United States of America

Bible texts used by Ellen G. White are from either the King James Version or the Revised Version (identified R.V.).

You can obtain additional copies of this book by calling toll-free 1-800-765-6955 or by visiting http://www.adventistbookcenter.com.

ISBN 13: 978-0-8163-5737-6
ISBN 10: 0-8163-5737-4

May 2015

Contents

MARCH — SURRENDER AND ACCEPTANCE

APRIL — VICTORY IN CHRIST

MAY — KEY TO HEAVEN'S STOREHOUSE

JUNE — LAW AND SABBATH: DUAL TEST OF LOYALITY

JULY — PRACTICAL CHRISTIAN LIVING

AUGUST — A UNITED CHURCH

SEPTEMBER — THE FAMILY OF GOD

OCTOBER — JESUS, OUR HIGH PRIEST

NOVEMBER — THE GREAT CONTROVERSY

DECEMBER — THE BEGINNING OF ETERNITY

Foreword

Revelation 14:6–11 presents the three angels' messages, in which Seventh-day Adventists find their commission. Then verse 12 helps provide their identity: "Here is the patience of the saints; here are those who keep the commandments of God and the faith of Jesus." Immediately after, the very next verse includes this blessing: " 'Blessed are the dead who die in the Lord from now on' . . . 'that they may rest from their labors, and their works follow them' " (v. 13). Ellen G. White, one of the founders of the Seventh-day Adventist movement, who helped proclaim those three messages and urged keeping the commandments and the faith of Jesus, died in 1915. Her works have followed her, especially in the writings she left with us.

Those writings have inspired and instructed the church since its beginning. They have given us important insights into Scripture, enriching our Bible understanding. They have contributed significant instruction on organization, education, publishing, and other matters relating to church structure. They have presented key principles regarding diet, health, spiritual growth, and other topics of personal benefit to Christ's followers. Where the church has taken these writings seriously, the members and the organization have been blessed.

In Ellen White's later years, she often included an autographed note in copies of her books that she gave away (see a photo of one of her notes at the end of this foreword). The opening words on this note were "We are homeward bound." This unshakeable belief in the return of Christ and the promise of heaven was a hallmark of her life and ministry. It therefore seems appropriate that the title and focus of this collection of daily meditative thoughts, released during the centennial year of her death, is *Homeward Bound.*

As we mark a century's passing since Ellen White's death, it is fitting that *Homeward Bound* provides a retrospective of some of the major themes she dealt with in those writings. Each month's readings will take up one of these themes. In doing so, this book may depart in some respects from the customary devotional book pattern. The readings are not aimed solely at providing inspirational uplift, but at presenting matters that Ellen White deemed important. Sometimes these will call on the readers to do or to avoid certain things as part of their faithful service for the Lord. Sometimes they will highlight particular aspects of Seventh-day Adventist teaching and Bible understanding, such as Satan's fate during the millennium and at its close. Items like this are included here because they are a part of Ellen White's emphasis on the given theme.

In keeping with recent practice in the devotional books, the readings here have reduced her generic use of such words as *man, men, brethren, he, him,* and *his,* which were widely used in Ellen White's time to refer to men and women in general, but which usage is much less common today. Without altering Ellen White's meaning, these adjustments in meaning will avoid distracting the reader from the message of the passage.

Ellen G. White famously wrote, "We have nothing to fear for the future, except as we shall forget the way the Lord has led us, and His teaching in our past history" (*Life Sketches of Ellen G. White,* p. 196). It is our prayer that this volume may remind us not only of how the Lord has led us but also of His teaching through His servant Ellen G. White.

—The Ellen G. White Estate Board of Trustees

We are homeward bound. A little longer, and the strife will be over. May we who stand in the heat of the conflict, ever keep before us a vision of things unseen—of that time when the world will be bathed in the light of heaven, when the years will move on in gladness, when over the scene the morning stars will sing together and the sons of God will shout for joy, while God and Christ will unite in proclaiming, "There shall be no more sin, neither shall there be any more death." "Forgetting those things which are behind, and reaching forth unto those things which are before," let us "press toward the mark for the prize of the high calling of God in Christ Jesus."

Ellen G. White.

The Book of Books

January 1

For the Common People

The words that I speak to you are spirit, and they are life.—John 6:63.

The Bible was not written for the scholar alone; on the contrary, it was designed for the common people. The great truths necessary for salvation are made as clear as noonday; and none will mistake and lose their way except those who follow their own judgment instead of the plainly revealed will of God.

We should not take the testimony of anyone as to what the Scriptures teach, but should study the words of God for ourselves. If we allow others to do our thinking, we shall have crippled energies and contracted abilities. The noble powers of the mind may be so dwarfed by lack of exercise on themes worthy of their concentration as to lose their ability to grasp the deep meaning of the word of God. The mind will enlarge if it is employed in tracing out the relation of the subjects of the Bible, comparing scripture with scripture and spiritual things with spiritual.

There is nothing more calculated to strengthen the intellect than the study of the Scriptures. No other book is so potent to elevate the thoughts, to give vigor to the faculties, as the broad, ennobling truths of the Bible. If God's word were studied as it should be, people would have a breadth of mind, a nobility of character, and a stability of purpose rarely seen in these times.

But there is but little benefit derived from a hasty reading of the Scriptures. One may read the whole Bible through and yet fail to see its beauty or comprehend its deep and hidden meaning. One passage studied until its significance is clear to the mind and its relation to the plan of salvation is evident, is of more value than the perusal of many chapters with no definite purpose in view and no positive instruction gained. Keep your Bible with you. As you have opportunity, read it; fix the texts in your memory. Even while you are walking the streets you may read a passage and meditate upon it, thus fixing it in the mind.

We cannot obtain wisdom without earnest attention and prayerful study. . . . There must be careful research and prayerful reflection. And such study will be richly repaid. . . .

Never should the Bible be studied without prayer. Before opening its pages we should ask for the enlightenment of the Holy Spirit, and it will be given.—*Steps to Christ*, pp. 89–91.

Food for the Soul

It is written, "Man shall not live by bread alone, but by every word of God."
—Luke 4:4.

Education is but a preparation of the physical, intellectual, and spiritual powers for the best performance of all the duties of life. The powers of endurance, and the strength and activity of the brain, are lessened or increased by the way in which they are employed. The mind should be so disciplined that all its powers will be symmetrically developed. . . .

The nature of one's religious experience is revealed by the character of the books one chooses to read in one's leisure moments. In order to have a healthy tone of mind and sound religious principles, the youth must live in communion with God through His word. Pointing out the way of salvation through Christ, the Bible is our guide to a higher, better life. It contains the most interesting and the most instructive history and biography that were ever written. Those whose imagination has not become perverted by the reading of fiction will find the Bible the most interesting of books.

The Bible is the book of books. If you love the Word of God, searching it as you have opportunity, that you may come into possession of its rich treasures, and be thoroughly furnished unto all good works, then you may be assured that Jesus is drawing you to Himself. But to read the Scriptures in a casual way, without seeking to comprehend Christ's lesson that you may comply with His requirements, is not enough. There are treasures in the word of God that can be discovered only by sinking the shaft deep into the mine of truth.

The carnal mind rejects the truth; but the soul that is converted undergoes a marvelous change. The book that before was unattractive because it revealed truths which testified against the sinner, now becomes the food of the soul, the joy and consolation of the life. The Sun of righteousness illuminates the sacred pages, and the Holy Spirit speaks through them to the soul. . . .

Let all who have cultivated a love for light reading, now turn their attention to the sure word of prophecy. Take your Bibles, and begin to study with fresh interest the sacred records of the Old and New Testaments. The oftener and more diligently you study the Bible, the more beautiful will it appear, and the less relish you will have for light reading. Bind this precious volume to your hearts. It will be to you a friend and guide.—*Messages to Young People*, pp. 271, 273, 274.

JANUARY 3

ONLY RULE OF FAITH

He who hears My word and believes in Him who sent Me has everlasting life.
—John 5:24.

The Bible is the only rule of faith and doctrine. . . .

Those who are teaching the most solemn message ever given to the world, should discipline the mind to comprehend its significance. The theme of redemption will bear the most concentrated study, and its depth will never be fully explored. You need not fear that you will exhaust this wonderful theme. Drink deep of the well of salvation. Go to the fountain for yourself, that you may be filled with refreshment, that Jesus may be in you a well of water, springing up unto everlasting life. Only Bible truth and Bible religion will stand the test of the judgment. We are not to pervert the word of God to suit our convenience, and worldly interests, but to honestly inquire, "What wilt thou have me to do?" "Ye are not your own, for ye are bought with a price." And what a price! Not "with corruptible things, as silver and gold, . . . but with the precious blood of Christ." When the human race was lost, the Son of God said, I will redeem them, I will become their surety and substitute. He laid aside His royal robes, clothed His divinity with humanity, stepped down from the royal throne, that He might reach the very depth of human woe and temptation, lift up our fallen natures, and make it possible for us to be overcomers—the sons and daughers of God, the heirs of the eternal kingdom. Shall we then allow any consideration of earth to turn us away from the path of truth? Shall we not challenge every doctrine and theory, and put it to the test of God's word?

We should not allow any human argument to turn us away from a thorough investigation of Bible truth. Human opinions and customs are not to be received as of divine authority. God has revealed in His word what is the whole duty of man, and we are not to be swayed from the great standard of righteousness. He sent His only begotten Son to be our example, and bade us to hear and to follow Him. We must not be influenced from the truth as it is in Jesus, because great and professedly good people urge their ideas above the plain statements of the word of God.

The work of Christ is to draw us from the false and spurious to the true and genuine. "He that followeth me shall not walk in darkness, but shall have the light of life." (John 8:12.)—*Fundamentals of Christian Education*, pp. 126–128.

January 4

Behold Wondrous Things

Stand still and consider the wondrous works of God.—Job 37:14.

People of piety and talent catch views of eternal realities, but often they fail of understanding, because the things that are seen eclipse the glory of the unseen. Those who would seek successfully for the hidden treasure must rise to higher pursuits than the things of this world. Their affections and all their capabilities must be consecrated to the search.

Disobedience has closed the door to a vast amount of knowledge that might have been gained from the Scriptures. Understanding means obedience to God's commandments. The Scriptures are not to be adapted to meet human prejudice and jealousy. They can be understood only by those who are humbly seeking for a knowledge of the truth that they may obey it.

Do you ask, What shall I do to be saved? You must lay your preconceived opinions, your hereditary and cultivated ideas, at the door of investigation. If you search the Scriptures to vindicate your own opinions, you will never reach the truth. Search in order to learn what the Lord says. If conviction comes as you search, if you see that your cherished opinions are not in harmony with the truth, do not misinterpret the truth in order to suit your own belief, but accept the light given. Open mind and heart that you may behold wondrous things out of God's word.

Faith in Christ as the world's Redeemer calls for an acknowledgment of the enlightened intellect controlled by a heart that can discern and appreciate the heavenly treasure. This faith is inseparable from repentance and transformation of character. To have faith means to find and accept the gospel treasure, with all the obligations which it imposes. . . .

We need the enlightenment of the Holy Spirit in order to discern the truths in God's word. The lovely things of the natural world are not seen until the sun, dispelling the darkness, floods them with its light. So the treasures in the word of God are not appreciated until they are revealed by the bright beams of the Sun of Righteousness.

The Holy Spirit, sent from heaven by the benevolence of infinite love, takes the things of God and reveals them to every soul that has an implicit faith in Christ. By His power the vital truths upon which the salvation of the soul depends are impressed upon the mind, and the way of life is made so plain that none need err therein.—*Christ's Object Lessons,* pp. 112, 113.

January 5, 2016

Live in the Atmosphere of Heaven

Call to Me, and I will answer you, and show you great and mighty things.
—*Jeremiah 33:3.*

All who with sincere and teachable spirit study God's word, seeking to comprehend its truths, will be brought in touch with its Author; and, except by their own choice, there is no limit to the possibilities of their development.

In its wide range of style and subjects the Bible has something to interest every mind and appeal to every heart. In its pages are found history the most ancient; biography the truest to life; principles of government for the control of the state, for the regulation of the household—principles that human wisdom has never equaled. It contains philosophy the most profound, poetry the sweetest and the most sublime, the most impassioned and the most pathetic [touching]. Immeasurably superior in value to the productions of any human author are the Bible writings, even when thus considered; but of infinitely wider scope, of infinitely greater value, are they when viewed in their relation to the grand central thought. Viewed in the light of this thought, every topic has a new significance. In the most simply stated truths are involved principles that are as high as heaven and that compass eternity. . . .

With the word of God in their hands, all human beings, wherever their lot in life may be cast, may have such companionship as they shall choose. In its pages they may hold converse with the noblest and best of the human race, and may listen to the voice of the Eternal as He speaks with humanity. As they study and meditate upon the themes into which "the angels desire to look" (1 Peter 1:12), they may have their companionship. They may follow the steps of the heavenly Teacher, and listen to His words as when He taught on mountain and plain and sea. They may dwell in this world in the atmosphere of heaven, imparting to earth's sorrowing and tempted ones thoughts of hope and longings for holiness; themselves coming closer and still closer into fellowship with the Unseen; like him of old who walked with God, drawing nearer and nearer the threshold of the eternal world, until the portals shall open, and they shall enter there. They will find themselves no strangers. The voices that will greet them are the voices of the holy ones, who, unseen, were on earth their companions—voices that here they learned to distinguish and to love. Those who through the word of God have lived in fellowship with heaven, will find themselves at home in heaven's companionship.—*Education,* pp. 125, 127.

January 6

A Transcript of God's Will

Your word I have hidden in my heart, that I might not sin against You.
—Psalm 119:11.

In the precepts of His holy law, God has given a perfect rule of life; and He has declared that until the close of time this law, unchanged in a single jot or tittle, is to maintain its claim upon human beings. Christ came to magnify the law and make it honorable. He showed that it is based upon the broad foundation of love to God and love to man, and that obedience to its precepts comprises the whole duty of man. In His own life He gave an example of obedience to the law of God. In the Sermon on the Mount He showed how its requirements extend beyond the outward acts and take cognizance of the thoughts and intents of the heart.

The law, obeyed, leads us to deny "ungodliness and worldly lusts," and to "live soberly, righteously, and godly, in this present world." (Titus 2:12.) But the enemy of all righteousness has taken the world captive and has led men and women to disobey the law. As Paul foresaw, multitudes have turned from the plain, searching truths of God's word and have chosen teachers who present to them the fables they desire. Many among both ministers and people are trampling under their feet the commandments of God. Thus the Creator of the world is insulted, and Satan laughs in triumph at the success of his devices.

With the growing contempt for God's law there is an increasing distaste for religion, an increase of pride, love of pleasure, disobedience to parents, and self-indulgence; and thoughtful minds everywhere are anxiously inquiring, What can be done to correct these alarming evils? The answer is found in Paul's exhortation to Timothy, "Preach the word." (2 Timothy 4:2.) In the Bible are found the only safe principles of action. It is a transcript of the will of God, an expression of divine wisdom. It opens to our understanding the great problems of life, and to all who heed its precepts it will prove an unerring guide, keeping them from wasting their lives in misdirected effort.

God has made known His will, and it is folly for anyone to question that which has gone out of His lips. After Infinite Wisdom has spoken, there can be no doubtful questions for us to settle, no wavering possibilities for us to adjust. All that is required of us is a frank, earnest concurrence in the expressed will of God. Obedience is the highest dictate of reason as well as of conscience.—*The Acts of the Apostles,* pp. 505, 506.

January 7

The Plan of Salvation Made Plain

Fear God and keep His commandments, for this is man's all.
—Ecclesiastes 12:13.

In the Bible the whole duty of man is defined. Solomon says, "Fear God, and keep his commandments: for this is the whole duty of man." The will of God is revealed in His written word, and this is the essential knowledge. Human wisdom, familiarity with the languages of different nations, is a help in the missionary work. An understanding of the customs of the people, of the location and time of events, is practical knowledge; for it aids in making the figures of the Bible clear, in bringing out the force of Christ's lessons; but it is not positively necessary to know these things. The wayfaring man may find the pathway cast up for the ransomed to walk in, and there will be no excuse found for any one who perishes through misapprehension of the Scriptures.

In the Bible every vital principle is declared, every duty made plain, every obligation made evident. The whole duty of man is summed up by the Saviour. He says, "Thou shalt love the Lord thy God with all thy heart, and with all thy soul, and with all thy mind. . . . Thou shalt love thy neighbor as thyself." In the word the plan of salvation is plainly delineated. The gift of eternal life is promised on condition of saving faith in Christ. The drawing power of the Holy Spirit is pointed out as an agent in the work of our salvation. The rewards of the faithful, the punishment of the guilty, are all laid out in clear lines. The Bible contains the science of salvation for all those who will hear and do the words of Christ.

The apostle says, "All scripture is given by inspiration of God, and is profitable for doctrine, for reproof, for correction, for instruction in righteousness: that the man of God may be perfect, throughly furnished unto all good works." The Bible is its own expositor. One passage will prove to be a key that will unlock other passages, and in this way light will be shed upon the hidden meaning of the word. By comparing different texts treating on the same subject, viewing their bearing on every side, the true meaning of the Scriptures will be made evident. . . .

The Lord God, the Creator of the worlds, at infinite cost has given the gospel to the world.—*Fundamentals of Christian Education,* pp. 186–188.

January 8

Hearing Jesus' Voice

You search the Scriptures, for in them you think you have eternal life; and these are they which testify of Me.—John 5:39.

God speaks to us in His word. Here we have in clearer lines the revelation of His character, of His dealings with us, and the great work of redemption. Here is open before us the history of patriarchs and prophets and other holy believers of old. They were "subject to like passions as we are." (James 5:17.) We see how they struggled through discouragements like our own, how they fell under temptation as we have done, and yet took heart again and conquered through the grace of God; and, beholding, we are encouraged in our striving after righteousness. As we read of the precious experiences granted them, of the light and love and blessing it was theirs to enjoy, and of the work they wrought through the grace given them, the spirit that inspired them kindles a flame of holy emulation in our hearts and a desire to be like them in character—like them to walk with God.

Jesus said of the Old Testament Scriptures—and how much more is it true of the New—"They are they which testify of Me," the Redeemer, Him in whom our hopes of eternal life are centered. (John 5:39.) Yes, the whole Bible tells of Christ. From the first record of creation—for "without Him was not anything made that was made"—to the closing promise, "Behold, I come quickly," we are reading of His works and listening to His voice. (John 1:3; Revelation 22:12.) If you would become acquainted with the Saviour, study the Holy Scriptures.

Fill the whole heart with the words of God. They are the living water, quenching your burning thirst. They are the living bread from heaven. Jesus declares, "Except ye eat the flesh of the Son of man, and drink His blood, ye have no life in you." And He explains Himself by saying, "The words that I speak unto you, they are spirit, and they are life." (John 6:53, 63.) Our bodies are built up from what we eat and drink; and as in the natural economy, so in the spiritual economy: it is what we meditate upon that will give tone and strength to our spiritual nature.

The theme of redemption is one that the angels desire to look into; it will be the science and the song of the redeemed throughout the ceaseless ages of eternity. Is it not worthy of careful thought and study now?—*Steps to Christ*, pp. 87–89.

January 9, 2016

The Keys of Heaven

And I will give you the keys of the kingdom of heaven.
—Matthew 16:19.

Jesus continued: "I say also unto thee, That thou art Peter, and upon this rock I will build My church; and the gates of hell shall not prevail against it." (Matthew 16:18.) The word Peter signifies a stone—a rolling stone. Peter was not the rock upon which the church was founded. The gates of hell did prevail against him when he denied his Lord with cursing and swearing. The church was built upon One against whom the gates of hell could not prevail. . . .

"Upon this rock," said Jesus, "I will build My church." In the presence of God, and all the heavenly intelligences, in the presence of the unseen army of hell, Christ founded His church upon the living Rock. That Rock is Himself—His own body, for us broken and bruised. Against the church built upon this foundation, the gates of hell shall not prevail.

How feeble the church appeared when Christ spoke these words! There was only a handful of believers, against whom all the power of demons and evil men would be directed; yet the followers of Christ were not to fear. Built upon the Rock of their strength, they could not be overthrown.

For six thousand years, faith has builded upon Christ. For six thousand years the floods and tempests of satanic wrath have beaten upon the Rock of our salvation; but it stands unmoved. Peter had expressed the truth which is the foundation of the church's faith, and Jesus now honored him as the representative of the whole body of believers. He said, "I will give unto thee the keys of the kingdom of heaven: and whatsoever thou shalt bind on earth shall be bound in heaven: and whatsoever thou shalt loose on earth shall be loosed in heaven." (Verse 19.)

"The keys of the kingdom of heaven" are the words of Christ. All the words of Holy Scripture are His, and are here included. These words have power to open and to shut heaven. They declare the conditions upon which people are received or rejected. Thus the work of those who preach God's word is a savor of life unto life or of death unto death. Theirs is a mission weighted with eternal results.—*The Desire of Ages,* pp. 412–414.

January 10

Without Rival

Your testimonies also are my delight and my counselors.
—Psalm 119:24.

No other study will so ennoble every thought, feeling, and aspiration as the study of the Scriptures. This Sacred Word is the will of God revealed to humanity. Here we may learn what God expects of the beings formed in His image. Here we learn how to improve the present life and how to secure the future life. No other book can satisfy the questionings of the mind and the craving of the heart. By obtaining a knowledge of God's word, and giving heed thereto, we may rise from the lowest depths of ignorance and degradation to become the sons and daughters of God, the associates of sinless angels.

A clear conception of what God is, and what He requires us to be, will give us humble views of self. Those who study aright the Sacred Word will learn that human intellect is not omnipotent; that, without the help which none but God can give, human strength and wisdom are but weakness and ignorance.

As an educating power the Bible is without a rival. Nothing will so impart vigor to all the faculties as requiring students to grasp the stupendous truths of revelation. The mind gradually adapts itself to the subjects upon which it is allowed to dwell. If occupied with commonplace matters only, to the exclusion of grand and lofty themes, it will become dwarfed and enfeebled. If never required to grapple with difficult problems, or put to the stretch to comprehend important truths, it will, after a time, almost lose the power of growth.

The Bible is the most comprehensive and the most instructive history which mankind possesses. It came fresh from the fountain of eternal truth, and a divine hand has preserved its purity through all the ages. Its bright rays shine into the far distant past, where human research seeks vainly to penetrate. In God's word alone we find an authentic account of creation. Here we behold the power that laid the foundation of the earth and that stretched out the heavens. Here only can we find a history of our race, unsullied by human prejudice or human pride.

In the word of God the mind finds subject for the deepest thought, the loftiest aspiration. Here we may hold communion with patriarchs and prophets, and listen to the voice of the Eternal as he speaks with mortals. Here we behold the Majesty of heaven.—*Testimonies for the Church,* vol. 5, pp. 24, 25.

January 11

Creative Energy

By the word of the Lord the heavens were made, and all the host of them by the breath of His mouth.—Psalm 33:6.

The creative energy that called the worlds into existence is in the word of God. This word imparts power; it begets life. Every command is a promise; accepted by the will, received into the soul, it brings with it the life of the Infinite One. It transforms the nature and re-creates the soul in the image of God.

The life thus imparted is in like manner sustained. "By every word that proceedeth out of the mouth of God" (Matthew 4:4) shall man live.

The mind, the soul, is built up by that upon which it feeds; and it rests with us to determine upon what it shall be fed. It is within the power of everyone to choose the topics that shall occupy the thoughts and shape the character. Of every human being privileged with access to the Scriptures, God says, "I have written to him the great things of My law." "Call unto Me, and I will answer thee, and show thee great and mighty things, which thou knowest not." (Hosea 8:12; Jeremiah 33:3.) . . .

The word of God, like the character of its Author, presents mysteries that can never be fully comprehended by finite beings. But God has given in the Scriptures sufficient evidence of their divine authority. His own existence, His character, the truthfulness of His word, are established by testimony that appeals to our reason; and this testimony is abundant. True, He has not removed the possibility of doubt; faith must rest upon evidence, not demonstration; those who wish to doubt have opportunity; but those who desire to know the truth find ample ground for faith.

We have no reason to doubt God's word because we cannot understand the mysteries of His providence. In the natural world we are constantly surrounded with wonders beyond our comprehension. Should we then be surprised to find in the spiritual world also mysteries that we cannot fathom? The difficulty lies solely in the weakness and narrowness of the human mind.

The mysteries of the Bible, so far from being an argument against it, are among the strongest evidences of its divine inspiration.—*Education,* pp. 126, 127, 169, 170.

2016

JANUARY 12

DEATH OF THE EARTHLY NATURE

This is my comfort in my affliction, for Your word has given me life.
—Psalm 119:50.

The life of Christ that gives life to the world is in His word. It was by His word that Jesus healed disease and cast out demons; by His word He stilled the sea, and raised the dead; and the people bore witness that His word was with power. He spoke the word of God, as He had spoken through all the prophets and teachers of the Old Testament. The whole Bible is a manifestation of Christ, and the Saviour desired to fix the faith of His followers on the word. When His visible presence should be withdrawn, the word must be their source of power. Like their Master, they were to live "by every word that proceedeth out of the mouth of God." (Matthew 4:4.) . . .

As faith thus receives and assimilates the principles of truth, they become a part of the being and the motive power of the life. The word of God, received into the soul, molds the thoughts, and enters into the development of character.

By looking constantly to Jesus with the eye of faith, we shall be strengthened. God will make the most precious revelations to His hungering, thirsting people. They will find that Christ is a personal Saviour. As they feed upon His word, they find that it is spirit and life. The word destroys the natural, earthly nature, and imparts a new life in Christ Jesus. The Holy Spirit comes to the soul as a Comforter. By the transforming agency of His grace, the image of God is reproduced in the disciples; they become new creatures. Love takes the place of hatred, and the heart receives the divine similitude. This is what it means to live "by every word that proceedeth out of the mouth of God." This is eating the Bread that comes down from heaven.

Christ had spoken a sacred, eternal truth regarding the relation between Himself and His followers. He knew the character of those who claimed to be His disciples, and His words tested their faith. He declared that they were to believe and act upon His teaching. All who received Him would partake of His nature, and be conformed to His character. This involved the relinquishment of their cherished ambitions. It required the complete surrender of themselves to Jesus. They were called to become self-sacrificing, meek and lowly in heart. They must walk in the narrow path traveled by the Man of Calvary, if they would share in the gift of life and the glory of heaven.—*The Desire of Ages,* pp. 390, 391.

January 13

A Fortress Against Temptation

How can a young man cleanse his way? By taking heed according to Your word.
—Psalm 119:9.

The whole Bible is a revelation of the glory of God in Christ. Received, believed, obeyed, it is the great instrumentality in the transformation of character. It is the grand stimulus, the constraining force, that quickens the physical, mental, and spiritual powers, and directs the life into right channels.

The reason why the youth, and even those of mature years, are so easily led into temptation and sin, is that they do not study the word of God and meditate upon it as they should. The lack of firm, decided will power, which is manifest in life and character, results from neglect of the sacred instruction of God's word. They do not by earnest effort direct the mind to that which would inspire pure, holy thought and divert it from that which is impure and untrue. There are few who choose the better part, who sit at the feet of Jesus, as did Mary, to learn of the divine Teacher. Few treasure His words in the heart and practice them in the life.

The truths of the Bible, received, will uplift mind and soul. If the word of God were appreciated as it should be, both young and old would possess an inward rectitude, a strength of principle, that would enable them to resist temptation.

Let us teach and write the precious things of the Holy Scriptures. Let the thought, the aptitude, the keen exercise of brain power, be given to the study of the thoughts of God. Study not the philosophy of human conjectures, but study the philosophy of Him who is truth. No other literature can compare with this in value.

The mind that is earthly finds no pleasure in contemplating the word of God; but for the mind renewed by the Holy Spirit, divine beauty and celestial light shine from the sacred page. That which to the earthly mind was a desolate wilderness, to the spiritual mind becomes a land of living streams.

The knowledge of God as revealed in His word is the knowledge to be given to our children. From the earliest dawn of reason they should be made familiar with the name and the life of Jesus. Their first lessons should teach them that God is their Father.—*The Ministry of Healing*, pp. 458–460.

JANUARY 14

DIG DEEP

Through Your precepts I get understanding.—Psalm 119:104.

For the mind and the soul, as well as for the body, it is God's law that strength is acquired by effort. It is exercise that develops. In harmony with this law, God has provided in His word the means for mental and spiritual development.

The Bible contains all the principles that we need to understand in order to be fitted either for this life or for the life to come. And these principles may be understood by all. No one with a spirit to appreciate its teaching can read a single passage from the Bible without gaining from it some helpful thought. But the most valuable teaching of the Bible is not to be gained by occasional or disconnected study. Its great system of truth is not so presented as to be discerned by the hasty or careless reader. Many of its treasures lie far beneath the surface, and can be obtained only by diligent research and continuous effort. The truths that go to make up the great whole must be searched out and gathered up, "here a little, and there a little." (Isaiah 28:10.)

When thus searched out and brought together, they will be found to be perfectly fitted to one another. Each Gospel is a supplement to the others, every prophecy an explanation of another, every truth a development of some other truth. The types of the Jewish economy are made plain by the gospel. Every principle in the word of God has its place, every fact its bearing. And the complete structure, in design and execution, bears testimony to its Author. Such a structure no mind but that of the Infinite could conceive or fashion.

In searching out the various parts and studying their relationship, the highest faculties of the human mind are called into intense activity. No one can engage in such study without developing mental power.

And not alone in searching out truth and bringing it together does the mental value of Bible study consist. It consists also in the effort required to grasp the themes presented. The mind occupied with commonplace matters only, becomes dwarfed and enfeebled. If never tasked to comprehend grand and far-reaching truths, it after a time loses the power of growth. As a safeguard against this degeneracy, and a stimulus to development, nothing else can equal the study of God's word.—*Education,* pp. 123, 124.

January 15

Side by Side

So it was, while they conversed and reasoned, that Jesus Himself drew near and went with them.—Luke 24:15.

Those who are seeking the righteousness of Christ will be dwelling upon the themes of the great salvation. The Bible is the storehouse that supplies their souls with nourishing food. They meditate upon the incarnation of Christ, they contemplate the great sacrifice made to save them from perdition, to bring in pardon, peace, and everlasting righteousness. The soul is aglow with these grand and elevating themes. Holiness and truth, grace and righteousness, occupy the thoughts. Self dies, and Christ lives in His servants. In contemplation of the word their hearts burn within them as did the hearts of the two disciples while they went to Emmaus and Christ walked with them by the way and opened to them the scriptures concerning Himself.

How few realize that Jesus, unseen, is walking by their side! How ashamed many would be to hear His voice speaking to them and to know that He heard all their foolish, common talk! And how many hearts would burn with holy joy if they only knew that the Saviour was by their side, that the holy atmosphere of His presence was surrounding them, and they were feeding on the bread of life! How pleased the Saviour would be to hear His followers talking on His precious lessons of instruction and to know that they had a relish for holy things!

When the truth abides in the heart, there is no place for criticism of God's servants, or for picking flaws with the message He sends. That which is in the heart will flow from the lips. It cannot be repressed. The things that God has prepared for those that love Him will be the theme of conversation. The love of Christ is in the soul as a well of water, springing up into everlasting life, sending forth living streams that bring life and gladness wherever they flow.—*Counsels to Parents, Teachers, and Students,* pp. 341, 342.

And even greater is the power of the Bible in the development of the spiritual nature. We are created for fellowship with God, and can only in such fellowship find our real life and development. Created to find in God our highest joy, we can find in nothing else that which can quiet the cravings of the heart, can satisfy the hunger and thirst of the soul. Those who with sincere and teachable spirit study God's word, seeking to comprehend its truths, will be brought in touch with its Author.—*Education,* pp. 124, 125.

January 16

The Bible's Central Theme

Beloved, now we are the children of God; and it has not yet been revealed what we shall be, but we know that when He is revealed, we shall be like Him, for we shall see Him as He is.—1 John 3:2.

As an educator no part of the Bible is of greater value than are its biographies. These biographies differ from all others in that they are absolutely true to life. It is impossible for any finite mind to interpret rightly, in all things, the workings of another. None but He who reads the heart, who discerns the secret springs of motive and action, can with absolute truth delineate character, or give a faithful picture of a human life. In God's word alone is found such delineation.

No truth does the Bible more clearly teach than that what we do is the result of what we are. To a great degree the experiences of life are the fruition of our own thoughts and deeds. . . .

The central theme of the Bible, the theme about which every other in the whole book clusters, is the redemption plan, the restoration in the human soul of the image of God. From the first intimation of hope in the sentence pronounced in Eden to that last glorious promise of the Revelation, "They shall see His face; and His name shall be in their foreheads" (Revelation 22:4), the burden of every book and every passage of the Bible is the unfolding of this wondrous theme—humanity's uplifting—the power of God, "which giveth us the victory through our Lord Jesus Christ." (1 Corinthians 15:57.)

Those who grasp this thought have before them an infinite field for study. They have the key that will unlock to them the whole treasure house of God's word.

The science of redemption is the science of all sciences; the science that is the study of the angels and of all the intelligences of the unfallen worlds; the science that engages the attention of our Lord and Saviour; the science that enters into the purpose brooded in the mind of the Infinite—"kept in silence through times eternal" (Romans 16:25, R.V.); the science that will be the study of God's redeemed throughout endless ages.

This is the highest study in which it is possible for man to engage. As no other study can, it will quicken the mind and uplift the soul. . . .

The creative energy that called the worlds into existence is in the word of God. This word imparts power; it begets life. Every command is a promise; accepted by the will, received into the soul, it brings with it the life of the Infinite One. It transforms the nature and re-creates the soul in the image of God.—*Education,* pp. 146, 125, 126.

January 17

The Great Controversy in Scripture

And war broke out in heaven.
—Revelation 12:7.

The Bible is its own expositor. Scripture is to be compared with scripture. Students should learn to view the word as a whole, and to see the relation of its parts. They should gain a knowledge of its grand central theme, of God's original purpose for the world, of the rise of the great controversy, and of the work of redemption. They should understand the nature of the two principles that are contending for supremacy, and should learn to trace their working through the records of history and prophecy, to the great consummation. They should see how this controversy enters into every phase of human experience; how in every act of life they themselves reveal the one or the other of the two antagonistic motives; and how, whether willingly or not, they are even now deciding upon which side of the controversy they will be found.

Every part of the Bible is given by inspiration of God and is profitable. The Old Testament no less than the New should receive attention. As we study the Old Testament we shall find living springs bubbling up where the careless reader discerns only a desert.

The book of Revelation, in connection with the book of Daniel, especially demands study. Let every God-fearing teacher consider how most clearly to comprehend and to present the gospel that our Saviour came in person to make known to His servant John—"The Revelation of Jesus Christ, which God gave unto Him, to show unto His servants things which must shortly come to pass." (Revelation 1:1.) None should become discouraged in the study of the Revelation because of its apparently mystical symbols. "If any of you lack wisdom, let him ask of God, that giveth to all men liberally, and upbraideth not." (James 1:5.)

"Blessed is he that readeth, and they that hear the words of this prophecy, and keep those things which are written therein: for the time is at hand." (Revelation 1:3.)

When a real love for the Bible is awakened, and the students begin to realize how vast is the field and how precious its treasure, they will desire to seize upon every opportunity for acquainting themselves with God's word. Its study will be restricted to no special time or place. And this continuous study is one of the best means of cultivating a love for the Scriptures.—*Education,* pp. 190, 191.

January 18

Verse by Verse

Blessed are You, O Lord! Teach me Your statutes.
—Psalm 119:12.

The student of the Bible should be taught to approach it in the spirit of a learner. We are to search its pages, not for proof to sustain our opinions, but in order to know what God says.

A true knowledge of the Bible can be gained only through the aid of that Spirit by whom the word was given. And in order to gain this knowledge we must live by it. All that God's word commands, we are to obey. All that it promises, we may claim. The life which it enjoins is the life that, through its power, we are to live. Only as the Bible is thus held can it be studied effectively.

The study of the Bible demands our most diligent effort and persevering thought. As the miner digs for the golden treasure in the earth, so earnestly, persistently, must we seek for the treasure of God's word.

In daily study the verse-by-verse method is often most helpful. Let the students take one verse, and concentrate the mind on ascertaining the thought that God has put into that verse for them, and then dwell upon the thought until it becomes their own. One passage thus studied until its significance is clear is of more value than the perusal of many chapters with no definite purpose in view and no positive instruction gained.

One of the chief causes of mental inefficiency and moral weakness is the lack of concentration for worthy ends. We pride ourselves on the wide distribution of literature; but the multiplication of books, even books that in themselves are not harmful, may be a positive evil. With the immense tide of printed matter constantly pouring from the press, old and young form the habit of reading hastily and superficially, and the mind loses its power of connected and vigorous thought. Furthermore, a large share of the periodicals and books that, like the frogs of Egypt, are overspreading the land, are not merely commonplace, idle, and enervating, but unclean and degrading. Their effect is not merely to intoxicate and ruin the mind, but to corrupt and destroy the soul. The mind, the heart, that is indolent, aimless, falls an easy prey to evil. It is on diseased, lifeless organisms that fungus roots. It is the idle mind that is Satan's workshop. Let the mind be directed to high and holy ideals, let the life have a noble aim, an absorbing purpose, and evil finds little foothold.—*Education,* pp. 189, 190.

January 19

God's Hand in History

He removes kings and raises up kings.
—Daniel 2:21.

The Bible is the most ancient and the most comprehensive history that we possess. It came fresh from the fountain of eternal truth, and throughout the ages a divine hand has preserved its purity. It lights up the far-distant past, where human research in vain seeks to penetrate. In God's word only do we behold the power that laid the foundations of the earth and that stretched out the heavens. Here only do we find an authentic account of the origin of nations. Here only is given a history of our race unsullied by human pride or prejudice.

In the annals of human history the growth of nations, the rise and fall of empires, appear as dependent on the will and prowess of man. The shaping of events seems, to a great degree, to be determined by his power, ambition, or caprice. But in the word of God the curtain is drawn aside, and we behold, behind, above, and through all the play and counterplay of human interests and power and passions, the agencies of the all-merciful One, silently, patiently working out the counsels of His own will.

The Bible reveals the true philosophy of history. In those words of matchless beauty and tenderness spoken by the apostle Paul to the sages of Athens is set forth God's purpose in the creation and distribution of races and nations: He "hath made of one blood all nations of men for to dwell on all the face of the earth, and hath determined the times before appointed, and the bounds of their habitation; that they should seek the Lord, if haply they might feel after Him, and find Him." (Acts 17:26, 27.) God declares that whosoever will may come "into the bond of the covenant." (Ezekiel 20:37.) In the creation it was His purpose that the earth be inhabited by beings whose existence should be a blessing to themselves and to one another, and an honor to their Creator. All who will may identify themselves with this purpose. Of them it is spoken, "This people have I formed for Myself; they shall show forth My praise." (Isaiah 43:21.)

God has revealed in His law the principles that underlie all true prosperity both of nations and of individuals. "This is your wisdom and your understanding," Moses declared to the Israelites of the law of God. "It is not a vain thing for you; because it is your life." (Deuteronomy 4:6; 32:47.) The blessings thus assured to Israel are, on the same conditions and in the same degree, assured to every nation and every individual.—*Education*, pp. 173, 174.

January 20

Why Doubt?

O you of little faith, why did you doubt?
—Matthew 14:31.

The Word of God, like the character of its divine Author, presents mysteries that can never be fully comprehended by finite beings. The entrance of sin into the world, the incarnation of Christ, regeneration, the resurrection, and many other subjects presented in the Bible, are mysteries too deep for the human mind to explain, or even fully to comprehend. But we have no reason to doubt God's Word because we cannot understand the mysteries of His providence. In the natural world we are constantly surrounded with mysteries that we cannot fathom. The very humblest forms of life present a problem that the wisest of philosophers is powerless to explain. Everywhere are wonders beyond our ken. Should we then be surprised to find that in the spiritual world also there are mysteries that we cannot fathom? . . .

The difficulties of Scripture have been urged by skeptics as an argument against the Bible; but so far from this, they constitute a strong evidence of its divine inspiration. If it contained no account of God but that which we could easily comprehend; if His greatness and majesty could be grasped by finite minds, then the Bible would not bear the unmistakable credentials of divine authority. The very grandeur and mystery of the themes presented should inspire faith in it as the Word of God.

The Bible unfolds truth with a simplicity and a perfect adaptation to the needs and longings of the human heart, that has astonished and charmed the most highly cultivated minds, while it enables the humblest and uncultured to discern the way of salvation. And yet these simply stated truths lay hold upon subjects so elevated, so far-reaching, so infinitely beyond the power of human comprehension, that we can accept them only because God has declared them. Thus the plan of redemption is laid open to us, so that every soul may see the steps to take in repentance toward God and faith toward our Lord Jesus Christ, in order to be saved in God's appointed way; yet beneath these truths, so easily understood, lie mysteries that are the hiding of His glory—mysteries that overpower the mind in its research, yet inspire the sincere seeker for truth with reverence and faith. The more we search the Bible, the deeper is the conviction that it is the Word of the living God, and human reason bows before the majesty of divine revelation.—*Steps to Christ,* pp. 106–108.

January 21

Good-Ground Hearers

But others fell on good ground and yielded a crop: some a hundredfold, some sixty, some thirty. —Matthew 13:8.

A knowledge of the truth depends not so much upon strength of intellect as upon pureness of purpose, the simplicity of an earnest, dependent faith. To those who in humility of heart seek for divine guidance, angels of God draw near. The Holy Spirit is given to open to them the rich treasures of the truth.

The good-ground hearers, having heard the word, keep it. Satan with all his agencies of evil is not able to catch it away.

Merely to hear or to read the word is not enough. Those who desire to be profited by the Scriptures must meditate upon the truth that has been presented to them. By earnest attention and prayerful thought they must learn the meaning of the words of truth, and drink deep of the spirit of the holy oracles.

God bids us fill the mind with great thoughts, pure thoughts. He desires us to meditate upon His love and mercy, to study His wonderful work in the great plan of redemption. Then clearer and still clearer will be our perception of truth, higher, holier, our desire for purity of heart and clearness of thought. The soul dwelling in the pure atmosphere of holy thought will be transformed by communion with God through the study of Scriptures.

"And bring forth fruit." (Mark 4:20.) Those who, having heard the word, keep it, will bring forth fruit in obedience. The word of God, received into the soul, will be manifest in good works. Its results will be seen in a Christ-like character and life. Christ said of Himself, "I delight to do Thy will, O My God; yea, Thy law is within My heart." (Psalm 40:8.) "I seek not Mine own will, but the will of the Father which hath sent Me." (John 5:30.) And the Scripture says, "He that saith he abideth in Him ought himself also so to walk, even as He walked." (1 John 2:6.)

The word of God often comes in collision with our hereditary and cultivated traits of character and our habits of life. But the good-ground hearer, in receiving the word, accepts all its conditions and requirements.—*Christ's Object Lessons,* pp. 59, 60.

January 22

Get Acquainted With Truth

You shall know the truth, and the truth shall make you free.
—John 8:32.

The Scriptures need not be read by the dim light of tradition or human speculation. As well might we try to give light to the sun with a torch as to explain the Scriptures by human tradition or imagination. God's holy word needs not the torchlight glimmer of earth to make its glories distinguishable. It is light in itself—the glory of God revealed, and beside it every other light is dim.

But there must be earnest study and close investigation. Sharp, clear perceptions of truth will never be the reward of indolence. No earthy blessing can be obtained without earnest, patient, persevering effort. If people attain success in business, they must have a will to do and a faith to look for results. And we cannot expect to gain spiritual knowledge without earnest toil. Those who desire to find the treasures of truth must dig for them as the miner digs for the treasure hidden in the earth. No halfhearted, indifferent work will avail. It is essential for old and young, not only to read God's word, but to study it with wholehearted earnestness, praying and searching for truth as for hidden treasure. Those who do this will be rewarded, for Christ will quicken the understanding.

Our salvation depends on a knowledge of the truth contained in the Scriptures. It is God's will that we should possess this. Search, O search the precious Bible with hungry hearts. Explore God's word as the miner explores the earth to find veins of gold. Never give up the search until you have ascertained your relation to God and His will in regard to you. Christ declared, "Whatsoever ye shall ask in My name, that will I do, that the Father may be glorified in the Son. If ye shall ask anything in My name, I will do it." (John 14:13, 14.)

People of piety and talent catch views of eternal realities, but often they fail of understanding, because the things that are seen eclipse the glory of the unseen. Those who would seek successfully for the hidden treasure must rise to higher pursuits than the things of this world. Their affections and all their capabilities must be consecrated to the search. . . .

The Scriptures are not to be adapted to meet human prejudice and jealousy. They can be understood only by those who are humbly seeking for a knowledge of the truth that they may obey it.—*Christ's Object Lessons*, pp. 111, 112.

2016

January 23

Example of the Bereans

They received the word with all readiness, and searched the Scriptures daily to find out whether these things were so.—Acts 17:11.

At Berea Paul found Jews who were willing to investigate the truths he taught. Luke's record declares of them: "These were more noble than those in Thessalonica, in that they received the word with all readiness of mind, and searched the Scriptures daily, whether those things were so. Therefore many of them believed; also of honorable women which were Greeks, and of men, not a few." (Acts 17:11, 12.)

The minds of the Bereans were not narrowed by prejudice. They were willing to investigate the truthfulness of the doctrines preached by the apostles. They studied the Bible, not from curiosity, but in order that they might learn what had been written concerning the promised Messiah. Daily they searched the inspired records, and as they compared scripture with scripture, heavenly angels were beside them, enlightening their minds and impressing their hearts.

Wherever the truths of the gospel are proclaimed, those who honestly desire to do right are led to a diligent searching of the Scriptures. If, in the closing scenes of this earth's history, those to whom testing truths are proclaimed would follow the example of the Bereans, searching the Scriptures daily, and comparing with God's word the messages brought them, there would today be a large number loyal to the precepts of God's law, where now there are comparatively few. But when unpopular Bible truths are presented, many refuse to make this investigation. Though unable to controvert the plain teachings of Scripture, they yet manifest the utmost reluctance to study the evidences offered. Some assume that even if these doctrines are indeed true, it matters little whether or not they accept the new light, and they cling to pleasing fables which the enemy uses to lead souls astray. Thus their minds are blinded by error, and they become separated from heaven.

All will be judged according to the light that has been given. The Lord sends forth His ambassadors with a message of salvation, and those who hear He will hold responsible for the way in which they treat the words of His servants. Those who are sincerely seeking for truth will make a careful investigation, in the light of God's word, of the doctrines presented to them.—*The Acts of the Apostles,* pp. 231, 232.

January 24

Have an Elevating Influence

Those who fear You will be glad when they see me, because I have hoped in Your word.—Psalm 119:74.

If the truths of the Bible are woven into practical life, they will bring the mind up from its earthliness and debasement. Those who are conversant with the Scriptures, will be found to be men and women who exert an elevating influence. In searching for the heaven-revealed truths, the Spirit of God is brought into close connection with the sincere searcher of the Scriptures. An understanding of the revealed will of God, enlarges the mind, expands, elevates, and endows it with new vigor, by bringing its faculties in contact with stupendous truths. If the study of the Scriptures is made a secondary consideration, great loss is sustained. The Bible was for a time excluded from our schools, and Satan found a rich field, in which he worked with marvelous rapidity, and gathered a harvest to his liking.

The understanding takes the level of the things with which it becomes familiar. If all would make the Bible their study, we should see a people further developed, capable of thinking more deeply, and showing a greater degree of intelligence, than the most earnest efforts in studying merely the sciences and histories of the world could make them. The Bible gives the true seeker an advanced mental discipline, and he comes from contemplation of divine things with his faculties enriched; self is humbled, while God and His revealed truth are exalted. It is because people are unacquainted with the precious Bible histories, that there is so much lifting up of the human, and so little honor given to God. The Bible contains just that quality of food that the Christian needs in order to grow strong in spirit and intellect. The searching of all books of philosophy and science cannot do for the mind and morals what the Bible can do, if it is studied and practiced. Through the study of the Bible, converse is held with patriarchs and prophets. The truth is clothed in elevated language, which exerts a fascinating power over the mind; the thought is lifted up from the things of earth, and brought to contemplate the glory of the future immortal life. What wisdom of man can compare with the grandeur of the revelation of God? Finite man, who knows not God, may seek to lessen the value of the Scriptures, and may bury the truth beneath the supposed knowledge of science.—*Fundamentals of Christian Education,* pp. 129, 130.

January 25

The Great Educator

Trust in the Lord with all your heart, and lean not on your own understanding.
—Proverbs 3:5.

The Bible unfolds truth with a simplicity and an adaptation to the needs and longings of the human heart that has astonished and charmed the most highly cultivated minds, while to the humble and uncultured also it makes plain the way of life. "The wayfaring men, though fools, shall not err therein." (Isaiah 35:8.) No child need mistake the path. Not one trembling seeker need fail of walking in pure and holy light. Yet the most simply stated truths lay hold upon themes elevated, far-reaching, infinitely beyond the power of human comprehension—mysteries that are the hiding of His glory, mysteries that overpower the mind in its research—while they inspire the sincere seeker for truth with reverence and faith. The more we search the Bible, the deeper is our conviction that it is the word of the living God, and human reason bows before the majesty of divine revelation.

God intends that to the earnest seeker the truths of His word shall be ever unfolding. While "the secret things belong unto the Lord our God," "those things which are revealed belong unto us and to our children." (Deuteronomy 29:29.) The idea that certain portions of the Bible cannot be understood has led to neglect of some of its most important truths. The fact needs to be emphasized, and often repeated, that the mysteries of the Bible are not such because God has sought to conceal truth, but because our own weakness or ignorance makes us incapable of comprehending or appropriating truth. The limitation is not in His purpose, but in our capacity. Of those very portions of Scripture often passed by as impossible to be understood, God desires us to understand as much as our minds are capable of receiving. "All Scripture is given by inspiration of God," that we may be "throughly furnished unto all good works." (2 Timothy 3:16, 17.)

It is impossible for any human mind to exhaust even one truth or promise of the Bible. One catches the glory from one point of view, another from another point; yet we can discern only gleamings. The full radiance is beyond our vision.

As we contemplate the great things of God's word, we look into a fountain that broadens and deepens beneath our gaze. Its breadth and depth pass our knowledge. As we gaze, the vision widens; stretched out before us we behold a boundless, shoreless sea.—*Education,* pp. 170, 171.

January 26

2016

The Science of Salvation

Our God is the God of salvation.
—Psalm 68:20.

This is the treasure that is found in the Scriptures. The Bible is God's great lesson book, His great educator. The foundation of all true science is contained in the Bible. Every branch of knowledge may be found by searching the word of God. And above all else it contains the science of all sciences, the science of salvation. The Bible is the mine of the unsearchable riches of Christ.

The true higher education is gained by studying and obeying the word of God. But when God's word is laid aside for books that do not lead to God and the kingdom of heaven, the education acquired is a perversion of the name.

There are wonderful truths in nature. The earth, the sea, and the sky are full of truth. They are our teachers. Nature utters her voice in lessons of heavenly wisdom and eternal truth. But fallen human beings will not understand. Sin has obscured their vision, and they cannot of themselves interpret nature without placing it above God. Correct lessons cannot impress the minds of those who reject the word of God. The teaching of nature is by them so perverted that it turns the mind away from the Creator.

By many, human wisdom is thought to be higher than the wisdom of the divine Teacher, and God's lesson book is looked upon as old-fashioned, stale, and uninteresting. But by those who have been vivified by the Holy Spirit it is not so regarded. They see the priceless treasure, and would sell all to buy the field that contains it. Instead of books containing the suppositions of reputedly great authors, they choose the word of Him who is the greatest Author and the greatest Teacher the world has ever known, who gave His life for us, that through Him we might have everlasting life. . . .

Christ is the truth. His words are truth, and they have a deeper significance than appears on the surface. All the sayings of Christ have a value beyond their unpretending appearance. Minds that are quickened by the Holy Spirit will discern the value of these sayings. They will discern the precious gems of truth, though these may be buried treasures.—*Christ's Object Lessons,* pp. 107, 108, 110.

January 27

Science and the Bible

Where were you when I laid the foundations of the earth?
—Job 38:4.

Since the book of nature and the book of revelation bear the impress of the same master mind, they cannot but speak in harmony. By different methods, and in different languages, they witness to the same great truths. Science is ever discovering new wonders; but she brings from her research nothing that, rightly understood, conflicts with divine revelation. The book of nature and the written word shed light upon each other. They make us acquainted with God by teaching us something of the laws through which He works.

Inferences erroneously drawn from facts observed in nature have, however, led to supposed conflict between science and revelation; and in the effort to restore harmony, interpretations of Scripture have been adopted that undermine and destroy the force of the word of God. Geology has been thought to contradict the literal interpretation of the Mosaic record of the creation. Millions of years, it is claimed, were required for the evolution of the earth from chaos; and in order to accommodate the Bible to this supposed revelation of science, the days of creation are assumed to have been vast, indefinite periods, covering thousands or even millions of years.

Such a conclusion is wholly uncalled for. The Bible record is in harmony with itself and with the teaching of nature. Of the first day employed in the work of creation is given the record, "The evening and the morning were the first day." (Genesis 1:5.) And the same in substance is said of each of the first six days of creation week. Each of these periods Inspiration declares to have been a day consisting of evening and morning, like every other day since that time. In regard to the work of creation itself the divine testimony is, "He spake, and it was done; He commanded, and it stood fast." (Psalm 33:9.) With Him who could thus call into existence unnumbered worlds, how long a time would be required for the evolution of the earth from chaos? In order to account for His works, must we do violence to His word? . . .

Only by the aid of that Spirit who in the beginning "was brooding upon the face of the waters;" of that Word by whom "all things were made;" of that "true Light, which lighteth every man that cometh into the world," can the testimony of science be rightly interpreted.—*Education,* pp. 128, 129, 134.

January 28

Keep Your Eyes on Christ

For assuredly, I say to you that many prophets and righteous men desired to see what you see, and did not see it.—Matthew 13:17.

The warnings of the word of God regarding the perils surrounding the Christian church belong to us today. As in the days of the apostles men tried by tradition and philosophy to destroy faith in the Scriptures, so today, by the pleasing sentiments of higher criticism, evolution, spiritualism, theosophy, and pantheism, the enemy of righteousness is seeking to lead souls into forbidden paths. To many the Bible is as a lamp without oil, because they have turned their minds into channels of speculative belief that bring misunderstanding and confusion. The work of higher criticism, in dissecting, conjecturing, reconstructing, is destroying faith in the Bible as a divine revelation. It is robbing God's word of power to control, uplift, and inspire human lives. By spiritualism, multitudes are taught to believe that desire is the highest law, that license is liberty, and that they are accountable only to themselves.

The followers of Christ will meet with the "enticing words" against which the apostle warned the Colossian believers. They will meet with spiritualistic interpretations of the Scriptures, but they are not to accept them. Their voices are to be heard in clear affirmation of the eternal truths of the Scriptures. Keeping their eyes fixed on Christ, they are to move steadily forward in the path marked out, discarding all ideas that are not in harmony with His teaching. The truth of God is to be the subject for their contemplation and meditation. They are to regard the Bible as the voice of God speaking directly to them. Thus they will find the wisdom which is divine.

The knowledge of God as revealed in Christ is the knowledge that all who are saved must have. This is the knowledge that works transformation of character. Received into the life, it will re-create the soul in the image of Christ. This is the knowledge that God invites His children to receive, beside which all else is vanity and nothingness.

In every generation and in every land the true foundation for character building has been the same—the principles contained in the word of God. The only safe and sure rule is to do what God says. "The statutes of the Lord are right," and "he that doeth these things shall never be moved." (Psalm 19:8; 15:5.) It was with the word of God that the apostles met the false theories of their day.—*The Acts of the Apostles*, pp. 474, 475.

January 29

Last Day Deceptions

You have a little strength, have kept My word, and have not denied My name.
—Revelation 3:8.

Popular revivals are too often carried by appeals to the imagination, by exciting the emotions, by gratifying the love for what is new and startling. Converts thus gained have little desire to listen to Bible truth, little interest in the testimony of prophets and apostles. Unless a religious service has something of a sensational character, it has no attractions for them. A message which appeals to unimpassioned reason awakens no response. The plain warnings of God's word, relating directly to their eternal interests, are unheeded.

With every truly converted soul the relation to God and to eternal things will be the great topic of life. But where, in the popular churches of today, is the spirit of consecration to God? . . .

In many of the revivals which have occurred during the last half century, the same influences have been at work, to a greater or less degree, that will be manifest in the more extensive movements of the future. There is an emotional excitement, a mingling of the true with the false, that is well adapted to mislead. Yet none need be deceived. In the light of God's word it is not difficult to determine the nature of these movements. Wherever people neglect the testimony of the Bible, turning away from those plain, soul-testing truths which require self-denial and renunciation of the world, there we may be sure that God's blessing is not bestowed. And by the rule which Christ Himself has given, "Ye shall know them by their fruits" (Matthew 7:16), it is evident that these movements are not the work of the Spirit of God.

In the truths of His word, God has given us a revelation of Himself; and to all who accept them they are a shield against the deceptions of Satan. It is a neglect of these truths that has opened the door to the evils which are now becoming so widespread in the religious world. The nature and the importance of the law of God have been, to a great extent, lost sight of. A wrong conception of the character, the perpetuity, and the obligation of the divine law has led to errors in relation to conversion and sanctification, and has resulted in lowering the standard of piety in the church. Here is to be found the secret of the lack of the Spirit and power of God in the revivals of our time.—*The Great Controversy,* pp. 463–465.

JANUARY 30

THE SCRIPTURES OUR SAFEGUARD

To the law and to the testimony! If they do not speak according to this word, it is because there is no light in them.—Isaiah 8:20.

The people of God are directed to the Scriptures as their safeguard against the influence of false teachers and the delusive power of spirits of darkness. Satan employs every possible device to prevent people from obtaining a knowledge of the Bible; for its plain utterances reveal his deceptions. At every revival of God's work the prince of evil is aroused to more intense activity; he is now putting forth his utmost efforts for a final struggle against Christ and His followers. The last great delusion is soon to open before us. Antichrist is to perform his marvelous works in our sight. So closely will the counterfeit resemble the true that it will be impossible to distinguish between them except by the Holy Scriptures. By their testimony every statement and every miracle must be tested.

Those who endeavor to obey all the commandments of God will be opposed and derided. They can stand only in God. In order to endure the trial before them, they must understand the will of God as revealed in His word; they can honor Him only as they have a right conception of His character, government, and purposes, and act in accordance with them. None but those who have fortified the mind with the truths of the Bible will stand through the last great conflict. To every soul will come the searching test: Shall I obey God rather than men? The decisive hour is even now at hand. Are our feet planted on the rock of God's immutable word? Are we prepared to stand firm in defense of the commandments of God and the faith of Jesus? . . .

The truth and the glory of God are inseparable; it is impossible for us, with the Bible within our reach, to honor God by erroneous opinions. Many claim that it matters not what one believes, if the life is only right. But the life is molded by the faith. If light and truth is within our reach, and we neglect to improve the privilege of hearing and seeing it, we virtually reject it; we are choosing darkness rather than light. . . .

God has given us His word that we may become acquainted with its teachings and know for ourselves what He requires of us. When the lawyer came to Jesus with the inquiry, "What shall I do to inherit eternal life?" the Saviour referred him to the Scriptures, saying: "What is written in the law? how readest thou?" (Luke 10:25, 26.)—*The Great Controversy,* pp. 593, 594, 597, 598.

January 31

Our First Duty

If anyone wills to do His will, he shall know concerning the doctrine.
—John 7:17.

It is the first and highest duty of every rational being to learn from the Scriptures what is truth, and then to walk in the light and encourage others to follow this example. We should day by day study the Bible diligently, weighing every thought and comparing scripture with scripture. With divine help we are to form our opinions for ourselves as we are to answer for ourselves before God.

The truths most plainly revealed in the Bible have been involved in doubt and darkness by learned scholars, who, with a pretense of great wisdom, teach that the Scriptures have a mystical, a secret, spiritual meaning not apparent in the language employed. These are false teachers. It was to such a class that Jesus declared: "Ye know not the Scriptures, neither the power of God." (Mark 12:24.) The language of the Bible should be explained according to its obvious meaning, unless a symbol or figure is employed. Christ has given the promise: "If any man will do His will, he shall know of the doctrine." (John 7:17.) If people would but take the Bible as it reads, if there were no false teachers to mislead and confuse their minds, a work would be accomplished that would make angels glad and that would bring into the fold of Christ thousands upon thousands who are now wandering in error.

We should exert all the powers of the mind in the study of the Scriptures and should task the understanding to comprehend, as far as mortals can, the deep things of God; yet we must not forget that the docility and submission of a child is the true spirit of the learner. Scriptural difficulties can never be mastered by the same methods that are employed in grappling with philosophical problems. We should not engage in the study of the Bible with that self-reliance with which so many enter the domains of science, but with a prayerful dependence upon God and a sincere desire to learn His will. We must come with a humble and teachable spirit to obtain knowledge from the great I AM. Otherwise, evil angels will so blind our minds and harden our hearts that we shall not be impressed by the truth.

Many a portion of Scripture which scholars pronounce a mystery, or pass over as unimportant, is full of comfort and instruction to those who have been taught in the school of Christ.—*The Great Controversy,* pp. 598, 599.

Jesus, God's Gift

February 1

A Voluntary Sacrifice

The preaching of Jesus Christ, according to the revelation of the mystery kept secret since the world began.
—Romans 16:25.

The plan for our redemption was not an afterthought, a plan formulated after the fall of Adam. It was a revelation of "the mystery which hath been kept in silence through times eternal." (Romans 16:25, R.V.) It was an unfolding of the principles that from eternal ages have been the foundation of God's throne. From the beginning, God and Christ knew of the apostasy of Satan, and of the fall of man through the deceptive power of the apostate. God did not ordain that sin should exist, but He foresaw its existence, and made provision to meet the terrible emergency. So great was His love for the world, that He covenanted to give His only-begotten Son, "that whosoever believeth in Him should not perish, but have everlasting life." (John 3:16.) . . .

This was a voluntary sacrifice. Jesus might have remained at the Father's side. He might have retained the glory of heaven, and the homage of the angels. But He chose to give back the scepter into the Father's hands, and to step down from the throne of the universe, that He might bring light to the benighted, and life to the perishing.

Nearly two thousand years ago, a voice of mysterious import was heard in heaven, from the throne of God, "Lo, I come." "Sacrifice and offering Thou wouldest not, but a body hast Thou prepared Me. . . . Lo, I come (in the volume of the Book it is written of Me,) to do Thy will, O God." (Hebrews 10:5–7.) In these words is announced the fulfillment of the purpose that had been hidden from eternal ages. Christ was about to visit our world, and to become incarnate. He says, "A body hast Thou prepared Me." Had He appeared with the glory that was His with the Father before the world was, we could not have endured the light of His presence. That we might behold it and not be destroyed, the manifestation of His glory was shrouded. His divinity was veiled with humanity—the invisible glory in the visible human form. . . .

So Christ set up His tabernacle in the midst of our human encampment. He pitched His tent by the side of the tents of humanity, that He might dwell among us, and make us familiar with His divine character and life.—*The Desire of Ages*, pp. 22, 23.

FEBRUARY 2

AN UNBREAKABLE TIE

And without controversy great is the mystery of godliness: God was manifested in the flesh.—1 Timothy 3:16.

By His life and His death, Christ has achieved even more than recovery from the ruin wrought through sin. It was Satan's purpose to bring about an eternal separation between God and mankind; but in Christ we become more closely united to God than if we had never fallen. In taking our nature, the Saviour has bound Himself to humanity by a tie that is never to be broken. Through the eternal ages He is linked with us. "God so loved the world, that He gave His only-begotten Son." (John 3:16.) He gave Him not only to bear our sins, and to die as our sacrifice; He gave Him to the fallen race. To assure us of His immutable counsel of peace, God gave His only-begotten Son to become one of the human family, forever to retain His human nature. This is the pledge that God will fulfill His word. . . . God has adopted human nature in the person of His Son, and has carried the same into the highest heaven. It is the "Son of man" who shares the throne of the universe. . . . The I AM is the Daysman between God and humanity, laying His hand upon both. He who is "holy, harmless, undefiled, separate from sinners," is not ashamed to call us brethren. (Hebrews 7:26; 2:11.) In Christ the family of earth and the family of heaven are bound together. Christ glorified is our brother. Heaven is enshrined in humanity, and humanity is enfolded in the bosom of Infinite Love. . . .

By love's self-sacrifice, the inhabitants of earth and heaven are bound to their Creator in bonds of indissoluble union.

The work of redemption will be complete. In the place where sin abounded, God's grace much more abounds. The earth itself, the very field that Satan claims as his, is to be not only ransomed but exalted. Our little world, under the curse of sin the one dark blot in His glorious creation, will be honored above all other worlds in the universe of God. Here, where the Son of God tabernacled in humanity; where the King of glory lived and suffered and died—here, when He shall make all things new, the tabernacle of God shall be with men, "and He will dwell with them, and they shall be His people, and God Himself shall be with them, and be their God." (Revelation 21:3.) And through endless ages as the redeemed walk in the light of the Lord, they will praise Him for His unspeakable Gift—*Immanuel, "God with us."—The Desire of Ages,* pp. 25, 26.

February 3

Greater Works

Believe Me that I am in the Father and the Father in Me, or else believe Me for the sake of the works themselves.—John 14:11.

As Christ was speaking these words, the glory of God was shining from His countenance, and all present felt a sacred awe as they listened with rapt attention to His words. Their hearts were more decidedly drawn to Him; and as they were drawn to Christ in greater love, they were drawn to one another. They felt that heaven was very near, and that the words to which they listened were a message to them from their heavenly Father.

"Verily, verily, I say unto you," Christ continued, "He that believeth on Me, the works that I do shall he do also." (John 14:12.) The Saviour was deeply anxious for His disciples to understand for what purpose His divinity was united to humanity. He came to the world to display the glory of God, that we might be uplifted by its restoring power. God was manifested in Him that He might be manifested in us. Jesus revealed no qualities, and exercised no powers, that we may not have through faith in Him. His perfect humanity is that which all His followers may possess, if they will be in subjection to God as He was.

"And greater works than these shall he do; because I go unto My Father." (Verse 12.) By this Christ did not mean that the disciples' work would be of a more exalted character than His, but that it would have greater extent. He did not refer merely to miracle working, but to all that would take place under the working of the Holy Spirit.

After the Lord's ascension, the disciples realized the fulfillment of His promise. The scenes of the crucifixion, resurrection, and ascension of Christ were a living reality to them. They saw that the prophecies had been literally fulfilled. They searched the Scriptures, and accepted their teaching with a faith and assurance unknown before. They knew that the divine Teacher was all that He had claimed to be. As they told their experience, and exalted the love of God, hearts were melted and subdued, and multitudes believed on Jesus.

The Saviour's promise to His disciples is a promise to His church to the end of time. God did not design that His wonderful plan to redeem humanity should achieve only insignificant results. All who will go to work, trusting not in what they themselves can do, but in what God can do for and through them, will certainly realize the fulfillment of His promise. "Greater works than these shall ye do," He declares; "because I go unto My Father."—*The Desire of Ages*, pp. 664, 667.

February 4

Divinity Needed Humanity

And the Word became flesh and dwelt among us.
—John 1:14.

As His representatives among us, Christ does not choose angels who have never fallen, but human beings, of like passions with those they seek to save. Christ took upon Himself humanity, that He might reach humanity. Divinity needed humanity; for it required both the divine and the human to bring salvation to the world. Divinity needed humanity, that humanity might afford a channel of communication between God and mankind. So with the servants and messengers of Christ. We need a power outside of and beyond ourselves, to restore us to the likeness of God, and enable us to do the work of God; but this does not make the human agency unessential. Humanity lays hold upon divine power, Christ dwells in the heart by faith; and through cooperation with the divine, human power becomes efficient for good.

He who called the fisherman of Galilee is still calling followers to His service. And He is just as willing to manifest His power through us as through the first disciples. However imperfect and sinful we may be, the Lord holds out to us the offer of partnership with Himself, of apprenticeship to Christ. He invites us to come under the divine instruction, that, uniting with Christ, we may work the works of God.

"We have this treasure in earthen vessels, that the exceeding greatness of the power may be of God, and not from ourselves." (2 Corinthians 4:7, R.V.) This is why the preaching of the gospel was committed to erring mortals rather than to the angels. It is manifest that the power which works through the weakness of humanity is the power of God; and thus we are encouraged to believe that the power which can help others as weak as ourselves can help us. And those who are themselves "compassed with infirmity" should be able to "have compassion on the ignorant, and on them that are out of the way." (Hebrews 5:2.) Having been in peril themselves, they are acquainted with the dangers and difficulties of the way, and for this reason are called to reach out for others in like peril. There are souls perplexed with doubt, burdened with infirmities, weak in faith, and unable to grasp the Unseen; but a friend whom they can see, coming to them in Christ's stead, can be a connecting link to fasten their trembling faith upon Christ.

We are to be laborers together with the heavenly angels in presenting Jesus to the world.—*The Desire of Ages,* pp. 296, 297.

February 5

The Divine Teacher

His name will be called Wonderful, Counselor, Mighty God, Everlasting Father, Prince of Peace.—Isaiah 9:6.

In the Teacher sent from God, heaven gave us its best and greatest. He who had stood in the councils of the Most High, who had dwelt in the innermost sanctuary of the Eternal, was the One chosen to reveal in person to humanity the knowledge of God.

Through Christ had been communicated every ray of divine light that had ever reached our fallen world. It was He who had spoken through everyone that throughout the ages had declared God's word to mankind. Of Him all the excellences manifest in the earth's greatest and noblest souls were reflections. The purity and beneficence of Joseph, the faith and meekness and long-suffering of Moses, the steadfastness of Elisha, the noble integrity and firmness of Daniel, the ardor and self-sacrifice of Paul, the mental and spiritual power manifest in all these men, and in all others who had ever dwelt on the earth, were but gleams from the shining of His glory. In Him was found the perfect ideal.

To reveal this ideal as the only true standard for attainment; to show what every human being might become; what, through the indwelling of humanity by divinity, all who received Him would become—for this, Christ came to the world. He came to show how we are to be trained as befits the sons and daughters of God; how on earth we are to practice the principles and to live the life of heaven.

God's greatest gift was bestowed to meet our greatest need. The Light appeared when the world's darkness was deepest. Through false teaching people's minds had long been turned away from God. In the prevailing systems of education, human philosophy had taken the place of divine revelation. Instead of the heaven-given standard of truth, people had accepted a standard of their own devising. From the Light of life they had turned aside to walk in the sparks of the fire which they had kindled. . . .

Anyone who seeks to transform humanity must himself understand humanity. Only through sympathy, faith, and love can people be reached and uplifted. Here Christ stands revealed as the master teacher; of all that ever dwelt on the earth, He alone has perfect understanding of the human soul.
—*Education,* pp. 73, 74, 78.

February 6

Self-Renouncing Love

For God did not send His Son into the world to condemn the world, but that the world through Him might be saved.—John 3:17.

The light of the knowledge of the glory of God" is seen "in the face of Jesus Christ." (2 Corinthians 4:6.) From the days of eternity the Lord Jesus Christ was one with the Father; He was "the image of God," the image of His greatness and majesty, "the outshining of His glory." It was to manifest this glory that He came to our world. To this sin-darkened earth He came to reveal the light of God's love—to be "God with us." Therefore it was prophesied of Him, "His name shall be called Immanuel."

By coming to dwell with us, Jesus was to reveal God both to humanity and to angels. He was the Word of God—God's thought made audible. In His prayer for His disciples He says, "I have declared unto them Thy name,"—"merciful and gracious, long-suffering, and abundant in goodness and truth,"—"that the love wherewith Thou hast loved Me may be in them, and I in them." (John 17:26; Exodus 34:6.) But not alone for His earthborn children was this revelation given. Our little world is the lesson book of the universe. God's wonderful purpose of grace, the mystery of redeeming love, is the theme into which "angels desire to look," and it will be their study throughout endless ages. Both the redeemed and the unfallen beings will find in the cross of Christ their science and their song. It will be seen that the glory shining in the face of Jesus is the glory of self-sacrificing love. In the light from Calvary it will be seen that the law of self-renouncing love is the law of life for earth and heaven; that the love which "seeketh not her own" has its source in the heart of God; and that in the meek and lowly One is manifested the character of Him who dwelleth in the light which no man can approach unto.

In the beginning, God was revealed in all the works of creation. It was Christ that spread the heavens, and laid the foundations of the earth. It was His hand that hung the worlds in space, and fashioned the flowers of the field. "His strength setteth fast the mountains." "The sea is His, and He made it." (Psalm 65:6; 95:5.) It was He that filled the earth with beauty, and the air with song. And upon all things in earth, and air, and sky, He wrote the message of the Father's love.—*The Desire of Ages,* pp. 19, 20.

February 7

Lucifer Exposed

Having disarmed principalities and powers, He made a public spectacle of them, triumphing over them in it.—Colossians 2:15.

In the banishment of Satan from heaven, God declared His justice and maintained the honor of His throne. But when mankind had sinned through yielding to the deceptions of this apostate spirit, God gave an evidence of His love by yielding up His only-begotten Son to die for the fallen race. In the atonement the character of God is revealed. The mighty argument of the cross demonstrates to the whole universe that the course of sin which Lucifer had chosen was in no wise chargeable upon the government of God.

In the contest between Christ and Satan, during the Saviour's earthly ministry, the character of the great deceiver was unmasked. Nothing could so effectually have uprooted Satan from the affections of the heavenly angels and the whole loyal universe as did his cruel warfare upon the world's Redeemer. The daring blasphemy of his demand that Christ should pay him homage, his presumptuous boldness in bearing Him to the mountain summit and the pinnacle of the temple, the malicious intent betrayed in urging Him to cast Himself down from the dizzy height, the unsleeping malice that hunted Him from place to place, inspiring the hearts of priests and people to reject His love, and at the last to cry, "Crucify Him! crucify Him!"—all this excited the amazement and indignation of the universe.

It was Satan that prompted the world's rejection of Christ. The prince of evil exerted all his power and cunning to destroy Jesus; for he saw that the Saviour's mercy and love, His compassion and pitying tenderness, were representing to the world the character of God. Satan contested every claim put forth by the Son of God and employed human beings as his agents to fill the Saviour's life with suffering and sorrow. The sophistry and falsehood by which he had sought to hinder the work of Jesus, the hatred manifested through the children of disobedience, his cruel accusations against Him whose life was one of unexampled goodness, all sprang from deep-seated revenge. The pent-up fires of envy and malice, hatred and revenge, burst forth on Calvary against the Son of God, while all heaven gazed upon the scene in silent horror. . . .

Now the guilt of Satan stood forth without excuse. He had revealed his true character as a liar and a murderer.—*The Great Controversy,* pp. 500–502.

February 8

Selfishness Cannot Understand Love

I will exalt my throne above the stars of God; . . . I will be like the Most High.
—Isaiah 14:13, 14.

At the birth of Jesus, Satan knew that One had come with a divine commission to dispute his dominion. He trembled at the angel's message attesting the authority of the newborn King. Satan well knew the position that Christ had held in heaven as the Beloved of the Father. That the Son of God should come to this earth as a man filled him with amazement and with apprehension. He could not fathom the mystery of this great sacrifice. His selfish soul could not understand such love for the deceived race. The glory and peace of heaven, and the joy of communion with God, were but dimly comprehended by human beings; but they were well known to Lucifer, the covering cherub. Since he had lost heaven, he was determined to find revenge by causing others to share his fall. This he would do by causing them to undervalue heavenly things, and to set the heart upon things of earth. . . .

The image of God was manifest in Christ, and in the councils of Satan it was determined that He should be overcome. No human being had come into the world and escaped the power of the deceiver. The forces of the confederacy of evil were set upon His track to engage in warfare against Him, and if possible to prevail over Him.

At the Saviour's baptism, Satan was among the witnesses. He saw the Father's glory overshadowing His Son. He heard the voice of Jehovah testifying to the divinity of Jesus. Ever since Adam's sin, the human race had been cut off from direct communion with God; the communication between heaven and earth had been through Christ; but now that Jesus had come "in the likeness of sinful flesh" (Romans 8:3), the Father Himself spoke. He had before communicated with humanity *through* Christ; now He communicated with humanity *in* Christ. Satan had hoped that God's abhorrence of evil would bring an eternal separation between heaven and earth. But now it was manifest that the connection between God and humanity had been restored.

Satan saw that he must either conquer or be conquered. The issues of the conflict involved too much to be entrusted to his confederate angels. He must personally conduct the warfare. All the energies of apostasy were rallied against the Son of God. Christ was made the mark of every weapon of hell.—*The Desire of Ages,* pp. 115, 116.

February 9

God Understands

Of His fullness we have all received, and grace for grace.—John 1:16.

Since Jesus came to dwell with us, we know that God is acquainted with our trials, and sympathizes with our griefs. Every son and daughter of Adam may understand that our Creator is the friend of sinners. For in every doctrine of grace, every promise of joy, every deed of love, every divine attraction presented in the Saviour's life on earth, we see "God with us."

Satan represents God's law of love as a law of selfishness. He declares that it is impossible for us to obey its precepts. The fall of our first parents, with all the woe that has resulted, he charges upon the Creator, leading people to look upon God as the author of sin, and suffering, and death. Jesus was to unveil this deception. As one of us He was to give an example of obedience. For this He took upon Himself our nature, and passed through our experiences. "In all things it behooved Him to be made like unto His brethren." (Hebrews 2:17.) If we had to bear anything which Jesus did not endure, then upon this point Satan would represent the power of God as insufficient for us. Therefore Jesus was "in all points tempted like as we are." (Hebrews 4:15.) He endured every trial to which we are subject. And He exercised in His own behalf no power that is not freely offered to us. As a human, He met temptation, and overcame in the strength given Him from God. He says, "I delight to do Thy will, O My God: yea, Thy law is within My heart." (Psalm 40:8.) As He went about doing good, and healing all who were afflicted by Satan, He made plain to all the character of God's law and the nature of His service. His life testifies that it is possible for us also to obey the law of God.

By His humanity, Christ touched humanity; by His divinity, He lays hold upon the throne of God. As the Son of man, He gave us an example of obedience; as the Son of God, He gives us power to obey. It was Christ who from the bush on Mount Horeb spoke to Moses saying, "I AM THAT I AM." . . . And to us He says: "I AM the Good Shepherd." "I AM the living Bread." "I AM the Way, the Truth, and the Life." "All power is given unto Me in heaven and in earth." (John 10:11; 6:51; 14:6; Matthew 28:18.) I AM the assurance of every promise. I AM; be not afraid. "God with us" is the surety of our deliverance from sin, the assurance of our power to obey the law of heaven.—*The Desire of Ages,* pp. 24, 25.

February 10

The Story of Bethlehem

"For there is born to you this day in the city of David a Savior, who is Christ the Lord."
—Luke 2:11.

Heaven and earth are no wider apart today than when shepherds listened to the angels' song. Humanity is still as much the object of heaven's solicitude as when common people of common occupations met angels at noonday, and talked with the heavenly messengers in the vineyards and the fields. To us in the common walks of life, heaven may be very near. Angels from the courts above will attend the steps of those who come and go at God's command.

The story of Bethlehem is an exhaustless theme. In it is hidden "the depth of the riches both of the wisdom and knowledge of God." (Romans 11:33.) We marvel at the Saviour's sacrifice in exchanging the throne of heaven for the manger, and the companionship of adoring angels for the beasts of the stall. Human pride and self-sufficiency stand rebuked in His presence. Yet this was but the beginning of His wonderful condescension. It would have been an almost infinite humiliation for the Son of God to take human nature, even when Adam stood in his innocence in Eden. But Jesus accepted humanity when the race had been weakened by four thousand years of sin. Like every child of Adam He accepted the results of the working of the great law of heredity. What these results were is shown in the history of His earthly ancestors. He came with such a heredity to share our sorrows and temptations, and to give us the example of a sinless life.

Satan in heaven had hated Christ for His position in the courts of God. He hated Him the more when he himself was dethroned. He hated Him who pledged Himself to redeem a race of sinners. Yet into the world where Satan claimed dominion God permitted His Son to come, a helpless babe, subject to the weakness of humanity. He permitted Him to meet life's peril in common with every human soul, to fight the battle as every child of humanity must fight it, at the risk of failure and eternal loss. . . .

God gave His only-begotten Son, that the path of life might be made sure for our little ones. "Herein is love." Wonder, O heavens! and be astonished, O earth!—*The Desire of Ages,* pp. 48, 49.

February 11

Understanding His Mission

And when He was twelve years old, they went up to Jerusalem according to the custom of the feast.—Luke 2:42.

The Passover was followed by the seven days' feast of unleavened bread. On the second day of the feast, the first fruits of the year's harvest, a sheaf of barley, was presented before the Lord. All the ceremonies of the feast were types of the work of Christ. The deliverance of Israel from Egypt was an object lesson of redemption, which the Passover was intended to keep in memory. The slain lamb, the unleavened bread, the sheaf of first fruits, represented the Saviour.

With most of the people in the days of Christ, the observance of this feast had degenerated into formalism. But what was its significance to the Son of God!

For the first time the child Jesus looked upon the temple. He saw the white-robed priests performing their solemn ministry. He beheld the bleeding victim upon the altar of sacrifice. With the worshipers He bowed in prayer, while the cloud of incense ascended before God. He witnessed the impressive rites of the paschal service. Day by day He saw their meaning more clearly. Every act seemed to be bound up with His own life. New impulses were awakening within Him. Silent and absorbed, He seemed to be studying out a great problem. The mystery of His mission was opening to the Saviour.

Rapt in the contemplation of these scenes, He did not remain beside His parents. He sought to be alone. When the paschal services were ended, He still lingered in the temple courts; and when the worshipers departed from Jerusalem, He was left behind.

In this visit to Jerusalem, the parents of Jesus wished to bring Him in connection with the great teachers in Israel. While He was obedient in every particular to the word of God, He did not conform to the rabbinical rites and usages. Joseph and Mary hoped that He might be led to reverence the learned rabbis, and give more diligent heed to their requirements. But Jesus in the temple had been taught by God. That which He had received, He began at once to impart. . . .

If followed, the lines of truth He pointed out would have worked a reformation in the religion of the day. A deep interest in spiritual things would have been awakened; and when Jesus began His ministry, many would have been prepared to receive Him.—*The Desire of Ages,* pp. 77–79.

February 12

"My Father's Business"

Why did you seek Me? Did you not know that I must be about My Father's business?
—Luke 2:49.

How is it that ye sought Me?" answered Jesus. "Wist ye not that I must be about My Father's business?" And as they seemed not to understand His words, He pointed upward. On His face was a light at which they wondered. Divinity was flashing through humanity. On finding Him in the temple, they had listened to what was passing between Him and the rabbis, and they were astonished at His questions and answers. His words started a train of thought that would never be forgotten. . . .

It was natural for the parents of Jesus to look upon Him as their own child. He was daily with them, His life in many respects was like that of other children, and it was difficult for them to realize that He was the Son of God. They were in danger of failing to appreciate the blessing granted them in the presence of the world's Redeemer. The grief of their separation from Him, and the gentle reproof which His words conveyed, were designed to impress them with the sacredness of their trust.

In the answer to His mother, Jesus showed for the first time that He understood His relation to God. Before His birth the angel had said to Mary, "He shall be great, and shall be called the Son of the Highest: and the Lord God shall give unto Him the throne of His father David: and He shall reign over the house of Jacob forever." (Luke 1:32, 33.) These words Mary had pondered in her heart; yet while she believed that her child was to be Israel's Messiah, she did not comprehend His mission. Now she did not understand His words; but she knew that He had disclaimed kinship to Joseph, and had declared His Sonship to God.

Jesus did not ignore His relation to His earthly parents. From Jerusalem He returned home with them, and aided them in their life of toil. He hid in His own heart the mystery of His mission, waiting submissively for the appointed time for Him to enter upon His work. For eighteen years after He had recognized that He was the Son of God, He acknowledged the tie that bound Him to the home at Nazareth, and performed the duties of a son, a brother, a friend, and a citizen.—*The Desire of Ages,* pp. 81, 82.

February 13

Family Problems

For even His brothers did not believe in Him.
—John 7:5.

At a very early age, Jesus had begun to act for Himself in the formation of His character, and not even respect and love for His parents could turn Him from obedience to God's word. "It is written" was His reason for every act that varied from the family customs. But the influence of the rabbis made His life a bitter one. Even in His youth He had to learn the hard lesson of silence and patient endurance.

His brothers, as the sons of Joseph were called, sided with the rabbis. They insisted that the traditions must be heeded, as if they were the requirements of God. They even regarded the human precepts more highly than the word of God, and they were greatly annoyed at the clear penetration of Jesus in distinguishing between the false and the true. His strict obedience to the law of God they condemned as stubbornness. They were surprised at the knowledge and wisdom He showed in answering the rabbis. They knew that He had not received instruction from the wise men, yet they could not but see that He was an instructor to them. They recognized that His education was of a higher type than their own. But they did not discern that He had access to the tree of life, a source of knowledge of which they were ignorant. . . .

At all times and in all places He manifested a loving interest in people, and shed about Him the light of a cheerful piety. All this was a rebuke to the Pharisees. It showed that religion does not consist in selfishness, and that their morbid devotion to personal interest was far from being true godliness. This had roused their enmity against Jesus, so that they tried to enforce His conformity to their regulations. . . .

All this displeased His brothers. Being older than Jesus, they felt that He should be under their dictation. They charged Him with thinking Himself superior to them, and reproved Him for setting Himself above their teachers and the priests and rulers of the people. Often they threatened and tried to intimidate Him; but He passed on, making the Scriptures His guide.

Jesus loved His brothers, and treated them with unfailing kindness; but they were jealous of Him, and manifested the most decided unbelief and contempt. They could not understand His conduct.—*The Desire of Ages,* pp. 86, 87.

Patience

Are You able to drink the cup that I drink?
—Mark 10:38.

Of the bitterness that falls to the lot of humanity, there was no part which Christ did not taste. There were those who tried to cast contempt upon Him because of His birth, and even in His childhood He had to meet their scornful looks and evil whisperings. If He had responded by an impatient word or look, if He had conceded to His brothers by even one wrong act, He would have failed of being a perfect example. Thus He would have failed of carrying out the plan for our redemption. Had He even admitted that there could be an excuse for sin, Satan would have triumphed, and the world would have been lost. This is why the tempter worked to make His life as trying as possible, that He might be led to sin.

But to every temptation He had one answer, "It is written." He rarely rebuked any wrongdoing of His brothers, but He had a word from God to speak to them. Often He was accused of cowardice for refusing to unite with them in some forbidden act; but His answer was, It is written, "The fear of the Lord, that is wisdom; and to depart from evil is understanding." (Job 28:28.)

There were some who sought His society, feeling at peace in His presence; but many avoided Him, because they were rebuked by His stainless life. . . .

Often He was asked, Why are you bent on being so singular, so different from us all? It is written, He said, "Blessed are the undefiled in the way, who walk in the law of the Lord. Blessed are they that keep His testimonies, and that seek Him with the whole heart. They also do no iniquity; they walk in His ways." (Psalm 119:1–3.)

When questioned why He did not join in the frolics of the youth of Nazareth, He said, It is written, "I have rejoiced in the way of Thy testimonies, as much as in all riches. I will meditate in Thy precepts, and have respect unto Thy ways. I will delight myself in Thy statutes; I will not forget Thy word." (Psalm 119:14–16.)

Jesus did not contend for His rights. Often His work was made unnecessarily severe because He was willing and uncomplaining. Yet He did not fail nor become discouraged. He lived above these difficulties, as if in the light of God's countenance. He did not retaliate when roughly used, but bore insult patiently.—*The Desire of Ages,* pp. 88, 89.

February 15

Stay Focused on Christ

Therefore, if anyone is in Christ, he is a new creation.
—2 Corinthians 5:17.

When Christ took human nature upon Him, He bound humanity to Himself by a tie of love that can never be broken by any power save the choice of man himself. Satan will constantly present allurements to induce us to break this tie—to choose to separate ourselves from Christ. Here is where we need to watch, to strive, to pray, that nothing may entice us to choose another master; for we are always free to do this. But let us keep our eyes fixed upon Christ, and He will preserve us. Looking unto Jesus, we are safe. Nothing can pluck us out of His hand. In constantly beholding Him, we "are changed into the same image from glory to glory, even as by the Spirit of the Lord." (2 Corinthians 3:18.)

It was thus that the early disciples gained their likeness to the dear Saviour. When those disciples heard the words of Jesus, they felt their need of Him. They sought, they found, they followed Him. They were with Him in the house, at the table, in the closet, in the field. They were with Him as pupils with a teacher, daily receiving from His lips lessons of holy truth. They looked to Him, as servants to their master, to learn their duty. Those disciples were men "subject to like passions as we are." (James 5:17.) They had the same battle with sin to fight. They needed the same grace, in order to live a holy life.

Even John, the beloved disciple, the one who most fully reflected the likeness of the Saviour, did not naturally possess that loveliness of character. He was not only self-assertive and ambitious for honor, but impetuous, and resentful under injuries. But as the character of the Divine One was manifested to him, he saw his own deficiency and was humbled by the knowledge. The strength and patience, the power and tenderness, the majesty and meekness, that he beheld in the daily life of the Son of God, filled his soul with admiration and love. Day by day his heart was drawn out toward Christ, until he lost sight of self in love for his Master. His resentful, ambitious temper was yielded to the molding power of Christ. The regenerating influence of the Holy Spirit renewed his heart. The power of the love of Christ wrought a transformation of character. This is the sure result of union with Jesus. When Christ abides in the heart, the whole nature is transformed. Christ's Spirit, His love, softens the heart, subdues the soul, and raises the thoughts and desires toward God and heaven.—*Steps to Christ,* pp. 72, 73.

Love Stronger Than Death

Now hope does not disappoint, because the love of God has been poured out in our hearts by the Holy Spirit who was given to us.—Romans 5:5.

We must fall upon the Rock and be broken before we can be uplifted in Christ. Self must be dethroned, pride must be humbled, if we would know the glory of the spiritual kingdom. . . .

In the light of the Saviour's life, the hearts of all, even from the Creator to the prince of darkness, are revealed. Satan has represented God as selfish and oppressive, as claiming all, and giving nothing, as requiring the service of His creatures for His own glory, and making no sacrifice for their good. But the gift of Christ reveals the Father's heart. It testifies that the thoughts of God toward us are "thoughts of peace, and not of evil." (Jeremiah 29:11.) It declares that while God's hatred of sin is as strong as death, His love for the sinner is stronger than death. Having undertaken our redemption, He will spare nothing, however dear, which is necessary to the completion of His work. No truth essential to our salvation is withheld, no miracle of mercy is neglected, no divine agency is left unemployed. Favor is heaped upon favor, gift upon gift. The whole treasury of heaven is open to those He seeks to save. Having collected the riches of the universe, and laid open the resources of infinite power, He gives them all into the hands of Christ, and says, All these are for mankind. Use these gifts to convince them that there is no love greater than Mine in earth or heaven. Their greatest happiness will be found in loving Me.

At the cross of Calvary, love and selfishness stood face to face. Here was their crowning manifestation. Christ had lived only to comfort and bless, and in putting Him to death, Satan manifested the malignity of his hatred against God. He made it evident that the real purpose of his rebellion was to dethrone God, and to destroy Him through whom the love of God was shown.

By the life and the death of Christ, the thoughts of men and women also are brought to view. From the manger to the cross, the life of Jesus was a call to self-surrender, and to fellowship in suffering. It unveiled the purposes of everyone. Jesus came with the truth of heaven, and all who were listening to the voice of the Holy Spirit were drawn to Him. The worshipers of self belonged to Satan's kingdom. In their attitude toward Christ, all would show on which side they stood. And thus all pass judgment on themselves.—*The Desire of Ages,* p. 57.

February 17

The Good Shepherd

I am the good shepherd.
—John 10:11.

Every soul is as fully known to Jesus as if he or she were the only one for whom the Saviour died. The distress of every one touches His heart. The cry for aid reaches His ear. He came to draw all unto Himself. He bids them, "Follow Me," and His Spirit moves upon their hearts to draw them to come to Him. Many refuse to be drawn. Jesus knows who they are. He also knows who gladly hear His call, and are ready to come under His pastoral care. He says, "My sheep hear My voice, and I know them, and they follow Me." (John 10:27.) He cares for each one as if there were not another on the face of the earth. . . .

It is not the fear of punishment, or the hope of everlasting reward, that leads the disciples of Christ to follow Him. They behold the Saviour's matchless love, revealed throughout His pilgrimage on earth, from the manger of Bethlehem to Calvary's cross, and the sight of Him attracts, it softens and subdues the soul. Love awakens in the heart of the beholders. They hear His voice, and they follow Him.

As the shepherd goes before his sheep, himself first encountering the perils of the way, so does Jesus with His people. "When He putteth forth His own sheep, He goeth before them." (John 10:4.) The way to heaven is consecrated by the Saviour's footprints. The path may be steep and rugged, but Jesus has traveled that way; His feet have pressed down the cruel thorns, to make the pathway easier for us. Every burden that we are called to bear He Himself has borne.

Though now He has ascended to the presence of God, and shares the throne of the universe, Jesus has lost none of His compassionate nature. Today the same tender, sympathizing heart is open to all the woes of humanity. Today the hand that was pierced is reached forth to bless more abundantly His people that are in the world. "And they shall never perish, neither shall any man pluck them out of My hand." (John 10:28.) The soul that has given himself to Christ is more precious in His sight than the whole world. The Saviour would have passed through the agony of Calvary that one might be saved in His kingdom. He will never abandon one for whom He has died. Unless His followers choose to leave Him, He will hold them fast.—*The Desire of Ages,* pp. 480–483.

The Test of Christ's Divinity

Lazarus, come forth!
—John 11:43.

He felt every pang of anguish, as He said to His disciples, "Lazarus is dead." But Christ had not only the loved ones at Bethany to think of; He had the training of His disciples to consider. They were to be His representatives to the world, that the Father's blessing might embrace all. For their sake He permitted Lazarus to die. Had He restored him from illness to health, the miracle that is the most positive evidence of His divine character, would not have been performed. . . .

In delaying to come to Lazarus, Christ had a purpose of mercy toward those who had not received Him. He tarried, that by raising Lazarus from the dead He might give to His stubborn, unbelieving people another evidence that He was indeed "the resurrection, and the life." . . . In His mercy He purposed to give them one more evidence that He was the Restorer, the One who alone could bring life and immortality to light. This was to be an evidence that the priests could not misinterpret. This was the reason of His delay in going to Bethany. This crowning miracle, the raising of Lazarus, was to set the seal of God on His work and on His claim to divinity. . . .

Lazarus had been laid in a cave in a rock, and a massive stone had been placed before the entrance. "Take ye away the stone," Christ said. Thinking that He only wished to look upon the dead, Martha objected, saying that the body had been buried four days, and corruption had already begun its work. This statement, made before the raising of Lazarus, left no room for Christ's enemies to say that a deception had been practiced. . . .

"And when He thus had spoken, He cried with a loud voice, Lazarus, come forth." His voice, clear and penetrating, pierces the ear of the dead. As He speaks, divinity flashes through humanity. In His face, which is lighted up by the glory of God, the people see the assurance of His power. Every eye is fastened on the entrance to the cave. Every ear is bent to catch the slightest sound. With intense and painful interest all wait for the test of Christ's divinity, the evidence that is to substantiate His claim to be the Son of God, or to extinguish the hope forever.

There is a stir in the silent tomb, and he who was dead stands at the door of the sepulcher.—*The Desire of Ages,* pp. 528, 529, 534, 536.

February 19

Triumphal Entry

Behold, your King is coming to you; He is just and having salvation,
lowly and riding on a donkey, a colt, the foal of a donkey.
—Zechariah 9:9.

Christ was following the Jewish custom for a royal entry. The animal on which He rode was that ridden by the kings of Israel, and prophecy had foretold that thus the Messiah should come to His kingdom. No sooner was He seated upon the colt than a loud shout of triumph rent the air. The multitude hailed Him as Messiah, their King. Jesus now accepted the homage which He had never before permitted, and the disciples received this as proof that their glad hopes were to be realized by seeing Him established on the throne. The multitude were convinced that the hour of their emancipation was at hand. In imagination they saw the Roman armies driven from Jerusalem, and Israel once more an independent nation. All were happy and excited; the people vied with one another in paying Him homage. They could not display outward pomp and splendor, but they gave Him the worship of happy hearts. They were unable to present Him with costly gifts, but they spread their outer garments as a carpet in His path, and they also strewed the leafy branches of the olive and the palm in the way. They could lead the triumphal procession with no royal standards, but they cut down the spreading palm boughs, Nature's emblem of victory, and waved them aloft with loud acclamations and hosannas.

As they proceeded, the multitude was continually increased by those who had heard of the coming of Jesus and hastened to join the procession. . . . They had all heard of Jesus, and expected Him to go to Jerusalem; but they knew that He had heretofore discouraged all effort to place Him on the throne, and they were greatly astonished to learn that this was He. They wondered what could have wrought this change in Him who had declared that His kingdom was not of this world. . . .

Never before in His earthly life had Jesus permitted such a demonstration. He clearly foresaw the result. It would bring Him to the cross. . . . It was necessary, then, that the eyes of all people should now be directed to Him; the events which preceded His great sacrifice must be such as to call attention to the sacrifice itself. After such a demonstration as that attending His entry into Jerusalem, all eyes would follow His rapid progress to the final scene.—*The Desire of Ages,* pp. 570, 571.

February 20

Jesus Came to Glorify God

For this purpose I came to this hour. Father, glorify Your name.
—John 12:27, 28.

The message of the Greeks, foreshadowing as it did the gathering in of the Gentiles, brought to the mind of Jesus His entire mission. The work of redemption passed before Him, from the time when in heaven the plan was laid, to the death that was now so near at hand. A mysterious cloud seemed to enshroud the Son of God. Its gloom was felt by those near Him. He sat rapt in thought. . . .

Then came divine submission to His Father's will. "For this cause," He said, "came I unto this hour. Father, glorify Thy name." Only through the death of Christ could Satan's kingdom be overthrown. Only thus could we be redeemed, and God be glorified. Jesus consented to the agony, He accepted the sacrifice. The Majesty of heaven consented to suffer as the Sin Bearer. "Father, glorify Thy name," He said. As Christ spoke these words, a response came from the cloud which hovered above His head: "I have both glorified it, and will glorify it again." Christ's whole life, from the manger to the time when these words were spoken, had glorified God; and in the coming trial His divine-human sufferings would indeed glorify His Father's name.

As the voice was heard, a light darted from the cloud, and encircled Christ, as if the arms of Infinite Power were thrown about Him like a wall of fire. The people beheld this scene with terror and amazement. No one dared to speak. With silent lips and bated breath all stood with eyes fixed upon Jesus. The testimony of the Father having been given, the cloud lifted, and scattered in the heavens. For the time the visible communion between the Father and the Son was ended.

"The people therefore, that stood by, and heard it, said that it thundered: others said, An angel spake to Him." But the inquiring Greeks saw the cloud, heard the voice, comprehended its meaning, and discerned Christ indeed; to them He was revealed as the Sent of God.

The voice of God had been heard at the baptism of Jesus at the beginning of His ministry, and again at His transfiguration on the mount. Now at the close of His ministry it was heard for the third time, by a larger number of persons, and under peculiar circumstances.—*The Desire of Ages,* pp. 624, 625.

February 21

The Gospel to the World

And this gospel of the kingdom will be preached in all the world as a witness to all the nations, and then the end will come.—Matthew 24:14.

Christ has given signs of His coming. He declares that we may know when He is near, even at the doors. He says of those who see these signs, "This generation shall not pass, till all these things be fulfilled." These signs have appeared. Now we know of a surety that the Lord's coming is at hand. "Heaven and earth shall pass away," He says, "but My words shall not pass away." . . .

The exact time of the second coming of the Son of man is God's mystery. . . .

In the prophecy of Jerusalem's destruction Christ said, "Because iniquity shall abound, the love of many shall wax cold. But he that shall endure unto the end, the same shall be saved. And this gospel of the kingdom shall be preached in all the world for a witness unto all nations; and then shall the end come." This prophecy will again be fulfilled. The abounding iniquity of that day finds its counterpart in this generation. So with the prediction in regard to the preaching of the gospel. Before the fall of Jerusalem, Paul, writing by the Holy Spirit, declared that the gospel was preached to "every creature which is under heaven." (Colossians 1:23.) So now, before the coming of the Son of man, the everlasting gospel is to be preached "to every nation, and kindred, and tongue, and people." (Revelation 14:6, 14.) God "hath appointed a day, in the which He will judge the world." (Acts 17:31.) Christ tells us when that day shall be ushered in. He does not say that all the world will be converted, but that "this gospel of the kingdom shall be preached in all the world for a witness unto all nations; and then shall the end come." By giving the gospel to the world it is in our power to hasten our Lord's return. We are not only to look for but to hasten the coming of the day of God. (2 Peter 3:12, margin.) Had the church of Christ done her appointed work as the Lord ordained, the whole world would before this have been warned, and the Lord Jesus would have come to our earth in power and great glory. . . .

Those who watch for the Lord's coming are not waiting in idle expectancy. . . . With vigilant watching they combine earnest working. Because they know that the Lord is at the door, their zeal is quickened to co-operate with the divine intelligences in working for the salvation of souls.—*The Desire of Ages*, pp. 632–634.

You Are Clean

He who is bathed needs only to wash his feet,
but is completely clean; and you are clean.
—John 13:10.

These words mean more than bodily cleanliness. Christ is still speaking of the higher cleansing as illustrated by the lower. He who came from the bath was clean, but the sandaled feet soon became dusty, and again needed to be washed. So Peter and his brethren had been washed in the great fountain opened for sin and uncleanness. Christ acknowledged them as His. But temptation had led them into evil, and they still needed His cleansing grace. When Jesus girded Himself with a towel to wash the dust from their feet, He desired by that very act to wash the alienation, jealousy, and pride from their hearts. This was of far more consequence than the washing of their dusty feet. With the spirit they then had, not one of them was prepared for communion with Christ. Until brought into a state of humility and love, they were not prepared to partake of the paschal supper, or to share in the memorial service which Christ was about to institute. Their hearts must be cleansed. Pride and self-seeking create dissension and hatred, but all this Jesus washed away in washing their feet. A change of feeling was brought about. Looking upon them, Jesus could say, "Ye are clean." Now there was union of heart, love for one another. They had become humble and teachable. . . .

When believers assemble to celebrate the ordinances, there are present messengers unseen by human eyes. There may be a Judas in the company, and if so, messengers from the prince of darkness are there, for they attend all who refuse to be controlled by the Holy Spirit. Heavenly angels also are present. These unseen visitants are present on every such occasion. There may come into the company persons who are not in heart servants of truth and holiness, but who may wish to take part in the service. They should not be forbidden. There are witnesses present who were present when Jesus washed the feet of the disciples and of Judas. More than human eyes beheld the scene. . . .

None should exclude themselves from the Communion because some who are unworthy may be present. Every disciple is called upon to participate publicly, and thus bear witness of accepting Christ as a personal Saviour. It is at these, His own appointments, that Christ meets His people, and energizes them by His presence.—*The Desire of Ages,* pp. 646, 656.

February 23

The Penitent Thief

Lord, remember me when You come into Your kingdom.
—Luke 23:42.

To Jesus in His agony on the cross there came one gleam of comfort. It was the prayer of the penitent thief. Both the men who were crucified with Jesus had at first railed upon Him; and one under his suffering only became more desperate and defiant. But not so with his companion. This man was not a hardened criminal; he had been led astray by evil associations, but he was less guilty than many of those who stood beside the cross reviling the Saviour. He had seen and heard Jesus, and had been convicted by His teaching, but he had been turned away from Him by the priests and rulers. Seeking to stifle conviction, he had plunged deeper and deeper into sin, until he was arrested, tried as a criminal, and condemned to die on the cross. In the judgment hall and on the way to Calvary he had been in company with Jesus. He had heard Pilate declare, "I find no fault in Him." (John 19:4.) He had marked His godlike bearing, and His pitying forgiveness of His tormentors. On the cross he sees the many great religionists shoot out the tongue with scorn, and ridicule the Lord Jesus. . . . Among the passers-by he hears many defending Jesus. He hears them repeat His words, and tell of His works. The conviction comes back to him that this is the Christ. Turning to his fellow criminal he says, "Dost not thou fear God, seeing thou art in the same condemnation?" The dying thieves have no longer anything to fear from man. But upon one of them presses the conviction that there is a God to fear, a future to cause him to tremble. And now, all sin-polluted as it is, his life history is about to close. "And we indeed justly," he moans; "for we receive the due reward of our deeds: but this Man hath done nothing amiss." . . .

The Holy Spirit illuminates his mind, and little by little the chain of evidence is joined together. In Jesus, bruised, mocked, and hanging upon the cross, he sees the Lamb of God, that taketh away the sin of the world. Hope is mingled with anguish in his voice as the helpless, dying soul casts himself upon a dying Saviour. "Lord, remember me," he cries, "when Thou comest into Thy kingdom."

Quickly the answer came. Soft and melodious the tone, full of love, compassion, and power the words: Verily I say unto thee today, Thou shalt be with Me in paradise.—*The Desire of Ages,* pp. 749, 750.

February 24

It Is Finished

So when Jesus had received the sour wine, He said, "It is finished!"
And bowing His head, He gave up His spirit.
—John 19:30.

Satan with his fierce temptations wrung the heart of Jesus. The Saviour could not see through the portals of the tomb. Hope did not present to Him His coming forth from the grave a conqueror, or tell Him of the Father's acceptance of the sacrifice. He feared that sin was so offensive to God that Their separation was to be eternal. Christ felt the anguish which the sinner will feel when mercy shall no longer plead for the guilty race. It was the sense of sin, bringing the Father's wrath upon Him as our substitute, that made the cup He drank so bitter, and broke the heart of the Son of God. . . .

God and His holy angels were beside the cross. The Father was with His Son. Yet His presence was not revealed. Had His glory flashed forth from the cloud, every human beholder would have been destroyed. And in that dreadful hour Christ was not to be comforted with the Father's presence. He trod the wine press alone. . . .

To the angels and the unfallen worlds the cry, "It is finished," had a deep significance. It was for them as well as for us that the great work of redemption had been accomplished. They with us share the fruits of Christ's victory.

Not until the death of Christ was the character of Satan clearly revealed to the angels or to the unfallen worlds. The archapostate had so clothed himself with deception that even holy beings had not understood his principles. They had not clearly seen the nature of his rebellion. . . .

It was God's purpose to place things on an eternal basis of security, and in the councils of heaven it was decided that time must be given for Satan to develop the principles which were the foundation of his system of government. He had claimed that these were superior to God's principles. Time was given for the working of Satan's principles, that they might be seen by the heavenly universe. . . .

Well, then, might the angels rejoice as they looked upon the Saviour's cross; for though they did not then understand all, they knew that the destruction of sin and Satan was forever made certain, that the redemption of man was assured, and that the universe was made eternally secure.—*The Desire of Ages,* pp. 753, 754, 758, 759, 764.

February 25

He Is Risen

He is not here: for He is risen, as He said. Come, see the place where the Lord lay.—Matthew 28:6.

An earthquake marked the hour when Christ laid down His life, and another earthquake witnessed the moment when He took it up in triumph. He who had vanquished death and the grave came forth from the tomb with the tread of a conqueror, amid the reeling of the earth, the flashing of lightning, and the roaring of thunder. . . .

Christ came forth from the tomb glorified, and the Roman guard beheld Him. Their eyes were riveted upon the face of Him whom they had so recently mocked and derided. In this glorified Being they beheld the prisoner whom they had seen in the judgment hall, the one for whom they had plaited a crown of thorns. . . .

At sight of the angels and the glorified Saviour the Roman guard had fainted and become as dead men. When the heavenly train was hidden from their view, they arose to their feet, and as quickly as their trembling limbs could carry them, made their way to the gate of the garden. Staggering like drunken men, they hurried on to the city, telling those whom they met the wonderful news. They were making their way to Pilate, but their report had been carried to the Jewish authorities, and the chief priests and rulers sent for them to be brought first into their presence. A strange appearance those soldiers presented. Trembling with fear, their faces colorless, they bore testimony to the resurrection of Christ. The soldiers told all, just as they had seen it; they had not had time to think or speak anything but the truth. With painful utterance they said, It was the Son of God who was crucified; we have heard an angel proclaiming Him as the Majesty of heaven, the King of glory.

The faces of the priests were as those of the dead. Caiaphas tried to speak. His lips moved, but they uttered no sound. . . . A lying report was then given to the soldiers. . . .

When Jesus was laid in the grave, Satan triumphed. He dared to hope that the Saviour would not take up His life again. He claimed the Lord's body, and set his guard about the tomb, seeking to hold Christ a prisoner. He was bitterly angry when his angels fled at the approach of the heavenly messenger. When he saw Christ come forth in triumph, he knew that his kingdom would have an end, and that he must finally die.—*The Desire of Ages,* pp. 780–782.

He Is the King of Glory

Lift up your heads, O you gates! And be lifted up, you everlasting doors! And the King of glory shall come in.—Psalm 24:7.

The time had come for Christ to ascend to His Father's throne. As a divine conqueror He was about to return with the trophies of victory to the heavenly courts. . . .

Now with the eleven disciples Jesus made His way toward the mountain. As they passed through the gate of Jerusalem, many wondering eyes looked upon the little company, led by One whom a few weeks before the rulers had condemned and crucified. . . .

With hands outstretched in blessing, and as if in assurance of His protecting care, He slowly ascended from among them, drawn heavenward by a power stronger than any earthly attraction. . . .

While the disciples were still gazing upward, voices addressed them which sounded like richest music. They turned, and saw two angels in the form of men, who spoke to them, saying, "Ye men of Galilee, why stand ye gazing up into heaven? this same Jesus, which is taken up from you into heaven, shall so come in like manner as ye have seen Him go into heaven." (Acts 1:11.)

These angels were of the company that had been waiting in a shining cloud to escort Jesus to His heavenly home. The most exalted of the angel throng, they were the two who had come to the tomb at Christ's resurrection, and they had been with Him throughout His life on earth. With eager desire all heaven had waited for the end of His tarrying in a world marred by the curse of sin. . . .

All heaven was waiting to welcome the Saviour to the celestial courts. As He ascended, He led the way, and the multitude of captives set free at His resurrection followed. The heavenly host, with shouts and acclamations of praise and celestial song, attended the joyous train.

As they drew near to the city of God, the challenge is given by the escorting angels,—

"Lift up your heads, O ye gates;
And be ye lift up, ye everlasting doors;
And the King of glory shall come in."

—*The Desire of Ages*, pp. 829–833.

February 27

Christ's Coronation and Its Results

Jesus . . . has sat down at the right hand of the throne of God.
—Hebrews 12:2.

Christ's ascension to heaven was the signal that His followers were to receive the promised blessing. For this they were to wait before they entered upon their work. When Christ passed within the heavenly gates, He was enthroned amidst the adoration of the angels. As soon as this ceremony was completed, the Holy Spirit descended upon the disciples in rich currents, and Christ was indeed glorified, even with the glory which He had with the Father from all eternity. The Pentecostal outpouring was Heaven's communication that the Redeemer's inauguration was accomplished. According to His promise He had sent the Holy Spirit from heaven to His followers as a token that He had, as priest and king, received all authority in heaven and on earth, and was the Anointed One over His people. . . .

During His life on this earth He had sown the seed of truth and had watered it with His blood. The conversions that took place on the Day of Pentecost were the result of this sowing, the harvest of Christ's work, revealing the power of His teaching.

The arguments of the apostles alone, though clear and convincing, would not have removed the prejudice that had withstood so much evidence. But the Holy Spirit sent the arguments home to hearts with divine power. The words of the apostles were as sharp arrows of the Almighty, convicting the hearers of their terrible guilt in rejecting and crucifying the Lord of glory.

Under the training of Christ the disciples had been led to feel their need of the Spirit. Under the Spirit's teaching they received the final qualification, and went forth to their lifework. No longer were they ignorant and uncultured. No longer were they a collection of independent units or discordant, conflicting elements. No longer were their hopes set on worldly greatness. They were of "one accord," "of one heart and of one soul." (Acts 2:46; 4:32.) Christ filled their thoughts; the advancement of His kingdom was their aim. In mind and character they had become like their Master. . . .

Pentecost brought them the heavenly illumination. The truths they could not understand while Christ was with them were now unfolded. With a faith and assurance that they had never before known, they accepted the teachings of the Sacred Word.—*The Acts of the Apostles,* pp. 38, 39, 45, 46.

February 28

The Intercession of Christ

Let us therefore come boldly to the throne of grace, that we may obtain mercy and find grace to help in time of need.—Hebrews 4:16.

The sanctuary in heaven is the very center of Christ's work in our behalf. It concerns every soul living upon the earth. It opens to view the plan of redemption, bringing us down to the very close of time and revealing the triumphant issue of the contest between righteousness and sin. It is of the utmost importance that all should thoroughly investigate these subjects and be able to give an answer to everyone that asketh them a reason of the hope that is in them.

The intercession of Christ in our behalf in the sanctuary above is as essential to the plan of salvation as was His death upon the cross. By His death He began that work which after His resurrection He ascended to complete in heaven. We must by faith enter within the veil, "whither the forerunner is for us entered." (Hebrews 6:20.) There the light from the cross of Calvary is reflected. There we may gain a clearer insight into the mysteries of redemption. The salvation of sinners is accomplished at an infinite expense to heaven; the sacrifice made is equal to the broadest demands of the broken law of God. Jesus has opened the way to the Father's throne, and through His mediation the sincere desire of all who come to Him in faith may be presented before God. . . .

We are now living in the great day of atonement. In the typical service, while the high priest was making the atonement for Israel, all were required to afflict their souls by repentance of sin and humiliation before the Lord, lest they be cut off from among the people. In like manner, all who would have their names retained in the book of life should now, in the few remaining days of their probation, afflict their souls before God by sorrow for sin and true repentance. There must be deep, faithful searching of heart. The light, frivolous spirit indulged by so many professed Christians must be put away. There is earnest warfare before all who would subdue the evil tendencies that strive for the mastery. The work of preparation is an individual work. We are not saved in groups. The purity and devotion of one will not offset the want of these qualities in another. Though all nations are to pass in judgment before God, yet He will examine the case of each individual with as close and searching scrutiny as if there were not another being upon the earth.—*The Great Controversy*, pp. 488–490.

February 29

Christ's Heavenly Ministry

Now this is the main point of the things we are saying: We have such a High Priest, who is seated at the right hand of the throne of the Majesty in the heavens.—Hebrews 8:1.

For eighteen centuries this work of ministration continued in the first apartment of the sanctuary. The blood of Christ, pleaded in behalf of penitent believers, secured their pardon and acceptance with the Father, yet their sins still remained upon the books of record. As in the typical service there was a work of atonement at the close of the year, so before Christ's work for the redemption of sinners is completed there is a work of atonement for the removal of sin from the sanctuary. This is the service which began when the 2300 days ended. At that time, as foretold by Daniel the prophet, our High Priest entered the most holy, to perform the last division of His solemn work—to cleanse the sanctuary.

As anciently the sins of the people were by faith placed upon the sin offering and through its blood transferred, in figure, to the earthly sanctuary, so in the new covenant the sins of the repentant are by faith placed upon Christ and transferred, in fact, to the heavenly sanctuary. And as the typical cleansing of the earthly was accomplished by the removal of the sins by which it had been polluted, so the actual cleansing of the heavenly is to be accomplished by the removal, or blotting out, of the sins which are there recorded. But before this can be accomplished, there must be an examination of the books of record to determine who, through repentance of sin and faith in Christ, are entitled to the benefits of His atonement. The cleansing of the sanctuary therefore involves a work of investigation—a work of judgment. This work must be performed prior to the coming of Christ to redeem His people; for when He comes, His reward is with Him to give to every man according to his works. (Revelation 22:12.)

Thus those who followed in the light of the prophetic word saw that, instead of coming to the earth at the termination of the 2300 days in 1844, Christ then entered the most holy place of the heavenly sanctuary to perform the closing work of atonement preparatory to His coming.

It was seen, also, that while the sin offering pointed to Christ as a sacrifice, and the high priest represented Christ as a mediator, the scapegoat typified Satan, the author of sin, upon whom the sins of the truly penitent will finally be placed.—*The Great Controversy,* pp. 421, 422.

Surrender and Acceptance

MARCH 1

JUST AS WE ARE

Come to Me, all you who labor and are heavy laden.
—Matthew 11:28.

Some seem to feel that they must be on probation, and must prove to the Lord that they are reformed, before they can claim His blessing. But they may claim the blessing of God even now. They must have His grace, the Spirit of Christ, to help their infirmities, or they cannot resist evil. Jesus loves to have us come to Him just as we are, sinful, helpless, dependent. We may come with all our weakness, our folly, our sinfulness, and fall at His feet in penitence. It is His glory to encircle us in the arms of His love and to bind up our wounds, to cleanse us from all impurity.

Here is where thousands fail; they do not believe that Jesus pardons them personally, individually. They do not take God at His word. It is the privilege of all who comply with the conditions to know for themselves that pardon is freely extended for every sin. Put away the suspicion that God's promises are not meant for you. They are for every repentant transgressor. Strength and grace have been provided through Christ to be brought by ministering angels to every believing soul. None are so sinful that they cannot find strength, purity, and righteousness in Jesus, who died for them. He is waiting to strip them of their garments stained and polluted with sin, and to put upon them the white robes of righteousness; He bids them live and not die.

God does not deal with us as finite human beings deal with one another. His thoughts are thoughts of mercy, love, and tenderest compassion. He says, "Let the wicked forsake his way, and the unrighteous man his thoughts: and let him return unto the Lord, and He will have mercy upon him; and to our God, for He will abundantly pardon." "I have blotted out, as a thick cloud, thy transgressions, and, as a cloud, thy sins." (Isaiah 55:7; 44:22.)

"I have no pleasure in the death of him that dieth, saith the Lord God: wherefore turn yourselves, and live ye." (Ezekiel 18:32.) Satan is ready to steal away the blessed assurances of God. He desires to take every glimmer of hope and every ray of light from the soul; but you must not permit him to do this. Do not give ear to the tempter, but say, "Jesus has died that I might live. He loves me, and wills not that I should perish. I have a compassionate heavenly Father."—*Steps to Christ,* pp. 52, 53.

March 2

Perfection

Therefore you shall be perfect, just as your Father in heaven is perfect.
—Matthew 5:48.

The condition of eternal life is now just what it always has been—just what it was in Paradise before the fall of our first parents—perfect obedience to the law of God, perfect righteousness. If eternal life were granted on any condition short of this, then the happiness of the whole universe would be imperiled. The way would be open for sin, with all its train of woe and misery, to be immortalized.

It was possible for Adam, before the fall, to form a righteous character by obedience to God's law. But he failed to do this, and because of his sin our natures are fallen and we cannot make ourselves righteous. Since we are sinful, unholy, we cannot perfectly obey the holy law. We have no righteousness of our own with which to meet the claims of the law of God. But Christ has made a way of escape for us. He lived on earth amid trials and temptations such as we have to meet. He lived a sinless life. He died for us, and now He offers to take our sins and give us His righteousness. If you give yourself to Him, and accept Him as your Saviour, then, sinful as your life may have been, for His sake you are accounted righteous. Christ's character stands in place of your character, and you are accepted before God just as if you had not sinned.

More than this, Christ changes the heart. He abides in your heart by faith. You are to maintain this connection with Christ by faith and the continual surrender of your will to Him; and so long as you do this, He will work in you to will and to do according to His good pleasure. So you may say, "The life which I now live in the flesh I live by the faith of the Son of God, who loved me, and gave Himself for me." (Galatians 2:20.) So Jesus said to His disciples, "It is not ye that speak, but the Spirit of your Father which speaketh in you." (Matthew 10:20.) Then with Christ working in you, you will manifest the same spirit and do the same good works—works of righteousness, obedience.

So we have nothing in ourselves of which to boast. We have no ground for self-exaltation. Our only ground of hope is in the righteousness of Christ imputed to us, and in that wrought by His Spirit working in and through us.—*Steps to Christ,* pp. 62, 63.

March 3

By Grace Alone

My grace is sufficient for you, for My strength is made perfect in weakness.—2 Corinthians 12:9.

It is impossible for us, of ourselves, to escape from the pit of sin in which we are sunken. Our hearts are evil, and we cannot change them. "Who can bring a clean thing out of an unclean? not one." "The carnal mind is enmity against God: for it is not subject to the law of God, neither indeed can be." (Job 14:4; Romans 8:7.) Education, culture, the exercise of the will, human effort, all have their proper sphere, but here they are powerless. They may produce an outward correctness of behavior, but they cannot change the heart; they cannot purify the springs of life. There must be a power working from within, a new life from above, before we can be changed from sin to holiness. That power is Christ. His grace alone can quicken the lifeless faculties of the soul, and attract it to God, to holiness.

The Saviour said, "Except a man be born from above," unless he shall receive a new heart, new desires, purposes, and motives, leading to a new life, "he cannot see the kingdom of God." (John 3:3, margin.) The idea that it is necessary only to develop the good that exists in us by nature, is a fatal deception. "The natural man receiveth not the things of the Spirit of God: for they are foolishness unto him: neither can he know them, because they are spiritually discerned." "Marvel not that I said unto thee, Ye must be born again." (1 Corinthians 2:14; John 3:7.) Of Christ it is written, "In Him was life; and the life was the light of men"—the only "name under heaven given among men, whereby we must be saved." (John 1:4; Acts 4:12.)

It is not enough to perceive the loving-kindness of God, to see the benevolence, the fatherly tenderness, of His character. It is not enough to discern the wisdom and justice of His law, to see that it is founded upon the eternal principle of love. Paul the apostle saw all this when he exclaimed, "I consent unto the law that it is good." "The law is holy, and the commandment holy, and just, and good." But he added, in the bitterness of his soul-anguish and despair, "I am carnal, sold under sin." (Romans 7:16, 12, 14.) He longed for the purity, the righteousness, to which in himself he was powerless to attain, and cried out, "O wretched man that I am! who shall deliver me from this body of death?" (Romans 7:24, margin.) Such is the cry that has gone up from burdened hearts in all lands and in all ages. To all, there is but one answer, "Behold the Lamb of God, which taketh away the sin of the world." (John 1:29.)—*Steps to Christ,* pp. 18, 19.

March 4

It's Your Choice

Choose for yourselves this day whom you will serve.
—Joshua 24:15.

All who refuse to give themselves to God are under the control of another power. They are not their own. They may talk of freedom, but they are in the most abject slavery. They are not allowed to see the beauty of truth, for their minds are under the control of Satan. While they flatter themselves that they are following the dictates of their own judgment, they obey the will of the prince of darkness. Christ came to break the shackles of sin-slavery from the soul. "If the Son therefore shall make you free, ye shall be free indeed." "The law of the Spirit of life in Christ Jesus" sets us "free from the law of sin and death." (John 8:36; Romans 8:2.)

In the work of redemption there is no compulsion. No external force is employed. Under the influence of the Spirit of God, we are left free to choose whom we will serve. In the change that takes place when the soul surrenders to Christ, there is the highest sense of freedom. The expulsion of sin is the act of the soul itself. True, we have no power to free ourselves from Satan's control; but when we desire to be set free from sin, and in our great need cry out for a power out of and above ourselves, the powers of the soul are imbued with the divine energy of the Holy Spirit, and they obey the dictates of the will in fulfilling the will of God.

The only condition upon which our freedom is possible is that of becoming one with Christ. "The truth shall make you free" (John 8:32); and Christ is the truth. Sin can triumph only by enfeebling the mind, and destroying the liberty of the soul. Subjection to God is restoration to one's self—to the true glory and dignity of humanity. The divine law, to which we are brought into subjection, is "the law of liberty." (James 2:12.)

The Pharisees had declared themselves the children of Abraham. Jesus told them that this claim could be established only by doing the works of Abraham. The true children of Abraham would live, as he did, a life of obedience to God. They would not try to kill One who was speaking the truth that was given Him from God. In plotting against Christ, the rabbis were not doing the works of Abraham. A mere lineal descent from Abraham was of no value. Without a spiritual connection with him, which would be manifested in possessing the same spirit, and doing the same works, they were not his children.—*The Desire of Ages*, pp. 466, 467.

March 5

It's Either Or

He who is not with Me is against Me.
—Matthew 12:30.

Satan is continually seeking to overcome the people of God by breaking down the barriers which separate them from the world. Ancient Israel were enticed into sin when they ventured into forbidden association with the heathen. In a similar manner are modern Israel led astray. "The god of this world hath blinded the minds of them which believe not, lest the light of the glorious gospel of Christ, who is the image of God, should shine unto them." (2 Corinthians 4:4.) All who are not decided followers of Christ are servants of Satan. In the unregenerate heart there is love of sin and a disposition to cherish and excuse it. In the renewed heart there is hatred of sin and determined resistance against it. When Christians choose the society of the ungodly and unbelieving, they expose themselves to temptation. Satan conceals himself from view and stealthily draws his deceptive covering over their eyes. They cannot see that such company is calculated to do them harm; and while all the time assimilating to the world in character, words, and actions, they are becoming more and more blinded.

Conformity to worldly customs converts the church to the world; it never converts the world to Christ. Familiarity with sin will inevitably cause it to appear less repulsive. He who chooses to associate with the servants of Satan will soon cease to fear their master. When in the way of duty we are brought into trial, as was Daniel in the king's court, we may be sure that God will protect us; but if we place ourselves under temptation we shall fall sooner or later.

The tempter often works most successfully through those who are least suspected of being under his control. The possessors of talent and education are admired and honored, as if these qualities could atone for the absence of the fear of God or entitle anyone to His favor. Talent and culture, considered in themselves, are gifts of God; but when these are made to supply the place of piety, when, instead of bringing the soul nearer to God, they lead away from Him, then they become a curse and a snare. The opinion prevails with many that all which appears like courtesy or refinement must, in some sense, pertain to Christ. Never was there a greater mistake. These qualities should grace the character of every Christian, for they would exert a powerful influence in favor of true religion; but they must be consecrated to God, or they also are a power for evil.—*The Great Controversy,* pp. 508, 509.

March 6

No Excuse for Sinning

Neither do I condemn you; go and sin no more.
—John 8:11.

God's ideal for His children is higher than the highest human thought can reach. "Be ye therefore perfect, even as your Father which is in heaven is perfect." (Matthew 5:48.) This command is a promise. The plan of redemption contemplates our complete recovery from the power of Satan. Christ always separates the contrite soul from sin. He came to destroy the works of the devil, and He has made provision that the Holy Spirit shall be imparted to every repentant soul, to keep that one from sinning.

The tempter's agency is not to be accounted an excuse for one wrong act. Satan is jubilant when he hears the professed followers of Christ making excuses for their deformity of character. It is these excuses that lead to sin. There is no excuse for sinning. A holy temper, a Christlike life, is accessible to every repenting, believing child of God.

The ideal of Christian character is Christlikeness. As the Son of man was perfect in His life, so His followers are to be perfect in their life. Jesus was in all things made like unto His brethren. He became flesh, even as we are. He was hungry and thirsty and weary. He was sustained by food and refreshed by sleep. He shared the lot of humanity; yet He was the blameless Son of God. He was God in the flesh. His character is to be ours. The Lord says of those who believe in Him, "I will dwell in them, and walk in them; and I will be their God, and they shall be My people." (2 Corinthians 6:16.)

Christ is the ladder that Jacob saw, the base resting on the earth, and the topmost round reaching to the gate of heaven, to the very threshold of glory. If that ladder had failed by a single step of reaching the earth, we should have been lost. But Christ reaches us where we are. He took our nature and overcame, that we through taking His nature might overcome. Made "in the likeness of sinful flesh" (Romans 8:3), He lived a sinless life. Now by His divinity He lays hold upon the throne of heaven, while by His humanity He reaches us. He bids us by faith in Him attain to the glory of the character of God. Therefore are we to be perfect, even as our "Father which is in heaven is perfect."—*The Desire of Ages,* pp. 311, 312.

March 7

The Greatest Battle We Face

Let everyone who names the name of Christ depart from iniquity.
—2 Timothy 2:19.

The whole heart must be yielded to God, or the change can never be wrought in us by which we are to be restored to His likeness. By nature we are alienated from God. The Holy Spirit describes our condition in such words as these: "Dead in trespasses and sins;" "the whole head is sick, and the whole heart faint;" "no soundness in it." We are held fast in the snare of Satan, "taken captive by him at his will." (Ephesians 2:1; Isaiah 1:5, 6; 2 Timothy 2:26.) God desires to heal us, to set us free. But since this requires an entire transformation, a renewing of our whole nature, we must yield ourselves wholly to Him.

The warfare against self is the greatest battle that was ever fought. The yielding of self, surrendering all to the will of God, requires a struggle; but the soul must submit to God before it can be renewed in holiness.

The government of God is not, as Satan would make it appear, founded upon a blind submission, an unreasoning control. It appeals to the intellect and the conscience. "Come now, and let us reason together" is the Creator's invitation to the beings He has made. (Isaiah 1:18.) God does not force the will of His creatures. He cannot accept an homage that is not willingly and intelligently given. A mere forced submission would prevent all real development of mind or character; it would make us mere automatons. Such is not the purpose of the Creator. He desires that human beings, the crowning work of His creative power, shall reach the highest possible development. He sets before us the height of blessing to which He desires to bring us through His grace. He invites us to give ourselves to Him, that He may work His will in us. It remains for us to choose whether we will be set free from the bondage of sin, to share the glorious liberty of the sons of God.

In giving ourselves to God, we must necessarily give up all that would separate us from Him. Hence the Saviour says, "Whosoever he be of you that forsaketh not all that he hath, he cannot be My disciple." (Luke 14:33.) Whatever shall draw away the heart from God must be given up. . . .

A profession of Christ without this deep love is mere talk, dry formality, and heavy drudgery.—*Steps to Christ,* pp. 43, 44.

MARCH 8

PREPARATION FOR THE TIME OF TROUBLE

The LORD is good, a stronghold in the day of trouble; and He knows those who trust in Him.—Nahum 1:7.

The "time of trouble, such as never was" (Daniel 12:1), is soon to open upon us; and we shall need an experience which we do not now possess and which many are too indolent to obtain. It is often the case that trouble is greater in anticipation than in reality; but this is not true of the crisis before us. The most vivid presentation cannot reach the magnitude of the ordeal. In that time of trial, every soul must stand individually before God. "Though Noah, Daniel, and Job" were in the land, "as I live, saith the Lord God, they shall deliver neither son nor daughter; they shall but deliver their own souls by their righteousness." (Ezekiel 14:20.)

Now, while our great High Priest is making the atonement for us, we should seek to become perfect in Christ. Not even by a thought could our Saviour be brought to yield to the power of temptation. Satan finds in human hearts some point where he can gain a foothold; some sinful desire is cherished, by means of which his temptations assert their power. But Christ declared of Himself: "The prince of this world cometh, and hath nothing in Me." (John 14:30.) Satan could find nothing in the Son of God that would enable him to gain the victory. He had kept His Father's commandments, and there was no sin in Him that Satan could use to his advantage. This is the condition in which those must be found who shall stand in the time of trouble.

It is in this life that we are to separate sin from us, through faith in the atoning blood of Christ. Our precious Saviour invites us to join ourselves to Him, to unite our weakness to His strength, our ignorance to His wisdom, our unworthiness to His merits. God's providence is the school in which we are to learn the meekness and lowliness of Jesus. The Lord is ever setting before us, not the way we would choose, which seems easier and pleasanter to us, but the true aims of life. It rests with us to cooperate with the agencies which Heaven employs in the work of conforming our characters to the divine model. None can neglect or defer this work but at the most fearful peril to their souls. . . .

The wrath of Satan increases as his time grows short, and his work of deceit and destruction will reach its culmination in the time of trouble.—*The Great Controversy,* pp. 622, 623.

March 9

The Self-Righteous

There is none righteous, no, not one.
—Romans 3:10.

The claim to be without sin is, in itself, evidence that the one who makes this claim is far from holy. It is because people have no true conception of the infinite purity and holiness of God or of what they must become who shall be in harmony with His character; because they have no true conception of the purity and exalted loveliness of Jesus, and the malignity and evil of sin, that human beings can regard themselves as holy. The greater the distance between them and Christ, and the more inadequate their conceptions of the divine character and requirements, the more righteous they appear in their own eyes.

The sanctification set forth in the Scriptures embraces the entire being—spirit, soul, and body. Paul prayed for the Thessalonians that their "whole spirit and soul and body be preserved blameless unto the coming of our Lord Jesus Christ." (1 Thessalonians 5:23.) Again he writes to believers: "I beseech you therefore, brethren, by the mercies of God, that ye present your bodies a living sacrifice, holy, acceptable unto God." (Romans 12:1.) In the time of ancient Israel every offering brought as a sacrifice to God was carefully examined. If any defect was discovered in the animal presented, it was refused; for God had commanded that the offering be "without blemish." So Christians are bidden to present their bodies, "a living sacrifice, holy, acceptable unto God." In order to do this, all their powers must be preserved in the best possible condition. Every practice that weakens physical or mental strength unfits us for the service of our Creator. And will God be pleased with anything less than the best we can offer? Said Christ: "Thou shalt love the Lord thy God with all thy heart." Those who do love God with all the heart will desire to give Him the best service of their life, and they will be constantly seeking to bring every power of their being into harmony with the laws that will promote their ability to do His will. They will not, by the indulgence of appetite or passion, enfeeble or defile the offering which they present to their heavenly Father. . . .

Every sinful gratification tends to benumb the faculties and deaden the mental and spiritual perceptions, and the word or the Spirit of God can make but a feeble impression upon the heart.—*The Great Controversy,* pp. 473, 474.

What God Can Do With You

And the Lord added to the church daily those who were being saved.
—Acts 2:47.

In the apostles of our Lord there was nothing to bring glory to themselves. It was evident that the success of their labors was due only to God. The lives of these men, the characters they developed, and the mighty work that God wrought through them, are a testimony to what He will do for all who are teachable and obedient.

Those who love Christ the most will do the greatest amount of good. There is no limit to the usefulness of those who, by putting self aside, make room for the working of the Holy Spirit upon their hearts, and live their lives wholly consecrated to God. If men and women will endure the necessary discipline, without complaining or fainting by the way, God will teach them hour by hour, and day by day. He longs to reveal His grace. If His people will remove the obstructions, He will pour forth the waters of salvation in abundant streams through the human channels. If those in humble life were encouraged to do all the good they could do, if restraining hands were not laid upon them to repress their zeal, there would be a hundred workers for Christ where now there is one.

God takes people as they are, and educates them for His service, if they will yield themselves to Him. The Spirit of God, received into the soul, will quicken all its faculties. Under the guidance of the Holy Spirit, the mind that is devoted unreservedly to God develops harmoniously, and is strengthened to comprehend and fulfill the requirements of God. The weak, vacillating character becomes changed to one of strength and steadfastness. Continual devotion establishes so close a relation between Jesus and His disciple that the Christian becomes like Him in mind and character. Through a connection with Christ believers will have clearer and broader views. Their discernment will be more penetrative, their judgment better balanced. Those who long to be of service to Christ are so quickened by the life-giving power of the Sun of Righteousness that they are enabled to bear much fruit to the glory of God.

People of the highest education in the arts and sciences have learned precious lessons from Christians in humble life who were designated by the world as unlearned. But these obscure disciples had obtained an education in the highest of all schools. They had sat at the feet of Him who spoke as "never man spake." (John 7:46.)—*The Desire of Ages,* pp. 250, 251.

March 11

The Gospel Is for Everyone

And I, if I am lifted up from the earth, will draw all peoples to Myself.
—John 12:32.

God is a Spirit: and they that worship Him must worship Him in spirit and in truth." (John 4:24.)

Here is declared the same truth that Jesus had revealed to Nicodemus when He said, "Except a man be born from above, he cannot see the kingdom of God." (John 3:3, margin.) Not by seeking a holy mountain or a sacred temple are people brought into communion with heaven. Religion is not to be confined to external forms and ceremonies. The religion that comes from God is the only religion that will lead to God. In order to serve Him aright, we must be born of the divine Spirit. This will purify the heart and renew the mind, giving us a new capacity for knowing and loving God. It will give us a willing obedience to all His requirements. This is true worship. It is the fruit of the working of the Holy Spirit. By the Spirit every sincere prayer is indited, and such prayer is acceptable to God. Wherever a soul reaches out after God, there the Spirit's working is manifest, and God will reveal Himself to that soul. For such worshipers He is seeking. He waits to receive them, and to make them His sons and daughters. . . .

The gospel invitation is not to be narrowed down, and presented only to a select few, who, we suppose, will do us honor if they accept it. The message is to be given to all. Wherever hearts are open to receive the truth, Christ is ready to instruct them. He reveals to them the Father, and the worship acceptable to Him who reads the heart. For such He uses no parables. To them, as to the woman at the well, He says, "I that speak unto thee am He." (John 4:26.) . . .

The Saviour did not wait for congregations to assemble. Often He began His lessons with only a few gathered about Him, but one by one the passers-by paused to listen, until a multitude heard with wonder and awe the words of God through the heaven-sent Teacher. Those who work for Christ should not feel that they cannot speak with the same earnestness to a few hearers as to a larger company. There may be only one to hear the message; but who can tell how far-reaching will be its influence? It seemed a small matter, even to His disciples, for the Saviour to spend His time upon a woman of Samaria. But He reasoned more earnestly and eloquently with her than with kings, councilors, or high priests. The lessons He gave to that woman have been repeated to the earth's remotest bounds.—*The Desire of Ages*, pp. 189, 194, 195.

2016

March 12

The Work of the Holy Spirit

However, when He, the Spirit of truth, has come, He will guide you into all truth.—John 16:13.

The office of the Holy Spirit is distinctly specified in the words of Christ: "When He is come, He will reprove the world of sin, and of righteousness, and of judgment." (John 16:8.) It is the Holy Spirit that convicts of sin. If sinners respond to the quickening influence of the Spirit, they will be brought to repentance and aroused to the importance of obeying the divine requirements.

To the repentant sinner, hungering and thirsting for righteousness, the Holy Spirit reveals the Lamb of God that taketh away the sin of the world. "He shall receive of Mine, and shall show it unto you," Christ said. "He shall teach you all things, and bring all things to your remembrance, whatsoever I have said unto you." (John 16:14; 14:26.)

The Spirit is given as a regenerating agency, to make effectual the salvation wrought by the death of our Redeemer. The Spirit is constantly seeking to draw people's attention to the great offering that was made on the cross of Calvary, to unfold to the world the love of God, and to open to the convicted soul the precious things of the Scriptures.

Having brought conviction of sin, and presented before the mind the standard of righteousness, the Holy Spirit withdraws the affections from the things of this earth and fills the soul with a desire for holiness. "He will guide you into all truth" (John 16:13), the Saviour declared. If we are willing to be molded, there will be brought about a sanctification of the whole being. The Spirit will take the things of God and stamp them on the soul. By His power the way of life will be made so plain that none need err therein.

From the beginning, God has been working by His Holy Spirit through human instrumentalities for the accomplishment of His purpose in behalf of the fallen race. . . .

The Spirit of the Almighty is moving upon human hearts, and those who respond to its influence become witnesses for God and His truth. In many places consecrated men and women may be seen communicating to others the light that has made plain to them the way of salvation through Christ. And as they continue to let their light shine, as did those who were baptized with the Spirit on the Day of Pentecost, they receive more and still more of the Spirit's power. Thus the earth is to be lightened with the glory of God.
—*The Acts of the Apostles,* pp. 52–54.

March 13

Spiritual Healing

And you He made alive, who were dead in trespasses and sins.
—Ephesians 2:1.

But the Saviour saw one case of supreme wretchedness. It was that of a man who had been a helpless cripple for thirty-eight years. His disease was in a great degree the result of his own sin, and was looked upon as a judgment from God. Alone and friendless, feeling that he was shut out from God's mercy, the sufferer had passed long years of misery. . . .

Jesus does not ask this sufferer to exercise faith in Him. He simply says, "Rise, take up thy bed, and walk." (John 5:8.) But the man's faith takes hold upon that word. Every nerve and muscle thrills with new life, and healthful action comes to his crippled limbs. Without question he sets his will to obey the command of Christ, and all his muscles respond to his will. Springing to his feet, he finds himself an active man.

Jesus had given him no assurance of divine help. The man might have stopped to doubt, and lost his one chance of healing. But he believed Christ's word, and in acting upon it he received strength.

Through the same faith we may receive spiritual healing. By sin we have been severed from the life of God. Our souls are palsied. Of ourselves we are no more capable of living a holy life than was the impotent man capable of walking. There are many who realize their helplessness, and who long for that spiritual life which will bring them into harmony with God; they are vainly striving to obtain it. In despair they cry, "O wretched man that I am! who shall deliver me from this body of death?" (Romans 7:24, margin.) Let these desponding, struggling ones look up. The Saviour is bending over the purchase of His blood, saying with inexpressible tenderness and pity, "Wilt thou be made whole?" (John 5:6.) He bids you arise in health and peace. Do not wait to feel that you are made whole. Believe His word, and it will be fulfilled. Put your will on the side of Christ. Will to serve Him, and in acting upon His word you will receive strength. Whatever may be the evil practice, the master passion which through long indulgence binds both soul and body, Christ is able and longs to deliver. He will impart life to the soul that is "dead in trespasses." (Ephesians 2:1.) He will set free the captive that is held by weakness and misfortune and the chains of sin.—*The Desire of Ages*, pp. 202, 203.

Cleansing the Temple

Do you not know that you are the temple of God?
—1 Corinthians 3:16.

In the cleansing of the temple, Jesus was announcing His mission as the Messiah, and entering upon His work. That temple, erected for the abode of the divine Presence, was designed to be an object lesson for Israel and for the world. From eternal ages it was God's purpose that every created being, from the bright and holy seraph to individual men and women, should be a temple for the indwelling of the Creator. Because of sin, humanity ceased to be a temple for God. Darkened and defiled by evil, the human heart no longer revealed the glory of the Divine One. But by the incarnation of the Son of God, the purpose of Heaven is fulfilled. God dwells in humanity, and through saving grace people's hearts become again His temple. God designed that the temple at Jerusalem should be a continual witness to the high destiny open to every soul. But the Jews had not understood the significance of the building they regarded with so much pride. They did not yield themselves as holy temples for the Divine Spirit. The courts of the temple at Jerusalem, filled with the tumult of unholy traffic, represented all too truly the temple of the heart, defiled by the presence of sensual passion and unholy thoughts. In cleansing the temple from the world's buyers and sellers, Jesus announced His mission to cleanse the heart from the defilement of sin—from the earthly desires, the selfish lusts, the evil habits, that corrupt the soul. "The Lord, whom ye seek, shall suddenly come to His temple, even the Messenger of the covenant, whom ye delight in: behold, He shall come, saith the Lord of hosts. But who may abide the day of His coming? and who shall stand when He appeareth? for He is like a refiner's fire, and like fullers' soap: and He shall sit as a refiner and purifier of silver: and He shall purify the sons of Levi, and purge them as gold and silver." (Malachi 3:1–3.) . . .

We cannot by ourselves cast out the evil throng that have taken possession of the heart. Only Christ can cleanse the soul temple. But He will not force an entrance. He comes not into the heart as to the temple of old; but He says, "Behold, I stand at the door, and knock: if any man hear My voice, and open the door, I will come in to him." (Revelation 3:20.) . . . His presence will cleanse and sanctify the soul, so that it may be a holy temple unto the Lord, and "an habitation of God through the Spirit." (Ephesians 2:21, 22.)—*The Desire of Ages,* pp. 161, 162.

March 15

Holiness Is . . . !

Therefore, having these promises, beloved, let us cleanse ourselves from all filthiness of the flesh and spirit, perfecting holiness in the fear of God.
—2 Corinthians 7:1.

Since this is the means by which we are to receive power, why do we not hunger and thirst for the gift of the Spirit? Why do we not talk of it, pray for it, and preach concerning it? The Lord is more willing to give the Holy Spirit to those who serve Him than parents are to give good gifts to their children. For the daily baptism of the Spirit every worker should offer petitions to God. Companies of Christian workers should gather to ask for special help, for heavenly wisdom, that they may know how to plan and execute wisely. Especially should they pray that God will baptize His chosen ambassadors in mission fields with a rich measure of His Spirit. The presence of the Spirit with God's workers will give the proclamation of truth a power that not all the honor or glory of the world could give.

With the consecrated workers for God, in whatever place they may be, the Holy Spirit abides. The words spoken to the disciples are spoken also to us. The Comforter is ours as well as theirs. The Spirit furnishes the strength that sustains striving, wrestling souls in every emergency, amidst the hatred of the world, and the realization of their own failures and mistakes. In sorrow and affliction, when the outlook seems dark and the future perplexing, and we feel helpless and alone—these are the times when, in answer to the prayer of faith, the Holy Spirit brings comfort to the heart.

It is not a conclusive evidence that people are Christians because they manifest spiritual ecstasy under extraordinary circumstances. Holiness is not rapture: it is an entire surrender of the will to God; it is living by every word that proceeds from the mouth of God; it is doing the will of our heavenly Father; it is trusting God in trial, in darkness as well as in the light; it is walking by faith and not by sight; it is relying on God with unquestioning confidence, and resting in His love.

It is not essential for us to be able to define just what the Holy Spirit is. Christ tells us that the Spirit is the Comforter, "the Spirit of truth, which proceedeth from the Father." It is plainly declared regarding the Holy Spirit that, in His work of guiding us into all truth, "He shall not speak of Himself." (John 15:26; 16:13.)—*The Acts of the Apostles*, pp. 50, 51.

2016

Righteousness Is . . . !

Blessed are those who hunger and thirst for righteousness.
—Matthew 5:6.

Righteousness is holiness, likeness to God, and "God is love." (1 John 4:16.) It is conformity to the law of God, for "all Thy commandments are righteousness" (Psalm 119:172), and "love is the fulfilling of the law." (Romans 13:10.) Righteousness is love, and love is the light and the life of God. The righteousness of God is embodied in Christ. We receive righteousness by receiving Him.

Not by painful struggles or wearisome toil, not by gift or sacrifice, is righteousness obtained; but it is freely given to every soul who hungers and thirsts to receive it. "Ho, every one that thirsteth, come ye to the waters, and he that hath no money; come ye, buy, and eat, . . . without money and without price." "Their righteousness is of Me, saith the Lord," and, "This is His name whereby He shall be called, The Lord Our Righteousness." (Isaiah 55:1; 54:17; Jeremiah 23:6.)

No human agent can supply that which will satisfy the hunger and thirst of the soul. But Jesus says, "Behold, I stand at the door, and knock: if any man hear My voice, and open the door, I will come in to him, and will sup with him, and he with Me." (Revelation 3:20.) . . .

As we need food to sustain our physical strength, so do we need Christ, the Bread from heaven, to sustain spiritual life and impart strength to work the works of God. As the body is continually receiving the nourishment that sustains life and vigor, so the soul must be constantly communing with Christ, submitting to Him and depending wholly upon Him. . . .

As we discern the perfection of our Saviour's character we shall desire to become wholly transformed and renewed in the image of His purity. The more we know of God, the higher will be our ideal of character and the more earnest our longing to reflect His likeness. A divine element combines with the human when the soul reaches out after God and the longing heart can say, "My soul, wait thou only upon God; for my expectation is from Him." (Psalm 62:5.)

If you have a sense of need in your soul, if you hunger and thirst after righteousness, this is an evidence that Christ has wrought upon your heart.—*Thoughts From the Mount of Blessing,* pp. 18, 19.

MARCH 17

SANCTIFICATION IS . . . !

For this is the will of God, your sanctification.
—1 Thessalonians 4:3.

As God is holy in His sphere, so fallen human beings, through faith in Christ, are to be holy in their sphere. . . .

The sanctification of the church is God's object in all His dealings with His people. He has chosen them from eternity, that they might be holy. He gave His Son to die for them, that they might be sanctified through obedience to the truth, divested of all the littleness of self. From them He requires a personal work, a personal surrender. God can be honored by those who profess to believe in Him, only as they are conformed to His image and controlled by His Spirit. Then, as witnesses for the Saviour, they may make known what divine grace has done for them.

True sanctification comes through the working out of the principle of love. "God is love; and he that dwelleth in love dwelleth in God, and God in him." (1 John 4:16.) The lives of those in whose hearts Christ abides, will reveal practical godliness. The character will be purified, elevated, ennobled, and glorified. Pure doctrine will blend with works of righteousness; heavenly precepts will mingle with holy practices.

Those who would gain the blessing of sanctification must first learn the meaning of self-sacrifice. . . . It is the fragrance of our love for others that reveals our love for God. It is patience in service that brings rest to the soul. It is through humble, diligent, faithful toil that the welfare of Israel is promoted. God upholds and strengthens the one who is willing to follow in Christ's way.

Sanctification is not the work of a moment, an hour, a day, but of a lifetime. It is not gained by a happy flight of feeling, but is the result of constantly dying to sin, and constantly living for Christ. Wrongs cannot be righted nor reformations wrought in the character by feeble, intermittent efforts. It is only by long, persevering effort, sore discipline, and stern conflict, that we shall overcome. We know not one day how strong will be our conflict the next. So long as Satan reigns, we shall have self to subdue, besetting sins to overcome; so long as life shall last, there will be no stopping place, no point which we can reach and say, I have fully attained. Sanctification is the result of lifelong obedience.—*The Acts of the Apostles,* pp. 559–561.

Sanctification Is a Bible Doctrine

Sanctify them by Your truth. Your word is truth.
—John 17:17.

Erroneous theories of sanctification, also, springing from neglect or rejection of the divine law, have a prominent place in the religious movements of the day. These theories are both false in doctrine and dangerous in practical results; and the fact that they are so generally finding favor, renders it doubly essential that all have a clear understanding of what the Scriptures teach upon this point.

True sanctification is a Bible doctrine. The apostle Paul, in his letter to the Thessalonian church, declares: "This is the will of God, even your sanctification." And he prays: "The very God of peace sanctify you wholly." (1 Thessalonians 4:3; 5:23.) The Bible clearly teaches what sanctification is and how it is to be attained. The Saviour prayed for His disciples: "Sanctify them through Thy truth: Thy word is truth." (John 17:17.) And Paul teaches that believers are to be "sanctified by the Holy Ghost." (Romans 15:16.) What is the work of the Holy Spirit? Jesus told His disciples: "When He, the Spirit of truth, is come, He will guide you into all truth." (John 16:13.) And the psalmist says: "Thy law is the truth." By the word and the Spirit of God are opened to us the great principles of righteousness embodied in His law. And since the law of God is "holy, and just, and good," a transcript of the divine perfection, it follows that a character formed by obedience to that law will be holy. Christ is a perfect example of such a character. He says: "I have kept My Father's commandments." "I do always those things that please Him." (John 15:10; 8:29.) The followers of Christ are to become like Him—by the grace of God to form characters in harmony with the principles of His holy law. This is Bible sanctification.

This work can be accomplished only through faith in Christ, by the power of the indwelling Spirit of God. Paul admonishes believers: "Work out your own salvation with fear and trembling. For it is God which worketh in you both to will and to do of His good pleasure." (Philippians 2:12, 13.) Christians will feel the promptings of sin, but they will maintain a constant warfare against it. Here is where Christ's help is needed. Human weakness becomes united to divine strength, and faith exclaims: "Thanks be to God, which giveth us the victory through our Lord Jesus Christ." (1 Corinthians 15:57.)—*The Great Controversy,* pp. 469, 470.

March 19

Repentance Is . . . !

For godly sorrow produces repentance leading to salvation.
—2 Corinthians 7:10.

How shall anyone be just with God? How shall the sinner be made righteous? It is only through Christ that we can be brought into harmony with God, with holiness; but how are we to come to Christ? Many are asking the same question as did the multitude on the Day of Pentecost, when, convicted of sin, they cried out, "What shall we do?" The first word of Peter's answer was, "Repent." (Acts 2:37, 38.) At another time, shortly after, he said, "Repent, . . . and be converted, that your sins may be blotted out." (Acts 3:19.)

Repentance includes sorrow for sin and a turning away from it. We shall not renounce sin unless we see its sinfulness; until we turn away from it in heart, there will be no real change in the life.

There are many who fail to understand the true nature of repentance. Multitudes sorrow that they have sinned and even make an outward reformation because they fear that their wrongdoing will bring suffering upon themselves. But this is not repentance in the Bible sense. They lament the suffering rather than the sin. Such was the grief of Esau when he saw that the birthright was lost to him forever. Balaam, terrified by the angel standing in his pathway with drawn sword, acknowledged his guilt lest he should lose his life; but there was no genuine repentance for sin, no conversion of purpose, no abhorrence of evil. Judas Iscariot, after betraying his Lord, exclaimed, "I have sinned in that I have betrayed the innocent blood." (Matthew 27:4.)

The confession was forced from his guilty soul by an awful sense of condemnation and a fearful looking for of judgment. The consequences that were to result to him filled him with terror, but there was no deep, heartbreaking grief in his soul, that he had betrayed the spotless Son of God and denied the Holy One of Israel. Pharaoh, when suffering under the judgments of God, acknowledged his sin in order to escape further punishment, but returned to his defiance of Heaven as soon as the plagues were stayed. These all lamented the results of sin, but did not sorrow for the sin itself.—*Steps to Christ,* pp. 23, 24.

March 20

Reaching Out After God

But seek first the kingdom of God and His righteousness.
—Matthew 6:33.

None of the apostles and prophets ever claimed to be without sin. Men and women who have lived the nearest to God, who would sacrifice life itself rather than knowingly commit a wrong act, whom God has honored with divine light and power, have confessed the sinfulness of their nature. They have put no confidence in the flesh, have claimed no righteousness of their own, but have trusted wholly in the righteousness of Christ.

So will it be with all who behold Christ. The nearer we come to Jesus, and the more clearly we discern the purity of His character, the more clearly shall we see the exceeding sinfulness of sin, and the less shall we feel like exalting ourselves. There will be a continual reaching out of the soul after God, a continual, earnest, heartbreaking confession of sin and humbling of the heart before Him. At every advance step in our Christian experience our repentance will deepen. We shall know that our sufficiency is in Christ alone and shall make the apostle's confession our own: "I know that in me (that is, in my flesh,) dwelleth no good thing." "God forbid that I should glory, save in the cross of our Lord Jesus Christ, by whom the world is crucified unto me, and I unto the world." (Romans 7:18; Galatians 6:14.)

Let the recording angels write the history of the holy struggles and conflicts of the people of God; let them record their prayers and tears; but let not God be dishonored by the declaration from human lips, "I am sinless; I am holy." Sanctified lips will never give utterance to such presumptuous words. . . .

Let those who feel inclined to make a high profession of holiness look into the mirror of God's law. As they see its far-reaching claims, and understand its work as a discerner of the thoughts and intents of the heart, they will not boast of sinlessness. "If we," says John, not separating himself from his brethren, "say that we have no sin, we deceive ourselves, and the truth is not in us." "If we say that we have not sinned, we make Him a liar, and His word is not in us." (1 John 1:10.) . . .

If we abide in Christ, if the love of God dwells in the heart, our feelings, our thoughts, our actions, will be in harmony with the will of God. The sanctified heart is in harmony with the precepts of God's law.—*The Acts of the Apostles,* pp. 561–563.

AN EXAMPLE OF REPENTANCE

Create in me a clean heart, O God.
—Psalm 51:10.

When the heart yields to the influence of the Spirit of God, the conscience will be quickened, and sinful human beings will discern something of the depth and sacredness of God's holy law, the foundation of His government in heaven and on earth. The "Light, which lighteth every man that cometh into the world," illumines the secret chambers of the soul, and the hidden things of darkness are made manifest. (John 1:9.) Conviction takes hold upon the mind and heart. Sinners have a sense of the righteousness of Jehovah and feel the terror of appearing, in their own guilt and uncleanness, before the Searcher of hearts. They see the love of God, the beauty of holiness, the joy of purity; they long to be cleansed and to be restored to communion with Heaven.

The prayer of David after his fall, illustrates the nature of true sorrow for sin. His repentance was sincere and deep. There was no effort to palliate his guilt; no desire to escape the judgment threatened, inspired his prayer. David saw the enormity of his transgression; he saw the defilement of his soul; he loathed his sin. It was not for pardon only that he prayed, but for purity of heart. He longed for the joy of holiness—to be restored to harmony and communion with God. . . .

A repentance such as this, is beyond the reach of our own power to accomplish; it is obtained only from Christ, who ascended up on high and has given gifts unto men. . . .

The Bible does not teach that sinners must repent before they can heed the invitation of Christ, "Come unto Me, all ye that labor and are heavy-laden, and I will give you rest." (Matthew 11:28.) It is the virtue that goes forth from Christ, that leads to genuine repentance. Peter made the matter clear in his statement to the Israelites when he said, "Him hath God exalted with His right hand to be a Prince and a Saviour, for to give repentance to Israel, and forgiveness of sins." (Acts 5:31.) We can no more repent without the Spirit of Christ to awaken the conscience than we can be pardoned without Christ.

Christ is the source of every right impulse. He is the only one that can implant in the heart enmity against sin. Every desire for truth and purity, every conviction of our own sinfulness, is an evidence that His Spirit is moving upon our hearts.—*Steps to Christ,* pp. 24–26.

March 22

The First Step in Acceptance

He who covers his sins will not prosper, but whoever confesses and forsakes them will have mercy.
—Proverbs 28:13.

Those who have not humbled their souls before God in acknowledging their guilt, have not yet fulfilled the first condition of acceptance. If we have not experienced that repentance which is not to be repented of, and have not with true humiliation of soul and brokenness of spirit confessed our sins, abhorring our iniquity, we have never truly sought for the forgiveness of sin; and if we have never sought, we have never found the peace of God. The only reason why we do not have remission of sins that are past is that we are not willing to humble our hearts and comply with the conditions of the word of truth. Explicit instruction is given concerning this matter. Confession of sin, whether public or private, should be heartfelt and freely expressed. It is not to be urged from the sinner. It is not to be made in a flippant and careless way, or forced from those who have no realizing sense of the abhorrent character of sin. The confession that is the outpouring of the inmost soul finds its way to the God of infinite pity. The psalmist says, "The Lord is nigh unto them that are of a broken heart; and saveth such as be of a contrite spirit." (Psalm 34:18.)

True confession is always of a specific character, and acknowledges particular sins. They may be of such a nature as to be brought before God only; they may be wrongs that should be confessed to individuals who have suffered injury through them; or they may be of a public character, and should then be as publicly confessed. But all confession should be definite and to the point, acknowledging the very sins of which you are guilty. . . .

Confession will not be acceptable to God without sincere repentance and reformation. There must be decided changes in the life; everything offensive to God must be put away. This will be the result of genuine sorrow for sin. The work that we have to do on our part is plainly set before us: "Wash you, make you clean; put away the evil of your doings from before mine eyes; cease to do evil." (Isaiah 1:16.) . . . Paul says, speaking of the work of repentance: "Ye sorrowed after a godly sort, what carefulness it wrought in you, yea, what clearing of yourselves." (2 Corinthians 7:11.)—*Steps to Christ,* pp. 37–39.

MARCH 23

ASK FOR REPENTANCE

The goodness of God leads you to repentance.
—Romans 2:4.

The same divine mind that is working upon the things of nature is speaking to the hearts of men and women and creating an inexpressible craving for something they have not. The things of the world cannot satisfy their longing. The Spirit of God is pleading with them to seek for those things that alone can give peace and rest—the grace of Christ, the joy of holiness. Through influences seen and unseen, our Saviour is constantly at work to attract minds of people from the unsatisfying pleasures of sin to the infinite blessings that may be theirs in Him. To all these souls, who are vainly seeking to drink from the broken cisterns of this world, the divine message is addressed, "Let him that is athirst come. And whosoever will, let him take the water of life freely." (Revelation 22:17.)

You who in heart long for something better than this world can give, recognize this longing as the voice of God to your soul. Ask Him to give you repentance, to reveal Christ to you in His infinite love, in His perfect purity. In the Saviour's life the principles of God's law—love to God and to others—were perfectly exemplified. Benevolence, unselfish love, was the life of His soul. It is as we behold Him, as the light from our Saviour falls upon us, that we see the sinfulness of our own hearts.

We may have flattered ourselves, as did Nicodemus, that our life has been upright, that our moral character is correct, and think that we need not humble the heart before God, like the common sinner: but when the light from Christ shines into our souls, we shall see how impure we are; we shall discern the selfishness of motive, the enmity against God, that has defiled every act of life. Then we shall know that our own righteousness is indeed as filthy rags, and that the blood of Christ alone can cleanse us from the defilement of sin, and renew our hearts in His own likeness.

One ray of the glory of God, one gleam of the purity of Christ, penetrating the soul, makes every spot of defilement painfully distinct. . . .

The soul thus touched will hate its selfishness, abhor its self-love, and will seek, through Christ's righteousness, for the purity of heart that is in harmony with the law of God and the character of Christ.—*Steps to Christ*, pp. 28, 29.

What's Wrong With Procrastination?

Go away for now; when I have a convenient time I will call for you.
—Acts 24:25.

Beware of procrastination. Do not put off the work of forsaking your sins and seeking purity of heart through Jesus. Here is where thousands upon thousands have erred to their eternal loss. I will not here dwell upon the shortness and uncertainty of life; but there is a terrible danger—a danger not sufficiently understood—in delaying to yield to the pleading voice of God's Holy Spirit, in choosing to live in sin; for such this delay really is. Sin, however small it may be esteemed, can be indulged in only at the peril of infinite loss. What we do not overcome, will overcome us and work out our destruction.

Adam and Eve persuaded themselves that in so small a matter as eating of the forbidden fruit there could not result such terrible consequences as God had declared. But this small matter was the transgression of God's immutable and holy law, and it separated mankind from God and opened the floodgates of death and untold woe upon our world. Age after age there has gone up from our earth a continual cry of mourning, and the whole creation groaneth and travaileth together in pain as a consequence of our first parents' disobedience. Heaven itself has felt the effects of human rebellion against God. Calvary stands as a memorial of the amazing sacrifice required to atone for the transgression of the divine law. Let us not regard sin as a trivial thing.

Every act of transgression, every neglect or rejection of the grace of Christ, is reacting upon yourself; it is hardening the heart, depraving the will, benumbing the understanding, and not only making you less inclined to yield, but less capable of yielding, to the tender pleading of God's Holy Spirit. . . .

Even one wrong trait of character, one sinful desire, persistently cherished, will eventually neutralize all the power of the gospel. Every sinful indulgence strengthens the soul's aversion to God. Those who manifest an infidel hardihood, or a stolid indifference to divine truth, are but reaping the harvest of that which they themselves have sown. In all the Bible there is not a more fearful warning against trifling with evil than the words of the wise man that the sinner "shall be holden with the cords of his sins." (Proverbs 5:22.)—*Steps to Christ,* pp. 32–34.

March 25

The Power of the Will

For it is God who works in you both to will and to do for His good pleasure.
—Philippians 2:13.

The world's Redeemer accepts sinners as they are, with all their wants, imperfections, and weaknesses; and He will not only cleanse from sin and grant redemption through His blood, but will satisfy the heart-longing of all who consent to wear His yoke, to bear His burden. It is His purpose to impart peace and rest to all who come to Him for the bread of life. He requires us to perform only those duties that will lead our steps to heights of bliss to which the disobedient can never attain. The true, joyous life of the soul is to have Christ formed within, the hope of glory.

Many are inquiring, "*How* am I to make the surrender of myself to God?" You desire to give yourself to Him, but you are weak in moral power, in slavery to doubt, and controlled by the habits of your life of sin. Your promises and resolutions are like ropes of sand. You cannot control your thoughts, your impulses, your affections. The knowledge of your broken promises and forfeited pledges weakens your confidence in your own sincerity, and causes you to feel that God cannot accept you; but you need not despair. What you need to understand is the true force of the will. This is the governing power in our nature, the power of decision, or of choice. Everything depends on the right action of the will. The power of choice God has given to us; it is ours to exercise. You cannot change your heart, you cannot of yourself give to God its affections; but you can *choose* to serve Him. You can give Him your will; He will then work in you to will and to do according to His good pleasure. Thus your whole nature will be brought under the control of the Spirit of Christ; your affections will be centered upon Him, your thoughts will be in harmony with Him.

Desires for goodness and holiness are right as far as they go; but if you stop here, they will avail nothing. Many will be lost while hoping and desiring to be Christians. They do not come to the point of yielding the will to God. They do not now *choose* to be Christians.

Through the right exercise of the will, an entire change may be made in your life. By yielding up your will to Christ, you ally yourself with the power that is above all principalities and powers. You will have strength from above to hold you steadfast, and thus through constant surrender to God you will be enabled to live the new life, even the life of faith.—*Steps to Christ*, pp. 46–48.

MARCH 26

THE NEW BIRTH

Most assuredly, I say to you, unless one is born again, he cannot see the kingdom of God.
—John 3:3.

The claim that Christ by His death abolished His Father's law is without foundation. Had it been possible for the law to be changed or set aside, then Christ need not have died to save us from the penalty of sin. The death of Christ, so far from abolishing the law, proves that it is immutable.

The law of God, from its very nature, is unchangeable. It is a revelation of the will and the character of its Author. God is love, and His law is love. Its two great principles are love to God and love to man. "Love is the fulfilling of the law." (Romans 13:10.) The character of God is righteousness and truth; such is the nature of His law. Says the psalmist: "Thy law is the truth:" "all Thy commandments are righteousness." (Psalm 119:142, 172.) And the apostle Paul declares: "The law is holy, and the commandment holy, and just, and good." (Romans 7:12.) Such a law, being an expression of the mind and will of God, must be as enduring as its Author.

It is the work of conversion and sanctification to reconcile men and women to God by bringing them into accord with the principles of His law. In the beginning, human beings were created in the image of God. They were in perfect harmony with the nature and the law of God; the principles of righteousness were written upon their hearts. But sin alienated them from their Maker. They no longer reflected the divine image. Their hearts were at war with the principles of God's law. "The carnal mind is enmity against God: for it is not subject to the law of God, neither indeed can be." (Romans 8:7.) But "God so loved the world, that He gave His only-begotten Son," that we might be reconciled to God. Through the merits of Christ we can be restored to harmony with our Maker. Our hearts must be renewed by divine grace; we must have a new life from above. This change is the new birth, without which, says Jesus, we "cannot see the kingdom of God."

The first step in reconciliation to God is the conviction of sin. "Sin is the transgression of the law." "By the law is the knowledge of sin." (1 John 3:4; Romans 3:20.) In order to see their guilt, sinners must test their character by God's great standard of righteousness. It is a mirror which shows the perfection of a righteous character and enables them to discern the defects in their own.—*The Great Controversy,* pp. 466, 467.

March 27

Believe What God Says

Do not be afraid; only believe.
—Mark 5:36.

You cannot atone for your past sins; you cannot change your heart and make yourself holy. But God promises to do all this for you through Christ. You *believe* that promise. You confess your sins and give yourself to God. You *will* to serve Him. Just as surely as you do this, God will fulfill His word to you. If you believe the promise—believe that you are forgiven and cleansed—God supplies the fact; you are made whole, just as Christ gave the paralytic power to walk when the man believed that he was healed. It *is* so if you believe it.

Do not wait to *feel* that you are made whole, but say, "I believe it; it *is* so, not because I feel it, but because God has promised."—*Steps to Christ,* p. 51.

The law reveals to us our sins, but it provides no remedy. While it promises life to the obedient, it declares that death is the portion of the transgressors. The gospel of Christ alone can free them from the condemnation or the defilement of sin. They must exercise repentance toward God, whose law has been transgressed; and faith in Christ, their atoning sacrifice. Thus they obtain "remission of sins that are past" and become partakers of the divine nature. They are children of God, having received the spirit of adoption, whereby they cry: "Abba, Father!" . . .

In the new birth the heart is brought into harmony with God, as it is brought into accord with His law. When this mighty change has taken place in sinners, they have passed from death unto life, from sin unto holiness, from transgression and rebellion to obedience and loyalty. The old life of alienation from God has ended; the new life of reconciliation, of faith and love, has begun. Then "the righteousness of the law" will "be fulfilled in us, who walk not after the flesh, but after the Spirit." (Romans 8:4.) And the language of the soul will be: "O how love I Thy law! it is my meditation all the day." (Psalm 119:97.) . . .

Without the law, people have no just conception of the purity and holiness of God or of their own guilt and uncleanness. They have no true conviction of sin and feel no need of repentance. Not seeing their lost condition as violators of God's law, they do not realize their need of the atoning blood of Christ. The hope of salvation is accepted without a radical change of heart or reformation of life. Thus superficial conversions abound, and multitudes are joined to the church who have never been united to Christ.—*The Great Controversy,* pp. 467, 468.

In the Shadow of the Cross

God forbid that I should boast except in the cross of our Lord Jesus Christ.
—Galatians 6:14.

There can be no self-exaltation, no boastful claim to freedom from sin, on the part of those who walk in the shadow of Calvary's cross. They feel that it was their sin which caused the agony that broke the heart of the Son of God, and this thought will lead them to self-abasement. Those who live nearest to Jesus discern most clearly the frailty and sinfulness of humanity, and their only hope is in the merit of a crucified and risen Saviour.

The sanctification now gaining prominence in the religious world carries with it a spirit of self-exaltation and a disregard for the law of God that mark it as foreign to the religion of the Bible. Its advocates teach that sanctification is an instantaneous work, by which, through faith alone, they attain to perfect holiness. "Only believe," say they, "and the blessing is yours." No further effort on the part of the receiver is supposed to be required. At the same time they deny the authority of the law of God, urging that they are released from obligation to keep the commandments. But is it possible to be holy, in accord with the will and character of God, without coming into harmony with the principles which are an expression of His nature and will, and which show what is well pleasing to Him?

The desire for an easy religion that requires no striving, no self-denial, no divorce from the follies of the world, has made the doctrine of faith, and faith only, a popular doctrine; but what saith the word of God? . . .

The testimony of the word of God is against this ensnaring doctrine of faith without works. It is not faith that claims the favor of Heaven without complying with the conditions upon which mercy is to be granted, it is presumption; for genuine faith has its foundation in the promises and provisions of the Scriptures.

Let none deceive themselves with the belief that they can become holy while willfully violating one of God's requirements. The commission of a known sin silences the witnessing voice of the Spirit and separates the soul from God. . . . We cannot accord holiness to any without bringing them to the measurement of God's only standard of holiness in heaven and in earth.—*The Great Controversy,* pp. 471, 472.

March 29

Grace From the Saviour

For by grace you have been saved through faith, and that not of yourselves; it is the gift of God.—Ephesians 2:8.

We must learn in the school of Christ. Nothing but His righteousness can entitle us to one of the blessings of the covenant of grace. We have long desired and tried to obtain these blessings, but have not received them because we have cherished the idea that we could do something to make ourselves worthy of them. We have not looked away from ourselves, believing that Jesus is a living Saviour. We must not think that our own grace and merits will save us; the grace of Christ is our only hope of salvation. Through His prophet the Lord promises, "Let the wicked forsake his way, and the unrighteous man his thoughts: and let him return unto the Lord, and he will have mercy upon him; and to our God, for he will abundantly pardon." (Isaiah 55:7.) We must believe the naked promise, and not accept feeling for faith. When we trust God fully, when we rely upon the merits of Jesus as a sin-pardoning Saviour, we shall receive all the help that we can desire.

We look to self, as though we had power to save ourselves; but Jesus died for us because we are helpless to do this. In Him is our hope, our justification, our righteousness. We should not despond, and fear that we have no Saviour, or that He has no thoughts of mercy toward us. At this very time He is carrying on His work in our behalf, inviting us to come to Him in our helplessness and be saved. We dishonor Him by our unbelief. It is astonishing how we treat our very best Friend, how little confidence we repose in Him who is able to save to the uttermost, and who has given us every evidence of His great love. . . .

Let none here feel that their case is hopeless; for it is not. You may see that you are sinful and undone; but it is just on this account that you need a Saviour. If you have sins to confess, lose no time. These moments are golden. "If we confess our sins, he is faithful and just to forgive us our sins, and to cleanse us from all unrighteousness." (1 John 1:9.) Those who hunger and thirst after righteousness will be filled; for Jesus has promised it. Precious Saviour! His arms are open to receive us, and His great heart of love is waiting to bless us.

Some seem to feel that they must be on probation and must prove to the Lord that they are reformed, before they can claim His blessing. But these dear souls may claim the blessing even now. They must have His grace, the Spirit of Christ, to help their infirmities, or they cannot form a Christian character. Jesus loves to have us come to Him, just as we are—sinful, helpless, dependent.—*Selected Messages,* book 1, pp. 351–353.

An Example of True Sanctification

Everyone who has this hope in Him purifies himself, just as He is pure.
—1 John 3:3.

In the life of the disciple John true sanctification is exemplified. During the years of his close association with Christ, he was often warned and cautioned by the Saviour; and these reproofs he accepted. As the character of the Divine One was manifested to him, John saw his own deficiencies, and was humbled by the revelation. Day by day, in contrast with his own violent spirit, he beheld the tenderness and forbearance of Jesus, and heard His lessons of humility and patience. Day by day his heart was drawn out to Christ, until he lost sight of self in love for his Master. The power and tenderness, the majesty and meekness, the strength and patience, that he saw in the daily life of the Son of God, filled his soul with admiration. He yielded his resentful, ambitious temper to the molding power of Christ, and divine love wrought in him a transformation of character. . . .

Such transformation of character as is seen in the life of John is ever the result of communion with Christ. There may be marked defects in people's characters, yet when they become true disciples of Christ, the power of divine grace transforms and sanctifies them. Beholding as in a glass the glory of the Lord, they are changed from glory to glory, until they are like Him whom they adore.

John was a teacher of holiness, and in his letters to the church he laid down unerring rules for the conduct of Christians. "Every man that hath this hope in him," he wrote, "purifieth himself, even as He is pure." "He that saith he abideth in Him ought himself also so to walk, even as He walked." (1 John 3:3; 2:6.) He taught that Christians must be pure in heart and life. Never should they be satisfied with an empty profession. As God is holy in His sphere, so fallen human beings, through faith in Christ, are to be holy in their sphere.

"This is the will of God," the apostle Paul wrote, "even your sanctification." (1 Thessalonians 4:3.) The sanctification of the church is God's object in all His dealings with His people. He has chosen them from eternity, that they might be holy. He gave His Son to die for them, that they might be sanctified through obedience to the truth, divested of all the littleness of self. From them He requires a personal work, a personal surrender.—*The Acts of the Apostles*, pp. 557, 559.

March 31

Conformed to God's Will

For whom He foreknew, He also predestined to be conformed to the image of His Son. —*Romans 8:29.*

Many commit the error of trying to define minutely the fine points of distinction between justification and sanctification. Into the definitions of these two terms they often bring their own ideas and speculations. Why try to be more minute than is Inspiration on the vital question of righteousness by faith? Why try to work out every minute point, as if the salvation of the soul depended upon all having exactly your understanding of this matter? All cannot see in the same line of vision. You are in danger of making a world of an atom, and an atom of a world.

As penitent sinners, contrite before God, discern Christ's atonement in their behalf, and accept this atonement as their only hope in this life and the future life, their sins are pardoned. This is justification by faith. Every believing soul is to conform his or her will entirely to God's will, and keep in a state of repentance and contrition, exercising faith in the atoning merits of the Redeemer, and advancing from strength to strength, from glory to glory.

Pardon and justification are one and the same thing. . . .

Justification is the opposite of condemnation. God's boundless mercy is exercised toward those who are wholly undeserving. He forgives transgressions and sins for the sake of Jesus, who has become the propitiation for our sins. Through faith in Christ the guilty transgressor is brought into favor with God and into the strong hope of life eternal.

David was pardoned of his transgression because he humbled his heart before God in repentance and contrition of soul and believed that God's promise to forgive would be fulfilled. He confessed his sin, repented, and was reconverted. In the rapture of the assurance of forgiveness he exclaimed, "Blessed is he whose transgression is forgiven, whose sin is covered. Blessed is the man unto whom the Lord imputeth not iniquity, and in whose spirit there is no guile." The blessing comes because of pardon; pardon comes through faith that the sin, confessed and repented of, is borne by the great Sin-bearer. Thus from Christ cometh all our blessings. His death is an atoning sacrifice for our sins. He is the great medium through whom we receive the mercy and favor of God. He, then, is indeed the Originator, the Author, as well as the Finisher, of our faith.—*Manuscript Releases,* vol. 9, pp. 300–302.

Victory in Christ

April 1

The Keynote of Victory

But also for this very reason, giving all diligence, add to your faith virtue, to virtue knowledge, to knowledge self-control.—2 Peter 1:5, 6.

These words are full of instruction, and strike the keynote of victory. The apostle presents before the believers the ladder of Christian progress, every step of which represents advancement in the knowledge of God, and in the climbing of which there is to be no standstill. Faith, virtue, knowledge, temperance, patience, godliness, brotherly kindness, and charity are the rounds of the ladder. We are saved by climbing round after round, mounting step after step, to the height of Christ's ideal for us. Thus He is made unto us wisdom, and righteousness, and sanctification, and redemption.

God has called His people to glory and virtue, and these will be manifest in the lives of all who are truly connected with Him. Having become partakers of the heavenly gift, they are to go on unto perfection, being "kept by the power of God through faith." (1 Peter 1:5.) It is the glory of God to give His virtue to His children. He desires to see men and women reaching the highest standard; and when by faith they lay hold of the power of Christ, when they plead His unfailing promises, and claim them as their own, when with an importunity that will not be denied they seek for the power of the Holy Spirit, they will be made complete in Him.

Having received the faith of the gospel, the next work of the believers is to add to their character virtue, and thus cleanse the heart and prepare the mind for the reception of the knowledge of God. This knowledge is the foundation of all true education and of all true service. It is the only real safeguard against temptation; and it is this alone that can make one like God in character. Through the knowledge of God and of His Son Jesus Christ, are given to the believer "all things that pertain unto life and godliness." No good gift is withheld from anyone who sincerely desires to obtain the righteousness of God. . . .

None of us need fail of attaining, in our sphere, to perfection of Christian character. By the sacrifice of Christ, provision has been made for the believer to receive all things that pertain to life and godliness.—*The Acts of the Apostles,* pp. 530, 531.

Lowliness Gives Victory

Blessed are the meek, for they shall inherit the earth.
—Matthew 5:5.

"Blessed are the meek." The difficulties we have to encounter may be very much lessened by that meekness which hides itself in Christ. If we possess the humility of our Master, we shall rise above the slights, the rebuffs, the annoyances, to which we are daily exposed, and they will cease to cast a gloom over the spirit. The highest evidence of nobility in a Christian is self-control. Those who under abuse or cruelty fail to maintain a calm and trustful spirit rob God of His right to reveal in them His own perfection of character. Lowliness of heart is the strength that gives victory to the followers of Christ; it is the token of their connection with the courts above.

"Though the Lord be high, yet hath He respect unto the lowly." (Psalm 138:6.) Those who reveal the meek and lowly spirit of Christ are tenderly regarded by God. They may be looked upon with scorn by the world, but they are of great value in His sight. Not only the wise, the great, the beneficent, will gain a passport to the heavenly courts; not only the busy worker, full of zeal and restless activity. No; the poor in spirit, who crave the presence of an abiding Christ, the humble in heart, whose highest ambition is to do God's will—these will gain an abundant entrance. They will be among that number who have washed their robes and made them white in the blood of the Lamb. "Therefore are they before the throne of God, and serve Him day and night in His temple: and He that sitteth on the throne shall dwell among them." (Revelation 7:15.) . . .

The merciful shall find mercy, and the pure in heart shall see God. Every impure thought defiles the soul, impairs the moral sense, and tends to obliterate the impressions of the Holy Spirit. It dims the spiritual vision, so that we cannot behold God. The Lord may and does forgive the repenting sinner; but though forgiven, the soul is marred. All impurity of speech or of thought must be shunned by those who would have clear discernment of spiritual truth.

But the words of Christ cover more than freedom from sensual impurity, more than freedom from that ceremonial defilement which the Jews so rigorously shunned. Selfishness prevents us from beholding God. . . . Only the unselfish heart, the humble and trustful spirit, shall see God as "merciful and gracious, long-suffering, and abundant in goodness and truth." (Exodus 34:6.)—*The Desire of Ages*, pp. 301, 302.

April 3

Victory in God Alone

This is the victory that has overcome the world—our faith.
—1 John 5:4.

The Christian life is a battle and a march. But the victory to be gained is not won by human power. The field of conflict is the domain of the heart. The battle which we have to fight—the greatest battle that was ever fought by human beings—is the surrender of self to the will of God, the yielding of the heart to the sovereignty of love. The old nature, born of blood and of the will of the flesh, cannot inherit the kingdom of God. The hereditary tendencies, the former habits, must be given up.

Those who determine to enter the spiritual kingdom will find that all the powers and passions of an unregenerate nature, backed by the forces of the kingdom of darkness, are arrayed against them. Selfishness and pride will make a stand against anything that would show them to be sinful. We cannot, of ourselves, conquer the evil desires and habits that strive for the mastery. We cannot overcome the mighty foe who holds us in his thrall. God alone can give us the victory. He desires us to have the mastery over ourselves, our own will and ways. But He cannot work in us without our consent and cooperation. The divine Spirit works through the faculties and powers given to us. Our energies are required to cooperate with God.

The victory is not won without much earnest prayer, without the humbling of self at every step. Our will is not to be forced into cooperation with divine agencies, but it must be voluntarily submitted. Were it possible to force upon you with a hundredfold greater intensity the influence of the Spirit of God, it would not make you a Christian, a fit subject for heaven. The stronghold of Satan would not be broken. The will must be placed on the side of God's will. You are not able, of yourself, to bring your purposes and desires and inclinations into submission to the will of God; but if you are "willing to be made willing," God will accomplish the work for you, even "casting down imaginations, and every high thing that exalteth itself against the knowledge of God, and bringing into captivity every thought to the obedience of Christ." (2 Corinthians 10:5.) Then you will "work out your own salvation with fear and trembling. For it is God which worketh in you both to will and to do of His good pleasure." (Philippians 2:12, 13.)—*Thoughts From the Mount of Blessing*, pp. 141–143.

Foundation for Victory

Thanks be to God, who gives us the victory through our Lord Jesus Christ.
—1 Corinthians 15:57.

To those who believe, Christ is the sure foundation. These are they who fall upon the Rock and are broken. Submission to Christ and faith in Him are here represented. To fall upon the Rock and be broken is to give up our self-righteousness and to go to Christ with the humility of a child, repenting of our transgressions, and believing in His forgiving love. And so also it is by faith and obedience that we build on Christ as our foundation.

Upon this living stone, Jews and Gentiles alike may build. This is the only foundation upon which we may securely build. It is broad enough for all, and strong enough to sustain the weight and burden of the whole world. And by connection with Christ, the living stone, all who build upon this foundation become living stones. Many persons are by their own endeavors hewn, polished, and beautified; but they cannot become "living stones," because they are not connected with Christ. Without this connection, no one can be saved. Without the life of Christ in us, we cannot withstand the storms of temptation. Our eternal safety depends upon our building upon the sure foundation. Multitudes are today building upon foundations that have not been tested. When the rain falls, and the tempest rages, and the floods come, their house will fall, because it is not founded upon the eternal Rock, the chief cornerstone Christ Jesus.

"To them which stumble at the word, being disobedient," Christ is a rock of offense. But "the stone which the builders disallowed, the same is made the head of the corner." (1 Peter 2:7, 8.) Like the rejected stone, Christ in His earthly mission had borne neglect and abuse. He was "despised and rejected of men; a man of sorrows, and acquainted with grief: . . . He was despised, and we esteemed Him not." (Isaiah 53:3.) But the time was near when He would be glorified. By the resurrection from the dead He would be declared "the Son of God with power." (Romans 1:4.) At His second coming He would be revealed as Lord of heaven and earth. Those who were now about to crucify Him would recognize His greatness. Before the universe the rejected stone would become the head of the corner. . . .

So it will be in the great final day, when judgment shall fall upon the rejecters of God's grace. Christ, their rock of offense, will then appear to them as an avenging mountain.—*The Desire of Ages,* pp. 599, 600.

Temptation Can Result in Victory

God is faithful, who will not allow you to be temped beyond what you are able, but with the temptation will also make the way of escape.—1 Corinthians 10:13.

We should not present our petitions to God to prove whether He will fulfill His word, but because He will fulfill it; not to prove that He loves us, but because He loves us.

"Again, the devil taketh him up into an exceeding high mountain . . . and saith unto him, All these things will I give thee, if thou wilt fall down and worship me."

This was Satan's crowning effort. Into this effort he threw all his beguiling power. It was the charm of the serpent. He exerted the power of his fascination upon Christ, striving to make Him yield His will to him. In His weakness Christ laid hold of God. Divinity flashed through humanity. Christ stood revealed as the Commander of heaven, and His words were the words of one who has all power. "Get thee behind me, Satan," He said, "for it is written, Thou shalt worship the Lord thy God, and Him only shalt thou serve."

Satan had questioned whether Jesus was the Son of God. In his summary dismissal he had proof that he could not gainsay. He had no power to resist the command. Writhing with humiliation and rage, he was forced to withdraw from the presence of the world's Redeemer. Christ's victory was as complete as had been the failure of Adam.

Christ knew of the long years of conflict in the future between human beings and their subtle foe. He is the refuge of all who, beset by temptation, call upon Him. Temptation and trial will come to us all, but we need never be worsted by the enemy. Our Saviour has conquered in our behalf. Satan is not invincible. Day by day he meets those who are on trial, striving by his wiles to gain the mastery over them. His accusing power is great, and it is in this line that he wins more victories than in any other. Christ was tempted, that He might know how to help every soul that should afterward be tempted. Temptation is not sin; the sin lies in yielding. To the soul who trusts in Jesus, temptation means victory and greater strength.

Christ is ready to pardon all who come to Him confessing their sins. . . . Thank God, we have a high priest who is touched with the feelings of our infirmities, for He was in all points tempted as we are.—*Christ Triumphant,* p. 218.

In Safe Paths

The Son can do nothing of Himself, but what He sees the Father do.
—John 5:19.

The words of Christ teach that we should regard ourselves as inseparably bound to our Father in heaven. Whatever our position, we are dependent upon God, who holds all destinies in His hands. He has appointed us our work, and has endowed us with faculties and means for that work. So long as we surrender the will to God, and trust in His strength and wisdom, we shall be guided in safe paths, to fulfill our appointed part in His great plan. But those who depend upon their own wisdom and power are separating themselves from God. Instead of working in unison with Christ, they are fulfilling the purpose of the enemy of God and mankind.

The Saviour continued: "What things soever He [the Father] doeth, these also doeth the Son likewise. . . . As the Father raiseth up the dead, and quickeneth them; even so the Son quickeneth whom He will." The Sadducees held that there would be no resurrection of the body; but Jesus tells them that one of the greatest works of His Father is raising the dead, and that He Himself has power to do the same work. "The hour is coming, and now is, when the dead shall hear the voice of the Son of God: and they that hear shall live." The Pharisees believed in the resurrection of the dead. Christ declares that even now the power which gives life to the dead is among them, and they are to behold its manifestation. This same resurrection power is that which gives life to the soul "dead in trespasses and sins." (Ephesians 2:1.) That spirit of life in Christ Jesus, "the power of His resurrection," sets us "free from the law of sin and death." (Philippians 3:10; Romans 8:2.) The dominion of evil is broken, and through faith the soul is kept from sin. All who open their hearts to the Spirit of Christ become partakers of that mighty power which shall bring forth their bodies from the grave. . . .

The priests and rulers had set themselves up as judges to condemn Christ's work, but He declared Himself their judge, and the judge of all the earth. The world has been committed to Christ, and through Him has come every blessing from God to the fallen race. He was the Redeemer before as after His incarnation. As soon as there was sin, there was a Saviour. He has given light and life to all, and according to the measure of light given, each is to be judged. And He who has given the light, He who has followed the soul with tenderest entreaty, seeking to win it from sin to holiness, is in one its advocate and judge.—*The Desire of Ages,* pp. 209, 210.

Satan Can't Make You Sin

Away with you, Satan! For it is written, "You shall worship the Lord your God."—Matthew 4:10.

The tempter can never compel us to do evil. He cannot control minds unless they are yielded to his control. The will must consent, faith must let go its hold upon Christ, before Satan can exercise his power upon us. But every sinful desire we cherish affords him a foothold. Every point in which we fail of meeting the divine standard is an open door by which he can enter to tempt and destroy us. And every failure or defeat on our part gives occasion for him to reproach Christ.

When Satan quoted the promise, "He shall give His angels charge over Thee," he omitted the words, "to keep Thee in all Thy ways;" that is, in all the ways of God's choosing. Jesus refused to go outside the path of obedience. While manifesting perfect trust in His Father, He would not place Himself, unbidden, in a position that would necessitate the interposition of His Father to save Him from death. He would not force Providence to come to His rescue, and thus fail of giving us an example of trust and submission.

Jesus declared to Satan, "It is written again, Thou shalt not tempt the Lord thy God." These words were spoken by Moses to the children of Israel when they thirsted in the desert, and demanded that Moses should give them water, exclaiming, "Is the Lord among us, or not?" (Exodus 17:7.) God had wrought marvelously for them; yet in trouble they doubted Him, and demanded evidence that He was with them. In their unbelief they sought to put Him to the test. And Satan was urging Christ to do the same thing. God had already testified that Jesus was His Son; and now to ask for proof that He was the Son of God would be putting God's word to the test—tempting Him. And the same would be true of asking for that which God had not promised. It would manifest distrust, and be really proving, or tempting, Him. We should not present our petitions to God to prove whether He will fulfill His word, but because He will fulfill it; not to prove that He loves us, but because He loves us. "Without faith it is impossible to please Him: for he that cometh to God must believe that He is, and that He is a rewarder of them that diligently seek Him." (Hebrews 11:6.)

But faith is in no sense allied to presumption. Only those who have true faith are secure against presumption. For presumption is Satan's counterfeit of faith.—*The Desire of Ages,* pp. 125, 126.

God Must Have Your Consent

The Lord is my strength and my shield; my heart trusted in Him, and I am helped.—Psalm 28:7.

Side by side with the preaching of the gospel, agencies are at work which are but the medium of lying spirits. Many tamper with these merely from curiosity, but seeing evidence of the working of a more than human power, they are lured on and on, until they are controlled by a will stronger than their own. They cannot escape from its mysterious power.

The defenses of their souls are broken down. They have no barrier against sin. When once the restraints of God's word and His Spirit are rejected, no one knows to what depths of degradation they may sink. Secret sin or master passion may hold them captives as helpless as was the demoniac of Capernaum. Yet their condition is not hopeless.

The means by which we can overcome the wicked one is that by which Christ overcame—the power of the word. God does not control our minds without our consent; but if we desire to know and to do His will, His promises are ours: "Ye shall know the truth, and the truth shall make you free." "If any man willeth to do His will, he shall know of the teaching." (John 8:32; 7:17, R.V.) Through faith in these promises, everyone may be delivered from the snares of error and the control of sin.

All of the human race are free to choose what power they will have to rule over them. None have fallen so low, none are so vile, but that they can find deliverance in Christ. The demoniac, in place of prayer, could utter only the words of Satan; yet the heart's unspoken appeal was heard. No cry from a soul in need, though it fail of utterance in words, will be unheeded. Those who will consent to enter into covenant relation with the God of heaven are not left to the power of Satan or to the infirmity of their own nature. They are invited by the Saviour, "Let him take hold of My strength, that he may make peace with Me; and he shall make peace with Me." (Isaiah 27:5.) The spirits of darkness will battle for the soul once under their dominion, but angels of God will contend for that soul with prevailing power. The Lord says, "Shall the prey be taken from the mighty, or the lawful captive delivered? . . . Thus saith the Lord, Even the captives of the mighty shall be taken away, and the prey of the terrible shall be delivered: for I will contend with him that contendeth with thee, and I will save thy children." (Isaiah 49:24, 25.)—*The Desire of Ages*, pp. 258, 259.

April 9

Stepping Over the Line

Do not love the world or the things in the world.
—1 John 2:15.

Christ does not say that people will not or shall not serve two masters, but that they cannot. The interests of God and the interests of mammon have no union or sympathy. Just where the conscience of Christians warn them to forbear, to deny self, to stop, just there the worldlings step over the line, to indulge their selfish propensities. On one side of the line are the self-denying followers of Christ; on the other side are the self-indulgent world lovers, pandering to fashion, engaging in frivolity, and pampering themselves in forbidden pleasure. On that side of the line the Christian cannot go.

No one can occupy a neutral position; there is no middle class, who neither love God nor serve the enemy of righteousness. Christ is to live in His human agents and work through their faculties and act through their capabilities. Their will must be submitted to His will; they must act with His Spirit. Then it is no more they that live, but Christ that lives in them. Those who do not give themselves wholly to God are under the control of another power, listening to another voice, whose suggestions are of an entirely different character. Half-and-half service places the human agent on the side of the enemy as a successful ally of the hosts of darkness. When those who claim to be soldiers of Christ engage with the confederacy of Satan, and help along his side, they prove themselves enemies of Christ. They betray sacred trusts. They form a link between Satan and the true soldiers, so that through these agencies the enemy is constantly working to steal away the hearts of Christ's soldiers.

The strongest bulwark of vice in our world is not the iniquitous life of the abandoned sinner or the degraded outcast; it is that life which otherwise appears virtuous, honorable, and noble, but in which one sin is fostered, one vice indulged. To the soul that is struggling in secret against some giant temptation, trembling upon the very verge of the precipice, such an example is one of the most powerful enticements to sin. Anyone who, endowed with high conceptions of life and truth and honor, does yet willfully transgress one precept of God's holy law, has perverted His noble gifts into a lure to sin. Genius, talent, sympathy, even generous and kindly deeds, may become decoys of Satan to entice other souls over the precipice of ruin for this life and the life to come.—*Thoughts From the Mount of Blessing*, pp. 93, 94.

Learn to Distrust Self

Therefore whoever humbles himself as this little child is the greatest in the kingdom of heaven.—Matthew 18:4.

The Saviour did not despise education; for when controlled by the love of God, and devoted to His service, intellectual culture is a blessing. But He passed by the wise men of His time, because they were so self-confident that they could not sympathize with suffering humanity, and become colaborers with the Man of Nazareth. . . . The first thing to be learned by all who would become workers together with God is the lesson of self-distrust; then they are prepared to have imparted to them the character of Christ. This is not to be gained through education in the most scientific schools. It is the fruit of wisdom that is obtained from the divine Teacher alone.

Jesus chose unlearned fishermen because they had not been schooled in the traditions and erroneous customs of their time. They were men of native ability, and they were humble and teachable,—men whom He could educate for His work. In the common walks of life there are many people patiently treading the round of daily toil, unconscious that they possess powers which, if called into action, would raise them to an equality with the world's most honored leaders. The touch of a skillful hand is needed to arouse those dormant faculties. It was such men that Jesus called to be His colaborers; and He gave them the advantage of association with Himself. Never had the world's great minds such a teacher. When the disciples came forth from the Saviour's training, they were no longer ignorant and uncultured. They had become like Him in mind and character, and others took knowledge of them that they had been with Jesus.

It is not the highest work of education to communicate knowledge merely, but to impart that vitalizing energy which is received through the contact of mind with mind, and soul with soul. It is only life that can beget life. What privilege, then, was theirs who for three years were in daily contact with that divine life from which has flowed every life-giving impulse that has blessed the world! Above all his companions, John the beloved disciple yielded himself to the power of that wondrous life. He says, "The life was manifested, and we have seen it, and bear witness, and show unto you that eternal life, which was with the Father, and was manifested unto us." (1 John 1:2.)—*The Desire of Ages,* pp. 249, 250.

April 11

Stay Focused on Jesus

Blessed are your eyes for they see.
—Matthew 13:16.

Walking side by side, Peter's hand in that of his Master, they stepped into the boat together. But Peter was now subdued and silent. He had no reason to boast over his companions, for through unbelief and self-exaltation he had very nearly lost his life. When he turned his eyes from Jesus, his footing was lost, and he sank amid the waves.

When trouble comes upon us, how often we are like Peter! We look upon the waves, instead of keeping our eyes fixed upon the Saviour. Our footsteps slide, and the proud waters go over our souls. Jesus did not bid Peter come to Him that he should perish; He does not call us to follow Him, and then forsake us. . . .

Jesus read the character of His disciples. He knew how sorely their faith was to be tried. In this incident on the sea He desired to reveal to Peter his own weakness—to show that his safety was in constant dependence upon divine power. Amid the storms of temptation he could walk safely only as in utter self-distrust he should rely upon the Saviour. It was on the point where he thought himself strong that Peter was weak; and not until he discerned his weakness could he realize his need of dependence upon Christ. Had he learned the lesson that Jesus sought to teach him in that experience on the sea, he would not have failed when the great test came upon him.

Day by day God instructs His children. By the circumstances of the daily life He is preparing them to act their part upon that wider stage to which His providence has appointed them. It is the issue of the daily test that determines their victory or defeat in life's great crisis.

Those who fail to realize their constant dependence upon God will be overcome by temptation. We may now suppose that our feet stand secure, and that we shall never be moved. We may say with confidence, "I know in whom I have believed; nothing can shake my faith in God and in His word." But Satan is planning to take advantage of our hereditary and cultivated traits of character, and to blind our eyes to our own necessities and defects. Only through realizing our own weakness and looking steadfastly unto Jesus can we walk securely.—*The Desire of Ages,* pp. 381, 382.

April 12

You Are Not Alone

I pray for them. I do not pray for the world but for those whom You have given Me, for they are Yours.
—John 17:9.

The only safeguard against evil is the indwelling of Christ in the heart through faith in His righteousness. It is because selfishness exists in our hearts that temptation has power over us. But when we behold the great love of God, selfishness appears to us in its hideous and repulsive character, and we desire to have it expelled from the soul. As the Holy Spirit glorifies Christ, our hearts are softened and subdued, the temptation loses its power, and the grace of Christ transforms the character.

Christ will never abandon the soul for whom He has died. The soul may leave Him and be overwhelmed with temptation, but Christ can never turn from one for whom He has paid the ransom of His own life. Could our spiritual vision be quickened, we should see souls bowed under oppression and burdened with grief, pressed as a cart beneath sheaves and ready to die in discouragement. We should see angels flying swiftly to aid these tempted ones, who are standing as on the brink of a precipice. The angels from heaven force back the hosts of evil that encompass these souls, and guide them to plant their feet on the sure foundation. The battles waging between the two armies are as real as those fought by the armies of this world, and on the issue of the spiritual conflict eternal destinies depend.

To us, as to Peter, the word is spoken, "Satan hath desired to have you, that he may sift you as wheat: but I have prayed for thee, that thy faith fail not." (Luke 22:31, 32.) Thank God, we are not left alone. He who "so loved the world, that He gave His only-begotten Son, that whosoever believeth in Him should not perish, but have everlasting life" (John 3:16), will not desert us in the battle with the adversary of God and mankind. "Behold," He says, "I give unto you power to tread on serpents and scorpions, and over all the power of the enemy: and nothing shall by any means hurt you." (Luke 10:19.)

Live in contact with the living Christ, and He will hold you firmly by a hand that will never let go. Know and believe the love that God has to us, and you are secure; that love is a fortress impregnable to all the delusions and assaults of Satan.—*Thoughts From the Mount of Blessing,* pp. 118, 119.

April 13

Fortresses for God

Finally, my brethren, be strong in the Lord and in the power of His might.
—Ephesians 6:10.

There were many in Christ's day, as there are today, over whom the control of Satan for the time seemed broken; through the grace of God they were set free from the evil spirits that had held dominion over the soul. They rejoiced in the love of God; but, like the stony-ground hearers of the parable, they did not abide in His love. They did not surrender themselves to God daily, that Christ might dwell in the heart; and when the evil spirit returned, with "seven other spirits more wicked than himself," they were wholly dominated by the power of evil.

When the soul surrenders itself to Christ, a new power takes possession of the new heart. A change is wrought which we can never accomplish for ourselves. It is a supernatural work, bringing a supernatural element into human nature. The soul that is yielded to Christ becomes His own fortress, which He holds in a revolted world, and He intends that no authority shall be known in it but His own. A soul thus kept in possession by the heavenly agencies is impregnable to the assaults of Satan. But unless we do yield ourselves to the control of Christ, we shall be dominated by the wicked one. We must inevitably be under the control of the one or the other of the two great powers that are contending for the supremacy of the world. It is not necessary for us deliberately to choose the service of the kingdom of darkness in order to come under its dominion. We have only to neglect to ally ourselves with the kingdom of light. If we do not cooperate with the heavenly agencies, Satan will take possession of the heart, and will make it his abiding place. The only defense against evil is the indwelling of Christ in the heart through faith in His righteousness. Unless we become vitally connected with God, we can never resist the unhallowed effects of self-love, self-indulgence, and temptation to sin. We may leave off many bad habits, for the time we may part company with Satan; but without a vital connection with God, through the surrender of ourselves to Him moment by moment, we shall be overcome. Without a personal acquaintance with Christ, and a continual communion, we are at the mercy of the enemy, and shall do his bidding in the end. . . .

The most common manifestation of the sin against the Holy Spirit is in persistently slighting Heaven's invitation to repent. Every step in the rejection of Christ is a step toward the rejection of salvation.—*The Desire of Ages*, pp. 323, 324.

Heart Obedience

If you love Me, keep My commandments.
—John 14:15.

But to pray in Christ's name means much. It means that we are to accept His character, manifest His spirit, and work His works. The Saviour's promise is given on condition. "If ye love Me," He says, "keep My commandments." He saves people, not in sin, but from sin; and those who love Him will show their love by obedience.

All true obedience comes from the heart. It was heart work with Christ. And if we consent, He will so identify Himself with our thoughts and aims, so blend our hearts and minds into conformity to His will, that when obeying Him we shall be but carrying out our own impulses. The will, refined and sanctified, will find its highest delight in doing His service. When we know God as it is our privilege to know Him, our life will be a life of continual obedience. Through an appreciation of the character of Christ, through communion with God, sin will become hateful to us.

As Christ lived the law in humanity, so we may do if we will take hold of the Strong for strength. But we are not to place the responsibility of our duty upon others, and wait for them to tell us what to do. We cannot depend for counsel upon humanity. The Lord will teach us our duty just as willingly as He will teach somebody else. If we come to Him in faith, He will speak His mysteries to us personally. Our hearts will often burn within us as One draws nigh to commune with us as He did with Enoch. Those who decide to do nothing in any line that will displease God, will know, after presenting their case before Him, just what course to pursue. And they will receive not only wisdom, but strength. Power for obedience, for service, will be imparted to them, as Christ has promised. Whatever was given to Christ—the "all things" to supply the need of fallen men and women—was given to Him as the head and representative of humanity. And "whatsoever we ask, we receive of Him, because we keep His commandments, and do those things that are pleasing in His sight." (1 John 3:22.)

Before offering Himself as the sacrificial victim, Christ sought for the most essential and complete gift to bestow upon His followers, a gift that would bring within their reach the boundless resources of grace. "I will pray the Father," He said, "and He shall give you another Comforter." (John 14:16.)—*The Desire of Ages,* pp. 668, 669.

April 15

Be True to Principle

I stand continually on the watchtower in the daytime:
I have sat at my post every night.—Isaiah 21:8.

Jesus Himself never purchased peace by compromise. His heart overflowed with love for the whole human race, but He was never indulgent to their sins. He was too much their friend to remain silent while they were pursuing a course that would ruin their souls—the souls He had purchased with His own blood. He labored that human beings should be true to themselves, true to their higher and eternal interest. The servants of Christ are called to the same work, and they should beware lest, in seeking to prevent discord, they surrender the truth. They are to "follow after the things which make for peace" (Romans 14:19); but real peace can never be secured by compromising principle. And no one can be true to principle without exciting opposition. A Christianity that is spiritual will be opposed by the children of disobedience. But Jesus bade His disciples, "Fear not them which kill the body, but are not able to kill the soul." Those who are true to God need not fear human power nor the enmity of Satan. In Christ their eternal life is secure. Their only fear should be lest they surrender the truth, and thus betray the trust with which God has honored them.

It is Satan's work to fill people's hearts with doubt. He leads them to look upon God as a stern judge. He tempts them to sin, and then to regard themselves as too vile to approach their heavenly Father or to excite His pity. The Lord understands all this. Jesus assures His disciples of God's sympathy for them in their needs and weaknesses. Not a sigh is breathed, not a pain felt, not a grief pierces the soul, but the throb vibrates to the Father's heart.

The Bible shows us God in His high and holy place, not in a state of inactivity, not in silence and solitude, but surrounded by ten thousand times ten thousand and thousands of thousands of holy intelligences, all waiting to do His will. Through channels which we cannot discern He is in active communication with every part of His dominion. But it is in this speck of a world, in the souls that He gave His only-begotten Son to save, that His interest and the interest of all heaven is centered. God is bending from His throne to hear the cry of the oppressed. To every sincere prayer He answers, "Here am I." He uplifts the distressed and downtrodden. In all our afflictions He is afflicted.—*The Desire of Ages,* p. 356.

How Do We Deny Jesus?

But whoever denies Me before men, him I will also deny before My Father who is in heaven.—Matthew 10:33.

Jesus continues: As you confess Me before men, so I will confess you before God and the holy angels. You are to be My witnesses upon earth, channels through which My grace can flow for the healing of the world. So I will be your representative in heaven. The Father beholds not your faulty character, but He sees you as clothed in My perfection. I am the medium through which Heaven's blessings shall come to you. And everyone who confesses Me by sharing My sacrifice for the lost shall be confessed as a sharer in the glory and joy of the redeemed.

All who would confess Christ must have Christ abiding in them. They cannot communicate that which they have not received. The disciples might speak fluently on doctrines, they might repeat the words of Christ Himself; but unless they possessed Christlike meekness and love, they were not confessing Him. A spirit contrary to the spirit of Christ would deny Him, whatever the profession. People may deny Christ by evilspeaking, by foolish talking, by words that are untruthful or unkind. They may deny Him by shunning life's burdens, by the pursuit of sinful pleasure. They may deny Him by conforming to the world, by uncourteous behavior, by the love of their own opinions, by justifying self, by cherishing doubt, borrowing trouble, and dwelling in darkness. In all these ways they declare that Christ is not in them. . . .

The Saviour bade His disciples not to hope that the world's enmity to the gospel would be overcome, and that after a time its opposition would cease. He said, "I came not to send peace, but a sword." This creating of strife is not the effect of the gospel, but the result of opposition to it. Of all persecution the hardest to bear is variance in the home, the estrangement of dearest earthly friends. But Jesus declares, "He that loveth father or mother more than Me is not worthy of Me: and he that loveth son or daughter more than Me is not worthy of Me." . . .

The mission of Christ's servants is a high honor, and a sacred trust. . . . No act of kindness shown to them in His name will fail to be recognized and rewarded. And in the same tender recognition He includes the feeblest and lowliest of the family of God.—*The Desire of Ages,* pp. 357, 358.

April 17

How Do We See Ourselves?

And my God shall supply all your need according to His riches in glory by Christ Jesus.—Philippians 4:19.

In the days of Christ the religious leaders of the people felt that they were rich in spiritual treasure. The prayer of the Pharisee, "God, I thank Thee, that I am not as the rest of men" (Luke 18:11, R.V.), expressed the feeling of his class and, to a great degree, of the whole nation. But in the throng that surrounded Jesus there were some who had a sense of their spiritual poverty. When in the miraculous draft of fishes the divine power of Christ was revealed, Peter fell at the Saviour's feet, exclaiming, "Depart from me; for I am a sinful man, O Lord" (Luke 5:8); so in the multitude gathered upon the mount there were souls who, in the presence of His purity, felt that they were "wretched, and miserable, and poor, and blind, and naked" (Revelation 3:17); and they longed for "the grace of God that bringeth salvation." (Titus 2:11.) In these souls, Christ's words of greeting awakened hope; they saw that their lives were under the benediction of God.

Jesus had presented the cup of blessing to those who felt that they were "rich, and increased with goods" (Revelation 3:17), and had need of nothing, and they had turned with scorn from the gracious gift. Those who feel whole, who think that they are reasonably good, and are contented with their condition, do not seek to become partakers of the grace and righteousness of Christ. Pride feels no need, and so it closes the heart against Christ and the infinite blessings He came to give. There is no room for Jesus in the heart of such a person. Those who are rich and honorable in their own eyes do not ask in faith, and receive the blessing of God. They feel that they are full, therefore they go away empty. Those who know that they cannot possibly save themselves, or of themselves do any righteous action, are the ones who appreciate the help that Christ can bestow. They are the poor in spirit, whom He declares to be blessed.

Whom Christ pardons, He first makes penitent, and it is the office of the Holy Spirit to convince of sin. Those whose hearts have been moved by the convicting Spirit of God see that there is nothing good in themselves. They see that all they have ever done is mingled with self and sin. Like the poor publican, they stand afar off, not daring to lift up so much as their eyes to heaven, and cry, "God, be merciful to me the sinner." (Luke 18:13, R.V., margin.) And they are blessed.—*Thoughts From the Mount of Blessing,* pp. 6–8.

Do We Sense Our Need?

He only is my rock and my salvation; He is my defense.
—Psalm 62:6.

As we need food to sustain our physical strength, so do we need Christ, the Bread from heaven, to sustain spiritual life and impart strength to work the works of God. As the body is continually receiving the nourishment that sustains life and vigor, so the soul must be constantly communing with Christ, submitting to Him and depending wholly upon Him.

As the weary travelers seek the spring in the desert and, finding it, quench their burning thirst, so will the Christian thirst for and obtain the pure water of life, of which Christ is the fountain.

As we discern the perfection of our Saviour's character we shall desire to become wholly transformed and renewed in the image of His purity. The more we know of God, the higher will be our ideal of character and the more earnest our longing to reflect His likeness. A divine element combines with the human when the soul reaches out after God and the longing heart can say, "My soul, wait thou only upon God; for my expectation is from Him." (Psalm 62:5.)

If you have a sense of need in your soul, if you hunger and thirst after righteousness, this is an evidence that Christ has wrought upon your heart, in order that He may be sought unto to do for you, through the endowment of the Holy Spirit, those things which it is impossible for you to do for yourself. We need not seek to quench our thirst at shallow streams; for the great fountain is just above us, of whose abundant waters we may freely drink, if we will rise a little higher in the pathway of faith.

The words of God are the wellsprings of life. As you seek unto those living springs you will, through the Holy Spirit, be brought into communion with Christ. Familiar truths will present themselves to your mind in a new aspect, texts of Scripture will burst upon you with a new meaning as a flash of light, you will see the relation of other truths to the work of redemption, and you will know that Christ is leading you, a divine Teacher is at your side. . . .

As the Holy Spirit opens to you the truth you will treasure up the most precious experiences and will long to speak to others of the comforting things that have been revealed to you. When brought into association with them you will communicate some fresh thought in regard to the character or the work of Christ.—*Thoughts From the Mount of Blessing,* pp. 19, 20.

A New Life

You must be born again.
—John 3:7.

Like Nicodemus, we must be willing to enter into life in the same way as the chief of sinners. Than Christ, "there is none other name under heaven given among men, whereby we must be saved." (Acts 4:12.) Through faith we receive the grace of God; but faith is not our Saviour. It earns nothing. It is the hand by which we lay hold upon Christ, and appropriate His merits, the remedy for sin. And we cannot even repent without the aid of the Spirit of God. The Scripture says of Christ, "Him hath God exalted with His right hand to be a Prince and a Saviour, for to give repentance to Israel, and forgiveness of sins." (Acts 5:31.) Repentance comes from Christ as truly as does pardon.

How, then, are we to be saved? "As Moses lifted up the serpent in the wilderness," so the Son of man has been lifted up, and everyone who has been deceived and bitten by the serpent may look and live. "Behold the Lamb of God, which taketh away the sin of the world." (John 1:29.) The light shining from the cross reveals the love of God. His love is drawing us to Himself. If we do not resist this drawing, we shall be led to the foot of the cross in repentance for the sins that have crucified the Saviour. Then the Spirit of God through faith produces a new life in the soul. The thoughts and desires are brought into obedience to the will of Christ. The heart, the mind, are created anew in the image of Him who works in us to subdue all things to Himself. Then the law of God is written in the mind and heart, and we can say with Christ, "I delight to do Thy will, O my God." (Psalm 40:8.)

In the interview with Nicodemus, Jesus unfolded the plan of salvation, and His mission to the world. In none of His subsequent discourses did He explain so fully, step by step, the work necessary to be done in the hearts of all who would inherit the kingdom of heaven. At the very beginning of His ministry He opened the truth to a member of the Sanhedrin, to the mind that was most receptive, and to an appointed teacher of the people. But the leaders of Israel did not welcome the light. Nicodemus hid the truth in his heart, and for three years there was little apparent fruit. . . .

Nicodemus related to John the story of that interview, and by his pen it was recorded for the instruction of millions.—*The Desire of Ages,* pp. 175–177.

From Victory to Victory

This is the victory that has overcome the world—our faith.
—1 John 5:4.

Through Christ, restoration as well as reconciliation is provided for us. The gulf that was made by sin has been spanned by the cross of Calvary. A full, complete ransom has been paid by Jesus, by virtue of which the sinner is pardoned and the justice of the law is maintained. All who believe that Christ is the atoning sacrifice may come and receive pardon for their sins; for through the merit of Christ, communication has been opened between God and mankind. God can accept me as His child, and I can claim Him and rejoice in Him as my loving Father.

We must center our hopes of heaven upon Christ alone, because He is our Substitute and Surety. We have transgressed the law of God, and by the deeds of the law shall no flesh be justified. The best efforts that we in our own strength can make are valueless to meet the holy and just law that we have transgressed; but through faith in Christ we may claim the righteousness of the Son of God as all-sufficient. Christ satisfied the demands of the law in His human nature. He bore the curse of the law for sinners, made an atonement for them, "that whosoever believeth in Him should not perish, but have everlasting life." Genuine faith appropriates the righteousness of Christ, and sinners are made overcomers with Christ; for they are made partakers of the divine nature, and thus divinity and humanity are combined.

All who are trying to reach heaven by their own works in keeping the law are attempting an impossibility. We cannot be saved without obedience, but our works should not be of ourselves; Christ should work in us to will and to do of His good pleasure. If we could save ourselves by our own works, we might have something in ourselves in which to rejoice. The effort that we make in our own strength to obtain salvation is represented by the offering of Cain. All that human beings can do without Christ is polluted with selfishness and sin; but that which is wrought through faith is acceptable to God. When we seek to gain heaven through the merits of Christ, the soul makes progress. "Looking unto Jesus, the author and finisher of our faith," we may go on from strength to strength, from victory to victory; for through Christ the grace of God has worked out our complete salvation.—*Review and Herald,* July 1, 1890 (*Selected Messages,* book 1, pp. 363, 364).

April 21

Sin No Longer Attractive

For if when we were enemies we were reconciled to God through the death of His Son, much more, having been reconciled, we shall be saved by His life.
—Romans 5:10.

It is the righteousness of Christ that makes penitent sinners acceptable to God and works their justification. However sinful have been their lives, if they believe in Jesus as their personal Saviour, they stand before God in the spotless robes of Christ's imputed righteousness.

The sinners so recently dead in trespasses and sins are quickened by faith in Christ. They see by faith that Jesus is their Saviour, and alive forevermore, able to save unto "the uttermost [all] that come unto God by Him." In the atonement made for them the believers see such breadth and length and height and depth of efficiency—see such completeness of salvation, purchased at such infinite cost, that their souls are filled with praise and thanksgiving. They see as in a glass the glory of the Lord and are changed into the same image as by the Spirit of the Lord. They see the robe of Christ's righteousness, woven in the loom of heaven, wrought by His obedience, and imputed to the repenting soul through faith in His name.

When sinners have a view of the matchless charms of Jesus, sin no longer looks attractive to them; for they behold the Chiefest among ten thousand, the One altogether lovely. They realize by a personal experience the power of the gospel, whose vastness of design is equaled only by its preciousness of purpose.

We have a living Saviour. He is not in Joseph's new tomb; He is risen from the dead and has ascended on high as a Substitute and Surety for every believing soul. "Therefore being justified by faith, we have peace with God through our Lord Jesus Christ." (Romans 5:1.) We are justified through the merits of Jesus, and this is God's acknowledgment of the perfection of the ransom paid us. That Christ was obedient even unto the death of the cross is a pledge of the repenting sinner's acceptance with the Father. Then shall we permit ourselves to have a vacillating experience of doubting and believing, believing and doubting? Jesus is the pledge of our acceptance with God. We stand in favor before God, not because of any merit in ourselves, but because of our faith in "the Lord our righteousness." . . .

We are complete in Him, accepted in the Beloved, only as we abide in Him by faith.—*Signs of the Times,* July 4, 1892 (*Faith and Works,* pp. 106, 107).

Race for the Crown

Do you not know that those who run in a race all run, but one receives the prize?—1 Corinthians 9:24.

In the epistle to the Hebrews is pointed out the single-hearted purpose that should characterize the Christian's race for eternal life: "Let us lay aside every weight, and the sin which doth so easily beset us, and let us run with patience the race that is set before us, looking unto Jesus the author and finisher of our faith." (Hebrews 12:1, 2.) Envy, malice, evil thinking, evilspeaking, covetousness—these are weights that Christians must lay aside if they would run successfully the race for immortality. Every habit or practice that leads into sin and brings dishonor upon Christ must be put away, whatever the sacrifice. The blessing of heaven cannot attend anyone in violating the eternal principles of right. One sin cherished is sufficient to work degradation of character and to mislead others. . . .

The competitors in the ancient games, after they had submitted to self-denial and rigid discipline, were not even then sure of the victory. "Know ye not," Paul asked, "that they which run in a race run all, but one receiveth the prize?" However eagerly and earnestly the runners might strive, the prize could be awarded to but one. One hand only could grasp the coveted garland. Some might put forth the utmost effort to obtain the prize, but as they reached forth the hand to secure it, another, an instant before them, might grasp the coveted treasure.

Such is not the case in the Christian warfare. Not one who complies with the conditions will be disappointed at the end of the race. Not one who is earnest and persevering will fail of success. The race is not to the swift, nor the battle to the strong. The weakest saint, as well as the strongest, may wear the crown of immortal glory. All may win who, through the power of divine grace, bring their lives into conformity to the will of Christ. The practice, in the details of life, of the principles laid down in God's word, is too often looked upon as unimportant—a matter too trivial to demand attention. But in view of the issue at stake, nothing is small that will help or hinder. Every act casts its weight into the scale that determines life's victory or defeat. And the reward given to those who win will be in proportion to the energy and earnestness with which they have striven.—*The Acts of the Apostles,* pp. 312–314.

April 23

Abiding Peace

Peace I leave with you, My peace I give to you; not as the world gives do I give to you.—John 14:27.

When we receive Christ as an abiding guest in the soul, the peace of God, which passeth all understanding, will keep our hearts and minds through Christ Jesus. The Saviour's life on earth, though lived in the midst of conflict, was a life of peace. While angry enemies were constantly pursuing Him, He said, "He that sent Me is with Me: the Father hath not left Me alone; for I do always those things that please Him." (John 8:29.) No storm of human or satanic wrath could disturb the calm of that perfect communion with God. And He says to us, "Peace I leave with you, My peace I give unto you." "Take My yoke upon you, and learn of Me; for I am meek and lowly in heart: and ye shall find rest." (John 14:27; Matthew 11:29.) Bear with Me the yoke of service for the glory of God and the uplifting of humanity, and you will find the yoke easy and the burden light.

It is the love of self that destroys our peace. While self is all alive, we stand ready continually to guard it from mortification and insult; but when we are dead, and our life is hid with Christ in God, we shall not take neglects or slights to heart. We shall be deaf to reproach and blind to scorn and insult. . . .

Happiness drawn from earthly sources is as changeable as varying circumstances can make it; but the peace of Christ is a constant and abiding peace. It does not depend upon any circumstances in life, on the amount of worldly goods or the number of earthly friends. Christ is the fountain of living water, and happiness drawn from Him can never fail.

The meekness of Christ, manifested in the home, will make the inmates happy; it provokes no quarrel, gives back no angry answer, but soothes the irritated temper and diffuses a gentleness that is felt by all within its charmed circle. Wherever cherished, it makes the families of earth a part of the one great family above.

Far better would it be for us to suffer under false accusation than to inflict upon ourselves the torture of retaliation upon our enemies. The spirit of hatred and revenge originated with Satan, and can bring only evil to him who cherishes it. Lowliness of heart, that meekness which is the fruit of abiding in Christ, is the true secret of blessing.—*Thoughts From the Mount of Blessing,* pp. 15–17.

Share What You Receive

God . . . comforts us in all our tribulation, that we may be able to comfort those who are in any trouble, with the comfort with which we ourselves are comforted by God.—2 Corinthians 1:3, 4.

To repenting sinners, God is ever ready to show His mercy and truth; He is ready to bestow upon them forgiveness and love; and He requires that those who have been blessed by His compassion, shall reveal the same mercy and love toward others; for this is doing the works of Christ, this is keeping the commandments of God. Those who show true gratitude glorify God by loving Him supremely and their neighbors as themselves. They manifest the fact that they have received not the spirit which is of the world, but the Spirit which is of God. By an experimental knowledge they know what are the good things freely given them of God; for they are illuminated by the Holy Spirit. They work out their own salvation with fear and trembling, knowing that it is God who worketh in them to will and to do of His good pleasure. Christ abides in the soul of the believer, a well of water springing up unto everlasting life.

When we look upon ourselves as the purchased possession of Christ, we shall more clearly realize our need of His constant presence in order that we may represent Him by manifesting sympathy and love to all who are brought within the sphere of our influence. Our life is charged with solemn responsibilities, and it is only when we are fully consecrated to God, only when He cleanses us, and puts His own life and spirit upon us, that we can rightly represent Him to others. Our accountability extends to our thoughts, words, and acts, as well as to our larger transactions among our fellow-men.

In order to fulfill the law, we are to carry out the golden rule, and do unto others as we would have them do unto us. Our influence must be sanctified by the Holy Spirit of God, if it is to be a blessing to humanity. We are not to be anxious as to what we will do for weeks or months or years ahead; for the future does not belong to us. One day alone is ours, and during this day we are to live for God, beautify our characters by faith in the righteousness of Christ. This one day we are to place in the hands of Christ in solemn service, in all our purposes and plans to be guided by Him. This one day we are to do unto others exactly as we wish them to do unto us. We are to be ready to speak kind words from hearts full of sympathy and love.—*Signs of the Times,* July 11, 1892.

April 25

Victory Through the Merits of Christ

For as in Adam all die, even so in Christ all shall be made alive.
—1 Corinthians 15:22.

It is at an immense cost that we have been placed on the high vantage ground where we can be liberated from the bondage of sin, which has been wrought by the fall of Adam. . . . Never can we understand the value of the human soul until we realize the great sacrifice made for the redemption of the soul upon Calvary. Adam's sin in Eden plunged the human race into hopeless misery. But in the scheme of salvation a way has been provided for all to escape if they comply with the requirements. A second probation has been granted by the sacrifice of the Son of God. We have a battle to fight, but we can come off victor through the merits of Christ's blood.

God saw that it was impossible for us to overcome and gain the victory in our own strength. The race has ever been growing weaker in every succeeding generation since the fall, and without the help of Christ we cannot resist the evil of intemperance. How thankful we should be that we have a Saviour and that He consented to lay off His royal robes and leave the royal throne, and to clothe His divinity with humanity and become a Man of sorrows and acquainted with grief. . . .

After His baptism, He was led by the Spirit into the wilderness and was tempted of the devil. Christ commenced the work of redemption just where the ruin began, and the future welfare of the world depended on that battle fought by the Prince of life in the wilderness. Thanks be to God that He came off victorious, passing over the same ground where Adam fell and redeeming Adam's disgraceful failure. Satan left the field of battle a conquered foe. This victory is an assurance to us that through divine help we may come off victorious in our behalf on our own account in the conflict with the enemy. . . .

Satan felt that all the power of this fallen planet was in his possession, but when Christ came to measure strength with the prince of darkness, Satan found One who was able to resist his temptations. The words of Christ are, "The prince of this world cometh, and hath nothing in me." . . . All heaven was watching the result of the controversy between Christ and Satan. . . . Now the question is, Will we take advantage of the situation and come off more than conquerors through Him who loved us?—*Christ Triumphant,* p. 215.

Victorious Over Trials

Beloved, do not think it strange concerning the fiery trial which is to try you, as though some strange thing happened to you.—1 *Peter 4:12.*

In this time of trial we need to be encouraged and comforted by one another. The temptations of Satan are greater now than ever before, for he knows that his time is short and that very soon every case will be decided, either for life or for death. It is no time now to sink down beneath discouragement and trial; we must bear up under all our afflictions and trust wholly in the Almighty God of Jacob. The Lord has shown me that His grace is sufficient for all our trials; and although they are greater than ever before, yet if we trust wholly in God, we can overcome every temptation and through His grace come off victorious.

If we overcome our trials and get victory over the temptations of Satan, then we endure the trial of our faith, which is more precious than gold, and are stronger and better prepared to meet the next. But if we sink down and give way to the temptations of Satan, we shall grow weaker and get no reward for the trial and shall not be so well prepared for the next. In this way we shall grow weaker and weaker, until we are led captive by Satan at his will.

We must have on the whole armor of God and be ready at any moment for a conflict with the powers of darkness. When temptations and trials rush in upon us, let us go to God and agonize with Him in prayer. He will not turn us away empty, but will give us grace and strength to overcome, and to break the power of the enemy. Oh, that all could see these things in their true light and endure hardness as good soldiers of Jesus! Then would Israel move forward, strong in God, and in the power of His might.

God has shown me that He gave His people a bitter cup to drink, to purify and cleanse them. It is a bitter draft, and they can make it still more bitter by murmuring, complaining, and repining. But those who receive it thus must have another draft, for the first does not have its designed effect upon the heart. And if the second does not effect the work, then they must have another, and another, until it does have its designed effect, or they will be left filthy, impure in heart. I saw that this bitter cup can be sweetened by patience, endurance, and prayer, and that it will have its designed effect upon the hearts of those who thus receive it, and God will be honored and glorified.—*Early Writings,* pp. 46, 47.

April 27

Crowns and Robes

He who overcomes shall be clothed in white garments.
—Revelation 3:5.

Every one of us may know that there is a power working with our efforts to overcome. Why will not men and women lay hold upon the help that has been provided, that they may become elevated and ennobled? Why do they degrade themselves by the indulgence of perverted appetite? Why do they not rise in the strength of Jesus, and be victorious in his name? The very feeblest prayer that we can offer, Jesus will hear. He pities the weakness of every soul. Help for every one has been laid upon Him who is mighty to save. I point you to Jesus Christ, the sinner's Saviour, who alone can give you power to overcome on every point.

Heaven is worth everything to us. We must not run any risk in this matter. We must take no venture here. We must know that our steps are ordered by the Lord. May God help us in the great work of overcoming. He has crowns for those that overcome. He has white robes for the righteous. He has an eternal world of glory for those who seek for glory, honor, and immortality. All who enter the city of God will enter it as conquerors. They will not enter it as condemned criminals, but as sons and daughters of God. And the welcome given to every one who enters there will be, "Come, ye blessed of my Father, inherit the kingdom prepared for you from the foundation of the world." (Matthew 25:34.)

Gladly would I speak words that would aid such trembling souls to fasten their grasp by faith upon the mighty Helper, that they might develop a character upon which God will be pleased to look. Heaven may invite them, and present its choicest blessings, and they may have every facility to develop a perfect character; but all will be in vain unless they are willing to help themselves. They must put forth their own God-given powers, or they will sink lower and lower, and be of no account for good, either in time or in eternity.

All who are weakened, and even degraded by sinful indulgence, may become children of God. It is in their power to be constantly doing good to others, and helping them to overcome temptation; and in so doing they will reap benefit to themselves. They may be bright and shining lights in the world, and at last hear the benediction, "Well done, good and faithful servant," from the lips of the King of Glory.—*Christian Temperance and Bible Hygiene,* pp. 148, 149.

Look Up, Not Down

Therefore strengthen the hands which hang down, and the feeble knees.—Hebrews 12:12.

The church, endowed with the righteousness of Christ, is His depositary, in which the riches of His mercy, His grace, and His love, are to appear in full and final display. Christ looks upon His people in their purity and perfection, as the reward of His humiliation, and the supplement of His glory—Christ, the great Center, from whom radiates all glory.—*The Desire of Ages,* p. 680.

All heaven is interested in the work going on in this world, which is to prepare men and women for the future, immortal life. It is God's plan that human agencies shall have the high honor of acting as coworkers with Jesus Christ in the salvation of souls. . . . They should look upon the work of God as sacred and holy, and should bring to Him, every day, offerings of joy and gratitude, in return for the power of His grace, by which they are enabled to make advancement in the divine life. . . .

It is not necessary that anyone should yield to the temptations of Satan and thus violate conscience and grieve the Holy Spirit. Every provision has been made in the Word of God whereby all may have divine help in their endeavors to overcome.

In the religious life of all who are finally victorious there will be scenes of terrible perplexity and trial; but their knowledge of the Scriptures will enable them to bring to mind the encouraging promises of God, which will comfort their hearts and strengthen their faith in the power of the Mighty One. They read: . . . "that the trial of your faith, being much more precious than of gold that perisheth, though it be tried with fire, might be found unto praise and honour and glory at the appearing of Jesus Christ." (1 Peter 1:7.) The trial of faith is more precious than gold. All should learn that this is a part of the discipline in the school of Christ. . . .

Summon all your powers to look up, not down at your difficulties; then you will never faint by the way. You will soon see Jesus behind the cloud, reaching out His hand to help you; and all you have to do is to give Him your hand in simple faith and let Him lead you. . . . A great name in the world is as letters traced in sand, but a spotless character will endure to all eternity. God gives you intelligence and a reasoning mind, whereby you may grasp His promises; and Jesus is ready to help you in forming a strong, symmetrical character.—*Testimonies for the Church,* vol. 5, pp. 573, 574, 578, 579.

April 29

Talk About God's Blessings

When you have returned to Me, strengthen your brethren.
—Luke 22:32.

Faith familiarizes the soul with the existence and presence of God, and, living with an eye single to the glory of God, more and more we discern the beauty of His character, the excellence of His grace. Our souls become strong in spiritual power; for we are breathing the atmosphere of heaven. . . . We are rising above the world, beholding Him who is the Chief among ten thousand, the One altogether lovely.—*Selected Messages,* book 1, p. 334.

Every one who loves God is to testify of the preciousness of His grace and truth. Those who receive the light of truth are to have lesson upon lesson to educate them not to keep silent, but to speak often one to another. They are to keep in mind the Sabbath meeting, when those who love and fear God, and who think upon His name, can have opportunity to express their thoughts in speaking one to another. . . .

The Majesty of heaven identifies His interests with those of the believers, however humble may be their circumstances. And whenever they are privileged to meet together, it is appropriate that they speak often one to another, giving utterance to the gratitude and love that is a result of thinking upon the name of the Lord. Thus shall God be glorified as He hearkens and hears, and the testimony meeting will be considered the most precious of all meetings; for the words spoken are recorded in the book of remembrance. . . .

Do not gratify the enemy by dwelling upon the dark side of your experience; trust Jesus more fully for help to resist temptation. If we thought and talked more of Jesus, and less of ourselves, we should have much more of His presence. If we abide in Him, we shall be so filled with peace, faith, and courage, and shall have so victorious an experience to relate when we come to meeting, that others will be refreshed by our clear, strong testimony for God. These precious acknowledgements to the praise of the glory of His grace, when supported by a Christlike life, have an irresistible power, which works for the salvation of souls. The bright and cheerful side of religion will be represented by all who are daily consecrated to God. We should not dishonor our Lord by a mournful relation of trials that appear grievous. All trials that are received as educators will produce joy. The whole religious life will be uplifting, elevating, ennobling, fragrant with good words and works.—*The Seventh-day Adventisst Bible Commentary,* vol. 4, p. 1183.

Finally: A Position Above Angels

To him who overcomes I will grant to sit with Me on My throne, as I also overcame and sat down with My Father on His throne.—Revelation 3:21.

For the joy that was set before Him, Christ endured the cross, despising the shame, and is forever set down at the right hand of God. He died on the cross as a sacrifice for the world, and through this sacrifice comes the greatest blessing that God could bestow—the gift of the Holy Spirit. This blessing is for all who will receive Christ. The fallen world is the battlefield for the greatest conflict the heavenly universe and earthly powers have ever witnessed. It was appointed as the theater on which would be fought out the grand struggle between good and evil, between heaven and hell. Every human being acts a part in this conflict. No one can stand on neutral ground. Everyone must either accept or reject the world's Redeemer. All are witnesses, either for or against Christ. Christ calls upon those who stand under His banner to engage in the conflict with Him as faithful soldiers, that they may inherit the crown of life. They have been adopted as sons and daughters of God. Christ has left them His assured promise that great will be the reward in the kingdom of heaven of those who partake of His humiliation and suffering for the truth's sake.

The cross of Calvary challenges, and will finally vanquish, every earthly and hellish power. In the cross all influence centers, and from it all influence goes forth. It is the great center of attraction, for on it Christ gave up His life for the human race. This sacrifice was offered for the purpose of restoring humanity to its original perfection; yea, more. It was offered to give us an entire transformation of character, making us more than conquerors. Those who in the strength of Christ overcome the great enemy of God and mankind, will occupy a position in the heavenly courts above angels who have never fallen. . . .

In the plan of God, we are to draw upon all the riches of heaven. Nothing in the treasury of divine resources is deemed too costly to accompany the great gift of the only begotten Son of God. "As many as received Him, to them gave He power to become the sons of God, even to them that believe on His name." Christ was empowered to breathe into fallen humanity the breath of life. Those who receive Him will never hunger, never thirst; for greater joy than that found in Christ there cannot be.—*General Conference Bulletin,* Second Quarter, 1899, p. 33.

Key to Heaven's Storehouse

May 1

What Do You Talk to God About?

For the eyes of the Lord are on the righteous, and His ears are open to their prayers.—1 Peter 3:12.

Through nature and revelation, through His providence, and by the influence of His Spirit, God speaks to us. But these are not enough; we need also to pour out our hearts to Him. In order to have spiritual life and energy, we must have actual communication with our heavenly Father. Our minds may be drawn out toward Him; we may meditate upon His works, His mercies, His blessings; but this is not, in the fullest sense, communing with Him. In order to commune with God, we must have something to say to Him concerning our actual life.

Prayer is the opening of the heart to God as to a friend. Not that it is necessary in order to make known to God what we are, but in order to enable us to receive Him. Prayer does not bring God down to us, but brings us up to Him.

When Jesus was upon the earth, He taught His disciples how to pray. He directed them to present their daily needs before God, and to cast all their care upon Him. And the assurance He gave them that their petitions should be heard, is assurance also to us.

Jesus Himself, while He dwelt among humanity, was often in prayer. Our Saviour identified Himself with our needs and weakness, in that He became a suppliant, a petitioner, seeking from His Father fresh supplies of strength, that He might come forth braced for duty and trial. He is our example in all things. He is a brother in our infirmities, "in all points tempted like as we are;" but as the sinless one His nature recoiled from evil; He endured struggles and torture of soul in a world of sin. His humanity made prayer a necessity and a privilege. He found comfort and joy in communion with His Father. And if the Saviour, the Son of God, felt the need of prayer, how much more should feeble, sinful mortals feel the necessity of fervent, constant prayer.

Our heavenly Father waits to bestow upon us the fullness of His blessing. It is our privilege to drink largely at the fountain of boundless love. What a wonder it is that we pray so little! God is ready and willing to hear the sincere prayer of the humblest of His children, and yet there is much manifest reluctance on our part to make known our wants to God.—*Steps to Christ*, pp. 93, 94.

The Key in the Hand of Faith

And whatever things you ask in prayer, believing, you will receive.—Matthew 21:22.

What can the angels of heaven think of poor helpless human beings, who are subject to temptation, when God's heart of infinite love yearns toward them, ready to give them more than they can ask or think, and yet they pray so little and have so little faith? . . .

The darkness of the evil one encloses those who neglect to pray. The whispered temptations of the enemy entice them to sin; and it is all because they do not make use of the privileges that God has given them in the divine appointment of prayer. Why should the sons and daughters of God be reluctant to pray, when prayer is the key in the hand of faith to unlock heaven's storehouse, where are treasured the boundless resources of Omnipotence? Without unceasing prayer and diligent watching we are in danger of growing careless and of deviating from the right path. The adversary seeks continually to obstruct the way to the mercy seat, that we may not by earnest supplication and faith obtain grace and power to resist temptation.

There are certain conditions upon which we may expect that God will hear and answer our prayers. One of the first of these is that we feel our need of help from Him. He has promised, "I will pour water upon him that is thirsty, and floods upon the dry ground." (Isaiah 44:3.) Those who hunger and thirst after righteousness, who long after God, may be sure that they will be filled. The heart must be open to the Spirit's influence, or God's blessing cannot be received.

Our great need is itself an argument and pleads most eloquently in our behalf. But the Lord is to be sought unto to do these things for us. He says, "Ask, and it shall be given you." And "He that spared not His own Son, but delivered Him up for us all, how shall He not with Him also freely give us all things?" (Matthew 7:7; Romans 8:32.)

If we regard iniquity in our hearts, if we cling to any known sin, the Lord will not hear us; but the prayer of the penitent, contrite soul is always accepted. When all known wrongs are righted, we may believe that God will answer our petitions. Our own merit will never commend us to the favor of God; it is the worthiness of Jesus that will save us, His blood that will cleanse us; yet we have a work to do in complying with the conditions of acceptance.—*Steps to Christ,* pp. 94, 95.

May 3

The Science of Prayer

Pray without ceasing, in everything give thanks.
—1 Thessalonians 5:17, 18.

Christ's lessons in regard to prayer should be carefully considered. There is a divine science in prayer, and His illustration [of the friend at midnight, Luke 11:5–8] brings to view principles that all need to understand. He shows what is the true spirit of prayer, He teaches the necessity of perseverance in presenting our requests to God, and assures us of His willingness to hear and answer prayer.

Our prayers are not to be a selfish asking, merely for our own benefit. We are to ask that we may give. The principle of Christ's life must be the principle of our lives. "For their sakes," He said, speaking of His disciples, "I sanctify Myself, that they also might be sanctified." (John 17:19.) The same devotion, the same self-sacrifice, the same subjection to the claims of the word of God, that were manifest in Christ, must be seen in His servants. Our mission to the world is not to serve or please ourselves; we are to glorify God by cooperating with Him to save sinners. We are to ask blessings from God that we may communicate to others. The capacity for receiving is preserved only by imparting. We cannot continue to receive heavenly treasure without communicating to those around us.

In the parable the petitioner was again and again repulsed, but he did not relinquish his purpose. So our prayers do not always seem to receive an immediate answer; but Christ teaches that we should not cease to pray. Prayer is not to work any change in God; it is to bring us into harmony with God. When we make request of Him, He may see that it is necessary for us to search our hearts and repent of sin. Therefore He takes us through test and trial, He brings us through humiliation, that we may see what hinders the working of His Holy Spirit through us.

There are conditions to the fulfillment of God's promises, and prayer can never take the place of duty. "If ye love Me," Christ says, "Keep My commandments." "He that hath My commandments, and keepeth them, he it is that loveth Me; and he that loveth Me shall be loved of My Father, and I will love him, and will manifest Myself to him." (John 14:15, 21.) Those who bring their petitions to God, claiming His promise while they do not comply with the conditions, insult Jehovah. They bring the name of Christ as their authority for the fulfillment of the promise, but they do not those things that would show faith in Christ and love for Him.—*Christ's Object Lessons,* pp. 142, 143.

2016

Another Condition

Whatever things you ask when you pray, believe that you receive them.
—Mark 11:24.

Another element of prevailing prayer is faith. "He that cometh to God must believe that He is, and that He is a rewarder of them that diligently seek Him." (Hebrews 11:6.) Jesus said to His disciples, "What things soever ye desire, when ye pray, believe that ye receive them, and ye shall have them." (Mark 11:24.) Do we take Him at His word?

The assurance is broad and unlimited, and He is faithful who has promised. When we do not receive the very things we asked for, at the time we ask, we are still to believe that the Lord hears and that He will answer our prayers. We are so erring and short-sighted that we sometimes ask for things that would not be a blessing to us, and our heavenly Father in love answers our prayers by giving us that which will be for our highest good—that which we ourselves would desire if with vision divinely enlightened we could see all things as they really are. When our prayers seem not to be answered, we are to cling to the promise; for the time of answering will surely come, and we shall receive the blessing we need most. But to claim that prayer will always be answered in the very way and for the particular thing that we desire, is presumption. God is too wise to err, and too good to withhold any good thing from them that walk uprightly. Then do not fear to trust Him, even though you do not see the immediate answer to your prayers. Rely upon His sure promise, "Ask, and it shall be given you."

If we take counsel with our doubts and fears, or try to solve everything that we cannot see clearly, before we have faith, perplexities will only increase and deepen. But if we come to God, feeling helpless and dependent, as we really are, and in humble, trusting faith make known our wants to Him whose knowledge is infinite, who sees everything in creation, and who governs everything by His will and word, He can and will attend to our cry, and will let light shine into our hearts. Through sincere prayer we are brought into connection with the mind of the Infinite. We may have no remarkable evidence at the time that the face of our Redeemer is bending over us in compassion and love, but this is even so. We may not feel His visible touch, but His hand is upon us in love and pitying tenderness.

When we come to ask mercy and blessing from God we should have a spirit of love and forgiveness in our own hearts.—*Steps to Christ,* pp. 96, 97.

May 5

Faith and Secret Prayer

Evening and morning and at noon I will pray, and cry aloud, and He shall hear my voice.—Psalm 55:17.

True faith lays hold of and claims the promised blessing before it is realized and felt. We must send up our petitions in faith within the second veil and let our faith take hold of the promised blessing and claim it as ours. We are then to believe that we receive the blessing, because our faith has hold of it, and according to the Word it is ours. "What things soever ye desire, when ye pray, believe that ye receive them, and ye shall have them." (Mark 11:24.) Here is faith, naked faith, to believe that we receive the blessing, even before we realize it. When the promised blessing is realized and enjoyed, faith is swallowed up. But many suppose they have much faith when sharing largely of the Holy Spirit and that they cannot have faith unless they feel the power of the Spirit. Such confound faith with the blessing that comes through faith. The very time to exercise faith is when we feel destitute of the Spirit. When thick clouds of darkness seem to hover over the mind, then is the time to let living faith pierce the darkness and scatter the clouds. True faith rests on the promises contained in the Word of God, and those only who obey that Word can claim its glorious promises. . . .

We should be much in secret prayer. Christ is the vine, ye are the branches. And if we would grow and flourish, we must continually draw sap and nourishment from the Living Vine; for separated from the Vine we have no strength.

I asked the angel why there was no more faith and power in Israel. He said, "Ye let go of the arm of the Lord too soon. Press your petitions to the throne, and hold on by strong faith. The promises are sure. Believe ye receive the things ye ask for, and ye shall have them." . . . I saw that we had doubted the sure promises, and wounded the Saviour by our lack of faith. . . . If the enemy can lead the desponding to take their eyes off from Jesus, and look to themselves, and dwell upon their own unworthiness, instead of dwelling upon the worthiness of Jesus, His love, His merits, and His great mercy, he will get away their shield of faith and gain his object; they will be exposed to his fiery temptations. The weak should therefore look to Jesus, and believe in Him; they then exercise faith.—*Early Writings*, pp. 72, 73.

Your Very First Work

My voice You shall hear in the morning, O Lord.
—Psalm 5:3.

By *faith* you became Christ's, and by faith you are to grow up in Him—by giving and taking. You are to *give* all—your heart, your will, your service—give yourself to Him to obey all His requirements; and you must *take* all—Christ, the fullness of all blessing, to abide in your heart, to be your strength, your righteousness, your everlasting helper—to give you power to obey.

Consecrate yourself to God in the morning; make this your very first work. Let your prayer be, "Take me, O Lord, as wholly Thine. I lay all my plans at Thy feet. Use me today in Thy service. Abide with me, and let all my work be wrought in Thee." This is a daily matter. Each morning consecrate yourself to God for that day. Surrender all your plans to Him, to be carried out or given up as His providence shall indicate. Thus day by day you may be giving your life into the hands of God, and thus your life will be molded more and more after the life of Christ.

A life in Christ is a life of restfulness. There may be no ecstasy of feeling, but there should be an abiding, peaceful trust. Your hope is not in yourself; it is in Christ. Your weakness is united to His strength, your ignorance to His wisdom, your frailty to His enduring might. So you are not to look to yourself, not to let the mind dwell upon self, but look to Christ. Let the mind dwell upon His love, upon the beauty, the perfection, of His character. Christ in His self-denial, Christ in His humiliation, Christ in His purity and holiness, Christ in His matchless love—this is the subject for the soul's contemplation. It is by loving Him, copying Him, depending wholly upon Him, that you are to be transformed into His likeness.

Jesus says, "Abide in Me." These words convey the idea of rest, stability, confidence. Again He invites, "Come unto Me, . . . and I will give you rest." (Matthew 11:28.) The words of the psalmist express the same thought: "Rest in the Lord, and wait patiently for Him." . . . (Psalm 37:7.) This rest is not found in inactivity; for in the Saviour's invitation the promise of rest is united with the call to labor: "Take My yoke upon you: . . . and ye shall find rest." (Matthew 11:29.) The heart that rests most fully upon Christ will be most earnest and active in labor for Him.—*Steps to Christ*, pp. 70, 71.

May 7

Include Prayer Meeting

These all continued with one accord in prayer and supplication.
—Acts 1:14.

Perseverance in prayer has been made a condition of receiving. We must pray always if we would grow in faith and experience. We are to be "instant in prayer," to "continue in prayer, and watch in the same with thanksgiving." (Romans 12:12; Colossians 4:2.) Peter exhorts believers to be "sober, and watch unto prayer." (1 Peter 4:7.) Paul directs, "In everything by prayer and supplication with thanksgiving let your requests be made known unto God." (Philippians 4:6.) "But ye, beloved," says Jude, "praying in the Holy Ghost, keep yourselves in the love of God." (Jude 20, 21.) Unceasing prayer is the unbroken union of the soul with God.

There is necessity for diligence in prayer; let nothing hinder you. Make every effort to keep open the communion between Jesus and your own soul. Seek every opportunity to go where prayer is wont to be made. Those who are really seeking for communion with God will be seen in the prayer meeting, faithful to do their duty and earnest and anxious to reap all the benefits they can gain. They will improve every opportunity of placing themselves where they can receive the rays of light from heaven.

We should pray in the family circle, and above all we must not neglect secret prayer, for this is the life of the soul. It is impossible for the soul to flourish while prayer is neglected. Family or public prayer alone is not sufficient. In solitude let the soul be laid open to the inspecting eye of God. Secret prayer is to be heard only by the prayer-hearing God. No curious ear is to receive the burden of such petitions. In secret prayer the soul is free from surrounding influences, free from excitement. Calmly, yet fervently, will it reach out after God. Sweet and abiding will be the influence emanating from Him who seeth in secret, whose ear is open to hear the prayer arising from the heart. By calm, simple faith the soul holds communion with God and gathers to itself rays of divine light to strengthen and sustain it in the conflict with Satan. God is our tower of strength.

Pray in your closet, and as you go about your daily labor let your heart be often uplifted to God. It was thus that Enoch walked with God. These silent prayers rise like precious incense before the throne of grace. Satan cannot overcome anyone whose heart is thus stayed upon God.—*Steps to Christ,* pp. 97–99.

2016

Pray Like Jacob

I will not let You go unless You bless me!
—Genesis 32:26.

The season of distress and anguish before us will require a faith that can endure weariness, delay, and hunger—a faith that will not faint though severely tried. The period of probation is granted to all to prepare for that time. Jacob prevailed because he was persevering and determined. His victory is an evidence of the power of importunate prayer. All who will lay hold of God's promises, as he did, and be as earnest and persevering as he was, will succeed as he succeeded. Those who are unwilling to deny self, to agonize before God, to pray long and earnestly for His blessing, will not obtain it. Wrestling with God—how few know what it is! How few have ever had their souls drawn out after God with intensity of desire until every power is on the stretch. When waves of despair which no language can express sweep over the suppliant, how few cling with unyielding faith to the promises of God.

Those who exercise but little faith now, are in the greatest danger of falling under the power of satanic delusions and the decree to compel the conscience. And even if they endure the test they will be plunged into deeper distress and anguish in the time of trouble, because they have never made it a habit to trust in God. The lessons of faith which they have neglected they will be forced to learn under a terrible pressure of discouragement.

We should now acquaint ourselves with God by proving His promises. Angels record every prayer that is earnest and sincere. We should rather dispense with selfish gratifications than neglect communion with God. The deepest poverty, the greatest self-denial, with His approval, is better than riches, honors, ease, and friendship without it. We must take time to pray. If we allow our minds to be absorbed by worldly interests, the Lord may give us time by removing from us our idols of gold, of houses, or of fertile lands.

The young would not be seduced into sin if they would refuse to enter any path save that upon which they could ask God's blessing. If the messengers who bear the last solemn warning to the world would pray for the blessing of God, not in a cold, listless, lazy manner, but fervently and in faith, as did Jacob, they would find many places where they could say: "I have seen God face to face, and my life is preserved." (Genesis 32:30.) They would be accounted of heaven as princes, having power to prevail with God and with men.—*The Great Controversy*, pp. 621, 622.

May 9

You Cannot Wear God Out

Hear my prayer, O Lord, give ear to my supplications!
—Psalm 143:1.

Let the soul be drawn out and upward, that God may grant us a breath of the heavenly atmosphere. We may keep so near to God that in every unexpected trial our thoughts will turn to Him as naturally as the flower turns to the sun.

Keep your wants, your joys, your sorrows, your cares, and your fears before God. You cannot burden Him; you cannot weary Him. He who numbers the hairs of your head is not indifferent to the wants of His children. "The Lord is very pitiful, and of tender mercy." (James 5:11.) His heart of love is touched by our sorrows and even by our utterances of them. Take to Him everything that perplexes the mind. Nothing is too great for Him to bear, for He holds up worlds, He rules over all the affairs of the universe. Nothing that in any way concerns our peace is too small for Him to notice. There is no chapter in our experience too dark for Him to read; there is no perplexity too difficult for Him to unravel. No calamity can befall the least of His children, no anxiety harass the soul, no joy cheer, no sincere prayer escape the lips, of which our heavenly Father is unobservant, or in which He takes no immediate interest. "He healeth the broken in heart, and bindeth up their wounds." (Psalm 147:3.) The relations between God and each soul are as distinct and full as though there were not another soul upon the earth to share His watchcare, not another soul for whom He gave His beloved Son.

Jesus said, "Ye shall ask in My name: and I say not unto you, that I will pray the Father for you: for the Father Himself loveth you." "I have chosen you: . . . that whatsoever ye shall ask of the Father in My name, He may give it you." (John 16:26, 27; 15:16.) But to pray in the name of Jesus is something more than a mere mention of that name at the beginning and the ending of a prayer. It is to pray in the mind and spirit of Jesus, while we believe His promises, rely upon His grace, and work His works.

God does not mean that any of us should become hermits or monks and retire from the world in order to devote ourselves to acts of worship. The life must be like Christ's life—between the mountain and the multitude. Those who do nothing but pray will soon cease to pray, or their prayers will become a formal routine.—*Steps to Christ,* pp. 99–101.

May 10

Prayer Enhances Spiritual Growth

Set your mind on things above, not on things on the earth.
—Colossians 3:2.

Those who have determined to enter the spiritual kingdom will find that all the powers and passions of unregenerate nature, backed by the forces of the kingdom of darkness, are arrayed against them. Each day they must renew their consecration, each day do battle with evil. Old habits, hereditary tendencies to wrong, will strive for the mastery, and against these they are to be ever on guard, striving in Christ's strength for victory. . . .

The letter to the Colossians is filled with lessons of highest value to all who are engaged in the service of Christ, lessons that show the singleness of purpose and the loftiness of aim which will be seen in the life of those who rightly represent the Saviour. Renouncing all that would hinder them from making progress in the upward way or that would turn the feet of others from the narrow path, the believers will reveal in their daily life mercy, kindness, humility, meekness, forbearance, and the love of Christ.

The power of a higher, purer, nobler life is our great need. The world has too much of our thought, and the kingdom of heaven too little.

In their efforts to reach God's ideal for them, Christians are to despair of nothing. Moral and spiritual perfection, through the grace and power of Christ, is promised to all. Jesus is the source of power, the fountain of life. He brings us to His word, and from the tree of life presents to us leaves for the healing of sin-sick souls. He leads us to the throne of God, and puts into our mouth a prayer through which we are brought into close contact with Himself. In our behalf He sets in operation the all-powerful agencies of heaven. At every step we touch His living power.

God fixes no limit to the advancement of those who desire to be "filled with the knowledge of His will in all wisdom and spiritual understanding." Through prayer, through watchfulness, through growth in knowledge and understanding, they are to be "strengthened with all might, according to His glorious power." Thus they are prepared to work for others. It is the Saviour's purpose that human beings, purified and sanctified, shall be His helping hand. For this great privilege let us give thanks to Him who "hath made us meet to be partakers of the inheritance of the saints in light: who hath delivered us from the power of darkness, and hath translated us into the kingdom of His dear Son."—*The Acts of the Apostles,* pp. 477, 478.

May 11

Study With Earnest Prayer

For whatever things were written before were written for our learning, that we through the patience and comfort of the Scriptures might have hope.
—*Romans 15:4.*

Those who are unwilling to accept the plain, cutting truths of the Bible are continually seeking for pleasing fables that will quiet the conscience. The less spiritual, self-denying, and humiliating the doctrines presented, the greater the favor with which they are received. These persons degrade the intellectual powers to serve their carnal desires. Too wise in their own conceit to search the Scriptures with contrition of soul and earnest prayer for divine guidance, they have no shield from delusion. Satan is ready to supply the heart's desire, and he palms off his deceptions in the place of truth. It was thus that the papacy gained its power over the minds of people; and by rejection of the truth because it involves a cross, Protestants are following the same path. All who neglect the word of God to study convenience and policy, that they may not be at variance with the world, will be left to receive damnable heresy for religious truth. Every conceivable form of error will be accepted by those who willfully reject the truth. A person who looks with horror upon one deception will readily receive another. The apostle Paul, speaking of a class who "received not the love of the truth, that they might be saved," declares: "For this cause God shall send them strong delusion, that they should believe a lie: that they all might be damned who believed not the truth, but had pleasure in unrighteousness." (2 Thessalonians 2:10–12.) With such a warning before us it behooves us to be on our guard as to what doctrines we receive.

Among the most successful agencies of the great deceiver are the delusive teachings and lying wonders of spiritualism. Disguised as an angel of light, he spreads his nets where least suspected. If people would but study the Book of God with earnest prayer that they might understand it, they would not be left in darkness to receive false doctrines. But as they reject the truth they fall a prey to deception.

Another dangerous error is the doctrine that denies the deity of Christ, claiming that He had no existence before His advent to this world. This theory is received with favor by a large class who profess to believe the Bible; yet it directly contradicts the plainest statements of our Saviour concerning His relationship with the Father, His divine character, and His pre-existence. —*The Great Controversy,* pp. 523, 524.

What We Need to Learn About Prayer

And there was a certain nobleman whose son was sick at Capernaum.
—John 4:46.

He [the Saviour] knew also that the father had, in his own mind, made conditions concerning his belief in Jesus. Unless his petition should be granted, he would not receive Him as the Messiah. . . .

Yet the nobleman had a degree of faith; for he had come to ask what seemed to him the most precious of all blessings. Jesus had a greater gift to bestow. He desired, not only to heal the child, but to make the officer and his household sharers in the blessings of salvation, and to kindle a light in Capernaum, which was so soon to be the field of His own labors. . . .

The nobleman longed to know more of Christ. As he afterward heard His teaching, he and all his household became disciples. Their affliction was sanctified to the conversion of the entire family. Tidings of the miracle spread; and in Capernaum, where so many of His mighty works were performed, the way was prepared for Christ's personal ministry.

He who blessed the nobleman at Capernaum is just as desirous of blessing us. But like the afflicted father, we are often led to seek Jesus by the desire for some earthly good; and upon the granting of our request we rest our confidence in His love. The Saviour longs to give us a greater blessing than we ask; and He delays the answer to our request that He may show us the evil of our own hearts, and our deep need of His grace. He desires us to renounce the selfishness that leads us to seek Him. Confessing our helplessness and bitter need, we are to trust ourselves wholly to His love.

The nobleman wanted to *see* the fulfillment of his prayer before he should believe; but he had to accept the word of Jesus that his request was heard and the blessing granted. This lesson we also have to learn. Not because we see or feel that God hears us are we to believe. We are to trust in His promises. When we come to Him in faith, every petition enters the heart of God. When we have asked for His blessing, we should believe that we receive it, and thank Him that we *have* received it. Then we are to go about our duties, assured that the blessing will be realized when we need it most. When we have learned to do this, we shall know that our prayers are answered. God will do for us "exceeding abundantly," "according to the riches of His glory," and "the working of His mighty power." (Ephesians 3:20, 16; 1:19.)—*The Desire of Ages,* pp. 198, 200.

May 13

Prayer Moves the Arm of Omnipotence

Nor did their own arm save them; but it was Your right hand, Your arm, and the light of Your countenance, because You favored them.—Psalm 44:3.

When trials arise that seem unexplainable, we should not allow our peace to be spoiled. However unjustly we may be treated, let not passion arise. . . .

While the world is progressing in wickedness, none of us need flatter ourselves that we shall have no difficulties. But it is these very difficulties that bring us into the audience chamber of the Most High. We may seek counsel of One who is infinite in wisdom.

The Lord says, "Call upon Me in the day of trouble." (Psalm 50:15.) He invites us to present to Him our perplexities and necessities, and our need of divine help. He bids us be instant in prayer. As soon as difficulties arise, we are to offer to Him our sincere, earnest petitions. By our importunate prayers we give evidence of our strong confidence in God. The sense of our need leads us to pray earnestly, and our heavenly Father is moved by our supplications.

Often those who suffer reproach or persecution for their faith are tempted to think themselves forsaken by God. To human eyes they are in the minority. To all appearance their enemies triumph over them. But let them not violate their conscience. He who has suffered in their behalf, and has borne their sorrows and afflictions, has not forsaken them.

The children of God are not left alone and defenseless. Prayer moves the arm of Omnipotence. Prayer has "subdued kingdoms, wrought righteousness, obtained promises, stopped the mouths of lions, quenched the violence of fire"—we shall know what it means when we hear the reports of the martyrs who died for their faith—"turneth to flight the armies of the aliens." (Hebrews 11:33, 34.)

If we surrender our lives to His service, we can never be placed in a position for which God has not made provision. Whatever may be our situation, we have a Guide to direct our way; whatever our perplexities, we have a sure Counselor; whatever our sorrow, bereavement, or loneliness, we have a sympathizing Friend. If in our ignorance we make missteps, Christ does not leave us. His voice, clear and distinct, is heard saying, "I am the Way, the Truth, and the Life." (John 14:6.) "He shall deliver the needy when he crieth; the poor also, and him that hath no helper." (Psalm 72:12.)—*Christ's Object Lessons,* pp. 171–173.

May 14

No Prayer Lost

O You who hear prayer, to You all flesh will come.
—Psalm 65:2.

The Lord declares that He will be honored by those who draw nigh to Him, who faithfully do His service. "Thou wilt keep him in perfect peace whose mind is stayed on Thee, because he trusteth in Thee." (Isaiah 26:3.) The arm of Omnipotence is outstretched to lead us onward and still onward. Go forward, the Lord says; I will send you help. It is for My name's glory that you ask, and you shall receive. I will be honored before those who are watching for your failure. They shall see My word triumph gloriously. "All things, whatsoever ye shall ask in prayer, believing, ye shall receive." (Matthew 21:22.)

Let all who are afflicted or unjustly used, cry to God. Turn away from those whose hearts are as steel, and make your requests known to your Maker. Never is one repulsed who comes to Him with a contrite heart. Not one sincere prayer is lost. Amid the anthems of the celestial choir, God hears the cries of the weakest human being. We pour out our heart's desire in our closets, we breathe a prayer as we walk by the way, and our words reach the throne of the Monarch of the universe. They may be inaudible to any human ear, but they cannot die away into silence, nor can they be lost through the activities of business that are going on. Nothing can drown the soul's desire. It rises above the din of the street, above the confusion of the multitude, to the heavenly courts. It is God to whom we are speaking, and our prayer is heard.

You who feel the most unworthy, fear not to commit your case to God. When He gave Himself in Christ for the sin of the world, He undertook the case of every soul. "He that spared not His own Son, but delivered Him up for us all, how shall He not with Him also freely give us all things?" (Romans 8:32.) Will He not fulfill the gracious word given for our encouragement and strength?

Christ desires nothing so much as to redeem His heritage from the dominion of Satan. But before we are delivered from Satan's power without, we must be delivered from his power within. . . .

There is no danger that the Lord will neglect the prayers of His people. The danger is that in temptation and trial they will become discouraged, and fail to persevere in prayer.—*Christ's Object Lessons,* pp. 173–175.

May 15

Beautiful Prayers

The twenty-four elders fell down before the Lamb, each having a harp, and golden bowls full of incense, which are the prayers of the saints.
—Revelation 5:8.

As yet the disciples were unacquainted with the Saviour's unlimited resources and power. He said to them, "Hitherto have ye asked nothing in My name." (John 16:24.) He explained that the secret of their success would be in asking for strength and grace in His name. He would be present before the Father to make request for them. The prayer of the humble suppliant He presents as His own desire in that soul's behalf. Every sincere prayer is heard in heaven. It may not be fluently expressed; but if the heart is in it, it will ascend to the sanctuary where Jesus ministers, and He will present it to the Father without one awkward, stammering word, beautiful and fragrant with the incense of His own perfection.

The path of sincerity and integrity is not a path free from obstruction, but in every difficulty we are to see a call to prayer. There is no one living who has any power that has not come from God, and the source whence it comes is open to the weakest human being. "Whatsoever ye shall ask in My name," said Jesus, "that will I do, that the Father may be glorified in the Son. If ye shall ask anything in My name, I will do it."

"In My name," Christ bade His disciples pray. In Christ's name His followers are to stand before God. Through the value of the sacrifice made for them, they are of value in the Lord's sight. Because of the imputed righteousness of Christ they are accounted precious. For Christ's sake the Lord pardons those that fear Him. He does not see in them the vileness of the sinner. He recognizes in them the likeness of His Son, in whom they believe.

The Lord is disappointed when His people place a low estimate upon themselves. He desires His chosen heritage to value themselves according to the price He has placed upon them. God wanted them, else He would not have sent His Son on such an expensive errand to redeem them. He has a use for them, and He is well pleased when they make the very highest demands upon Him, that they may glorify His name. They may expect large things if they have faith in His promises.—*The Desire of Ages,* pp. 667, 668.

Christ's Remedy for Lifeless Prayers

The effective, fervent prayer of a righteous man avails much.
—James 5:16.

As believers in Christ we need greater faith. We need to be more fervent in prayer. Many wonder why their prayers are so lifeless, their faith so feeble and wavering, their Christian experience so dark and uncertain. Have we not fasted, they say, and "walked mournfully before the Lord of hosts?" In the fifty-eighth chapter of Isaiah Christ has shown how this condition of things may be changed. He says: "Is not this the fast that I have chosen? to loose the bands of wickedness, to undo the heavy burdens, and to let the oppressed go free, and that ye break every yoke? Is it not to deal thy bread to the hungry, and that thou bring the poor that are cast out to thy house? when thou seest the naked, that thou cover him; and that thou hide not thyself from thine own flesh?" (Verses 6, 7.) This is the recipe that Christ has prescribed for the fainthearted, doubting, trembling soul. Let the sorrowful ones, who walk mournfully before the Lord, arise and help someone who needs help.

Every church is in need of the controlling power of the Holy Spirit, and now is the time to pray for it. But in all God's work for us He plans that we shall cooperate with Him. To this end the Lord calls upon the church to have a higher piety, a more just sense of duty, a clearer realization of their obligations to their Creator. He calls upon them to be a pure, sanctified, working people. And the Christian help work is one means of bringing this about, for the Holy Spirit communicates with all who are doing God's service. . . .

All that heaven contains is awaiting the draft of every soul who will labor in Christ's lines. As the members of our churches individually take up their appointed work, they will be surrounded with an entirely different atmosphere. A blessing and a power will attend their labors. They will experience a higher culture of mind and heart. The selfishness that has bound up their souls will be overcome. Their faith will be a living principle. Their prayers will be more fervent. The quickening, sanctifying influence of the Holy Spirit will be poured out upon them, and they will be brought nearer to the kingdom of heaven.

The Saviour ignores both rank and caste, worldly honor and riches. It is character and devotedness of purpose that are of high value with Him.—*Testimonies for the Church,* vol. 6, pp. 266–268.

May 17

Live Your Prayers

Live according to God in the spirit.
—1 Peter 4:6.

Many have not a living faith. This is why they do not see more of the power of God. Their weakness is the result of their unbelief. They have more faith in their own working than in the working of God for them. They take themselves into their own keeping. They plan and devise, but pray little, and have little real trust in God. They think they have faith, but it is only the impulse of the moment. Failing to realize their own need, or God's willingness to give, they do not persevere in keeping their requests before the Lord.

Our prayers are to be as earnest and persistent as was the petition of the needy friend who asked for the loaves at midnight. The more earnestly and steadfastly we ask, the closer will be our spiritual union with Christ. We shall receive increased blessings because we have increased faith.

Our part is to pray and believe. Watch unto prayer. Watch, and cooperate with the prayer-hearing God. Bear in mind that "we are labourers together with God." (1 Corinthians 3:9.) Speak and act in harmony with your prayers. It will make an infinite difference with you whether trial shall prove your faith to be genuine, or show that your prayers are only a form.

When perplexities arise, and difficulties confront you, look not for help to humanity. Trust all with God. The practice of telling our difficulties to others only makes us weak, and brings no strength to them. It lays upon them the burden of our spiritual infirmities, which they cannot relieve. We seek the strength of erring, finite human beings, when we might have the strength of the unerring, infinite God.

You need not go to the ends of the earth for wisdom, for God is near. It is not the capabilities you now possess or ever will have that will give you success. It is that which the Lord can do for you. We need to have far less confidence in what human power can do and far more confidence in what God can do for every believing soul. He longs to have you reach after Him by faith. He longs to have you expect great things from Him. He longs to give you understanding in temporal as well as in spiritual matters. He can sharpen the intellect. He can give tact and skill. Put your talents into the work, ask God for wisdom, and it will be given you.—*Christ's Object Lessons*, pp. 145, 146.

2016

Promises and Prayer

By which have been given to us exceedingly great and precious promises, that through these you may be partakers of the divine nature.—2 Peter 1:4.

When we beseech the Lord to pity us in our distress, and to guide us by His Holy Spirit, He will never turn away our prayer. It is possible even for parents to turn away from their hungry child, but God can never reject the cry of the needy and longing heart. With what wonderful tenderness He has described His love! To those who in days of darkness feel that God is unmindful of them, this is the message from the Father's heart: "Zion said, The Lord hath forsaken me, and my Lord hath forgotten me. Can a woman forget her sucking child, that she should not have compassion on the son of her womb? Yea, they may forget, yet will I not forget thee. Behold, I have graven thee upon the palms of My hands." (Isaiah 49:14–16.)

Every promise in the word of God furnishes us with subject matter for prayer, presenting the pledged word of Jehovah as our assurance. Whatever spiritual blessing we need, it is our privilege to claim through Jesus. We may tell the Lord, with the simplicity of a child, exactly what we need. We may state to Him our temporal matters, asking Him for bread and raiment as well as for the bread of life and the robe of Christ's righteousness. Your heavenly Father knows that you have need of all these things, and you are invited to ask Him concerning them. It is through the name of Jesus that every favor is received. . . .

But do not forget that in coming to God as a father you acknowledge your relation to Him as a child. You not only trust His goodness, but in all things yield to His will, knowing that His love is changeless. You give yourself to do His work. It was to those whom He had bidden to seek first the kingdom of God and His righteousness that Jesus gave the promise, "Ask, and ye shall receive." (John 16:24.)

The gifts of Him who has all power in heaven and earth are in store for the children of God. Gifts so precious that they come to us through the costly sacrifice of the Redeemer's blood; gifts that will satisfy the deepest craving of the heart, gifts lasting as eternity, will be received and enjoyed by all who will come to God as little children. Take God's promises as your own, plead them before Him as His own words, and you will receive fullness of joy.—*Thoughts From the Mount of Blessing,* pp. 132–134.

Power of Secret Prayer

When you pray, go into your room, and when you have shut your door, pray to your Father who is in the secret place; and your Father who sees in secret will reward you openly.—Matthew 6:6.

Have a place for secret prayer. Jesus had select places for communion with God, and so should we. We need often to retire to some spot, however humble, where we can be alone with God.

"Pray to thy Father which is in secret." In the name of Jesus we may come into God's presence with the confidence of a child. No mortal is needed to act as a mediator. Through Jesus we may open our hearts to God as to one who knows and loves us.

In the secret place of prayer, where no eye but God's can see, no ear but His can hear, we may pour out our most hidden desires and longings to the Father of infinite pity, and in the hush and silence of the soul that voice which never fails to answer the cry of human need will speak to our hearts. . . .

Those who seek God in secret telling the Lord their needs and pleading for help, will not plead in vain. "Thy Father which seeth in secret Himself shall reward thee openly." As we make Christ our daily companion we shall feel that the powers of an unseen world are all around us; and by looking unto Jesus we shall become assimilated to His image. By beholding we become changed. The character is softened, refined, and ennobled for the heavenly kingdom. The sure result of our communication and fellowship with our Lord will be to increase piety, purity, and fervor. There will be a growing intelligence in prayer. We are receiving a divine education, and this is illustrated in a life of diligence and zeal.

The soul that turns to God for its help, its support, its power, by daily, earnest prayer, will have noble aspirations, clear perceptions of truth and duty, lofty purposes of action, and a continual hungering and thirsting after righteousness. By maintaining a connection with God, we shall be enabled to diffuse to others, through our association with them, the light, the peace, the serenity, that rule in our hearts. The strength acquired in prayer to God, united with persevering effort in training the mind in thoughtfulness and care-taking, prepares one for daily duties and keeps the spirit in peace under all circumstances.—*Thoughts From the Mount of Blessing,* pp. 84, 85.

May 20

God-Inspired Prayers

Show me Your ways, O Lord; teach me Your paths.
—Psalm 25:4.

But because this experience [of being a new creature in Christ] is theirs, Christians are not therefore to fold their hands, content with that which has been accomplished for them. Those who have determined to enter the spiritual kingdom will find that all the powers and passions of unregenerate nature, backed by the forces of the kingdom of darkness, are arrayed against them. Each day they must renew their consecration, each day do battle with evil. Old habits, hereditary tendencies to wrong, will strive for the mastery, and against these they are to be ever on guard, striving in Christ's strength for victory. . . .

Renouncing all that would hinder them from making progress in the upward way or that would turn the feet of another from the narrow path, the believers will reveal in their daily life mercy, kindness, humility, meekness, forbearance, and the love of Christ.

The power of a higher, purer, nobler life is our great need. The world has too much of our thought, and the kingdom of heaven too little.

In their efforts to reach God's ideal for them, Christians are to despair of nothing. Moral and spiritual perfection, through the grace and power of Christ, is promised to all. Jesus is the source of power, the fountain of life. He brings us to His word, and from the tree of life presents to us leaves for the healing of sin-sick souls. He leads us to the throne of God, and puts into our mouth a prayer through which we are brought into close contact with Himself. In our behalf He sets in operation the all-powerful agencies of heaven. At every step we touch His living power.

God fixes no limit to the advancement of those who desire to be "filled with the knowledge of His will in all wisdom and spiritual understanding." Through prayer, through watchfulness, through growth in knowledge and understanding, they are to be "strengthened with all might, according to His glorious power." Thus they are prepared to work for others. It is the Saviour's purpose that human beings, purified and sanctified, shall be His helping hand. For this great privilege let us give thanks to Him who "hath made us meet to be partakers of the inheritance of the saints in light: who hath delivered us from the power of darkness, and hath translated us into the kingdom of His dear Son."—*The Acts of the Apostles,* pp. 476–478.

May 21

What Should We Pray For?

We do not know what we should pray for as we ought, but the Spirit Himself makes intercession for us with groanings which cannot be uttered.—Romans 8:26.

There are many who, though striving to obey God's commandments, have little peace or joy. This lack in their experience is the result of a failure to exercise faith. They walk as it were in a salt land, a parched wilderness. They claim little, when they might claim much; for there is no limit to the promises of God. Such ones do not correctly represent the sanctification that comes through obedience to the truth. The Lord would have all His sons and daughters happy, peaceful, and obedient. Through the exercise of faith the believer comes into possession of these blessings. Through faith, every deficiency of character may be supplied, every defilement cleansed, every fault corrected, every excellence developed.

Prayer is heaven's ordained means of success in the conflict with sin and the development of Christian character. The divine influences that come in answer to the prayer of faith will accomplish in the soul of the suppliant all for which he pleads. For the pardon of sin, for the Holy Spirit, for a Christlike temper, for wisdom and strength to do His work, for any gift He has promised, we may ask; and the promise is, "Ye shall receive."

It was in the mount with God that Moses beheld the pattern of that wonderful building that was to be the abiding place of His glory. It is in the mount with God—in the secret place of communion—that we are to contemplate His glorious ideal for humanity. In all ages, through the medium of communion with heaven, God has worked out His purpose for His children, by unfolding gradually to their minds the doctrines of grace. His manner of imparting truth is illustrated in the words, "His going forth is prepared as the morning." (Hosea 6:3.) All who place themselves where God can enlighten them, advance, as it were, from the partial obscurity of dawn to the full radiance of noonday.

True sanctification means perfect love, perfect obedience, perfect conformity to the will of God. We are to be sanctified to God through obedience to the truth. Our conscience must be purged from dead works to serve the living God. We are not yet perfect; but it is our privilege to cut away from the entanglements of self and sin, and advance to perfection.—*The Acts of the Apostles,* pp. 563, 564.

The Importance of Family Worship

For I have known him, in order that he may command his children and his household after him, that they keep the way of the Lord, to do righteousness and justice.—Genesis 18:19.

In every family there should be a fixed time for morning and evening worship. How appropriate it is for parents to gather their children about them before the fast is broken, to thank the heavenly Father for His protection during the night, and to ask Him for His help and guidance and watch care during the day! How fitting, also, when evening comes, for parents and children to gather once more before Him and thank Him for the blessings of the day that is past!

Family worship should not be governed by circumstances. You are not to pray occasionally and, when you have a large day's work to do, neglect it. In thus doing you lead your children to look upon prayer as of no special consequence. Prayer means very much to the children of God, and thank offerings should come up before God morning and evening. Says the psalmist, "O come, let us sing unto the Lord: let us make a joyful noise to the rock of our salvation. Let us come before his presence with thanksgiving, and make a joyful noise unto him with psalms." (Psalm 95:1, 2.)

Fathers and mothers, however pressing your business, do not fail to gather your family around God's altar. Ask for the guardianship of holy angels in your home. Remember that your dear ones are exposed to temptations.

In our efforts for the comfort and happiness of guests, let us not overlook our obligations to God. The hour of prayer should not be neglected for any consideration. Do not talk and amuse yourselves till all are too weary to enjoy the season of devotion. To do this is to present to God a lame offering. At an early hour of the evening, when we can pray unhurriedly and understandingly, we should present our supplications and raise our voices in happy, grateful praise.

Let all who visit Christians see that the hour of prayer is the most precious, the most sacred, and the happiest hour of the day. These seasons of devotion exert a refining, elevating influence upon all who participate in them. They bring a peace and rest grateful to the spirit.—*Child Guidance,* pp. 520, 521.

May 23

Prayer for the Sick

Is anyone among you sick? Let him call for the elders of the church, and let them pray over him, anointing him with oil in the name of the Lord.—James 5:14.

Many who seek the Lord's healing mercy think that they must have a direct and immediate answer to their prayers or their faith is defective. For this reason, those who are weakened by disease need to be counseled wisely, that they may act with discretion. They should not disregard their duty to the friends who may survive them, or neglect to employ nature's agencies for the restoration of health.

Often there is danger of error here. Believing that they will be healed in answer to prayer, some fear to do anything that might seem to indicate a lack of faith. But they should not neglect to set their affairs in order as they would desire to do if they expected to be removed by death. Nor should they fear to utter words of encouragement or counsel which at the parting hour they wish to speak to their loved ones.

Those who seek healing by prayer should not neglect to make use of the remedial agencies within their reach. It is not a denial of faith to use such remedies as God has provided to alleviate pain and to aid nature in her work of restoration. It is no denial of faith to cooperate with God, and to place themselves in the condition most favorable to recovery. God has put it in our power to obtain a knowledge of the laws of life. This knowledge has been placed within our reach for use. We should employ every facility for the restoration of health, taking every advantage possible, working in harmony with natural laws. When we have prayed for the recovery of the sick, we can work with all the more energy, thanking God that we have the privilege of cooperating with Him, and asking His blessing on the means which He Himself has provided. . . .

When we have prayed for the recovery of the sick, whatever the outcome of the case, let us not lose faith in God. If we are called upon to meet bereavement, let us accept the bitter cup, remembering that a Father's hand holds it to our lips. But should health be restored, it should not be forgotten that the recipient of healing mercy is placed under renewed obligation to the Creator.—*The Ministry of Healing,* pp. 232–234.

May God's Will Be Done

Your will be done.
—Matthew 26:42.

To those who desire prayer for their restoration to health, it should be made plain that the violation of God's law, either natural or spiritual, is sin, and that in order for them to receive His blessing, sin must be confessed and forsaken. . . .

In prayer for the sick it should be remembered that "we know not what we should pray for as we ought." (Romans 8:26.) We do not know whether the blessing we desire will be best or not. . . .

The consistent course is to commit our desires to our all-wise heavenly Father, and then, in perfect confidence, trust all to Him. We know that God hears us if we ask according to His will. But to press our petitions without a submissive spirit is not right; our prayers must take the form, not of command, but of intercession.

There are cases where God works decidedly by His divine power in the restoration of health. But not all the sick are healed. Many are laid away to sleep in Jesus. John on the Isle of Patmos was bidden to write: "Blessed are the dead which die in the Lord from henceforth: Yea, saith the Spirit, that they may rest from their labors; and their works do follow them." (Revelation 14:13.) From this we see that if persons are not raised to health, they should not on this account be judged as wanting in faith.

We all desire immediate and direct answers to our prayers, and are tempted to become discouraged when the answer is delayed or comes in an unlooked-for form. But God is too wise and good to answer our prayers always at just the time and in just the manner we desire. He will do more and better for us than to accomplish all our wishes. And because we can trust His wisdom and love, we should not ask Him to concede to our will, but should seek to enter into and accomplish His purpose. Our desires and interests should be lost in His will. These experiences that test faith are for our benefit. By them it is made manifest whether our faith is true and sincere, resting on the word of God alone, or whether depending on circumstances, it is uncertain and changeable. Faith is strengthened by exercise. We must let patience have its perfect work, remembering that there are precious promises in the Scriptures for those who wait upon the Lord.—*The Ministry of Healing,* pp. 228–231.

May 25

No Prosy Prayer Meetings

Beware of the scribes, who . . . for a pretense make long prayers.
—*Luke 20:46, 47.*

The prayer meetings should be the most interesting gatherings that are held, but these are frequently poorly managed. Many attend preaching, but neglect the prayer meeting. Here, again, thought is required. Wisdom should be sought of God, and plans should be laid to conduct the meetings so that they will be interesting and attractive. The people hunger for the bread of life. If they find it at the prayer meeting they will go there to receive it.

Long, prosy talks and prayers are out of place anywhere, and especially in the social meeting. Those who are forward and ever ready to speak are allowed to crowd out the testimony of the timid and retiring. Those who are most superficial generally have the most to say. Their prayers are long and mechanical. They weary the angels and the people who listen to them. Our prayers should be short and right to the point. Let the long, tiresome petitions be left for the closet, if any have such to offer. Let the Spirit of God into your hearts, and it will sweep away all dry formality.

Christ impressed upon His disciples the idea that their prayers should be short, expressing just what they wanted, and no more. He gives the length and substance of their prayers, expressing their desires for temporal and spiritual blessings, and their gratitude for the same. How comprehensive this sample prayer! It covers the actual need of all. One or two minutes is long enough for any ordinary prayer. There may be instances where prayer is in a special manner indited by the Spirit of God, where supplication is made in the Spirit. The yearning soul becomes agonized and groans after God. The spirit wrestles as did Jacob and will not be at rest without special manifestations of the power of God. This is as God would have it.

But many offer prayer in a dry, sermonizing manner. These pray to other persons, not to God. If they were praying to God, and really understood what they were doing, they would be alarmed at their audacity; for they deliver a discourse to the Lord in the mode of prayer, as though the Creator of the universe needed special information upon general questions in relation to things transpiring in the world. All such prayers are as sounding brass and a tinkling cymbal. They are made no account of in heaven. Angels of God are wearied with them, as well as mortals who are compelled to listen to them.
—*Counsels for the Church,* pp. 292, 293.

Daniel's Example in Prayer

Then I set my face toward the Lord God to make request by prayer and supplications, with fasting, sackcloth, and ashes.
—Daniel 9:3.

Daniel does not proclaim his own fidelity before the Lord. Instead of claiming to be pure and holy, this honored prophet humbly identifies himself with the really sinful of Israel. The wisdom which God had imparted to him was as far superior to the wisdom of the great men of the world as the light of the sun shining in the heavens at noonday is brighter than the feeblest star. Yet ponder the prayer from the lips of this man so highly favored of Heaven. With deep humiliation, with tears and rending of heart, he pleads for himself and for his people. He lays his soul open before God, confessing his own unworthiness and acknowledging the Lord's greatness and majesty. . . .

As Daniel's prayer is going forth, the angel Gabriel comes sweeping down from the heavenly courts to tell him that his petitions are heard and answered. This mighty angel has been commissioned to give him skill and understanding—to open before him the mysteries of future ages. Thus, while earnestly seeking to know and understand the truth, Daniel was brought into communion with Heaven's delegated messenger.

In answer to his petition, Daniel received not only the light and truth which he and his people most needed, but a view of the great events of the future, even to the advent of the world's Redeemer. Those who claim to be sanctified, while they have no desire to search the Scriptures or to wrestle with God in prayer for a clearer understanding of Bible truth, know not what true sanctification is.

Daniel talked with God. Heaven was opened before him. But the high honors granted him were the result of humiliation and earnest seeking. All who believe with the heart the word of God will hunger and thirst for a knowledge of His will. God is the author of truth. He enlightens the darkened understanding and gives to the human mind power to grasp and comprehend the truths which He has revealed. . . .

Daniel was a devoted servant of the Most High. His long life was filled up with noble deeds of service for his Master. His purity of character and unwavering fidelity are equaled only by his humility of heart and his contrition before God.—*The Sanctified Life,* pp. 46–49, 52.

May 27

Golden Moments

To You, O Lord, I lift up my soul. O my God, I trust in You.
—Psalm 25:1, 2

Several times each day precious, golden moments should be consecrated to prayer and the study of the Scriptures, if it is only to commit a text to memory, that spiritual life may exist in the soul. The varied interests of the cause furnish us with food for reflection and inspiration for our prayers. Communion with God is highly essential for spiritual health, and here only may be obtained that wisdom and correct judgment so necessary in the performance of every duty.

Some, fearing they will suffer loss of earthly treasure, neglect prayer and the assembling of themselves together for the worship of God, that they may have more time to devote to their farms or their business. They show by their works which world they place the highest estimate upon. They sacrifice religious privileges, which are essential to their spiritual advancement, for the things of this life and fail to obtain a knowledge of the divine will. They come short of perfecting Christian character and do not meet the measurement of God. They make their temporal, worldly interests first, and rob God of the time which they should devote to His service. Such persons God marks, and they will receive a curse rather than a blessing. . . .

Do not take your sorrows and difficulties to other persons. Present yourself to Him who is able to do "exceeding abundantly." He knows just how to help you. Do not turn from the loving, compassionate Redeemer to human friends, who, though they may give you the best they have, may lead you into wrong paths. Take all your troubles to Jesus.

He will receive and strengthen and comfort you. He is the great Healer of all maladies. His great heart of infinite love yearns over you. He sends you the message that you may recover yourself from the snare of the enemy. You may regain your self-respect. You may stand where you regard yourself, not as a failure, but as a conqueror, in and through the uplifting influence of the Spirit of God.

It is just as convenient, just as essential, for us to pray three times a day as it was for Daniel. Prayer is the life of the soul, the foundation of spiritual growth. In your home, before your family, and before your workmen, you should testify to this truth. And when you are privileged to meet with others in the church, tell them of the necessity of keeping open the channel of communication between God and the soul.—*Daughters of God,* pp. 82–84.

2016

Nights in Prayer

Now it came to pass in those days that He went out to the mountain to pray, and continued all night in prayer to God.
—Luke 6:12.

The Majesty of heaven, while engaged in His earthly ministry, prayed much to His Father. He was frequently bowed all night in prayer. His spirit was often sorrowful as He felt the powers of the darkness of this world, and He left the busy city and the noisy throng, to seek a retired place to make His intercessions. The Mount of Olives was the favorite resort of the Son of God for His devotions. Frequently after the multitude had left Him for the retirement of the night, He rested not, though weary with the labors of the day. In the Gospel of John we read: "And every man went unto his own house. Jesus went unto the Mount of Olives." While the city was hushed in silence, and the disciples had returned to their homes to obtain refreshment in sleep, Jesus slept not. His divine pleadings were ascending to His Father from the Mount of Olives that His disciples might be kept from the evil influences which they would daily encounter in the world, and that His own soul might be strengthened and braced for the duties and trials of the coming day. All night, while His followers were sleeping, was their divine Teacher praying. The dew and frost of night fell upon His head bowed in prayer. His example is left for His followers.

The Majesty of heaven, while engaged in His mission, was often in earnest prayer. He did not always visit Olivet, for His disciples had learned His favorite retreat, and often followed Him. He chose the stillness of night, when there would be no interruption. Jesus could heal the sick and raise the dead. He was Himself a source of blessing and strength. He commanded even the tempests, and they obeyed Him. He was unsullied with corruption, a stranger to sin; yet He prayed, and that often with strong crying and tears. He prayed for His disciples and for Himself, thus identifying Himself with our needs, our weaknesses, and our failings, which are so common with humanity. He was a mighty petitioner, not possessing the passions of our human, fallen natures, but compassed with like infirmities, tempted in all points even as we are. Jesus endured agony which required help and support from His Father.—*Testimonies for the Church,* vol. 2, pp. 508, 509.

May 29

Pray With Bible in Hand

Be diligent to present yourself approved to God, a worker who does not need to be ashamed, rightly dividing the word of truth.—2 Timothy 2:15.

Let every one who claims to believe that the Lord is soon coming, search the Scriptures as never before; for Satan is determined to try every device possible to keep souls in darkness, and blind the mind to the perils of the times in which we are living. Let all the believers take up their Bibles with earnest prayer, that they may be enlightened by the Holy Spirit as to what is truth, that they may know more of God and of Jesus Christ whom He has sent. Search for the truth as for hidden treasures, and disappoint the enemy. The time of test is just upon us, for the loud cry of the third angel has already begun in the revelation of the righteousness of Christ, the sin-pardoning Redeemer. This is the beginning of the light of the angel whose glory shall fill the whole earth. For it is the work of every one to whom the message of warning has come, to lift up Jesus, to present Him to the world as revealed in types, as shadowed in symbols, as manifested in the revelations of the prophets, as unveiled in the lessons given to His disciples and in the wonderful miracles wrought for the sons of men. Search the Scriptures; for they are they that testify of Him.

If you would stand through the time of trouble, you must know Christ, and appropriate the gift of His righteousness, which He imputes to the repentant sinner. Human wisdom will not avail to devise a plan of salvation. Human philosophy is vain, the fruits of the loftiest human powers are worthless, aside from the great plan of the divine Teacher. No glory is to redound to us; all human help and glory lies in the dust; for the truth as it is in Jesus is the only available agent by which we may be saved. We are privileged to connect with Christ, and then the divine and the human combine; and in this union our hope must rest alone; for it is as the Spirit of God touches the soul that the powers of the soul are quickened, and we become new creatures in Christ Jesus. He was manifested to bring life and immortality to light. He says, "The words that I speak unto you, they are spirit and they are life." The psalmist declares, "The entrance of thy words giveth light; it giveth understanding unto the simple."—*Review and Herald,* November 2, 1892.

Prayer and Moral Courage

If anyone desires to come after Me, let him deny himself, and take up his cross, and follow Me.—Matthew 16:24.

It requires moral courage to take a position to keep the commandments of the Lord. An opposer of the truth once said that it was only weak-minded people, foolish, ignorant persons, who would turn away from the churches to keep the seventh day as the Sabbath; but a minister who had embraced the truth, replied, "If you think it takes weak-minded persons, just try it." It takes moral courage, firmness, decision, perseverance, and very much prayer to step out on the unpopular side. We are thankful that we can come to Christ as the poor suffering ones came to Christ in the temple. We hope that this house will be a house of prayer, and that those who enter here will realize that they are coming to meet with God. Christ has said, "For where two or three are gathered together in my name, there am I in the midst of them." We do not expect to be able to furnish you with a minister always; but you must have root in yourselves. You must learn to draw for yourselves from the fountain of life. You have not dared to trample under foot the commandments of God, and have stepped out on unpopular truth, let the result be what it may. Will the Saviour ever turn away to leave you to struggle alone?—No, never. But He never told His disciples that they should have no trials, no self-denial to endure, no sacrifices to make. The Master was a man of sorrows, and acquainted with grief. "Ye know the grace of our Lord Jesus Christ, that, though He was rich, yet for your sakes He became poor, that ye through His poverty, might be rich." We thank God that in your poverty, you can call God your Father. Poverty is coming upon this world, and there will be a time of trouble such as never was since there was a nation. There will be wars and rumors of wars, and the faces of people will gather paleness. You may have to suffer distress, you may go hungry sometimes; but God will not forsake you in your suffering. He will test your faith. We are not to live to please ourselves. We are here to manifest Christ to the world, to represent Him and His power to mankind. . . .

Christ is testing us today to see if we will be obedient to the law of God as He was, and be fitted up for the society of heavenly angels. God wants a loyal people.—*Review and Herald,* September 3, 1895.

May 31 2016

Prayer and a Revived Church

And when they had prayed, the place where they were assembled together was shaken; and they were all filled with the Holy Spirit, and they spoke the word of God with boldness.—Acts 4:31.

A revival of true godliness among us is the greatest and most urgent of all our needs. To seek this should be our first work. There must be earnest effort to obtain the blessing of the Lord, not because God is not willing to bestow His blessing upon us, but because we are unprepared to receive it. Our Heavenly Father is more willing to give His Holy Spirit to them that ask Him, than are earthly parents to give good gifts to their children. But it is our work, by confession, humiliation, repentance, and earnest prayer, to fulfill the conditions upon which God has promised to grant us His blessing. A revival need be expected only in answer to prayer. While the people are so destitute of God's Holy Spirit, they cannot appreciate the preaching of the word; but when the Spirit's power touches their hearts, then the discourses given will not be without effect. Guided by the teachings of God's word, with the manifestation of His Spirit, in the exercise of sound discretion, those who attend our meetings will gain a precious experience, and returning home, will be prepared to exert a healthful influence.

The old standard bearers knew what it was to wrestle with God in prayer, and to enjoy the outpouring of His Spirit. But these are passing off from the stage of action; and who are coming up to fill their places? How is it with the rising generation? Are they converted to God? Are we awake to the work that is going on in the heavenly sanctuary, or are we waiting for some compelling power to come upon the church before we shall arouse? Are we hoping to see the whole church revived? That time will never come.

There are persons in the church who are not converted, and who will not unite in earnest, prevailing prayer. We must enter upon the work individually. We must pray more, and talk less. Iniquity abounds, and the people must be taught not to be satisfied with a form of godliness without the spirit and power. If we are intent upon searching our own hearts, putting away our sins, and correcting our evil tendencies, our souls will not be lifted up unto vanity; we shall be distrustful of ourselves, having an abiding sense that our sufficiency is of God. . . .

The great deceiver has prepared his wiles for every soul that is not braced for trial and guarded by constant prayer and living faith.—*Selected Messages*, book 1, pp. 121–123.

Law and Sabbath: Dual Test of Loyalty

JUNE 1 2016

GOD'S LAW

Blessed are the undefiled in the way, who walk in the law of the LORD!
—Psalm 119:1.

From the very beginning of the great controversy in heaven it has been Satan's purpose to overthrow the law of God. It was to accomplish this that he entered upon his rebellion against the Creator, and though he was cast out of heaven he has continued the same warfare upon the earth. To deceive men and women, and thus lead them to transgress God's law, is the object which he has steadfastly pursued. Whether this be accomplished by casting aside the law altogether, or by rejecting one of its precepts, the result will be ultimately the same. Those who offend "in one point," manifest contempt for the whole law; their influence and example are on the side of transgression; they become "guilty of all." (James 2:10.)

In seeking to cast contempt upon the divine statutes, Satan has perverted the doctrines of the Bible, and errors have thus become incorporated into the faith of thousands who profess to believe the Scriptures. The last great conflict between truth and error is but the final struggle of the long-standing controversy concerning the law of God. Upon this battle we are now entering—a battle between human laws and the precepts of Jehovah, between the religion of the Bible and the religion of fable and tradition.

The agencies which will unite against truth and righteousness in this contest are now actively at work. God's holy word, which has been handed down to us at such a cost of suffering and blood, is but little valued. The Bible is within the reach of all, but there are few who really accept it as the guide of life. Infidelity prevails to an alarming extent, not in the world merely, but in the church. Many have come to deny doctrines which are the very pillars of the Christian faith. The great facts of creation as presented by the inspired writers, the fall of mankind, the atonement, and the perpetuity of the law of God, are practically rejected, either wholly or in part, by a large share of the professedly Christian world. Thousands who pride themselves upon their wisdom and independence regard it as an evidence of weakness to place implicit confidence in the Bible; they think it a proof of superior talent and learning to cavil at the Scriptures and to spiritualize and explain away their most important truths.—*The Great Controversy*, pp. 582, 583.

The Sabbath a Test

Hallow My Sabbaths, and they will be a sign between Me and you, that you may know that I am the Lord your God.
—*Ezekiel 20:20.*

Not one is made to suffer the wrath of God until the truth has been brought home to the mind and conscience, and has been rejected. There are many who have never had an opportunity to hear the special truths for this time. The obligation of the fourth commandment has never been set before them in its true light. He who reads every heart and tries every motive will leave none who desire a knowledge of the truth, to be deceived as to the issues of the controversy. The decree is not to be urged upon the people blindly. All are to have sufficient light to make their decision intelligently.

The Sabbath will be the great test of loyalty, for it is the point of truth especially controverted. When the final test shall be brought to bear upon humanity, then the line of distinction will be drawn between those who serve God and those who serve Him not. While the observance of the false sabbath in compliance with the law of the state, contrary to the fourth commandment, will be an avowal of allegiance to a power that is in opposition to God, the keeping of the true Sabbath, in obedience to God's law, is an evidence of loyalty to the Creator. While one class, by accepting the sign of submission to earthly powers, receive the mark of the beast, the other choosing the token of allegiance to divine authority, receive the seal of God.

Heretofore those who presented the truths of the third angel's message have often been regarded as mere alarmists. Their predictions that religious intolerance would gain control in the United States, that church and state would unite to persecute those who keep the commandments of God, have been pronounced groundless and absurd. It has been confidently declared that this land could never become other than what it has been—the defender of religious freedom. But as the question of enforcing Sunday observance is widely agitated, the event so long doubted and disbelieved is seen to be approaching, and the third message will produce an effect which it could not have had before.

In every generation God has sent His servants to rebuke sin, both in the world and in the church. But the people desire smooth things spoken to them, and the pure, unvarnished truth is not acceptable.—*The Great Controversy,* pp. 605, 606.

June 3

Obedience, a Condition for Happiness

Now therefore, if you will indeed obey My voice and keep My covenant, then you shall be a special treasure to Me above all people; for all the earth is Mine.
—*Exodus 19:5.*

Our first parents, though created innocent and holy, were not placed beyond the possibility of wrongdoing. God made them free moral agents, capable of appreciating the wisdom and benevolence of His character and the justice of His requirements, and with full liberty to yield or to withhold obedience. . . . At the very beginning of mankind's existence a check was placed upon the desire for self-indulgence, the fatal passion that lay at the foundation of Satan's fall. The tree of knowledge, which stood near the tree of life in the midst of the garden, was to be a test of the obedience, faith, and love of our parents. While permitted to eat freely of every other tree, they were forbidden to taste of this, on pain of death. They were also to be exposed to the temptations of Satan; but if they endured the trial, they would finally be placed beyond his power, to enjoy perpetual favor with God.

God placed human beings under law, as an indispensable condition of their very existence. They were subjects of the divine government, and there can be no government without law. God might have created them without the power to transgress His law; He might have withheld the hand of Adam from touching the forbidden fruit; but in that case human beings would have been, not free moral agents, but mere automatons. Without freedom of choice, their obedience would not have been voluntary, but forced. There could have been no development of character. Such a course would have been contrary to God's plan in dealing with the inhabitants of other worlds. It would have been unworthy of humanity as intelligent beings, and would have sustained Satan's charge of God's arbitrary rule.

God made Adam and Eve upright; He gave them noble traits of character, with no bias toward evil. He endowed them with high intellectual powers, and presented before them the strongest possible inducements to be true to his allegiance. Obedience, perfect and perpetual, was the condition of eternal happiness. On this condition they were to have access to the tree of life.—*Patriarchs and Prophets,* pp. 48, 49.

2016

GOD'S SHIELD

Happy is he who keeps the law.
—Proverbs 29:18.

There was but one hope for the human race—that into this mass of discordant and corrupting elements might be cast a new leaven; that there might be brought to mankind the power of a new life; that the knowledge of God might be restored to the world.

Christ came to restore this knowledge. He came to set aside the false teaching by which those who claimed to know God had misrepresented Him. He came to manifest the nature of His law, to reveal in His own character the beauty of holiness.

Christ came to the world with the accumulated love of eternity. Sweeping away the exactions which had encumbered the law of God, He showed that the law is a law of love, an expression of the Divine Goodness. He showed that in obedience to its principles is involved the happiness of mankind, and with it the stability, the very foundation and framework, of human society.

So far from making arbitrary requirements, God's law is given to us as a hedge, a shield. Whoever accepts its principles is preserved from evil. Fidelity to God involves fidelity to others. Thus the law guards the rights, the individuality, of every human being. It restrains the superior from oppression, and the subordinate from disobedience. It ensures our well-being, both for this world and for the world to come. To the obedient it is the pledge of eternal life, for it expresses the principles that endure forever.

Christ came to demonstrate the value of the divine principles by revealing their power for the regeneration of humanity. He came to teach how these principles are to be developed and applied.

With the people of that age the value of all things was determined by outward show. As religion had declined in power, it had increased in pomp. The educators of the time sought to command respect by display and ostentation. To all this the life of Jesus presented a marked contrast. His life demonstrated the worthlessness of those things that others regarded as life's great essentials. Born amidst surroundings the rudest, sharing a peasant's home, a peasant's fare, a craftsman's occupation, living a life of obscurity . . .—amidst these conditions and surroundings—Jesus followed the divine plan of education.—*Education,* pp. 76, 77.

June 5

On Probation

Of the tree of the knowledge of good and evil you shall not eat, for in the day that you eat of it you shall surely die.—Genesis 2:17.

The law of God is as sacred as God Himself. It is a revelation of His will, a transcript of His character, the expression of divine love and wisdom. The harmony of creation depends upon the perfect conformity of all beings, of everything, animate and inanimate, to the law of the Creator. God has ordained laws for the government, not only of living beings, but of all the operations of nature. . . . To human beings, the crowning work of creation, God has given power to understand His requirements, to comprehend the justice and beneficence of His law, and its sacred claims upon them; and of them unswerving obedience is required.

Like the angels, the dwellers in Eden had been placed upon probation; their happy estate could be retained only on condition of fidelity to the Creator's law. They could obey and live, or disobey and perish. God had made them the recipients of rich blessings; but should they disregard His will, He who spared not the angels that sinned, could not spare them; transgression would forfeit His gifts and bring upon them misery and ruin.

The angels warned them to be on their guard against the devices of Satan, for his efforts to ensnare them would be unwearied. While they were obedient to God the evil one could not harm them; for, if need be, every angel in heaven would be sent to their help. If they steadfastly repelled his first insinuations, they would be as secure as the heavenly messengers. But should they once yield to temptation, their nature would become so depraved that in themselves they would have no power and no disposition to resist Satan.

The tree of knowledge had been made a test of their obedience and their love to God. The Lord had seen fit to lay upon them but one prohibition as to the use of all that was in the garden; but if they should disregard His will in this particular, they would incur the guilt of transgression. Satan was not to follow them with continual temptations; he could have access to them only at the forbidden tree. Should they attempt to investigate its nature, they would be exposed to his wiles. They were admonished to give careful heed to the warning which God had sent them and to be content with the instruction which He had seen fit to impart.—*Patriarchs and Prophets*, pp. 52, 53.

JUNE 6

THE LAW IS HOLY

The law is holy, and the commandment holy and just and good.
—*Romans 7:12.*

Since "the law of the Lord is perfect," every variation from it must be evil. Those who disobey the commandments of God, and teach others to do so, are condemned by Christ. The Saviour's life of obedience maintained the claims of the law; it proved that the law could be kept in humanity, and showed the excellence of character that obedience would develop. All who obey as He did are likewise declaring that the law is "holy, and just, and good." (Romans 7:12.) On the other hand, all who break God's commandments are sustaining Satan's claim that the law is unjust, and cannot be obeyed. Thus they second the deceptions of the great adversary, and cast dishonor upon God. They are the children of the wicked one, who was the first rebel against God's law. To admit them into heaven would again bring in the elements of discord and rebellion, and imperil the well-being of the universe. No one who willfully disregards one principle of the law shall enter the kingdom of heaven.

The rabbis counted their righteousness a passport to heaven; but Jesus declared it to be insufficient and unworthy. External ceremonies and a theoretical knowledge of truth constituted Pharisaical righteousness. The rabbis claimed to be holy through their own efforts in keeping the law; but their works had divorced righteousness from religion. While they were punctilious in ritual observances, their lives were immoral and debased. Their so-called righteousness could never enter the kingdom of heaven.

The greatest deception of the human mind in Christ's day was that a mere assent to the truth constitutes righteousness. In all human experience a theoretical knowledge of the truth has been proved to be insufficient for the saving of the soul. It does not bring forth the fruits of righteousness. A jealous regard for what is termed theological truth often accompanies a hatred of genuine truth as made manifest in life. The darkest chapters of history are burdened with the record of crimes committed by bigoted religionists. The Pharisees claimed to be children of Abraham, and boasted of their possession of the oracles of God; yet these advantages did not preserve them from selfishness, malignity, greed for gain, and the basest hypocrisy. They thought themselves the greatest religionists of the world, but their so-called orthodoxy led them to crucify the Lord of glory.—*The Desire of Ages,* pp. 308, 309.

Law of Love

Love is the fulfillment of the law.
—Romans 13:10.

It was Christ who, amid thunder and flame, had proclaimed the law upon Mount Sinai. The glory of God, like devouring fire, rested upon its summit, and the mountain quaked at the presence of the Lord. The hosts of Israel, lying prostrate upon the earth, had listened in awe to the sacred precepts of the law. What a contrast to the scene upon the mount of the Beatitudes! Under the summer sky, with no sound to break the stillness but the song of birds, Jesus unfolded the principles of His kingdom. Yet He who spoke to the people that day in accents of love, was opening to them the principles of the law proclaimed upon Sinai. . . .

The law given upon Sinai was the enunciation of the principle of love, a revelation to earth of the law of heaven. It was ordained in the hand of a Mediator—spoken by Him through whose power human hearts could be brought into harmony with its principles. God had revealed the purpose of the law when He declared to Israel, "Ye shall be holy men unto Me." (Exodus 22:31.)

But Israel had not perceived the spiritual nature of the law, and too often their professed obedience was but an observance of forms and ceremonies, rather than a surrender of the heart to the sovereignty of love. As Jesus in His character and work represented to the people the holy, benevolent, and paternal attributes of God, and presented the worthlessness of mere ceremonial obedience, the Jewish leaders did not receive or understand His words. They thought that He dwelt too lightly upon the requirements of the law; and when He set before them the very truths that were the soul of their divinely appointed service, they, looking only at the external, accused Him of seeking to overthrow it.

The words of Christ, though calmly spoken, were uttered with an earnestness and power that stirred the hearts of the people. They listened for a repetition of the lifeless traditions and exactions of the rabbis, but in vain. They "were astonished at His teaching: for He taught them as one having authority, and not as their scribes." (Matthew 7:29, R.V.) The Pharisees noted the vast difference between their manner of instruction and that of Christ. They saw that the majesty and purity and beauty of the truth, with its deep and gentle influence, was taking firm hold upon many minds.—*Thoughts From the Mount of Blessing*, pp. 45–47.

2016

God's Law Is Eternal

Do not think that I came to destroy the Law or the Prophets. I did not come to destroy but to fulfill.
—Matthew 5:17.

It is our Creator, the Giver of the law, who declares that it is not His purpose to set aside its precepts. Everything in nature, from the mote in the sunbeam to the worlds on high, is under law. And upon obedience to these laws the order and harmony of the natural world depend. So there are great principles of righteousness to control the life of all intelligent beings, and upon conformity to these principles the well-being of the universe depends. Before this earth was called into being, God's law existed. Angels are governed by its principles, and in order for earth to be in harmony with heaven, humanity also must obey the divine statutes. To Adam and Eve in Eden Christ made known the precepts of the law "when the morning stars sang together, and all the sons of God shouted for joy." (Job 38:7.) The mission of Christ on earth was not to destroy the law, but by His grace to bring us back to obedience to its precepts.

The beloved disciple, who listened to the words of Jesus on the mount, writing long afterward under the inspiration of the Holy Spirit, speaks of the law as of perpetual obligation. He says that "sin is the transgression of the law" and that "whosoever committeth sin transgresseth also the law." (1 John 3:4.) He makes it plain that the law to which he refers is "an old commandment which ye had from the beginning." (1 John 2:7.) He is speaking of the law that existed at the creation and was reiterated upon Mount Sinai.

Speaking of the law, Jesus said, "I am not come to destroy, but to fulfill." He here used the word "fulfill" in the same sense as when He declared to John the Baptist His purpose to "fulfill all righteousness" (Matthew 3:15); that is, to fill up the measure of the law's requirement, to give an example of perfect conformity to the will of God.

His mission was to "magnify the law, and make it honorable." (Isaiah 42:21.) He was to show the spiritual nature of the law, to present its far-reaching principles, and to make plain its eternal obligation. . . .

Jesus, the express image of the Father's person, the effulgence of His glory; the self-denying Redeemer, throughout His pilgrimage of love on earth, was a living representation of the character of the law of God.—*Thoughts From the Mount of Blessing*, pp. 48, 49.

June 9

The Source of All Laws

Oh, how I love Your law! It is my meditation all the day.
—Psalm 119:97.

Upon all created things is seen the impress of the Deity. Nature testifies of God. The susceptible mind, brought in contact with the miracle and mystery of the universe, cannot but recognize the working of infinite power. Not by its own inherent energy does the earth produce its bounties, and year by year continue its motion around the sun. An unseen hand guides the planets in their circuit of the heavens. A mysterious life pervades all nature—a life that sustains the unnumbered worlds throughout immensity, that lives in the insect atom which floats in the summer breeze, that wings the flight of the swallow and feeds the young ravens which cry, that brings the bud to blossom and the flower to fruit.

The same power that upholds nature, is working also in us. The same great laws that guide alike the star and the atom control human life. The laws that govern the heart's action, regulating the flow of the current of life to the body, are the laws of the mighty Intelligence that has the jurisdiction of the soul. From Him all life proceeds. Only in harmony with Him can be found its true sphere of action. For all the objects of His creation the condition is the same—a life sustained by receiving the life of God, a life exercised in harmony with the Creator's will. To transgress His law, physical, mental, or moral, is to place one's self out of harmony with the universe, to introduce discord, anarchy, ruin.

To those who learn thus to interpret its teachings, all nature becomes illuminated; the world is a lesson book, life a school. The unity of the human race with nature and with God, the universal dominion of law, the results of transgression, cannot fail of impressing the mind and molding the character.

These are lessons that our children need to learn. To the little child, not yet capable of learning from the printed page or of being introduced to the routine of the schoolroom, nature presents an unfailing source of instruction and delight. The heart not yet hardened by contact with evil is quick to recognize the Presence that pervades all created things. The ear as yet undulled by the world's clamor is attentive to the Voice that speaks through nature's utterances.—*Education,* pp. 99, 100.

Exalting the Law

The law of the LORD is perfect, converting the soul.
—Psalm 19:7.

"Till heaven and earth pass," said Jesus, "one jot or one tittle shall in nowise pass from the law, till all be fulfilled." By His own obedience to the law, Christ testified to its immutable character and proved that through His grace it could be perfectly obeyed by every son and daughter of Adam. On the mount He declared that not the smallest iota should pass from the law till all things should be accomplished—all things that concern the human race, all that relates to the plan of redemption. He does not teach that the law is ever to be abrogated, but He fixes the eye upon the utmost verge of our horizon and assures us that until this point is reached the law will retain its authority so that none may suppose it was His mission to abolish the precepts of the law. So long as heaven and earth continue, the holy principles of God's law will remain. His righteousness, "like the great mountains" (Psalm 36:6), will continue, a source of blessing, sending forth streams to refresh the earth.

Because the law of the Lord is perfect, and therefore changeless, it is impossible for sinful human beings, in themselves, to meet the standard of its requirement. This was why Jesus came as our Redeemer. It was His mission, by making us partakers of the divine nature, to bring us into harmony with the principles of the law of heaven. When we forsake our sins and receive Christ as our Saviour, the law is exalted. The apostle Paul asks, "Do we then make void the law through faith? God forbid: yea, we establish the law." (Romans 3:31.)

The new-covenant promise is, "I will put My laws into their hearts, and in their minds will I write them." (Hebrews 10:16.) While the system of types which pointed to Christ as the Lamb of God that should take away the sin of the world was to pass away at His death, the principles of righteousness embodied in the Decalogue are as immutable as the eternal throne. Not one command has been annulled, not a jot or tittle has been changed. Those principles that were made known to our first parents in Paradise as the great law of life will exist unchanged in Paradise restored. When Eden shall bloom on earth again, God's law of love will be obeyed by all beneath the sun. —*Thoughts From the Mount of Blessing,* pp. 49, 50.

JUNE 11

WHAT DOES IT MEAN TO KEEP GOD'S COMMANDMENTS?

For this is the love of God, that we keep His commandments.—1 John 5:3.

A legal religion is insufficient to bring the soul into harmony with God. The hard, rigid orthodoxy of the Pharisees, destitute of contrition, tenderness, or love, was only a stumbling block to sinners. They were like the salt that had lost its savor; for their influence had no power to preserve the world from corruption. The only true faith is that which "worketh by love" (Galatians 5:6) to purify the soul. It is as leaven that transforms the character. . . .

The prophet Hosea had pointed out what constitutes the very essence of Pharisaism, in the words, "Israel is an empty vine, he bringeth forth fruit unto himself." (Hosea 10:1.) In their professed service to God, the Jews were really working for self. Their righteousness was the fruit of their own efforts to keep the law according to their own ideas and for their own selfish benefit. Hence it could be no better than they were. In their endeavor to make themselves holy, they were trying to bring a clean thing out of an unclean. The law of God is as holy as He is holy, as perfect as He is perfect. It presents to us the righteousness of God. It is impossible for us, of ourselves, to keep this law; for our nature is depraved, deformed, and wholly unlike the character of God. The works of the selfish heart are "as an unclean thing;" and "all our righteousnesses are as filthy rags." (Isaiah 64:6.)

While the law is holy, the Jews could not attain righteousness by their own efforts to keep the law. The disciples of Christ must obtain righteousness of a different character from that of the Pharisees, if they would enter the kingdom of heaven. God offered them, in His Son, the perfect righteousness of the law. If they would open their hearts fully to receive Christ, then the very life of God, His love, would dwell in them, transforming them into His own likeness; and thus through God's free gift they would possess the righteousness which the law requires. But the Pharisees rejected Christ; "being ignorant of God's righteousness, and going about to establish their own righteousness" (Romans 10:3), they would not submit themselves unto the righteousness of God.

Jesus proceeded to show His hearers what it means to keep the commandments of God—that it is a reproduction in themselves of the character of Christ. For in Him, God was daily made manifest before them.
—*Thoughts From the Mount of Blessing,* pp. 53–55.

Obedience Is the Fruit of Love

He who has My commandments and keeps them,
it is he who loves Me.—John 14:21.

Let those who feel inclined to make a high profession of holiness look into the mirror of God's law. As they see its far-reaching claims, and understand its work as a discerner of the thoughts and intents of the heart, they will not boast of sinlessness. . . .

There are those who profess holiness, who declare that they are wholly the Lord's, who claim a right to the promises of God, while refusing to render obedience to His commandments. These transgressors of the law claim everything that is promised to the children of God; but this is presumption on their part, for John tells us that true love for God will be revealed in obedience to all His commandments. It is not enough to believe the theory of truth, to make a profession of faith in Christ, to believe that Jesus is no impostor, and that the religion of the Bible is no cunningly devised fable. "He that saith, I know Him, and keepeth not His commandments," John wrote, "is a liar, and the truth is not in him. But whoso keepeth His word, in him verily is the love of God perfected: hereby know we that we are in Him." (1 John 2:4, 5.) . . .

John did not teach that salvation was to be earned by obedience; but that obedience was the fruit of faith and love. "Ye know that He was manifested to take away our sins," he said, "and in Him is no sin. Whosoever abideth in Him sinneth not: whosoever sinneth hath not seen Him, neither known Him." (1 John 3:5, 6.) If we abide in Christ, if the love of God dwells in the heart, our feelings, our thoughts, our actions, will be in harmony with the will of God. The sanctified heart is in harmony with the precepts of God's law.

There are many who, though striving to obey God's commandments, have little peace or joy. This lack in their experience is the result of a failure to exercise faith. They walk as it were in a salt land, a parched wilderness. They claim little, when they might claim much; for there is no limit to the promises of God. Such ones do not correctly represent the sanctification that comes through obedience to the truth. The Lord would have all His sons and daughters happy, peaceful, and obedient. Through the exercise of faith the believer comes into possession of these blessings. Through faith, every deficiency of character may be supplied, every defilement cleansed, every fault corrected, every excellence developed.—*The Acts of the Apostles,* pp. 562–564.

June 13

The Ten Commandments, With Sabbath at the Center

And in the ark you shall put the Testimony that I will give you.
—Exodus 25:21.

But the Lord gave me a view of the heavenly sanctuary. The temple of God was open in heaven, and I was shown the ark of God covered with the mercy seat. Two angels stood one at either end of the ark, with their wings spread over the mercy seat, and their faces turned toward it. This, my accompanying angel informed me, represented all the heavenly host looking with reverential awe toward the law of God, which had been written by the finger of God.

Jesus raised the cover of the ark, and I beheld the tables of stone on which the ten commandments were written. I was amazed as I saw the fourth commandment in the very center of the ten precepts, with a soft halo of light encircling it. Said the angel, "It is the only one of the ten which defines the living God who created the heavens and the earth and all things that are therein."

When the foundations of the earth were laid, then was also laid the foundation of the Sabbath. I was shown that if the true Sabbath had been kept, there would never have been an infidel or an atheist. The observance of the Sabbath would have preserved the world from idolatry.

The fourth commandment has been trampled upon, therefore we are called upon to repair the breach in the law and plead for the desecrated Sabbath. The man of sin, who exalted himself above God, and thought to change times and laws, brought about the change of the Sabbath from the seventh to the first day of the week. In doing this he made a breach in the law of God. Just prior to the great day of God, a message is sent forth to warn the people to come back to their allegiance to the law of God, which antichrist has broken down. Attention must be called to the breach in the law, by precept and example. . . .

I was shown that the third angel proclaiming the commandments of God and the faith of Jesus, represents the people who receive this message, and raise the voice of warning to the world to keep the commandments of God and His law as the apple of the eye; and that in response to this warning, many would embrace the Sabbath of the Lord.—*Life Sketches of Ellen G. White*, pp. 95, 96.

Sabbath, the Seal of God's Law

Bind up the testimony, seal the law among my disciples.
—Isaiah 8:16.

The Lord commands by the same prophet: "Bind up the testimony, seal the law among My disciples." (Isaiah 8:16.) The seal of God's law is found in the fourth commandment. This only, of all the ten, brings to view both the name and the title of the Lawgiver. It declares Him to be the Creator of the heavens and the earth, and thus shows His claim to reverence and worship above all others. Aside from this precept, there is nothing in the Decalogue to show by whose authority the law is given. When the Sabbath was changed by the papal power, the seal was taken from the law. The disciples of Jesus are called upon to restore it by exalting the Sabbath of the fourth commandment to its rightful position as the Creator's memorial and the sign of His authority.

"To the law and to the testimony." While conflicting doctrines and theories abound, the law of God is the one unerring rule by which all opinions, doctrines, and theories are to be tested. Says the prophet: "If they speak not according to this word, it is because there is no light in them." (Verse 20.) . . .

Again, the command is given: "Cry aloud, spare not, lift up thy voice like a trumpet, and show My people their transgression, and the house of Jacob their sins." It is not the wicked world, but those whom the Lord designates as "my people," that are to be reproved for their transgressions. He declares further: "Yet they seek Me daily, and delight to know My ways, as a nation that did righteousness, and forsook not the ordinance of their God." (Isaiah 58:1, 2.) . . .

The prophet thus points out the ordinance which has been forsaken: "Thou shalt raise up the foundations of many generations; and thou shalt be called, The repairer of the breach, The restorer of paths to dwell in. If thou turn away thy foot from the Sabbath, from doing thy pleasure on My holy day; and call the Sabbath a delight, the holy of the Lord, honorable; and shalt honor Him, not doing thine own ways, nor finding thine own pleasure, nor speaking thine own words: then shalt thou delight thyself in the Lord." (Verses 12–14.) This prophecy also applies in our time. The breach was made in the law of God when the Sabbath was changed by the Roman power. But the time has come for that divine institution to be restored. The breach is to be repaired and the foundation of many generations to be raised up.—*The Great Controversy,* pp. 452, 453.

June 15

The Sabbath Created by Christ

For by Him all things were created that are in heaven and that are on earth, visible and invisible.
—*Colossians 1:16.*

The Sabbath was hallowed at the creation. As ordained for humanity, it had its origin when "the morning stars sang together, and all the sons of God shouted for joy." (Job 38:7.) Peace brooded over the world; for earth was in harmony with heaven. "God saw everything that He had made, and, behold, it was very good;" and He rested in the joy of His completed work. (Genesis 1:31.)

Because He had rested upon the Sabbath, "God blessed the seventh day, and sanctified it"—set it apart to a holy use. He gave it to Adam as a day of rest. It was a memorial of the work of creation, and thus a sign of God's power and His love. The Scripture says, "He hath made His wonderful works to be remembered." "The things that are made," declare "the invisible things of Him since the creation of the world," "even His everlasting power and divinity." (Genesis 2:3; Psalm 111:4; Romans 1:20, R.V.)

All things were created by the Son of God. "In the beginning was the Word, and the Word was with God. . . . All things were made by Him; and without Him was not anything made that was made." (John 1:1–3.) And since the Sabbath is a memorial of the work of creation, it is a token of the love and power of Christ. . . .

The Sabbath was embodied in the law given from Sinai; but it was not then first made known as a day of rest. The people of Israel had a knowledge of it before they came to Sinai. On the way thither the Sabbath was kept. . . .

The Sabbath was not for Israel merely, but for the world. It had been made known to the human race in Eden, and, like the other precepts of the Decalogue, it is of imperishable obligation. Of that law of which the fourth commandment forms a part, Christ declares, "Till heaven and earth pass, one jot or one tittle shall in nowise pass from the law." So long as the heavens and the earth endure, the Sabbath will continue as a sign of the Creator's power. And when Eden shall bloom on earth again, God's holy rest day will be honored by all beneath the sun. "From one Sabbath to another" the inhabitants of the glorified new earth shall go up "to worship before Me, saith the Lord." (Matthew 5:18; Isaiah 66:23.)—*The Desire of Ages,* pp. 281, 283.

WORSHIP THE CREATOR

Worship Him who made heaven and earth, the sea and springs of water.
—Revelation 14:7.

The duty to worship God is based upon the fact that He is the Creator and that to Him all other beings owe their existence. And wherever, in the Bible, His claim to reverence and worship, above the gods of the heathen, is presented, there is cited the evidence of His creative power. . . .

In Revelation 14, we are called upon to worship the Creator; and the prophecy brings to view a class that, as the result of the threefold message, are keeping the commandments of God. One of these commandments points directly to God as the Creator. The fourth precept declares: "The seventh day is the Sabbath of the Lord thy God: . . . for in six days the Lord made heaven and earth, the sea, and all that in them is, and rested the seventh day: wherefore the Lord blessed the Sabbath day, and hallowed it." (Exodus 20:10, 11.) Concerning the Sabbath, the Lord says, further, that it is "a sign, . . . that ye may know that I am the Lord your God." (Ezekiel 20:20.) . . .

"The importance of the Sabbath as the memorial of creation is that it keeps ever present the true reason why worship is due to God"—because He is the Creator, and we are His creatures. "The Sabbath therefore lies at the very foundation of divine worship, for it teaches this great truth in the most impressive manner, and no other institution does this. The true ground of divine worship, not of that on the seventh day merely, but of all worship, is found in the distinction between the Creator and His creatures. This great fact can never become obsolete, and must never be forgotten." (J. N. Andrews, *History of the Sabbath*, chapter 27.) It was to keep this truth ever before our minds, that God instituted the Sabbath in Eden; and so long as the fact that He is our Creator continues to be a reason why we should worship Him, so long the Sabbath will continue as its sign and memorial. Had the Sabbath been universally kept, mankind's thoughts and affections would have been led to the Creator as the object of reverence and worship, and there would never have been an idolater, an atheist, or an infidel. The keeping of the Sabbath is a sign of loyalty to the true God, "Him that made heaven, and earth, and the sea, and the fountains of waters." It follows that the message which commands us to worship God and keep His commandments will especially call upon us to keep the fourth commandment.—*The Great Controversy,* pp. 436–438.

June 17

The Lord's Day

The Sabbath was made for man, and not man for the Sabbath. Therefore the Son of Man is also Lord of the Sabbath.—Mark 2:27, 28.

The Saviour had not come to set aside what patriarchs and prophets had spoken; for He Himself had spoken through these representative men. All the truths of God's word came from Him. But these priceless gems had been placed in false settings. Their precious light had been made to minister to error. God desired them to be removed from their settings of error and replaced in the framework of truth. This work only a divine hand could accomplish. By its connection with error, the truth had been serving the cause of the enemy of God and man. Christ had come to place it where it would glorify God, and work the salvation of humanity. . . .

"Wherefore the Son of man is Lord also of the Sabbath." These words are full of instruction and comfort. Because the Sabbath was made for mankind, it is the Lord's day. It belongs to Christ. For "all things were made by Him; and without Him was not anything made that was made." (John 1:3.) Since He made all things, He made the Sabbath. By Him it was set apart as a memorial of the work of creation. It points to Him as both the Creator and the Sanctifier. It declares that He who created all things in heaven and in earth, and by whom all things hold together, is the head of the church, and that by His power we are reconciled to God. For, speaking of Israel, He said, "I gave them My Sabbaths, to be a sign between Me and them, that they might know that I am the Lord that sanctify them"—make them holy. (Ezekiel 20:12.) Then the Sabbath is a sign of Christ's power to make us holy. And it is given to all whom Christ makes holy. As a sign of His sanctifying power, the Sabbath is given to all who through Christ become a part of the Israel of God.

And the Lord says, "If thou turn away thy foot from the Sabbath, from doing thy pleasure on My holy day; and call the Sabbath a delight, the holy of the Lord, honorable; . . . then shalt thou delight thyself in the Lord." (Isaiah 58:13, 14.) To all who receive the Sabbath as a sign of Christ's creative and redeeming power, it will be a delight. Seeing Christ in it, they delight themselves in Him. The Sabbath points them to the works of creation as an evidence of His mighty power in redemption. While it calls to mind the lost peace of Eden, it tells of peace restored through the Saviour.—*The Desire of Ages,* pp. 287–289.

Sabbath and the World of Nature

The heavens declare the glory of God; and the firmament shows His handiwork.—Psalm 19:1.

So through the creation we are to become acquainted with the Creator. The book of nature is a great lesson book, which in connection with the Scriptures we are to use in teaching others of His character, and guiding lost sheep back to the fold of God. As the works of God are studied, the Holy Spirit flashes conviction into the mind. It is not the conviction that logical reasoning produces; but unless the mind has become too dark to know God, the eye too dim to see Him, the ear too dull to hear His voice, a deeper meaning is grasped, and the sublime, spiritual truths of the written word are impressed on the heart. . . .

Christ's purpose in parable teaching was in direct line with the purpose of the Sabbath. God gave us the memorial of His creative power, that we might discern Him in the works of His hand. The Sabbath bids us behold in His created works the glory of the Creator. And it was because He desired us to do this that Jesus bound up His precious lessons with the beauty of natural things. On the holy rest day, above all other days, we should study the messages that God has written for us in nature. We should study the Saviour's parables where He spoke them, in the fields and groves, under the open sky, among the grass and flowers. As we come close to the heart of nature, Christ makes His presence real to us, and speaks to our hearts of His peace and love.

And Christ has linked His teaching, not only with the day of rest, but with the week of toil. He has wisdom for those who drive the plow and sow the seed. In the plowing and sowing, the tilling and reaping, He teaches us to see an illustration of His work of grace in the heart. So in every line of useful labor and every association of life, He desires us to find a lesson of divine truth. Then our daily toil will no longer absorb our attention and lead us to forget God; it will continually remind us of our Creator and Redeemer. The thought of God will run like a thread of gold through all our homely [common, domestic] cares and occupations. For us the glory of His face will again rest upon the face of nature. We shall ever be learning new lessons of heavenly truth, and growing into the image of His purity. Thus shall we "be taught of the Lord"; and in the lot wherein we are called, we shall "abide with God." (Isaiah 54:13; 1 Corinthians 7:24.)—*Christ's Object Lessons,* pp. 24–27.

June 19

An Expression of Thanks

Then God blessed the seventh day and sanctified it, because in it He rested from all His work which God had created and made.
—*Genesis 2:3.*

After resting upon the seventh day, God sanctified it, or set it apart, as a day of rest for the human family. Following the example of the Creator, they were to rest upon this sacred day, that as they should look upon the heavens and the earth, they might reflect upon God's great work of creation; and that as they should behold the evidences of God's wisdom and goodness, their hearts might be filled with love and reverence for their Maker.

In Eden, God set up the memorial of His work of creation, in placing His blessing upon the seventh day. The Sabbath was committed to Adam, the father and representative of the whole human family. Its observance was to be an act of grateful acknowledgment, on the part of all who should dwell upon the earth, that God was their Creator and their rightful Sovereign; that they were the work of His hands and the subjects of His authority. Thus the institution was wholly commemorative, and given to all mankind. There was nothing in it shadowy or of restricted application to any people.

God saw that a Sabbath was essential for mankind, even in Paradise. Human beings needed to lay aside their own interests and pursuits for one day of the seven, that they might more fully contemplate the works of God and meditate upon His power and goodness. They needed a Sabbath to remind them more vividly of God and to awaken gratitude because all that they enjoyed and possessed came from the beneficent hand of the Creator.

God designs that the Sabbath shall direct our minds to the contemplation of His created works. Nature speaks to our senses, declaring that there is a living God, the Creator, the Supreme Ruler of all. "The heavens declare the glory of God; and the firmament showeth His handiwork. Day unto day uttereth speech, and night unto night showeth knowledge." (Psalm 19:1, 2.) The beauty that clothes the earth is a token of God's love. We may behold it in the everlasting hills, in the lofty trees, in the opening buds and the delicate flowers. All speak to us of God. The Sabbath, ever pointing to Him who made them all, bids us open the great book of nature and trace therein the wisdom, the power, and the love of the Creator.—*Patriarchs and Prophets*, pp. 47, 48.

June 20

The Creation Week

So the evening and the morning were the first day.
—Genesis 1:5.

Like the Sabbath, the week originated at creation, and it has been preserved and brought down to us through Bible history. God Himself measured off the first week as a sample for successive weeks to the close of time. Like every other, it consisted of seven literal days. Six days were employed in the work of creation; upon the seventh, God rested, and He then blessed this day and set it apart as a day of rest for us.

In the law given from Sinai, God recognized the week, and the facts upon which it is based. After giving the command, "Remember the Sabbath day, to keep it holy," and specifying what shall be done on the six days, and what shall not be done on the seventh, He states the reason for thus observing the week, by pointing back to His own example: "For in six days the Lord made heaven and earth, the sea, and all that in them is, and rested the seventh day: wherefore the Lord blessed the Sabbath day, and hallowed it." (Exodus 20:8–11.) This reason appears beautiful and forcible when we understand the days of creation to be literal. The first six days of each week are given to us for labor, because God employed the same period of the first week in the work of creation. On the seventh day we are to refrain from labor, in commemoration of the Creator's rest.

But the assumption that the events of the first week required thousands upon thousands of years, strikes directly at the foundation of the fourth commandment. It represents the Creator as commanding us to observe the week of literal days in commemoration of vast, indefinite periods. This is unlike His method of dealing with His creatures. It makes indefinite and obscure that which He has made very plain. It is infidelity in its most insidious and hence most dangerous form; its real character is so disguised that it is held and taught by many who profess to believe the Bible.

The Bible recognizes no long ages in which the earth was slowly evolved from chaos. Of each successive day of creation, the sacred record declares that it consisted of the evening and the morning, like all other days that have followed. At the close of each day is given the result of the Creator's work. —*Patriarchs and Prophets,* pp. 111, 112.

June 21

Faith in Inspired History

This is the history of the heavens and the earth when they were created, in the day that the Lord God made the earth and the heavens.
—Genesis 2:4.

Geologists claim to find evidence from the earth itself that it is very much older than the Mosaic record teaches. Human and animal bones, as well as instruments of warfare, petrified trees, et cetera, much larger than any that now exist, or that have existed for thousands of years, have been discovered, and from this it is inferred that the earth was populated long before the time brought to view in the record of creation, and by a race of beings vastly superior in size to any persons now living. Such reasoning has led many professed Bible believers to adopt the position that the days of creation were vast, indefinite periods.

But apart from Bible history, geology can prove nothing. Those who reason so confidently upon its discoveries have no adequate conception of the size of humans, animals, and trees before the Flood, or of the great changes which then took place. Relics found in the earth do give evidence of conditions differing in many respects from the present, but the time when these conditions existed can be learned only from the Inspired Record. In the history of the Flood, inspiration has explained that which geology alone could never fathom. In the days of Noah, people, animals, and trees, many times larger than now exist, were buried, and thus preserved as an evidence to later generations that the antediluvians perished by a flood. God designed that the discovery of these things should establish faith in inspired history; but men and women, with their vain reasoning, fall into the same error as did the people before the Flood—the things which God gave them as a benefit, they turn into a curse by making a wrong use of them.

It is one of Satan's devices to lead the people to accept the fables of infidelity; for he can thus obscure the law of God, in itself very plain, and embolden them to rebel against the divine government. His efforts are especially directed against the fourth commandment, because it so clearly points to the living God, the Maker of the heavens and the earth.

There is a constant effort made to explain the work of creation as the result of natural causes; and human reasoning is accepted even by professed Christians, in opposition to plain Scripture facts.—*Patriarchs and Prophets*, pp. 112, 113.

2016

Sabbath Preparations

Remember the Sabbath day, to keep it holy.—Exodus 20:8.

At the very beginning of the fourth commandment the Lord said: "Remember." He knew that amid the multitude of cares and perplexities we would be tempted to excuse ourselves from meeting the full requirement of the law, or would forget its sacred importance. Therefore He said: "Remember the Sabbath day, to keep it holy." (Exodus 20:8.)

All through the week we are to have the Sabbath in mind and be making preparation to keep it according to the commandment. We are not merely to observe the Sabbath as a legal matter. We are to understand its spiritual bearing upon all the transactions of life. All who regard the Sabbath as a sign between them and God, showing that He is the God who sanctifies them, will represent the principles of His government. They will bring into daily practice the laws of His kingdom. Daily it will be their prayer that the sanctification of the Sabbath may rest upon them. Every day they will have the companionship of Christ and will exemplify the perfection of His character. Every day their light will shine forth to others in good works.

In all that pertains to the success of God's work, the very first victories are to be won in the home life. Here the preparation for the Sabbath must begin. Throughout the week let parents remember that their home is to be a school in which their children shall be prepared for the courts above. Let their words be right words. No words which their children should not hear are to escape their lips. Let the spirit be kept free from irritation. Parents, during the week live as in the sight of a holy God, who has given you children to train for Him. Train for Him the little church in your home, that on the Sabbath all may be prepared to worship in the Lord's sanctuary. Each morning and evening present your children to God as His blood-bought heritage. Teach them that it is their highest duty and privilege to love and serve God. . . .

When the Sabbath is thus remembered, the temporal will not be allowed to encroach upon the spiritual. No duty pertaining to the six working days will be left for the Sabbath. During the week our energies will not be so exhausted in temporal labor that on the day when the Lord rested and was refreshed we shall be too weary to engage in His service.—*Testimonies for the Church,* vol. 6, pp. 353, 354.

June 23

Double Manna

And so it was, on the sixth day, that they gathered twice as much bread.
—Exodus 16:22.

On the sixth day the people gathered two omers for every person. The rulers hastened to acquaint Moses with what had been done. His answer was, "This is that which the Lord hath said, Tomorrow is the rest of the holy Sabbath unto the Lord." . . .

God requires that His holy day be as sacredly observed now as in the time of Israel. The command given to the Hebrews should be regarded by all Christians as an injunction from Jehovah to them. The day before the Sabbath should be made a day of preparation, that everything may be in readiness for its sacred hours. In no case should our own business be allowed to encroach upon holy time. God has directed that the sick and suffering be cared for; the labor required to make them comfortable is a work of mercy, and no violation of the Sabbath; but all unnecessary work should be avoided. Many carelessly put off till the beginning of the Sabbath little things that might have been done on the day of preparation. This should not be. Work that is neglected until the beginning of the Sabbath should remain undone until it is past. This course might help the memory of these thoughtless ones, and make them careful to do their own work on the six working days.

Every week during their long sojourn in the wilderness the Israelites witnessed a threefold miracle, designed to impress their minds with the sacredness of the Sabbath: a double quantity of manna fell on the sixth day, none on the seventh, and the portion needed for the Sabbath was preserved sweet and pure, when if any were kept over at any other time it became unfit for use.

In the circumstances connected with the giving of the manna, we have conclusive evidence that the Sabbath was not instituted, as many claim, when the law was given at Sinai. Before the Israelites came to Sinai they understood the Sabbath to be obligatory upon them. In being obliged to gather every Friday a double portion of manna in preparation for the Sabbath, when none would fall, the sacred nature of the day of rest was continually impressed upon them. And when some of the people went out on the Sabbath to gather manna, the Lord asked, "How long *refuse ye* to keep My commandments and My laws?"—*Patriarchs and Prophets,* pp. 295–297.

2016

A Perpetual Covenant

You are a chosen generation, a royal priesthood,
a holy nation, His own special people.
—1 Peter 2:9.

When the Lord delivered His people Israel from Egypt and committed to them His law, He taught them that by the observance of the Sabbath they were to be distinguished from idolaters. It was this that made the distinction between those who acknowledge the sovereignty of God and those who refuse to accept Him as their Creator and King. . . .

As the Sabbath was the sign that distinguished Israel when they came out of Egypt to enter the earthly Canaan, so it is the sign that now distinguishes God's people as they come out from the world to enter the heavenly rest. The Sabbath is a sign of the relationship existing between God and His people, a sign that they honor His law. It distinguishes between His loyal subjects and transgressors.

From the pillar of cloud Christ declared concerning the Sabbath: "Verily My Sabbaths ye shall keep: for it is a sign between Me and you throughout your generations; that ye may know that I am the Lord that doth sanctify you." (Exodus 31:13.) The Sabbath given to the world as the sign of God as the Creator is also the sign of Him as the Sanctifier. The power that created all things is the power that re-creates the soul in His own likeness. To those who keep holy the Sabbath day it is the sign of sanctification. True sanctification is harmony with God, oneness with Him in character. It is received through obedience to those principles that are the transcript of His character. And the Sabbath is the sign of obedience. Those who from the heart obey the fourth commandment will obey the whole law. They are sanctified through obedience.

To us as to Israel the Sabbath is given "for a perpetual covenant." To those who reverence His holy day the Sabbath is a sign that God recognizes them as His chosen people. It is a pledge that He will fulfill to them His covenant. All who accept the sign of God's government place themselves under the divine, everlasting covenant. . . .

The fourth commandment alone of all the ten contains the seal of the great Lawgiver, the Creator of the heavens and the earth. Those who obey this commandment take upon themselves His name, and all the blessings it involves are theirs.—*Testimonies for the Church,* vol. 6, pp. 349, 350.

JUNE 25

2016

A JOYOUS WORK

Those who honor Me I will honor.
—1 Samuel 2:30.

When the Sabbath is thus remembered, the temporal will not be allowed to encroach upon the spiritual. No duty pertaining to the six working days will be left for the Sabbath. During the week our energies will not be so exhausted in temporal labor that on the day when the Lord rested and was refreshed we shall be too weary to engage in His service. . . .

On Friday let the preparation for the Sabbath be completed. See that all the clothing is in readiness and that all the cooking is done. Let the boots be blacked and the baths be taken. It is possible to do this. If you make it a rule you can do it. The Sabbath is not to be given to the repairing of garments, to the cooking of food, to pleasure seeking, or to any other worldly employment. Before the setting of the sun let all secular work be laid aside and all secular papers be put out of sight. Parents, explain your work and its purpose to your children, and let them share in your preparation to keep the Sabbath according to the commandment.

We should jealously guard the edges of the Sabbath. Remember that every moment is consecrated, holy time. Whenever it is possible, employers should give their workers the hours from Friday noon until the beginning of the Sabbath. Give them time for preparation, that they may welcome the Lord's day with quietness of mind. By such a course you will suffer no loss even in temporal things.

There is another work that should receive attention on the preparation day. On this day all differences between God's children, whether in the family or in the church, should be put away. Let all bitterness and wrath and malice be expelled from the soul. In a humble spirit, "confess your faults one to another, and pray one for another, that ye may be healed." (James 5:16.)

Before the Sabbath begins, the mind as well as the body should be withdrawn from worldly business. God has set His Sabbath at the end of the six working days, that we may stop and consider what we have gained during the week in preparation for the pure kingdom which admits no transgressor. We should each Sabbath reckon with our souls to see whether the week that has ended has brought spiritual gain or loss.

It means eternal salvation to keep the Sabbath holy unto the Lord. —*Testimonies for the Church,* vol. 6, pp. 354–356.

Satan's Attack on the Sabbath

He . . . shall intend to change times and law.
—Daniel 7:25.

The spirit of concession to paganism opened the way for a still further disregard of Heaven's authority. Satan, working through unconsecrated leaders of the church, tampered with the fourth commandment also, and essayed [tried] to set aside the ancient Sabbath, the day which God had blessed and sanctified (Genesis 2:2, 3), and in its stead to exalt the festival observed by the heathen as "the venerable day of the sun." This change was not at first attempted openly. In the first centuries the true Sabbath had been kept by all Christians. They were jealous for the honor of God, and, believing that His law is immutable, they zealously guarded the sacredness of its precepts. But with great subtlety Satan worked through his agents to bring about his object. That the attention of the people might be called to the Sunday, it was made a festival in honor of the resurrection of Christ. Religious services were held upon it; yet it was regarded as a day of recreation, the Sabbath being still sacredly observed.

To prepare the way for the work which he designed to accomplish, Satan had led the Jews, before the advent of Christ, to load down the Sabbath with the most rigorous exactions, making its observance a burden. Now, taking advantage of the false light in which he had thus caused it to be regarded, he cast contempt upon it as a Jewish institution. While Christians generally continued to observe the Sunday as a joyous festival, he led them, in order to show their hatred of Judaism, to make the Sabbath a fast, a day of sadness and gloom. . . .

The archdeceiver had not completed his work. He was resolved to gather the Christian world under his banner and to exercise his power through his vicegerent, the proud pontiff who claimed to be the representative of Christ. Through half-converted pagans, ambitious prelates, and world-loving churchmen he accomplished his purpose. Vast councils were held from time to time, in which the dignitaries of the church were convened from all the world. In nearly every council the Sabbath which God had instituted was pressed down a little lower, while the Sunday was correspondingly exalted. Thus the pagan festival came finally to be honored as a divine institution, while the Bible Sabbath was pronounced a relic of Judaism, and its observers were declared to be accursed.—*The Great Controversy,* pp. 52, 53.

June 27

Standing for God's Honor

A judgment was made in favor of the saints of the Most High.
—*Daniel 7:22.*

Among the leading causes that had led to the separation of the true church from Rome was the hatred of the latter toward the Bible Sabbath. As foretold by prophecy, the papal power cast down the truth to the ground. The law of God was trampled in the dust, while human traditions and customs were exalted. The churches that were under the rule of the papacy were early compelled to honor the Sunday as a holy day. Amid the prevailing error and superstition, many, even of the true people of God, became so bewildered that while they observed the Sabbath, they refrained from labor also on the Sunday. But this did not satisfy the papal leaders. They demanded not only that Sunday be hallowed, but that the Sabbath be profaned; and they denounced in the strongest language those who dared to show it honor. It was only by fleeing from the power of Rome that any could obey God's law in peace.

The Waldenses were among the first of the peoples of Europe to obtain a translation of the Holy Scriptures. . . . Hundreds of years before the Reformation they possessed the Bible in manuscript in their native tongue. They had the truth unadulterated, and this rendered them the special objects of hatred and persecution. They declared the Church of Rome to be the apostate Babylon of the Apocalypse, and at the peril of their lives they stood up to resist her corruptions. While, under the pressure of long-continued persecution, some compromised their faith, little by little yielding its distinctive principles, others held fast the truth. Through ages of darkness and apostasy there were Waldenses who denied the supremacy of Rome, who rejected image worship as idolatry, and who kept the true Sabbath. Under the fiercest tempests of opposition they maintained their faith. Though gashed by the Savoyard spear, and scorched by the Romish fagot, they stood unflinchingly for God's word and His honor.

Behind the lofty bulwarks of the mountains—in all ages the refuge of the persecuted and oppressed—the Waldenses found a hiding place. Here the light of truth was kept burning amid the darkness of the Middle Ages. . . .

God had provided for His people a sanctuary of awful grandeur, befitting the mighty truths committed to their trust. To those faithful exiles the mountains were an emblem of the immutable righteousness of Jehovah.—*The Great Controversy,* pp. 65, 66.

The Line in the Sand

Now he who keeps His commandments abides in Him, and He in him.
—1 John 3:24.

After the warning against the worship of the beast and his image the prophecy declares: "Here are they that keep the commandments of God, and the faith of Jesus." (Revelation 14:12.) Since those who keep God's commandments are thus placed in contrast with those that worship the beast and his image and receive his mark, it follows that the keeping of God's law, on the one hand, and its violation, on the other, will make the distinction between the worshipers of God and the worshipers of the beast.

The special characteristic of the beast, and therefore of his image, is the breaking of God's commandments. Says Daniel, of the little horn, the papacy: "He shall think to change times and the law." (Daniel 7:25, R.V.) And Paul styled the same power the "man of sin," who was to exalt himself above God. One prophecy is a complement of the other. Only by changing God's law could the papacy exalt itself above God; whoever should understandingly keep the law as thus changed would be giving supreme honor to that power by which the change was made. Such an act of obedience to papal laws would be a mark of allegiance to the pope in the place of God.

The papacy has attempted to change the law of God. The second commandment, forbidding image worship, has been dropped from the law, and the fourth commandment has been so changed as to authorize the observance of the first instead of the seventh day as the Sabbath. But papists urge, as a reason for omitting the second commandment, that it is unnecessary, being included in the first, and that they are giving the law exactly as God designed it to be understood. This cannot be the change foretold by the prophet. An intentional, deliberate change is presented: "He shall think to change the times and the law." The change in the fourth commandment exactly fulfills the prophecy. For this the only authority claimed is that of the church. Here the papal power openly sets itself above God.

While the worshipers of God will be especially distinguished by their regard for the fourth commandment—since this is the sign of His creative power and the witness to His claim upon man's reverence and homage—the worshipers of the beast will be distinguished by their efforts to tear down the Creator's memorial, to exalt the institution of Rome.—*The Great Controversy*, pp. 445, 446.

June 29

Sabbath Reform

Blessed is the man . . . who keeps from defiling the Sabbath.
—Isaiah 56:2.

The work of Sabbath reform to be accomplished in the last days is foretold in the prophecy of Isaiah: "Thus saith the Lord, Keep ye judgment, and do justice: for My salvation is near to come, and My righteousness to be revealed. Blessed is the man that doeth this, and the son of man that layeth hold on it; that keepeth the Sabbath from polluting it, and keepeth his hand from doing any evil." (Isaiah 56:1, 2.) . . .

These words apply in the Christian age, as shown by the context: "The Lord God which gathereth the outcasts of Israel saith, Yet will I gather others to him, beside those that are gathered unto him." (Verse 8.) Here is foreshadowed the gathering in of the Gentiles by the gospel. And upon those who then honor the Sabbath, a blessing is pronounced. Thus the obligation of the fourth commandment extends past the crucifixion, resurrection, and ascension of Christ, to the time when His servants should preach to all nations the message of glad tidings. . . .

Hallowed by the Creator's rest and blessing, the Sabbath was kept by Adam in his innocence in holy Eden; by Adam, fallen yet repentant, when he was driven from his happy estate. It was kept by all the patriarchs, from Abel to righteous Noah, to Abraham, to Jacob. When the chosen people were in bondage in Egypt, many, in the midst of prevailing idolatry, lost their knowledge of God's law; but when the Lord delivered Israel, He proclaimed His law in awful grandeur to the assembled multitude, that they might know His will and fear and obey Him forever.

From that day to the present the knowledge of God's law has been preserved in the earth, and the Sabbath of the fourth commandment has been kept. Though the "man of sin" succeeded in trampling underfoot God's holy day, yet even in the period of his supremacy there were, hidden in secret places, faithful souls who paid it honor. Since the Reformation, there have been some in every generation to maintain its observance. Though often in the midst of reproach and persecution, a constant testimony has been borne to the perpetuity of the law of God and the sacred obligation of the creation Sabbath.—*The Great Controversy,* pp. 451, 453.

JUNE 30

GOD'S LAW AND SABBATH VINDICATED

Who shall not fear You, O Lord, and glorify Your name? For You alone are holy.
—Revelation 15:4.

While these words of holy trust [Psalm 46:1–3] ascend to God, the clouds sweep back, and the starry heavens are seen, unspeakably glorious in contrast with the black and angry firmament on either side. The glory of the celestial city streams from the gates ajar. Then there appears against the sky a hand holding two tables of stone folded together. Says the prophet: "The heavens shall declare His righteousness: for God is judge Himself." (Psalm 50:6.) That holy law, God's righteousness, that amid thunder and flame was proclaimed from Sinai as the guide of life, is now revealed to the world as the rule of judgment. The hand opens the tables, and there are seen the precepts of the Decalogue, traced as with a pen of fire. The words are so plain that all can read them. Memory is aroused, the darkness of superstition and heresy is swept from every mind, and God's ten words, brief, comprehensive, and authoritative, are presented to the view of all the inhabitants of the earth.

It is impossible to describe the horror and despair of those who have trampled upon God's holy requirements. The Lord gave them His law; they might have compared their characters with it and learned their defects while there was yet opportunity for repentance and reform; but in order to secure the favor of the world, they set aside its precepts and taught others to transgress. They have endeavored to compel God's people to profane His Sabbath. Now they are condemned by that law which they have despised. With awful distinctness they see that they are without excuse. They chose whom they would serve and worship. "Then shall ye return, and discern between the righteous and the wicked, between him that serveth God and him that serveth Him not." (Malachi 3:18.)

The enemies of God's law, from the ministers down to the least among them, have a new conception of truth and duty. Too late they see that the Sabbath of the fourth commandment is the seal of the living God. Too late they see the true nature of their spurious sabbath and the sandy foundation upon which they have been building. They find that they have been fighting against God.—*The Great Controversy,* pp. 639, 640.

Practical Christian Living

God Is Owner

For every beast of the forest is Mine, and the cattle on a thousand hills.
—Psalm 50:10.

That which lies at the foundation of business integrity and of true success is the recognition of God's ownership. The Creator of all things, He is the original proprietor. We are His stewards. All that we have is a trust from Him, to be used according to His direction.

This is an obligation that rests upon every human being. It has to do with the whole sphere of human activity. Whether we recognize it or not, we are stewards, supplied from God with talents and facilities and placed in the world to do a work appointed by Him.

Money is not ours; houses and grounds, pictures and furniture, garments and luxuries, do not belong to us. We are pilgrims, we are strangers. We have only a grant of those things that are necessary for health and life. . . . Our temporal blessings are given us in trust, to prove whether we can be entrusted with eternal riches. If we endure the proving of God, then we shall receive that purchased possession which is to be our own—glory, honor, and immortality.

If our own people would only put into the cause of God the money that has been lent them in trust, that portion which they spend in selfish gratification, in idolatry, they would lay up treasure in heaven, and would be doing the very work God requires them to do. But like the rich man in the parable, they live sumptuously. The money God has lent them in trust, to be used to His name's glory, they spend extravagantly. They do not stop to consider their accountability to God. They do not stop to consider that there is to be a reckoning day not far hence, when they must give an account of their stewardship.

We should ever remember that in the judgment we must meet the record of the way we use God's money. Much is spent in self-pleasing, self-gratification, that does us no real good, but positive injury. If we realize that God is the giver of all good things, that the money is His, then we shall exercise wisdom in its expenditure, conforming to His holy will. The world, its customs, its fashions, will not be our standard. We shall not have a desire to conform to its practices; we shall not permit our own inclinations to control us.—*The Adventist Home,* pp. 367, 368.

How Does Money Impact You?

But a certain man named Ananias, with Sapphira his wife, sold a possession.—Acts 5:1.

Money is not necessarily a curse; it is of high value because if rightly appropriated, it can do good in the salvation of souls, in blessing others who are poorer than ourselves. By an improvident or unwise use, . . . money will become a snare to the user. He who employs money to gratify pride and ambition makes it a curse rather than a blessing. Money is a constant test of the affections. Whoever acquires more than sufficient for his real needs should seek wisdom and grace to know his own heart and to keep his heart diligently, lest he have imaginary wants and become an unfaithful steward, using with prodigality his Lord's entrusted capital.

When we love God supremely, temporal things will occupy their right place in our affections. If we humbly and earnestly seek for knowledge and ability in order to make a right use of our Lord's goods, we shall receive wisdom from above. When the heart leans to its own preferences and inclinations, when the thought is cherished that money can confer happiness without the favor of God, then the money becomes a tyrant, ruling us; it receives our confidence and esteem and is worshiped as a god. Honor, truth, righteousness, and justice are sacrificed upon its altar. The commands of God's word are set aside, and the world's customs and usages, which King Mammon has ordained, become a controlling power.

If the laws given by God had continued to be carried out, how different would be the present condition of the world, morally, spiritually, and temporally. Selfishness and self-importance would not be manifested as now, but each would cherish a kind regard for the happiness and welfare of others. . . . Instead of the poorer classes being kept under the iron heel of oppression by the wealthy, instead of having other's brains to think and plan for them in temporal as well as in spiritual things, they would have some chance for independence of thought and action.

The sense of being owners of their own homes would inspire them with a strong desire for improvement. They would soon acquire skill in planning and devising for themselves; their children would be educated to habits of industry and economy, and the intellect would be greatly strengthened. They would feel that they are men and women, not slaves, and would be able to regain to a great degree their lost self-respect and moral independence.—*The Adventist Home,* pp. 372, 373.

July 3

An Education in Stewardship

For where your treasure is, there your heart will be also.
—Luke 12:34.

Oh, how much money we waste on useless articles in the house, on ruffles and fancy dress, and on candies and other articles we do not need! Parents, teach your children that it is wrong to use God's money in self-gratification. . . . Encourage them to save their pennies wherever possible, to be used in missionary work. They will gain rich experiences through the practice of self-denial, and such lessons will often keep them from acquiring habits of intemperance.

The children may learn to show their love for Christ by denying themselves needless trifles, for the purchase of which much money slips through their fingers. In every family this work should be done. It requires tact and method, but it will be the best education the children can receive. And if all the little children would present their offerings to the Lord, their gifts would be as little rivulets which, when united and set flowing, would swell into a river.

Keep a little money box on the mantel or in some safe place where it can be seen, in which the children can place their offerings for the Lord. . . . Thus they may be trained for God.

Not only does the Lord claim the tithe as His own, but He tells us how it should be reserved for Him. He says, "Honour the Lord with thy substance, and with the firstfruits of all thine increase." (Proverbs 3:9.) This does not teach that we are to spend our means on ourselves and bring to the Lord the remnant, even though it should be otherwise an honest tithe. Let God's portion be first set apart. The directions given by the Holy Spirit through the Apostle Paul in regard to gifts present a principle that applies also to tithing. "Upon the first day of the week let every one of you lay by him in store, as God hath prospered him." (1 Corinthians 16:2.) Parents and children are here included. . . .

The very best legacy which parents can leave their children is a knowledge of useful labor and the example of a life characterized by disinterested benevolence. By such a life they show the true value of money, that it is only to be appreciated for the good that it will accomplish in relieving their own wants and the necessities of others, and in advancing the cause of God.—*The Adventist Home,* pp. 388–390.

2016

AVOID DEBT

Owe no one anything except to love one another.
—Romans 13:8.

The world has a right to expect strict integrity in those who profess to be Bible Christians. By one person's indifference in regard to paying his or her just dues all our people are in danger of being regarded as unreliable.

Those who make any pretensions to godliness should adorn the doctrine they profess, and not give occasion for the truth to be reviled through their inconsiderate course of action. "Owe no man any thing," says the apostle.

Be determined never to incur another debt. Deny yourself a thousand things rather than run in debt. This has been the curse of your life, getting into debt. Avoid it as you would the smallpox.

Make a solemn covenant with God that by His blessing you will pay your debts and then owe no one anything if you live on porridge and bread. It is so easy in preparing your table to throw out of your pocket twenty-five cents for extras. Take care of the pennies, and the dollars will take care of themselves. It is the mites here and the mites there that are spent for this, that, and the other that soon run up into dollars. Deny self at least while you are walled in with debts. . . . Do not falter, be discouraged, or turn back. Deny your taste, deny the indulgence of appetite, save your pence, and pay your debts. Work them off as fast as possible. When you can stand forth free again, owing no one anything, you will have achieved a great victory.

If some are found to be in debt and really unable to meet their obligations, they should not be pressed to do that which is beyond their power. They should be given a favorable chance to discharge their indebtedness, and not be placed in a position where they are utterly unable to free themselves from debt. Though such a course might be considered justice, it is not mercy and the love of God.

Some are not discreet and would incur debts that might be avoided. Others exercise a caution that savors of unbelief. By taking advantage of circumstances we may at times invest means to such advantage that the work of God will be strengthened and upbuilt, and yet keep strictly to right principles. —*The Adventist Home,* pp. 393, 394.

July 5

Remember the Poor

If you want to be perfect, go, sell what you have and give to the poor, and you will have treasure in heaven; and come, follow Me.—Matthew 19:21.

If we represent the character of Christ, every particle of selfishness must be expelled from the soul. In carrying forward the work He gave to our hands, it will be necessary for us to give every jot and tittle of our means that we can spare. Poverty and distress in families will come to our knowledge, and afflicted and suffering ones will have to be relieved. We know very little of the human suffering that exists everywhere about us; but as we have opportunity, we should be ready to render immediate assistance to those who are under a severe pressure.

The squandering of money in luxuries deprives the poor of the means necessary to supply them with food and clothing. That which is spent for the gratification of pride in dress, in buildings, in furniture, and in decorations would relieve the distress of many wretched, suffering families. God's stewards are to minister to the needy.

The giving that is the fruit of self-denial is a wonderful help to the giver. It imparts an education that enables us more fully to comprehend the work of Him who went about doing good, relieving the suffering, and supplying the needs of the destitute.

Constant, self-denying benevolence is God's remedy for the cankering sins of selfishness and covetousness. God has arranged systematic benevolence to sustain His cause and relieve the necessities of the suffering and needy. He has ordained that giving should become a habit, that it may counteract the dangerous and deceitful sin of covetousness. Continual giving starves covetousness to death. Systematic benevolence is designed in the order of God to tear away treasures from the covetous as fast as they are gained, and to consecrate them to the Lord, to whom they belong. . . .

The constant practice of God's plan of systematic benevolence weakens covetousness and strengthens benevolence. If riches increase, people, even those professing godliness, set their hearts upon them; and the more they have, the less they give to the treasury of the Lord. Thus riches make people selfish, and hoarding feeds covetousness; and these evils strengthen by active exercise. God knows our danger and has hedged us about with means to prevent our own ruin. He requires the constant exercise of benevolence.—*The Adventist Home,* pp. 370, 371.

2016

Remember God in Your Will

It is required in stewards that one be found faithful.
—I Corinthians 4:2.

Those who are faithful stewards of the Lord's means will know just how their business stands, and, like the wise, they will be prepared for any emergency. Should their probation close suddenly, they would not leave such great perplexity upon those who are called to settle their estate.

Many are not exercised upon the subject of making their wills while they are in apparent health. But this precaution should be taken. They should know their financial standing and should not allow their business to become entangled. They should arrange their property in such a manner that they may leave it at any time.

Wills should be made in a manner to stand the test of law. After they are drawn, they may remain for years and do no harm, if donations continue to be made from time to time as the cause has need. Death will not come one day sooner, brethren, because you have made your will. In disposing of your property by will to your relatives, be sure that you do not forget God's cause. You are His agents, holding His property; and His claims should have your first consideration. Your wife and children, of course, should not be left destitute; provision should be made for them if they are needy. But do not, simply because it is customary, bring into your will a long line of relatives who are not needy.

Let no one think that it will meet the mind of Christ to hoard up property through life and then at death make a bequest of a portion of it to some benevolent cause.

Some selfishly retain their means during their lifetime, trusting to make up for their neglect by remembering the cause in their wills. But not half the means thus bestowed in legacies ever benefits the object specified. Brethren and sisters, invest in the bank of heaven yourselves, and do not leave your stewardship upon another.

Parents should have great fear in entrusting children with the talents of means that God has placed in their hands, unless they have the surest evidence that their children have greater interest in, love for, and devotion to the cause of God than they themselves possess, and that these children will be more earnest and zealous in forwarding the work of God.—*The Adventist Home,* pp. 396–398.

July 7

Stewards of God's Grace

Having then gifts differing according to the grace that is given to us, let us use them.
—Romans 12:6.

Our Lord designed that His church should reflect to the world the fulness and sufficiency that we find in Him. We are constantly receiving of God's bounty, and by imparting of the same we are to represent to the world the love and beneficence of Christ. While all heaven is astir, dispatching messengers to all parts of the earth to carry forward the work of redemption, the church of the living God are also to be colaborers with Jesus Christ. We are members of His mystical body. He is the head, controlling all the members of the body. Jesus Himself, in His infinite mercy, is working on human hearts, effecting spiritual transformations so amazing that angels look on with astonishment and joy. The same unselfish love that characterizes the Master is seen in the character and life of His true followers. Christ expects that we will become partakers of His divine nature while in this world, thus not only reflecting His glory, to the praise of God, but illuminating the darkness of earth with the radiance of heaven. Thus will be fulfilled the words of Christ, "Ye are the light of the world."

"We are laborers together with God"—"stewards of the manifold grace of God." The knowledge of God's grace, the truths of His Word, and temporal gifts as well—time and means, talent and influence—are all a trust from God to be employed to His glory and for the salvation of others.

Wherever there is an impulse of love and sympathy, wherever the heart reaches out to uplift and bless others, there is revealed the working of God's Holy Spirit. In the depths of heathenism, those who have no knowledge of the written law of God, who have never even heard the name of Christ, have been kind to His servants, protecting them at the risk of their own lives. Their acts show the working of a divine power. The Holy Spirit has implanted the grace of Christ in the heart of the savages, quickening their sympathies contrary to their nature, contrary to their education. The "Light, which lighteth every man that cometh into the world," is shining in their souls; and this light, if heeded, will guide their feet to the kingdom of God.—*Review and Herald,* December 24, 1908.

The World's Greatest Want

Who may ascend into the hill of the Lord? Or who may stand in His holy place? He who has clean hands and a pure heart.
—Psalm 24:3, 4.

The same mighty truths that were revealed through these men [Joseph and Daniel], God desires to reveal through the youth and the children of today. The history of Joseph and Daniel is an illustration of what He will do for those who yield themselves to Him and with the whole heart seek to accomplish His purpose.

The greatest want of the world is the want of those men and women who will not be bought or sold, those who in their inmost souls are true and honest, those who do not fear to call sin by its right name, those whose conscience is as true to duty as the needle to the pole, those who will stand for the right though the heavens fall.

But such a character is not the result of accident; it is not due to special favors or endowments of Providence. A noble character is the result of self-discipline, of the subjection of the lower to the higher nature—the surrender of self for the service of love to God and to others.

The youth need to be impressed with the truth that their endowments are not their own. Strength, time, intellect, are but lent treasures. They belong to God, and it should be the resolve of every youth to put them to the highest use. The youth are branches, from which God expects fruit; stewards, whose capital must yield increase; lights, to illuminate the world's darkness.

Every youth, every child, has a work to do for the honor of God and the uplifting of humanity.

The early years of the prophet Elisha were passed in the quietude of country life, under the teaching of God and nature and the discipline of useful work. In a time of almost universal apostasy his father's household were among the number who had not bowed the knee to Baal. Theirs was a home where God was honored and where faithfulness to duty was the rule of daily life.

The son of a wealthy farmer, Elisha had taken up the work that lay nearest. While possessing the capabilities of a leader among men, he received a training in life's common duties. In order to direct wisely, he must learn to obey. By faithfulness in little things, he was prepared for weightier trusts. —*Education,* pp. 57, 58.

JULY 9

GOD IS SPEAKING

Be still, and know that I am God.
—Psalm 46:10.

It was in hours of solitary prayer that Jesus in His earth life received wisdom and power. Let the youth follow His example in finding at dawn and twilight a quiet season for communion with their Father in heaven. And throughout the day let them lift up their hearts to God. At every step of our way He says, "I the Lord thy God will hold thy right hand, . . . Fear not; I will help thee." (Isaiah 41:13.) Could our children learn these lessons in the morning of their years, what freshness and power, what joy and sweetness, would be brought into their lives!

These are lessons that only those who themselves have learned can teach. It is because so many parents and teachers profess to believe the word of God while their lives deny its power, that the teaching of Scripture has no greater effect upon the youth. At times the youth are brought to feel the power of the word. They see the preciousness of the love of Christ. They see the beauty of His character, the possibilities of a life given to His service. But in contrast they see the life of those who profess to revere God's precepts. Of how many are the words true that were spoken to the prophet Ezekiel:

Thy people "speak one to another, everyone to his brother, saying, Come, I pray you, and hear what is the word that cometh forth from the Lord. And they come unto thee as the people cometh, and they sit before thee as My people, and they hear thy words, but they will not do them." (Ezekiel 33:30, 31.)

It is one thing to treat the Bible as a book of good moral instruction, to be heeded so far as is consistent with the spirit of the times and our position in the world; it is another thing to regard it as it really is—the word of the living God, the word that is our life, the word that is to mold our actions, our words, and our thoughts. To hold God's word as anything less than this is to reject it. And this rejection by those who profess to believe it, is foremost among the causes of skepticism and infidelity in the youth. . . .

Many, even in their seasons of devotion, fail of receiving the blessing of real communion with God. They are in too great haste. With hurried steps they press through the circle of Christ's loving presence, pausing perhaps a moment within the sacred precincts, but not waiting for counsel. They have no time to remain with the divine Teacher.—*Education,* pp. 259, 260.

HELP ONE ANOTHER TO GROW

Be kindly affectionate to one another with brotherly love, in honor giving preference to one another.—Romans 12:10.

I have a deep interest in the youth, and I greatly desire to see them striving to perfect Christian characters, seeking by diligent study and earnest prayer to gain the training essential for acceptable service in the cause of God. I long to see them helping one another to reach a higher plane of Christian experience.

Christ came to teach the human family the way of salvation, and He made this way so plain that a little child can walk in it. He bids His disciples follow on to know the Lord; and as they daily follow His guidance, they learn that His going forth is prepared as the morning.

You have watched the rising sun, and the gradual break of day over earth and sky. Little by little the dawn increases, till the sun appears; then the light grows constantly stronger and clearer until the full glory of noontide is reached. This is a beautiful illustration of what God desires to do for His children in perfecting their Christian experience. As we walk day by day in the light He sends us, in willing obedience to all His requirements, our experience grows and broadens until we reach the full stature of men and women in Christ Jesus.

The youth need to keep ever before them the course that Christ followed. At every step it was a course of overcoming. Christ did not come to the earth as a king, to rule the nations. He came as a humble man, to be tempted, and to overcome temptation, to follow on, as we must, to know the Lord. In the study of His life we shall learn how much God through Him will do for His children. And we shall learn that, however great our trials may be, they cannot exceed what Christ endured that we might know the way, the truth, and the life. By a life of conformity to His example, we are to show our appreciation of His sacrifice in our behalf.

The youth have been bought with an infinite price, even the blood of the Son of God. Consider the sacrifice of the Father in permitting His Son to make this sacrifice. Consider what Christ gave up when He left the courts of heaven and the royal throne, to give His life a daily sacrifice for us. He suffered reproach and abuse. He bore all the insult and mockery that wicked people could heap upon Him. And when His earthly ministry was accomplished, He suffered the death of the cross.—*Messages to Young People,* pp. 15, 16.

2016

Choose Wisely

For what profit is it to a man if he gains the whole world, and loses his own soul?—Matthew 16:26.

God wants the youth to become people of earnest mind, to be prepared for action in His noble work, and fitted to bear responsibilities. God calls for young men with hearts uncorrupted, strong and brave, and determined to fight manfully in the struggle before them, that they may glorify God, and bless humanity. If the youth would but make the Bible their study, would but calm their impetuous desires, and listen to the voice of their Creator and Redeemer, they would not only be at peace with God, but would find themselves ennobled and elevated. It will be for your eternal interest, my young friend, to give heed to the instructions in the word of God, for they are of inestimable importance to you.

I entreat you to be wise, and consider what will be the result of leading a wild life, uncontrolled by the Spirit of God. "Be not deceived; God is not mocked: for whatsoever a man soweth, that shall he also reap. For he that soweth to his flesh shall of the flesh reap corruption." For your soul's sake, for Christ's sake, who gave Himself to save you from ruin, pause on the threshold of your life, and weigh well your responsibilities, your opportunities, your possibilities. God has given you an opportunity to fill a high destiny. Your influence may tell for the truth of God; you may be a co-laborer with God in the great work of human redemption. . . .

O that young men might appreciate the high destiny to which they are called! Ponder well the paths of your feet. Begin your work with high and holy purpose, and be determined that through the power of the grace of God, you will not diverge from the path of rectitude. If you begin to go in a wrong direction, every step will be fraught with peril and disaster, and you will go on straying from the path of truth, safety, and success. You need your intellect strengthened, your moral energies quickened, by divine power.

The cause of God demands the highest powers of the being, and there is urgent need in many fields for young men of literary qualifications. There is need of men who can be trusted to labor in extensive fields that are now white to the harvest. Young men of ordinary ability, who give themselves wholly to God, who are uncorrupted by vice and impurity, will be successful, and will be enabled to do a great work for God.—*Messages to Young People,* pp. 21, 22.

Prove Yourself

Preach the word! Be ready in season and out of season. Convince, rebuke, exhort, with all longsuffering and teaching.—2 Timothy 4:2.

You have within your reach more than finite possibilities. A man, as God applies the term, is a son of God. "Now are we the sons of God, and it doth not yet appear what we shall be. . . . And every man that hath this hope in him purifieth himself, even as He is pure." It is your privilege to turn away from that which is cheap and inferior, and rise to a high standard—to be respected by others and beloved by God.

The religious work which the Lord gives to young men, and to men of all ages, shows His respect for them as His children. He gives them the work of self-government. He calls them to be sharers with Him in the great work of redemption and uplifting. As a father takes his son into partnership in his business, so the Lord takes His children into partnership with Himself. We are made laborers together with God. Jesus says, "As Thou hast sent Me into the world, even so have I also sent them into the world." Would you not rather choose to be a child of God than a servant of Satan and sin, having your name registered as an enemy of Christ?

Young men and women need more of the grace of Christ, that they may bring the principles of Christianity into the daily life. The preparation for Christ's coming is a preparation made through Christ for the exercise of our highest qualities. It is the privilege of the youth to make of their character a beautiful structure. But there is a positive need of keeping close to Jesus. He is our strength and efficiency and power. We cannot depend on self for one moment. . . .

However large, however small, your talents, remember that what you have is yours only in trust. Thus God is testing you, giving you opportunity to prove yourself true. To Him you are indebted for all your capabilities. To Him belong your powers of body, mind, and soul, and for Him these powers are to be used. Your time, your influence, your capabilities, your skill—all must be accounted for to Him who gives all. Those use their gifts best who seek by earnest endeavor to carry out the Lord's great plan for the uplifting of humanity.

Persevere in the work that you have begun, until you gain victory after victory. Educate yourselves for a purpose. Keep in view the highest standard, that you may accomplish greater and still greater good, thus reflecting the glory of God.—*Messages to Young People*, pp. 47, 48.

July 13

God's Ideal

For as many as are led by the Spirit of God, these are sons of God.
—*Romans 8:14.*

A faithful obedience to God's requirements will have a surprising influence to elevate, develop, and strengthen all our faculties. Those who have in youth devoted themselves to the service of God, are found to be the people of sound judgment and keen discrimination. And why should it not be so? Communion with the greatest Teacher the world has ever known, strengthens the understanding, illuminates the mind, and purifies the heart—elevates, refines, and ennobles the whole person. "The entrance of Thy words giveth light; it giveth understanding unto the simple." . . .

God will do a great work for the youth, if they will by the aid of the Holy Spirit receive His word into the heart and obey it in the life. He is constantly seeking to attract them to Himself, the Source of all wisdom, the Fountain of goodness, purity, and truth. The mind which is occupied with exalted themes becomes itself ennobled.—*Signs of the Times,* December 1, 1881.

When the grace of God takes possession of the heart, it is seen that the inherited and cultivated tendencies to wrong must be crucified. A new life, under new control, must begin in the soul. All that is done must be done to the glory of God. This work includes the outward as well as the inward life. The entire being, body, soul, and spirit, must be brought into subjection to God, to be used by Him as an instrument of righteousness.

The natural man or woman is not subject to the law of God; neither, indeed, of themselves, can such people be. But by faith those who have been renewed live day by day the life of Christ. Day by day they show that they realize that they are God's property.

Body and soul belong to God. He gave His Son for the redemption of the world, and because of this we have been granted a new lease of life, a probation in which to develop characters of perfect loyalty. God has redeemed us from the slavery of sin, and has made it possible for us to live regenerated, transformed lives of service.

God's stamp is upon us. He has bought us, and He desires us to remember that our physical, mental, and moral powers belong to Him. Time and influence, reason, affection, and conscience, all are God's, and are to be used only in harmony with His will. They are not to be used in accordance with the direction of the world.—*The Youth's Instructor,* November 8, 1900.

Enlist in Christ's Army

2016

After these things I looked, and behold, a great multitude which no one could number, of all nations, tribes, peoples, and tongues, standing before the throne and before the Lamb, clothed with white robes, with palm branches in their hands.
—Revelation 7:9.

As sons and daughters of God, Christians should strive to reach the high ideal set before them in the gospel. They should be content with nothing less than perfection. . . .

Let us make God's holy word our study, bringing its holy principles into our lives. Let us walk before God in meekness and humility, daily correcting our faults. Let us not by selfish pride separate the soul from God. Cherish not a feeling of lofty supremacy, thinking yourself better than others. "Let him that thinketh he standeth take heed lest he fall." Peace and rest will come to you as you bring your will into subjection to the will of Christ. Then the love of Christ will rule in the heart, bringing into captivity to the Saviour the secret springs of action. The hasty, easily roused temper will be soothed and subdued by the oil of Christ's grace. The sense of sins forgiven will bring that peace that passeth all understanding. There will be an earnest striving to overcome all that is opposed to Christian perfection. Variance will disappear. Those who once found fault with others around them will see that far greater faults exist in their own characters.

There are those who listen to the truth, and are convinced that they have been living in opposition to Christ. They are condemned, and they repent of their transgressions. Relying upon the merits of Christ, exercising true faith in Him, they receive pardon for sin. As they cease to do evil and learn to do well, they grow in grace and in the knowledge of God. They see that they must sacrifice in order to separate from the world; and after counting the cost, they look upon all as loss if they may but win Christ. They have enlisted in Christ's army. The warfare is before them, and they enter it bravely and cheerfully, fighting against their natural inclinations and selfish desires, bringing the will into subjection to the will of Christ. Daily they seek the Lord for grace to obey Him, and they are strengthened and helped. This is true conversion. In humble, grateful dependence those who have been given a new heart rely upon the help of Christ. They reveal in their lives the fruit of righteousness. They once loved themselves. Worldly pleasure was their delight. Now their idol is dethroned, and God reigns supreme.—*The Youth's Instructor,* September 26, 1901.

July 15

Character Building

There is therefore now no condemnation to those who are in Christ Jesus, who do not walk according to the flesh, but according to the Spirit.—Romans 8:1.

True education does not ignore the value of scientific knowledge or literary acquirements; but above information it values power; above power, goodness; above intellectual acquirements, character. The world does not so much need people of great intellect as of noble character. It needs men and women in whom ability is controlled by steadfast principle.

"Wisdom is the principal thing; therefore get wisdom." "The tongue of the wise useth knowledge aright." (Proverbs 4:7; 15:2.) True education imparts this wisdom. It teaches the best use not only of one but of all our powers and acquirements. Thus it covers the whole circle of obligation—to ourselves, to the world, and to God.

Character building is the most important work ever entrusted to human beings; and never before was its diligent study so important as now. Never was any previous generation called to meet issues so momentous; never before were young men and young women confronted by perils so great as confront them today.

At such a time as this, what is the trend of the education given? To what motive is appeal most often made? To self-seeking. Much of the education given is a perversion of the name. In true education the selfish ambition, the greed for power, the disregard for the rights and needs of humanity, that are the curse of our world, find a counterinfluence. God's plan of life has a place for every human being. All are to improve their talents to the utmost; and faithfulness in doing this, be the gifts few or many, entitles one to honor. In God's plan there is no place for selfish rivalry. Those who measure themselves by themselves, and compare themselves among themselves, are not wise. (2 Corinthians 10:12.) Whatever we do is to be done "as of the ability which God giveth." (1 Peter 4:11.) It is to be done "heartily, as to the Lord, and not unto men; knowing that of the Lord ye shall receive the reward of the inheritance: for ye serve the Lord Christ." (Colossians 3:23, 24.) Precious the service done and the education gained in carrying out these principles. But how widely different is much of the education now given! From the child's earliest years it is an appeal to emulation and rivalry; it fosters selfishness, the root of all evil.—*Education,* pp. 225, 226.

2016

Lessons From the Rise and Fall of Nations

He reveals deep and secret things; He knows what is in the darkness, and light dwells with Him.
—Daniel 2:22.

The prophets to whom these great scenes were revealed longed to understand their import. They "inquired and searched diligently: . . . searching what, or what manner of time the Spirit of Christ which was in them did signify. . . . Unto whom it was revealed, that not unto themselves, but unto us they did minister the things, which are now reported unto you; . . . which things the angels desire to look into." (1 Peter 1:10–12.)

To us who are standing on the very verge of their fulfillment, of what deep moment, what living interest, are these delineations of the things to come—events for which, since our first parents turned their steps from Eden, God's children have watched and waited, longed and prayed! . . .

From the rise and fall of nations as made plain in the pages of Holy Writ, they need to learn how worthless is mere outward and worldly glory. Babylon, with all its power and its magnificence, the like of which our world has never since beheld—power and magnificence which to the people of that day seemed so stable and enduring—how completely has it passed away! As "the flower of the grass" it has perished. So perishes all that has not God for its foundation. Only that which is bound up with His purpose and expresses His character can endure. His principles are the only steadfast things our world knows.

It is these great truths that old and young need to learn. We need to study the working out of God's purpose in the history of nations and in the revelation of things to come, that we may estimate at their true value things seen and things unseen; that we may learn what is the true aim of life; that, viewing the things of time in the light of eternity, we may put them to their truest and noblest use. Thus, learning here the principles of His kingdom and becoming its subjects and citizens, we may be prepared at His coming to enter with Him into its possession.

The day is at hand. For the lessons to be learned, the work to be done, the transformation of character to be effected, the time remaining is but too brief a span.—*Education,* pp. 183, 184.

July 17

Gaining a Knowledge of God

The fear of the LORD is the beginning of wisdom,
and the knowledge of the Holy One is understanding.
—Proverbs 9:10.

Like our Saviour, we are in this world to do service for God. We are here to become like God in character, and by a life of service to reveal Him to the world. In order to be co-workers with God, in order to become like Him and to reveal His character, we must know Him aright. We must know Him as He reveals Himself.

A knowledge of God is the foundation of all true education and of all true service. It is the only real safeguard against temptation. It is this alone that can make us like God in character.

This is the knowledge needed by all who are working for the uplifting of others. Transformation of character, purity of life, efficiency in service, adherence to correct principles, all depend upon a right knowledge of God. This knowledge is the essential preparation both for this life and for the life to come. . . .

The things of nature that we now behold give us but a faint conception of Eden's glory. Sin has marred earth's beauty; on all things may be seen traces of the work of evil. Yet much that is beautiful remains. Nature testifies that One infinite in power, great in goodness, mercy, and love, created the earth, and filled it with life and gladness. Even in their blighted state, all things reveal the handiwork of the great Master Artist. Wherever we turn, we may hear the voice of God, and see evidences of His goodness.

From the solemn roll of the deep-toned thunder and old ocean's ceaseless roar, to the glad songs that make the forests vocal with melody, nature's ten thousand voices speak His praise. In earth and sea and sky, with their marvelous tint and color, varying in gorgeous contrast or blended in harmony, we behold His glory. The everlasting hills tell us of His power. The trees that wave their green banners in the sunlight, and the flowers in their delicate beauty, point to their Creator. The living green that carpets the brown earth tells of God's care for the humblest of His creatures. The caves of the sea and the depths of the earth reveal His treasures. . . . All the brightness and beauty that adorn the earth and light up the heavens, speak of God.—*The Ministry of Healing*, pp. 409, 411, 412.

Mind and Body

Let your heart keep my commands; for length of days and long life and peace they will add to you.—Proverbs 3:1, 2.

As the foundation principle of all education in these lines, the youth should be taught that the laws of nature are the laws of God—as truly divine as are the precepts of the Decalogue. The laws that govern our physical organism, God has written upon every nerve, muscle, and fiber of the body. Every careless or willful violation of these laws is a sin against our Creator. . . .

The influence of the mind on the body, as well as of the body on the mind, should be emphasized. The electric power of the brain, promoted by mental activity, vitalizes the whole system, and is thus an invaluable aid in resisting disease. This should be made plain. The power of the will and the importance of self-control, both in the preservation and in the recovery of health, the depressing and even ruinous effect of anger, discontent, selfishness, or impurity, and, on the other hand, the marvelous life-giving power to be found in cheerfulness, unselfishness, gratitude, should also be shown.

There is a physiological truth—truth that we need to consider—in the scripture, "A merry [rejoicing] heart doeth good like a medicine." (Proverbs 17:22.) . . .

The youth need to understand the deep truth underlying the Bible statement that with God "is the fountain of life." (Psalm 36:9.) Not only is He the originator of all, but He is the life of everything that lives. It is His life that we receive in the sunshine, in the pure, sweet air, in the food which builds up our bodies and sustains our strength. It is by His life that we exist, hour by hour, moment by moment. Except as perverted by sin, all His gifts tend to life, to health and joy.

"He hath made everything beautiful in its time" (Ecclesiastes 3:11, R.V.); and true beauty will be secured, not in marring God's work, but in coming into harmony with the laws of Him who created all things, and who finds pleasure in their beauty and perfection.

As the mechanism of the body is studied, attention should be directed to its wonderful adaptation of means to ends, the harmonious action and dependence of the various organs. As the interest of the students is thus awakened, and they are led to see the importance of physical culture, much can be done by the teacher to secure proper development and right habits. —*Education,* pp. 196–198.

July 19

Our Influence Is Vital

See that no one renders evil for evil to anyone, but always pursue what is good both for yourselves and for all.—1 Thessalonians 5:15.

There is an eloquence far more powerful than the eloquence of words in the quiet, consistent life of a pure, true Christian. What we are has more influence than what we say.

The officers who were sent to Jesus came back with the report that never man spoke as He spoke. But the reason for this was that never man lived as He lived. Had His life been other than it was, He could not have spoken as He did. His words bore with them a convincing power, because they came from a heart pure and holy, full of love and sympathy, benevolence and truth.

It is our own character and experience that determine our influence upon others. In order to convince others of the power of Christ's grace, we must know its power in our own hearts and lives. The gospel we present for the saving of souls must be the gospel by which our own souls are saved. Only through a living faith in Christ as a personal Saviour is it possible to make our influence felt in a skeptical world. If we would draw sinners out of the swift-running current, our own feet must be firmly set upon the Rock, Christ Jesus.

The badge of Christianity is not an outward sign, not the wearing of a cross or a crown, but it is that which reveals our union with God. By the power of His grace manifested in the transformation of character the world is to be convinced that God has sent His Son as its Redeemer. No other influence that can surround the human soul has such power as the influence of an unselfish life. The strongest argument in favor of the gospel is a loving and lovable Christian.

To live such a life, to exert such an influence, costs at every step effort, self-sacrifice, discipline. It is because they do not understand this that many are so easily discouraged in the Christian life. Many who sincerely consecrate their lives to God's service are surprised and disappointed to find themselves, as never before, confronted by obstacles and beset by trials and perplexities. They pray for Christlikeness of character, for a fitness for the Lord's work, and they are placed in circumstances that seem to call forth all the evil of their nature. Faults are revealed of which they did not even suspect the existence.—*The Ministry of Healing,* pp. 469, 470.

Power to Think and Do

The price of wisdom is above rubies.
—Job 28:18.

The Holy Scriptures are the perfect standard of truth, and as such should be given the highest place in education. To obtain an education worthy of the name, we must receive a knowledge of God, the Creator, and of Christ, the Redeemer, as they are revealed in the sacred word.

Every human being, created in the image of God, is endowed with a power akin to that of the Creator—individuality, power to think and to do. The people in whom this power is developed are the ones who bear responsibilities, who are leaders in enterprise, and who influence character. It is the work of true education to develop this power, to train the youth to be thinkers, and not mere reflectors of the thought of others. Instead of confining their study to that which others have said or written, let students be directed to the sources of truth, to the vast fields opened for research in nature and revelation. Let them contemplate the great facts of duty and destiny, and the mind will expand and strengthen. Instead of educated weaklings, institutions of learning may send forth people strong to think and to act, who are masters and not slaves of circumstances, who possess breadth of mind, clearness of thought, and the courage of their convictions.

Such an education provides more than mental discipline; it provides more than physical training. It strengthens the character, so that truth and uprightness are not sacrificed to selfish desire or worldly ambition. It fortifies the mind against evil. Instead of some master passion becoming a power to destroy, every motive and desire are brought into conformity to the great principles of right. As the perfection of His character is dwelt upon, the mind is renewed, and the soul is re-created in the image of God. . . .

Higher than the highest human thought can reach is God's ideal for His children. Godliness—godlikeness—is the goal to be reached. Before the students there is opened a path of continual progress. They have an object to achieve, a standard to attain, that includes everything good, and pure, and noble. They will advance as fast and as far as possible in every branch of true knowledge. But their efforts will be directed to objects as much higher than mere selfish and temporal interests as the heavens are higher than the earth.—*Education,* pp. 17–19.

July 21

The Power of Temperance

You were bought at a price; therefore glorify God in your body and in your spirit, which are God's.
—*1 Corinthians 6:20.*

Temperance in all things of this life is to be taught and practiced. Temperance in eating, drinking, sleeping, and dressing is one of the grand principles of the religious life. Truth brought into the sanctuary of the soul will guide in the treatment of the body. Nothing that concerns the health of the human agent is to be regarded with indifference. Our eternal welfare depends upon the use we make during this life of our time, strength, and influence.

Only one lease of life is granted us here; and the inquiry with everyone should be, How can I invest my life that it may yield the greatest profit?

Our first duty toward God and our fellow beings is that of self-development. Every faculty with which the Creator has endowed us should be cultivated to the highest degree of perfection, that we may be able to do the greatest amount of good of which we are capable. Hence that time is spent to good account which is directed to the establishment and preservation of sound physical and mental health. We cannot afford to dwarf or cripple a single function of mind or body by overwork or by abuse of any part of the living machinery. As surely as we do this, we must suffer the consequences. . . .

Every day people in positions of trust have decisions to make upon which depend results of great importance. Often they have to think rapidly, and this can be done successfully by those only who practice strict temperance. The mind strengthens under the correct treatment of the physical and mental powers. If the strain is not too great, new vigor comes with every taxation. . . .

Those who, like Daniel, refuse to defile themselves will reap the reward of their temperate habits. With their greater physical stamina and increased power of endurance, they have a bank of deposit upon which to draw in case of emergency.

Right physical habits promote mental superiority. Intellectual power, physical strength, and longevity depend upon immutable laws. There is no happen-so, no chance, about this matter. Nature's God will not interfere to preserve us from the consequences of violating nature's laws.—*Child Guidance,* pp. 394–396.

The Example of John the Baptist

For he will be great in the sight of the Lord, and shall drink neither wine nor strong drink. He will also be filled with the Holy Spirit, even from his mother's womb.—Luke 1:15.

As a prophet, John was "to turn the hearts of the fathers to the children, and the disobedient to the wisdom of the just; to make ready a people prepared for the Lord." In preparing the way for Christ's first advent, he was a representative of those who are to prepare a people for our Lord's second coming. The world is given to self-indulgence. Errors and fables abound. Satan's snares for destroying souls are multiplied. All who would perfect holiness in the fear of God must learn the lessons of temperance and self-control. The appetites and passions must be held in subjection to the higher powers of the mind. This self-discipline is essential to that mental strength and spiritual insight which will enable us to understand and to practice the sacred truths of God's word. For this reason temperance finds its place in the work of preparation for Christ's second coming.

In the natural order of things, the son of Zacharias would have been educated for the priesthood. But the training of the rabbinical schools would have unfitted him for his work. God did not send him to the teachers of theology to learn how to interpret the Scriptures. He called him to the desert, that he might learn of nature and nature's God.

It was a lonely region where he found his home, in the midst of barren hills, wild ravines, and rocky caves. But it was his choice to forgo the enjoyments and luxuries of life for the stern discipline of the wilderness. Here his surroundings were favorable to habits of simplicity and self-denial. Uninterrupted by the clamor of the world, he could here study the lessons of nature, of revelation, and of Providence. The words of the angel to Zacharias had been often repeated to John by his God-fearing parents. From childhood his mission had been kept before him, and he had accepted the holy trust. To him the solitude of the desert was a welcome escape from society in which suspicion, unbelief, and impurity had become well-nigh all-pervading. He distrusted his own power to withstand temptation, and shrank from constant contact with sin, lest he should lose the sense of its exceeding sinfulness.

Dedicated to God as a Nazarite from his birth, he made the vow his own in a life-long consecration.—*The Desire of Ages,* pp. 101, 102.

Parental Commitment

Walk as children of light.
—Ephesians 5:8.

A sacred trust is committed to parents, to guard the physical and moral constitutions of their children, so that the nervous system may be well balanced, and the soul not endangered. Fathers and mothers should understand the laws of life, that they may not, through ignorance, allow wrong tendencies to develop in their children. The diet affects both physical and moral health. How carefully, then, should mothers study to supply the table with the most simple, healthful food, in order that the digestive organs may not be weakened, the nerves unbalanced, or the instruction which they give their children counteracted.

Satan sees that he cannot have so great power over minds when the appetite is kept under control as when it is indulged, and he is constantly working to lead us to indulgence. Under the influence of unhealthful food, the conscience becomes stupefied, the mind is darkened, and its susceptibility to impressions is impaired. But the guilt of the transgressor is not lessened because the conscience has been violated till it has become insensible.

Since a healthy state of mind depends upon the normal condition of the vital forces, what care should be exercised that neither stimulants nor narcotics be used! Yet we see that a large number of those who profess to be Christians are using tobacco. They deplore the evils of intemperance; yet while speaking against the use of liquors, these very men will eject the juice of tobacco. There must be a change of sentiment with reference to tobacco-using before the root of the evil will be reached. We press the subject still closer. Tea and coffee are fostering the appetite for stronger stimulants. And then we come still closer home, to the preparation of food, and ask, Is temperance practiced in all things? are the reforms which are essential to health and happiness carried out here?

All true Christians will have control of their appetites and passions. Unless they are free from the bondage of appetite, they cannot be true, obedient servants of Christ. The indulgence of appetite and passion blunts the effect of truth upon the heart. It is impossible for the spirit and power of the truth to sanctify them, soul, body, and spirit, when they are controlled by sensual desires.—*Fundamentals of Christian Education,* pp. 143, 144.

2016

Appetite Cannot Be Trusted

Therefore, whether you eat or drink, or whatever you do, do all to the glory of God.—1 Corinthians 10:31.

Our bodies are built up from the food we eat. There is a constant breaking down of the tissues of the body; every movement of every organ involves waste, and this waste is repaired from our food. Each organ of the body requires its share of nutrition. The brain must be supplied with its portion; the bones, muscles, and nerves demand theirs. It is a wonderful process that transforms the food into blood and uses this blood to build up the varied parts of the body; but this process is going on continually, supplying with life and strength each nerve, muscle, and tissue.

Those foods should be chosen that best supply the elements needed for building up the body. In this choice, appetite is not a safe guide. Through wrong habits of eating, the appetite has become perverted. Often it demands food that impairs health and causes weakness instead of strength. We cannot safely be guided by the customs of society. The disease and suffering that everywhere prevail are largely due to popular errors in regard to diet.

In order to know what are the best foods, we must study God's original plan for our diet. He who created us and who understands our needs appointed Adam his food. "Behold," He said, "I have given you every herb yielding seed, . . . and every tree, in which is the fruit of a tree yielding seed; to you it shall be for food." (Genesis 1:29, A.R.V.) Upon leaving Eden to gain their livelihood by tilling the earth under the curse of sin, mankind received permission to eat also "the herb of the field." (Genesis 3:18.)

Grains, fruits, nuts, and vegetables constitute the diet chosen for us by our Creator. These foods, prepared in as simple and natural a manner as possible, are the most healthful and nourishing. They impart a strength, a power of endurance, and a vigor of intellect that are not afforded by a more complex and stimulating diet. . . .

Our bodies are Christ's purchased possession, and we are not at liberty to do with them as we please. All who understand the laws of health should realize their obligation to obey these laws which God has established in their being. Obedience to the laws of health is to be made a matter of personal duty.—*The Ministry of Healing,* pp. 295, 296, 310.

July 25

Be Consistent

Beloved, I pray that you may prosper in all things and be in health, just as your soul prospers.
—3 John 2.

In most cases two meals a day are preferable to three. Supper, when taken at an early hour, interferes with the digestion of the previous meal. When taken later, it is not itself digested before bedtime. Thus the stomach fails of securing proper rest. The sleep is disturbed, the brain and nerves are wearied, the appetite for breakfast is impaired, the whole system is unrefreshed and is unready for the day's duties.

The importance of regularity in the time for eating and sleeping should not be overlooked. Since the work of building up the body takes place during the hours of rest, it is essential, especially in youth, that sleep should be regular and abundant.

So far as possible we should avoid hurried eating. The shorter the time for a meal, the less should be eaten. It is better to omit a meal than to eat without proper mastication.

Mealtime should be a season for social interaction and refreshment. Everything that can burden or irritate should be banished. Let trust and kindliness and gratitude to the Giver of all good be cherished, and the conversation will be cheerful, a pleasant flow of thought that will uplift without wearying.

The observance of temperance and regularity in all things has a wonderful power. It will do more than circumstances or natural endowments in promoting that sweetness and serenity of disposition which count so much in smoothing life's pathway. At the same time the power of self-control thus acquired will be found one of the most valuable of equipments for grappling successfully with the stern duties and realities that await every human being.

Wisdom's "ways are ways of pleasantness, and all her paths are peace." (Proverbs 3:17.) Let all the youth in our land, with the possibilities before them of a destiny higher than that of crowned kings, ponder the lesson conveyed in the words of the wise man, "Blessed art thou, O land, when . . . thy princes eat in due season, for strength, and not for drunkenness!" (Ecclesiastes 10:17.)—*Education,* pp. 205, 206.

Touch Not, Taste Not

Fear the Lord and depart from evil. It will be health to your flesh, and strength to your bones.—Proverbs 3:7, 8.

There is work for mothers in helping their children to form correct habits and pure tastes. Educate the appetite; teach the children to abhor stimulants. Bring your children up to have moral stamina to resist the evil that surrounds them. Teach them that they are not to be swayed by others, that they are not to yield to strong influences, but to influence others for good.

Great efforts are made to put down intemperance; but there is much effort that is not directed to the right point. The advocates of temperance reform should be awake to the evils resulting from the use of unwholesome food, condiments, tea, and coffee. We bid all temperance workers Godspeed; but we invite them to look more deeply into the cause of the evil they war against and to be sure that they are consistent in reform.

It must be kept before the people that the right balance of the mental and moral powers depends in a great degree on the right condition of the physical system. All narcotics and unnatural stimulants that enfeeble and degrade the physical nature tend to lower the tone of the intellect and morals. Intemperance lies at the foundation of the moral depravity of the world. By the indulgence of perverted appetite, men and women lose their power to resist temptation.

Temperance reformers have a work to do in educating the people in these lines. Teach them that health, character, and even life, are endangered by the use of stimulants, which excite the exhausted energies to unnatural, spasmodic action.

In relation to tea, coffee, tobacco, and alcoholic drinks, the only safe course is to touch not, taste not, handle not. The tendency of tea, coffee, and similar drinks is in the same direction as that of alcoholic liquor and tobacco, and in some cases the habit is as difficult to break as it is for the drunkard to give up intoxicants. Those who attempt to leave off these stimulants will for a time feel a loss and will suffer without them. But by persistence they will overcome the craving and cease to feel the lack. Nature may require a little time to recover from the abuse she has suffered; but give her a chance, and she will again rally and perform her work nobly and well.—*The Ministry of Healing,* pp. 334, 335.

July 27

The Highway to Drunkenness

Do not look on the wine when it is red, when it sparkles in the cup, when it swirls around smoothly; at the last it bites like a serpent.
—*Proverbs 23:31, 32.*

Intoxication is just as really produced by wine, beer, and cider as by stronger drinks. The use of these drinks awakens the taste for those that are stronger, and thus the liquor habit is established. Moderate drinking is the school in which people are educated for the drunkard's career. Yet so insidious is the work of these milder stimulants that the highway to drunkenness is entered before the victim suspects his danger.

Some who are never considered really drunk are always under the influence of mild intoxicants. They are feverish, unstable in mind, unbalanced. Imagining themselves secure, they go on and on, until every barrier is broken down, every principle sacrificed. The strongest resolutions are undermined, the highest considerations are not sufficient to keep the debased appetite under the control of reason.

The Bible nowhere sanctions the use of intoxicating wine. The wine that Christ made from water at the marriage feast of Cana was the pure juice of the grape. This is the "new wine . . . found in the cluster," of which the Scripture says, "Destroy it not; for a blessing is in it." (Isaiah 65:8.)

It was Christ who, in the Old Testament, gave the warning to Israel, "Wine is a mocker, strong drink is raging: and whosoever is deceived thereby is not wise." (Proverbs 20:1.) He Himself provided no such beverage. Satan tempts us to indulgence that will becloud reason and benumb the spiritual perceptions, but Christ teaches us to bring the lower nature into subjection. He never places before us that which would be a temptation. His whole life was an example of self-denial. It was to break the power of appetite that in the forty days' fast in the wilderness He suffered in our behalf the severest test that humanity could endure. It was Christ who directed that John the Baptist should drink neither wine nor strong drink. It was He who enjoined similar abstinence upon the wife of Manoah. Christ did not contradict His own teaching. The unfermented wine that He provided for the wedding guests was a wholesome and refreshing drink. This is the wine that was used by our Saviour and His disciples in the first Communion.—*The Ministry of Healing*, pp. 332, 333.

July 28

Offensive to Others

We give no offense in anything.
—2 Corinthians 6:3.

Tobacco is a slow, insidious, but most malignant poison. In whatever form it is used, it tells upon the constitution; it is all the more dangerous because its effects are slow and at first hardly perceptible. It excites and then paralyzes the nerves. It weakens and clouds the brain. Often it affects the nerves in a more powerful manner than does intoxicating drink. It is more subtle, and its effects are difficult to eradicate from the system. Its use excites a thirst for strong drink and in many cases lays the foundation for the liquor habit.

The use of tobacco is inconvenient, expensive, uncleanly, defiling to the user, and offensive to others. Its devotees are encountered everywhere. You rarely pass through a crowd but some smoker puffs his poisoned breath in your face. It is unpleasant and unhealthful to remain in a railway car or in a room where the atmosphere is laden with the fumes of liquor and tobacco. Though some persist in using these poisons themselves, what right have they to defile the air that others must breathe?

Among children and youth the use of tobacco is working untold harm. The unhealthful practices of past generations affect the children and youth of today. Mental inability, physical weakness, disordered nerves, and unnatural cravings are transmitted as a legacy from parents to children. And the same practices, continued by the children, are increasing and perpetuating the evil results. To this cause in no small degree is owing the physical, mental, and moral deterioration which is becoming such a cause of alarm.

Boys begin the use of tobacco at a very early age. The habit thus formed when body and mind are especially susceptible to its effects, undermines the physical strength, dwarfs the body, stupefies the mind, and corrupts the morals. . . .

I appeal to those who profess to believe and obey the word of God: Can you as Christians indulge a habit that is paralyzing your intellect and robbing you of power rightly to estimate eternal realities? Can you consent daily to rob God of service which is His due, and to rob your fellow human beings, both of service you might render and of the power of example?

Have you considered your responsibility as God's stewards, for the means in your hands? How much of the Lord's money do you spend for tobacco? —*The Ministry of Healing*, pp. 327–330.

JULY 29 2016

DANGEROUS THEORIES

For You, LORD, are good, and ready to forgive, and abundant in mercy to all those who call upon You.—Psalm 86:5.

Today there are coming into educational institutions and into the churches everywhere spiritualistic teachings that undermine faith in God and in His word. The theory that God is an essence pervading all nature is received by many who profess to believe the Scriptures; but, however beautifully clothed, this theory is a most dangerous deception. It misrepresents God and is a dishonor to His greatness and majesty. And it surely tends not only to mislead, but to debase men and women. Darkness is its element, sensuality its sphere. The result of accepting it is separation from God. And to fallen human nature this means ruin.

Our condition through sin is unnatural, and the power that restores us must be supernatural, else it has no value. There is but one power that can break the hold of evil from human hearts, and that is the power of God in Jesus Christ. Only through the blood of the Crucified One is there cleansing from sin. His grace alone can enable us to resist and subdue the tendencies of our fallen nature. The spiritualistic theories concerning God make His grace of no effect. If God is an essence pervading all nature, then He dwells in everyone; and in order to attain holiness, we have only to develop the power within us.

These theories, followed to their logical conclusion, sweep away the whole Christian economy. They do away with the necessity for the atonement and make us our own savior. These theories regarding God make His word of no effect, and those who accept them are in great danger of being led finally to look upon the whole Bible as a fiction. They may regard virtue as better than vice; but, having shut out God from His rightful position of sovereignty, they place their dependence upon human power, which, without God, is worthless. The unaided human will has no real power to resist and overcome evil. The defenses of the soul are broken down. Mankind has no barrier against sin. When once the restraints of God's word and His Spirit are rejected, we know not to what depths one may sink. . . .

The revelation of Himself that God has given in His word is for our study. This we may seek to understand. But beyond this we are not to penetrate. —*The Ministry of Healing,* pp. 428, 429.

Effects of Gratitude and Praise

The fear of the Lord is a fountain of life.
—Proverbs 14:27.

Nothing tends more to promote health of body and of soul than does a spirit of gratitude and praise. It is a positive duty to resist melancholy, discontented thoughts and feelings—as much a duty as it is to pray. If we are heaven-bound, how can we go as a band of mourners, groaning and complaining all along the way to our Father's house?

Those professed Christians who are constantly complaining, and who seem to think cheerfulness and happiness a sin, have not genuine religion. Those who take a mournful pleasure in all that is melancholy in the natural world, who choose to look upon dead leaves rather than to gather the beautiful living flowers, who see no beauty in grand mountain heights and in valleys clothed with living green, who close their senses to the joyful voice which speaks to them in nature, and which is sweet and musical to the listening ear—these are not in Christ. They are gathering to themselves gloom and darkness, when they might have brightness, even the Sun of Righteousness arising in their hearts with healing in His beams.

Often your mind may be clouded because of pain. Then do not try to think. You know that Jesus loves you. He understands your weakness. You may do His will by simply resting in His arms.

It is a law of nature that our thoughts and feelings are encouraged and strengthened as we give them utterance. While words express thoughts, it is also true that thoughts follow words. If we would give more expression to our faith, rejoice more in the blessings that we know we have—the great mercy and love of God—we should have more faith and greater joy. No tongue can express, no finite mind can conceive, the blessing that results from appreciating the goodness and love of God. Even on earth we may have joy as a wellspring, never failing, because fed by the streams that flow from the throne of God.

Then let us educate our hearts and lips to speak the praise of God for His matchless love. Let us educate our souls to be hopeful and to abide in the light shining from the cross of Calvary. Never should we forget that we are children of the heavenly King, sons and daughters of the Lord of hosts. It is our privilege to maintain a calm repose in God.—*The Ministry of Healing*, pp. 251–253.

July 31

The Danger of Self-Trust

Yes, we had the sentence of death in ourselves, that we should not trust in ourselves but in God who raises the dead.
—2 Corinthians 1:9.

The thoughts must be centered upon God. We must put forth earnest effort to overcome the evil tendencies of the natural heart. Our efforts, our self-denial and perseverance, must be proportionate to the infinite value of the object of which we are in pursuit. Only by overcoming as Christ overcame shall we win the crown of life.

Our great danger is in being self-deceived, indulging self-sufficiency, and thus separating from God, the source of our strength. Our natural tendencies, unless corrected by the Holy Spirit of God, have in them the seeds of moral death. Unless we become vitally connected with God, we cannot resist the unhallowed effects of self-indulgence, self-love, and temptation to sin.

In order to receive help from Christ, we must realize our need. We must have a true knowledge of ourselves. It is only those who know themselves to be sinners that Christ can save. Only as we see our utter helplessness and renounce all self-trust, shall we lay hold on divine power.

It is not only at the beginning of the Christian life that this renunciation of self is to be made. At every advance step heavenward it is to be renewed. All our good works are dependent on a power outside of ourselves; therefore there needs to be a continual reaching out of the heart after God, a constant, earnest confession of sin and humbling of the soul before Him. Perils surround us; and we are safe only as we feel our weakness and cling with the grasp of faith to our mighty Deliverer.

We must turn away from a thousand topics that invite attention. There are matters that consume time and arouse inquiry, but end in nothing. The highest interests demand the close attention and energy that are so often given to comparatively insignificant things. . . .

The knowledge of God and of Jesus Christ expressed in character is an exaltation above everything else that is esteemed on earth or in heaven. It is the very highest education. It is the key that opens the portals of the heavenly city. This knowledge it is God's purpose that all who put on Christ shall possess.—*The Ministry of Healing,* pp. 455–457.

A United Church

August 1 2016

God's Chosen

Husbands, love your wives, just as Christ also loved the church and gave Himself for her.
—Ephesians 5:25.

God has a church upon the earth who are His chosen people, who keep His commandments. He is leading, not stray offshoots, not one here and one there, but a people. The truth is a sanctifying power; but the church militant is not the church triumphant. There are tares among the wheat. "Wilt thou then that we . . . gather them up?" was the question of the servant; but the master answered, "Nay; lest while ye gather up the tares, ye root up also the wheat with them." The gospel net draws not only good fish, but bad ones as well, and the Lord only knows who are His.

It is our individual duty to walk humbly with God. We are not to seek any strange, new message. We are not to think that the chosen ones of God who are trying to walk in the light compose Babylon.

Although there are evils existing in the church, and will be until the end of the world, the church in these last days is to be the light of the world that is polluted and demoralized by sin. The church, enfeebled and defective, needing to be reproved, warned, and counseled, is the only object upon earth upon which Christ bestows His supreme regard. The world is a workshop in which, through the cooperation of human and divine agencies, Jesus is making experiments by His grace and divine mercy upon human hearts.

God has a distinct people, a church on earth, second to none, but superior to all in their facilities to teach the truth, to vindicate the law of God. God has divinely appointed agencies—people whom He is leading, who have borne the heat and burden of the day, who are cooperating with heavenly instrumentalities to advance the kingdom of Christ in our world. Let all unite with these chosen agents, and be found at last among those who have the patience of the saints, who keep the commandments of God, and have the faith of Jesus.

The church of God below is one with the church of God above. Believers on the earth and the beings in heaven who have never fallen constitute one church.—*Counsels for the Church,* p. 240.

2016

God's Fortress

I write so that you may know how you ought to conduct yourself in the house of God, which is the church of the living God, the pillar and ground of the truth.—1 Timothy 3:15.

The church is God's appointed agency for our salvation. It was organized for service, and its mission is to carry the gospel to the world. From the beginning it has been God's plan that through His church shall be reflected to the world His fullness and His sufficiency. The members of the church, those whom He has called out of darkness into His marvelous light, are to show forth His glory. The church is the repository of the riches of the grace of Christ; and through the church will eventually be made manifest, even to "the principalities and powers in heavenly places," the final and full display of the love of God. (Ephesians 3:10.)

Many and wonderful are the promises recorded in the Scriptures regarding the church. "Mine house shall be called an house of prayer for all people." (Isaiah 56:7.) "I will make them and the places round about My hill a blessing; and I will cause the shower to come down in his season; there shall be showers of blessing." (Ezekiel 34:26.) . . .

The church is God's fortress, His city of refuge, which He holds in a revolted world. Any betrayal of the church is treachery to Him who has bought mankind with the blood of His only-begotten Son. From the beginning, faithful souls have constituted the church on earth. In every age the Lord has had His watchmen, who have borne a faithful testimony to the generation in which they lived. These sentinels gave the message of warning; and when they were called to lay off their armor, others took up the work. God brought these witnesses into covenant relation with Himself, uniting the church on earth with the church in heaven. He has sent forth His angels to minister to His church, and the gates of hell have not been able to prevail against His people.

Through centuries of persecution, conflict, and darkness, God has sustained His church. Not one cloud has fallen upon it that He has not prepared for; not one opposing force has risen to counterwork His work, that He has not foreseen. All has taken place as He predicted. He has not left His church forsaken, but has traced in prophetic declarations what would occur, and that which His Spirit inspired the prophets to foretell has been brought about. All His purposes will be fulfilled. His law is linked with His throne, and no power of evil can destroy it. Truth is inspired and guarded by God; and it will triumph over all opposition.—*The Acts of the Apostles,* pp. 9–12.

AUGUST 3

UNITY OF THE FAITH

Here is the patience of the saints; here are those who keep the commandments of God and the faith of Jesus.—Revelation 14:12.

God is leading a people out from the world upon the exalted platform of eternal truth, the commandments of God and the faith of Jesus. He will discipline and fit up His people. They will not be at variance, one believing one thing, and another having faith and views entirely opposite, each moving independently of the body. Through the diversity of the gifts and governments that He has placed in the church, they will all come to the unity of the faith. If one man takes his views of Bible truth without regard to the opinions of his brethren, and justifies his course, alleging that he has a right to his own peculiar views, and then presses them upon others, how can he be fulfilling the prayer of Christ? And if another and still another arises, each asserting his right to believe and talk what he pleases without reference to the faith of the body, where will be that harmony which existed between Christ and His Father, and which Christ prayed might exist among His brethren?

God is leading out a people and establishing them upon the one great platform of faith, the commandments of God and the testimony of Jesus. He has given His people a straight chain of Bible truth, clear and connected. This truth is of heavenly origin and has been searched for as for hidden treasure. It has been dug out through careful searching of the Scriptures and through much prayer. . . .

The heart of God never yearned toward His earthly children with deeper love and more compassionate tenderness than now. There never was a time when God was ready and waiting to do more for His people than now. And He will instruct and save all who choose to be saved in His appointed way. Those who are spiritual can discern spiritual things and see tokens of the presence and work of God everywhere. Satan, by his skillful and wicked strategy, led our first parents from the Garden of Eden—from their innocence and purity into sin and unspeakable wretchedness. He has not ceased to destroy; all the forces which he can command are diligently employed by him in these last days to compass the ruin of souls. . . .

But in order to be saved you must accept the yoke of Christ and lay off the yoke which you have fashioned for your neck. The victory that Jesus gained in the wilderness is a pledge to you of the victory that you may gain through His name. Your only hope and salvation is in overcoming as Christ overcame.—*Testimonies for the Church,* vol. 3, pp. 446, 447, 455–457.

2016

A CHANNEL OF LIGHT

Arise and go into the city, and you will be told what you must do.—Acts 9:6.

Ananias could scarcely credit the words of the angel; for the reports of Saul's bitter persecution of the saints at Jerusalem had spread far and wide. He presumed to expostulate: "Lord, I have heard by many of this man, how much evil he hath done to Thy saints at Jerusalem: and here he hath authority from the chief priests to bind all that call on Thy name." But the command was imperative: "Go thy way: for he is a chosen vessel unto Me, to bear My name before the Gentiles, and kings, and the children of Israel."

Obedient to the direction of the angel, Ananias sought out the man who had but recently breathed out threatenings against all who believed on the name of Jesus; and putting his hands on the head of the penitent sufferer, he said, "Brother Saul, the Lord, even Jesus, that appeared unto thee in the way as thou camest, hath sent me, that thou mightest receive thy sight, and be filled with the Holy Ghost." . . .

Thus Jesus gave sanction to the authority of His organized church and placed Saul in connection with His appointed agencies on earth. Christ had now a church as His representative on earth, and to it belonged the work of directing the repentant sinner in the way of life.

Many have an idea that they are responsible to Christ alone for their light and experience, independent of His recognized followers on earth. Jesus is the friend of sinners, and His heart is touched with their woe. He has all power, both in heaven and on earth; but He respects the means that He has ordained for our enlightenment and salvation; He directs sinners to the church, which He has made a channel of light to the world.

When, in the midst of his blind error and prejudice, Saul was given a revelation of the Christ whom he was persecuting, he was placed in direct communication with the church, which is the light of the world. In this case Ananias represents Christ, and also represents Christ's ministers upon the earth, who are appointed to act in His stead. In Christ's stead Ananias touches the eyes of Saul, that they may receive sight. In Christ's stead he places his hands upon him, and, as he prays in Christ's name, Saul receives the Holy Ghost. All is done in the name and by the authority of Christ. Christ is the fountain; the church is the channel of communication.—*The Acts of the Apostles*, pp. 121, 122.

August 5

Working Together

Seek out from among you seven men of good reputation, full of the Holy Spirit and wisdom, whom we may appoint over this business.
—*Acts 6:3.*

As disciples were multiplied, the enemy succeeded in arousing the suspicions of some who had formerly been in the habit of looking with jealousy on their brethren in the faith and of finding fault with their spiritual leaders, and so "there arose a murmuring of the Grecians against the Hebrews." The cause of complaint was an alleged neglect of the Greek widows in the daily distribution of assistance. . . .

The disciples of Jesus had reached a crisis in their experience. Under the wise leadership of the apostles, who labored unitedly in the power of the Holy Spirit, the work committed to the gospel messengers was developing rapidly. The church was continually enlarging, and this growth in membership brought increasingly heavy burdens upon those in charge. No one person, or even one set of persons, could continue to bear these burdens alone, without imperiling the future prosperity of the church. . . . Summoning a meeting of the believers, the apostles were led by the Holy Spirit to outline a plan for the better organization of all the working forces of the church. . . .

The appointment of the seven to take the oversight of special lines of work, proved a great blessing to the church. . . .

The proclamation of the gospel was to be world-wide in its extent, and the messengers of the cross could not hope to fulfill their important mission unless they should remain united in the bonds of Christian unity, and thus reveal to the world that they were one with Christ in God. Had not their divine Leader prayed to the Father, "Keep through Thine own name those whom Thou hast given Me, that they may be one, as We are"? . . .

Only as they were united with Christ could the disciples hope to have the accompanying power of the Holy Spirit and the co-operation of angels of heaven. With the help of these divine agencies they would present before the world a united front and would be victorious in the conflict they were compelled to wage unceasingly against the powers of darkness.—*The Acts of the Apostles,* pp. 87–89.

An Example of Church Unity

The Lord added to the church daily those who were being saved.
—Acts 2:47.

To the early church had been entrusted a constantly enlarging work—that of establishing centers of light and blessing wherever there were honest souls willing to give themselves to the service of Christ. The proclamation of the gospel was to be world-wide in its extent, and the messengers of the cross could not hope to fulfill their important mission unless they should remain united in the bonds of Christian unity, and thus reveal to the world that they were one with Christ in God. Had not their divine Leader prayed to the Father, "Keep through Thine own name those whom Thou hast given Me, that they may be one, as We are"? And had He not declared of His disciples, "The world hath hated them, because they are not of the world"? Had He not pleaded with the Father that they might be "made perfect in one," "that the world may believe that Thou hast sent Me"? (John 17:11, 14, 23, 21.) Their spiritual life and power was dependent on a close connection with the One by whom they had been commissioned to preach the gospel.

Only as they were united with Christ could the disciples hope to have the accompanying power of the Holy Spirit and the cooperation of angels of heaven. With the help of these divine agencies they would present before the world a united front and would be victorious in the conflict they were compelled to wage unceasingly against the powers of darkness. As they should continue to labor unitedly, heavenly messengers would go before them, opening the way; hearts would be prepared for the reception of truth, and many would be won to Christ. So long as they remained united, the church would go forth "fair as the moon, clear as the sun, and terrible as an army with banners." (Song of Solomon 6:10.) Nothing could withstand her onward progress. The church would advance from victory to victory, gloriously fulfilling her divine mission of proclaiming the gospel to the world.

The organization of the church at Jerusalem was to serve as a model for the organization of churches in every other place where messengers of truth should win converts to the gospel. Those to whom was given the responsibility of the general oversight of the church were not to lord it over God's heritage, but, as wise shepherds, were to "feed the flock of God." (1 Peter 5:2.)—*The Acts of the Apostles*, pp. 90, 91.

August 7

Church Order

Then the word of God spread, and the number of the disciples multiplied greatly.—Acts 6:7.

The same principles of piety and justice that were to guide the rulers among God's people in the time of Moses and of David, were also to be followed by those given the oversight of the newly organized church of God in the gospel dispensation. In the work of setting things in order in all the churches, and ordaining suitable men to act as officers, the apostles held to the high standards of leadership outlined in the Old Testament Scriptures. They maintained that one who is called to stand in a position of leading responsibility in the church "must be blameless, as the steward of God; not self-willed, not soon angry, not given to wine, no striker, not given to filthy lucre; but a lover of hospitality, a lover of good men, sober, just, holy, temperate; holding fast the faithful word as he hath been taught, that he may be able by sound doctrine both to exhort and to convince the gainsayers." (Titus 1:7–9.)

The order that was maintained in the early Christian church made it possible for them to move forward solidly as a well-disciplined army clad with the armor of God. The companies of believers, though scattered over a large territory, were all members of one body; all moved in concert and in harmony with one another. When dissension arose in a local church, as later it did arise in Antioch and elsewhere, and the believers were unable to come to an agreement among themselves, such matters were not permitted to create a division in the church, but were referred to a general council of the entire body of believers, made up of appointed delegates from the various local churches, with the apostles and elders in positions of leading responsibility. Thus the efforts of Satan to attack the church in isolated places, were met by concerted action on the part of all; and the plans of the enemy to disrupt and destroy were thwarted.

"God is not the author of confusion, but of peace, as in all churches of the saints." (1 Corinthians 14:33.) He requires that order and system be observed in the conduct of church affairs today no less than in the days of old. He desires His work to be carried forward with thoroughness and exactness so that He may place upon it the seal of His approval. Christian is to be united with Christian, church with church, the human instrumentality cooperating with the divine, every agency subordinate to the Holy Spirit, and all combined in giving to the world the good tidings of the grace of God.—*The Acts of the Apostles*, pp. 95, 96.

The Mission of the Church

2016

The Son of Man has come to seek and to save that which was lost.
—*Luke 19:10.*

The mission of the church of Christ is to save perishing sinners. It is to make known the love of God to men and women and to win them to Christ by the efficacy of that love. The truth for this time must be carried into the dark corners of the earth, and this work may begin at home. The followers of Christ should not live selfish lives; but, imbued with the Spirit of Christ, they should work in harmony with Him.

There are causes for the present coldness and unbelief. The love of the world and the cares of life separate the soul from God. The water of life must be in us, and flowing out from us, springing up into everlasting life. We must work out what God works in. If Christians would enjoy the light of life, they must increase their efforts to bring others to the knowledge of the truth. Their lives must be characterized by exertion and sacrifices to do others good; and then there will be no complaints of lack of enjoyment.

Angels are ever engaged in working for the happiness of others. This is their joy. That which selfish hearts would consider humiliating service, ministering to those who are wretched and in every way inferior in character and rank, is the work of the pure, sinless angels in the royal courts of heaven. The spirit of Christ's self-sacrificing love is the spirit which pervades heaven and is the very essence of its bliss.

Those who feel no special pleasure in seeking to be a blessing to others, in working, even at a sacrifice, to do them good, cannot have the spirit of Christ or of heaven; for they have no union with the work of heavenly angels and cannot participate in the bliss that imparts elevated joy to them. . . . If the joy of angels is to see sinners repent, will it not be the joy of sinners, saved by the blood of Christ, to see others repent and turn to Christ through their instrumentality? In working in harmony with Christ and the holy angels we shall experience a joy that cannot be realized aside from this work.

The principle of the cross of Christ brings all who believe under heavy obligations to deny self, to impart light to others, and to give of their means to extend the light. If they are in connection with heaven they will be engaged in the work in harmony with the angels.—*Testimonies for the Church,* vol. 3, pp. 381, 382.

August 9

Power in the Church

But you shall receive power when the Holy Spirit has come upon you.
—Acts 1:8.

When He [the Spirit of truth] is come, He will reprove the world of sin, and of righteousness, and of judgment." The preaching of the word will be of no avail without the continual presence and aid of the Holy Spirit. This is the only effectual teacher of divine truth. Only when the truth is accompanied to the heart by the Spirit will it quicken the conscience or transform the life. We might be able to present the letter of the word of God, we might be familiar with all its commands and promises; but unless the Holy Spirit sets home the truth, no souls will fall on the Rock and be broken. No amount of education, no advantages, however great, can make one a channel of light without the cooperation of the Spirit of God. The sowing of the gospel seed will not be a success unless the seed is quickened into life by the dew of heaven. Before one book of the New Testament was written, before one gospel sermon had been preached after Christ's ascension, the Holy Spirit came upon the praying apostles. Then the testimony of their enemies was, "Ye have filled Jerusalem with your doctrine." (Acts 5:28.)

Christ has promised the gift of the Holy Spirit to His church, and the promise belongs to us as much as to the first disciples. But like every other promise, it is given on conditions. There are many who believe and profess to claim the Lord's promise; they talk *about* Christ and *about* the Holy Spirit, yet receive no benefit. They do not surrender the soul to be guided and controlled by the divine agencies. We cannot use the Holy Spirit. The Spirit is to use us. Through the Spirit God works in His people "to will and to do of His good pleasure." (Philippians 2:13.) But many will not submit to this. They want to manage themselves. This is why they do not receive the heavenly gift. Only to those who wait humbly upon God, who watch for His guidance and grace, is the Spirit given. The power of God awaits their demand and reception. This promised blessing, claimed by faith, brings all other blessings in its train. It is given according to the riches of the grace of Christ, and He is ready to supply every soul according to the capacity to receive.

In His discourse to the disciples, Jesus made no mournful allusion to His own sufferings and death. His last legacy to them was a legacy of peace. He said, "Peace I leave with you, My peace I give unto you." (John 14:27.)—*The Desire of Ages,* pp. 671, 672.

Abide in Christ

If you keep My commandments, you will abide in My love.
—John 15:10.

This union with Christ, once formed, must be maintained. Christ said, "Abide in Me, and I in you. As the branch cannot bear fruit of itself, except it abide in the vine; no more can ye, except ye abide in Me." This is no casual touch, no off-and-on connection. The branch becomes a part of the living vine. The communication of life, strength, and fruitfulness from the root to the branches is unobstructed and constant. Separated from the vine, the branch cannot live. No more, said Jesus, can you live apart from Me. The life you have received from Me can be preserved only by continual communion. Without Me you cannot overcome one sin, or resist one temptation.

"Abide in Me, and I in you." Abiding in Christ means a constant receiving of His Spirit, a life of unreserved surrender to His service. The channel of communication must be open continually between us and our God. As the vine branch constantly draws the sap from the living vine, so are we to cling to Jesus, and receive from Him by faith the strength and perfection of His own character. . . .

The life of the vine will be manifest in fragrant fruit on the branches. "He that abideth in Me," said Jesus, "and I in him, the same bringeth forth much fruit: for without Me ye can do nothing." When we live by faith on the Son of God, the fruits of the Spirit will be seen in our lives; not one will be missing.

"My Father is the husbandman. Every branch in Me that beareth not fruit He taketh away." While the graft is outwardly united with the vine, there may be no vital connection. Then there will be no growth or fruitfulness. So there may be an apparent connection with Christ without a real union with Him by faith. A profession of religion places people in the church, but the character and conduct show whether they are in connection with Christ. If they bear no fruit, they are false branches. Their separation from Christ involves a ruin as complete as that represented by the dead branch. "If a man abide not in Me," said Christ, "he is cast forth as a branch, and is withered; and men gather them, and cast them into the fire, and they are burned."
—*The Desire of Ages,* p. 676.

August 11

Emptied of Self

He must increase, but I must decrease.
—John 3:30.

Looking in faith to the Redeemer, John had risen to the height of self-abnegation. He sought not to attract people to himself, but to lift their thoughts higher and still higher, until they should rest upon the Lamb of God. He himself had been only a voice, a cry in the wilderness. Now with joy he accepted silence and obscurity, that the eyes of all might be turned to the Light of life.

Those who are true to their calling as messengers for God will not seek honor for themselves. Love for self will be swallowed up in love for Christ. No rivalry will mar the precious cause of the gospel. They will recognize that it is their work to proclaim, as did John the Baptist, "Behold the Lamb of God, which taketh away the sin of the world." (John 1:29.) They will lift up Jesus, and with Him humanity will be lifted up. "Thus saith the high and lofty One that inhabiteth eternity, whose name is Holy; I dwell in the high and holy place, with him also that is of a contrite and humble spirit, to revive the spirit of the humble, and to revive the heart of the contrite ones." (Isaiah 57:15.)

The soul of the prophet, emptied of self, was filled with the light of the divine. As he witnessed to the Saviour's glory, his words were almost a counterpart of those that Christ Himself had spoken in His interview with Nicodemus. John said, "He that cometh from above is above all: he that is of the earth is earthly, and speaketh of the earth: He that cometh from heaven is above all. . . . For He whom God hath sent speaketh the words of God: for God giveth not the Spirit by measure unto Him." Christ could say, "I seek not Mine own will, but the will of the Father which hath sent Me." (John 5:30.) To Him it is declared, "Thou hast loved righteousness, and hated iniquity." (Hebrews 1:9.) . . .

So with the followers of Christ. We can receive of heaven's light only as we are willing to be emptied of self. We cannot discern the character of God, or accept Christ by faith, unless we consent to the bringing into captivity of every thought to the obedience of Christ. To all who do this the Holy Spirit is given without measure.—*The Desire of Ages,* pp. 179–181.

Self-Sacrifice in the Church

If we love one another, God abides in us, and His love has been perfected in us.—1 John 4:12.

The lawyer's question to Jesus had been, "What shall I do?" And Jesus, recognizing love to God and mankind as the sum of righteousness, had said, "This do, and thou shalt live." The Samaritan had obeyed the dictates of a kind and loving heart, and in this had proved himself a doer of the law. Christ bade the lawyer, "Go, and do thou likewise." (Luke 10:25, 28, 37.) Doing, and not saying merely, is expected of the children of God. "He that saith he abideth in Him ought himself also so to walk, even as He walked." (1 John 2:6.)

The lesson is no less needed in the world today than when it fell from the lips of Jesus. Selfishness and cold formality have well-nigh extinguished the fire of love, and dispelled the graces that should make fragrant the character. Many who profess His name have lost sight of the fact that Christians are to represent Christ. Unless there is practical self-sacrifice for the good of others, in the family circle, in the neighborhood, in the church, and wherever we may be, then whatever our profession, we are not Christians.

Christ has linked His interest with that of humanity, and He asks us to become one with Him for the saving of humanity. "Freely ye have received," He says, "freely give." (Matthew 10:8.) Sin is the greatest of all evils, and it is ours to pity and help the sinner. There are many who err, and who feel their shame and their folly. They are hungry for words of encouragement. They look upon their mistakes and errors, until they are driven almost to desperation. These souls we are not to neglect. If we are Christians, we shall not pass by on the other side, keeping as far as possible from the very ones who most need our help. When we see human beings in distress, whether through affliction or through sin, we shall never say, This does not concern me.

"Ye which are spiritual, restore such an one in the spirit of meekness." (Galatians 6:1.) By faith and prayer press back the power of the enemy. Speak words of faith and courage that will be as a healing balsam to the bruised and wounded one. Many, many, have fainted and become discouraged in the great struggle of life, when one word of kindly cheer would have strengthened them to overcome. Never should we pass by one suffering soul without seeking to impart to that one of the comfort wherewith we are comforted of God.—*The Desire of Ages,* pp. 504, 505.

August 13

God Leads His People

I will be their God, and they shall be My people.
—Jeremiah 31:33.

God is leading out a people to stand in perfect unity upon the platform of eternal truth. Christ gave Himself to the world that He might "purify unto Himself a peculiar people, zealous of good works." This refining process is designed to purge the church from all unrighteousness and the spirit of discord and contention, that they may build up instead of tear down, and concentrate their energies on the great work before them. God designs that His people should all come into the unity of the faith. The prayer of the Christ just prior to His crucifixion was that His disciples might be one, even as He was one with the Father, that the world might believe that the Father had sent Him. This most touching and wonderful prayer reaches down the ages, even to our day; for His words were: "Neither pray I for these alone, but for them also which shall believe on Me through their word."

How earnestly should the professed followers of Christ seek to answer this prayer in their lives. Many do not realize the sacredness of church relationship and are loath to submit to restraint and discipline. Their course of action shows that they exalt their own judgment above that of the united church, and they are not careful to guard themselves lest they encourage a spirit of opposition to its voice. Those who hold responsible positions in the church may have faults in common with other people and may err in their decisions; but notwithstanding this, the church of Christ on earth has given to them an authority that cannot be lightly esteemed. Christ, after His resurrection, delegated power unto His church, saying: "Whosesoever sins ye remit, they are remitted unto them; and whosesoever sins ye retain, they are retained." . . .

All believers should be wholehearted in their attachment to the church. Its prosperity should be their first interest, and unless they feel under sacred obligations to make their connection with the church a benefit to it in preference to themselves, it can do far better without them. It is in the power of all to do something for the cause of God. . . . The observance of external forms will never meet the great want of the human soul. A profession of Christ is not enough to enable one to stand the test of the day of judgment. There should be a perfect trust in God, a childlike dependence upon His promises, and an entire consecration to His will.—*Testimonies for the Church,* vol. 4, pp. 17, 18.

August 14

The Influence of Perfect Harmony

I, therefore, . . . beseech you to walk worthy of the calling with which you were called, . . . endeavoring to keep the unity of the Spirit in the bond of peace. —*Ephesians 4:1, 3.*

There is nothing too precious for us to give to Jesus. If we return to Him the talents of means which He has entrusted to our keeping, He will give more into our hands. Every effort we make for Christ will be rewarded by Him, and every duty we perform in His name will minister to our own happiness. God surrendered His dearly beloved Son to the agonies of the crucifixion, that all who believe on Him might become one through the name of Jesus. When Christ made so great a sacrifice to save us and bring us into unity with one another, even as He was united with the Father, what sacrifice is too great for His followers to make in order to preserve that unity?

If the world sees a perfect harmony existing in the church of God, it will be a powerful evidence to them in favor of the Christian religion. Dissensions, unhappy differences, and petty church trials dishonor our Redeemer. All these may be avoided if self is surrendered to God and the followers of Jesus obey the voice of the church. Unbelief suggests that individual independence increases our importance, that it is weak to yield our own ideas of what is right and proper to the verdict of the church; but to yield to such feelings and views is unsafe and will bring us into anarchy and confusion. Christ saw that unity and Christian fellowship were necessary to the cause of God, therefore He enjoined it upon His disciples. And the history of Christianity from that time until now proves conclusively that in union only is there strength. Let individual judgment submit to the authority of the church.

The apostles felt the necessity of strict unity, and they labored earnestly to this end. Paul exhorted his brethren in these words: "Now I beseech you, brethren, by the name of our Lord Jesus Christ, that ye all speak the same thing, and that there be no divisions among you; but that ye be perfectly joined together in the same mind and in the same judgment."

He also wrote to the Philippians: "If there be therefore any consolation in Christ, if any comfort of love, if any fellowship of the Spirit, if any bowels and mercies, fulfill ye my joy, that ye be like-minded, having the same love, being of one accord, of one mind."—*Testimonies for the Church,* vol. 4, pp. 19, 20.

August 15

Duty of the Church

If you instruct the brethren in these things, you will be a good minister of Jesus Christ.—1 Timothy 4:6.

The Holy Spirit is the breath of spiritual life in the soul. The impartation of the Spirit is the impartation of the life of Christ. It imbues the receiver with the attributes of Christ. Only those who are thus taught of God, those who possess the inward working of the Spirit, and in whose life the Christ-life is manifested, are to stand as representatives, to minister in behalf of the church.

"Whosesoever sins ye remit," said Christ, "they are remitted; . . . and whosesoever sins ye retain, they are retained." Christ here gives no liberty for anyone to pass judgment upon others. In the Sermon on the Mount He forbade this. It is the prerogative of God. But on the church in its organized capacity He places a responsibility for the individual members. Toward those who fall into sin, the church has a duty, to warn, to instruct, and if possible to restore. "Reprove, rebuke, exhort," the Lord says, "with all long-suffering and doctrine." (2 Timothy 4:2.) Deal faithfully with wrongdoing. Warn every soul that is in danger. Leave none to deceive themselves. Call sin by its right name. Declare what God has said in regard to lying, Sabbathbreaking, stealing, idolatry, and every other evil. "They which do such things shall not inherit the kingdom of God." (Galatians 5:21.) If they persist in sin, the judgment you have declared from God's word is pronounced upon them in heaven. In choosing to sin, they disown Christ; the church must show that she does not sanction their deeds, or she herself dishonors her Lord. She must say about sin what God says about it. She must deal with it as God directs, and her action is ratified in heaven. Anyone who despises the authority of the church despises the authority of Christ Himself.

But there is a brighter side to the picture. "Whosesoever sins ye remit, they are remitted." Let this thought be kept uppermost. In labor for the erring, let every eye be directed to Christ. . . .

Let the repentance of the sinner be accepted by the church with grateful hearts. Let the repenting one be led out from the darkness of unbelief into the light of faith and righteousness. Let his trembling hand be placed in the loving hand of Jesus. Such a remission is ratified in heaven.—*The Desire of Ages,* pp. 805, 806.

August 16

Dealing With Misunderstandings

Dare any of you, having a matter against another, go to law before the unrighteous, and not before the saints?
—1 Corinthians 6:1.

Whatever the character of the offense, this does not change the plan that God has made for the settlement of misunderstandings and personal injuries. Speaking alone and in the spirit of Christ to the one who is in fault will often remove the difficulty. Go to the erring one, with a heart filled with Christ's love and sympathy, and seek to adjust the matter. Reason with him calmly and quietly. Let no angry words escape your lips. Speak in a way that will appeal to his better judgment. Remember the words: "He which converteth the sinner from the error of his way shall save a soul from death, and shall hide a multitude of sins." (James 5:20.)

Take to your brother the remedy that will cure the disease of disaffection. Do your part to help him. For the sake of the peace and unity of the church, feel it a privilege as well as a duty to do this. If he will hear you, you have gained him as a friend.

All heaven is interested in the interview between the one who has been injured and the one who is in error. As the erring one accepts the reproof offered in the love of Christ, and acknowledges his wrong, asking forgiveness from God and from his brother, the sunshine of heaven fills his heart. The controversy is ended; friendship and confidence are restored. The oil of love removes the soreness caused by the wrong. The Spirit of God binds heart to heart, and there is music in heaven over the union brought about.

As those thus united in Christian fellowship offer prayer to God and pledge themselves to deal justly, to love mercy, and to walk humbly with God, great blessing comes to them. If they have wronged others they continue the work of repentance, confession, and restitution, fully set to do good to one another. This is the fulfilling of the law of Christ.

"But if he will not hear thee, then take with thee one or two more, that in the mouth of two or three witnesses every word may be established." (Matthew 18:16.) Take with you those who are spiritually minded, and talk with the one in error in regard to the wrong. He may yield to the united appeals of his brethren. As he sees their agreement in the matter, his mind may be enlightened.—*Testimonies for the Church,* vol. 7, pp. 261, 262.

August 17

Dealing With an Offender

I will forgive their iniquity, and their sin I will remember no more.
—*Jeremiah 31:34.*

If he will not hear them [see Matthew 18:15, 16], then, and not till then, the matter is to be brought before the whole body of believers. Let the members of the church, as the representatives of Christ, unite in prayer and loving entreaty that the offender may be restored. The Holy Spirit will speak through His servants, pleading with the wanderer to return to God. Paul the apostle, speaking by inspiration, says, "As though God did beseech you by us: we pray you in Christ's stead, be ye reconciled to God." (2 Corinthians 5:20.) Anyone who rejects this united overture has broken the tie that binds him to Christ, and thus has severed himself from the fellowship of the church. Henceforth, said Jesus, "let him be unto thee as an heathen man and a publican." But he is not to be regarded as cut off from the mercy of God. Let him not be despised or neglected by his former brothers and sisters in the church, but be treated with tenderness and compassion, as one of the lost sheep that Christ is still seeking to bring to His fold.

Christ's instruction as to the treatment of the erring repeats in more specific form the teaching given to Israel through Moses: "Thou shalt not hate thy brother in thine heart: thou shalt in anywise rebuke thy neighbor, that thou bear not sin for him." (Leviticus 19:17, margin.) That is, if others neglect the duty Christ has enjoined, of trying to restore those who are in error and sin, they become partakers in the sin. For evils that we might have checked, we are just as responsible as if we were guilty of the acts ourselves.

But it is to the wrongdoer himself that we are to present the wrong. We are not to make it a matter of comment and criticism among ourselves; nor even after it is told to the church, are we at liberty to repeat it to others. A knowledge of the faults of Christians will be only a cause of stumbling to the unbelieving world; and by dwelling upon these things, we ourselves can receive only harm; for it is by beholding that we become changed. While we seek to correct the errors of others, the Spirit of Christ will lead us to shield them, as far as possible, from the criticism of even their own brethren, and how much more from the censure of the unbelieving world. We ourselves are erring, and need Christ's pity and forgiveness, and just as we wish Him to deal with us, He bids us deal with one another.—*The Desire of Ages,* p. 441.

Press Together, Now

There should be no schism in the body, but . . . the members should have the same care for one another.—1 Corinthians 12:25.

Union is strength; division is weakness. When those who believe present truth are united, they exert a telling influence. Satan well understands this. Never was he more determined than now to make of none effect the truth of God by causing bitterness and dissension among the Lord's people.

The world is against us, the popular churches are against us, the laws of the land will soon be against us. If there was ever a time when the people of God should press together, it is now. God has committed to us the special truths for this time to make known to the world. The last message of mercy is now going forth. We are dealing with men and women who are judgment bound. How careful should we be in every word and act to follow closely the Pattern, that our example may lead people to Christ. With what care should we seek so to present the truth that others by beholding its beauty and simplicity may be led to receive it. If our characters testify of its sanctifying power, we shall be a continual light to others—living epistles, known and read of all men. We cannot afford now to give place to Satan by cherishing disunion, discord, and strife.

That union and love might exist among His disciples was the burden of our Saviour's last prayer for them prior to His crucifixion. With the agony of the cross before Him, His solicitude was not for Himself, but for those whom He should leave to carry forward His work in the earth. The severest trials awaited them, but Jesus saw that their greatest danger would be from a spirit of bitterness and division. . . .

All who have been benefited by the labors of God's servants should, according to their ability, unite with them in working for the salvation of souls. This is the work of all true believers, ministers and people. They should keep the grand object ever in view, all seeking to fill their proper position in the church, and all working together in order, harmony, and love. . . .

They will not neglect to labor for the strength and unity of the church. They will watch carefully lest opportunity be given for diversity and division to creep in.—*Testimonies for the Church,* vol. 5, pp. 236, 238.

August 19

The Church Is to Follow the Saviour's Rule

First be reconciled to your brother, and then come and offer your gift.
—*Matthew 5:24.*

Those who are appointed to guard the spiritual interests of the church should be careful to set a right example, giving no occasion for envy, jealousy, or suspicion, ever manifesting that same spirit of love, respect, and courtesy which they desire to encourage in their fellow church members. Diligent heed should be given to the instructions of God's word. Let every manifestation of animosity or unkindness be checked; let every root of bitterness be removed. When trouble arises between church members, the Saviour's rule should be strictly followed. All possible effort should be made to effect a reconciliation; but if the parties stubbornly persist in remaining at variance, they should be suspended till they can harmonize.

Upon the occurrence of trials in the church let all the members examine their own hearts to see if the cause of trouble does not exist within. By spiritual pride, a desire to dictate, an ambitious longing for honor or position, a lack of self-control, by the indulgence of passion or prejudice, by instability or lack of judgment, the church may be disturbed and her peace sacrificed.

Difficulties are often caused by the vendors of gossip, whose whispered hints and suggestions poison unsuspecting minds and separate the closest friends. Mischief-makers are seconded in their evil work by the many who stand with open ears and evil heart, saying: "Report, . . . and we will report it." This sin should not be tolerated among the followers of Christ. No Christian parent should permit gossip to be repeated in the family circle or remarks to be made disparaging the members of the church.

Christians should regard it as a religious duty to repress a spirit of envy or emulation. They should rejoice in the superior reputation or prosperity of their brethren, even when their own character or achievements seem to be cast in the shade. . . .

We should seek for true goodness rather than greatness. Those who possess the mind of Christ will have humble views of themselves. They will labor for the purity and prosperity of the church, and be ready to sacrifice their own interests and desires rather than to cause dissension among their fellow members.—*Testimonies for the Church,* vol. 5, pp. 241, 242.

AUGUST 20

THE GOSPEL NET

Again, the kingdom of heaven is like a dragnet that was cast into the sea and gathered some of every kind.—Matthew 13:47.

The kingdom of heaven is like unto a net, that was cast into the sea, and gathered of every kind; which, when it was full, they drew to shore, and sat down, and gathered the good into vessels, but cast the bad away. So shall it be at the end of the world: the angels shall come forth, and sever the wicked from among the just, and shall cast them into the furnace of fire: there shall be wailing and gnashing of teeth."

The casting of the net is the preaching of the gospel. This gathers both good and evil into the church. When the mission of the gospel is completed, the judgment will accomplish the work of separation. Christ saw how the existence of false members in the church would cause the way of truth to be evil spoken of. The world would revile the gospel because of the inconsistent lives of false professors. Even Christians would be caused to stumble as they saw that many who bore Christ's name were not controlled by His Spirit. Because these sinners were in the church, many would be in danger of thinking that God excused their sins. Therefore Christ lifts the veil from the future and bids all to behold that it is character, not position, which decides a person's destiny.

Both the parable of the tares and that of the net plainly teach that there is no time when all the wicked will turn to God. The wheat and the tares grow together until the harvest. The good and the bad fish are together drawn ashore for a final separation.

Again, these parables teach that there is to be no probation after the judgment. When the work of the gospel is completed, there immediately follows the separation between the good and the evil, and the destiny of each class is forever fixed.

God does not desire the destruction of any. "As I live, saith the Lord God, I have no pleasure in the death of the wicked; but that the wicked turn from his way and live. Turn ye, turn ye from your evil ways; for why will ye die?" (Ezekiel 33:11.) Throughout the period of probationary time His Spirit is entreating men and women to accept the gift of life. It is only those who reject His pleading that will be left to perish. God has declared that sin must be destroyed as an evil ruinous to the universe. Those who cling to sin will perish in its destruction.—*Christ's Object Lessons,* pp. 122, 123.

August 21

Christ's Love in the Church

Not as though I wrote a new commandment to you, but that which we have had from the beginning: that we love one another.—2 John 5.

This love is the evidence of their discipleship. "By this shall all men know that ye are My disciples," said Jesus, "if ye have love one to another." When people are bound together, not by force or self-interest, but by love, they show the working of an influence that is above every human influence. Where this oneness exists, it is evidence that the image of God is being restored in humanity, that a new principle of life has been implanted. It shows that there is power in the divine nature to withstand the supernatural agencies of evil, and that the grace of God subdues the selfishness inherent in the natural heart.

This love, manifested in the church, will surely stir the wrath of Satan. Christ did not mark out for His disciples an easy path. "If the world hate you," He said, "ye know that it hated Me before it hated you. If ye were of the world, the world would love his own: but because ye are not of the world, but I have chosen you out of the world, therefore the world hateth you. Remember the word that I said unto you, The servant is not greater than his lord. If they have persecuted Me, they will also persecute you; if they have kept My saying, they will keep yours also. But all these things will they do unto you for My name's sake, because they know not Him that sent Me." The gospel is to be carried forward by aggressive warfare, in the midst of opposition, peril, loss, and suffering. But those who do this work are only following in their Master's steps. . . .

Christ rejoiced that He could do more for His followers than they could ask or think. He spoke with assurance, knowing that an almighty decree had been given before the world was made. He knew that truth, armed with the omnipotence of the Holy Spirit, would conquer in the contest with evil; and that the bloodstained banner would wave triumphantly over His followers. He knew that the life of His trusting disciples would be like His, a series of uninterrupted victories, not seen to be such here, but recognized as such in the great hereafter. . . .

Christ did not fail, neither was He discouraged, and His followers are to manifest a faith of the same enduring nature. They are to live as He lived, and work as He worked, because they depend on Him as the great Master Worker.—*The Desire of Ages,* pp. 678, 679.

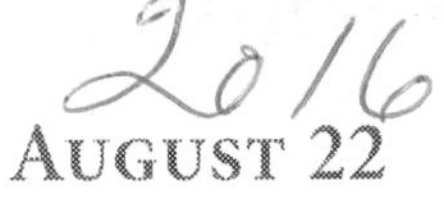

August 22

The Church Is Not One Man's Opinion

And if anyone thinks that he knows anything, he knows nothing yet as he ought to know.—1 Corinthians 8:2.

The world's Redeemer has invested great power with His church. He states the rules to be applied in cases of trial with its members. After He has given explicit directions as to the course to be pursued, He says: "Verily I say unto you, Whatsoever ye shall bind on earth shall be bound in heaven: and whatsoever [in church discipline] ye shall loose on earth shall be loosed in heaven." (Matthew 18:18.) Thus even the heavenly authority ratifies the discipline of the church in regard to its members when the Bible rule has been followed.

The word of God does not give license for lone individuals to set up their judgment in opposition to the judgment of the church, neither are they allowed to urge their opinions against the opinions of the church. If there were no church discipline and government, the church would go to fragments; it could not hold together as a body. There have ever been individuals of independent minds who have claimed that they were right, that God had especially taught, impressed, and led them. They each have a theory of their own, views peculiar to themselves, and they each claim that their views are in accordance with the word of God. Each one has a different theory and faith, yet each claims special light from God. These draw away from the body, and each one is a separate church individually. All these cannot be right, yet they all claim to be led of the Lord. The word of Inspiration is not Yea and Nay, but Yea and Amen in Christ Jesus.

Our Saviour follows His lessons of instruction with a promise that if two or three should be united in asking anything of God it should be given them. Christ here shows that there must be union with others, even in our desires for a given object. Great importance is attached to the united prayer, the union of purpose. God hears the prayers of individuals, but on this occasion Jesus was giving especial and important lessons that were to have a special bearing upon His newly organized church on the earth. There must be an agreement in the things which they desire and for which they pray. It was not merely the thoughts and exercises of one mind, liable to deception; but the petition was to be the earnest desire of several minds centered on the same point.—*Testimonies for the Church,* vol. 3, pp. 428, 429.

August 23

God's Spirit and Unity in the Church

Now all who believed were together, and had all things in common.
—Acts 2:44.

Christ declared that the divine influence of the Spirit was to be with His followers unto the end. But the promise is not appreciated as it should be; and therefore its fulfillment is not seen as it might be. The promise of the Spirit is a matter little thought of; and the result is only what might be expected—spiritual drought, spiritual darkness, spiritual declension and death. Minor matters occupy the attention, and the divine power which is necessary for the growth and prosperity of the church, and which would bring all other blessings in its train, is lacking, though offered in its infinite plenitude.

It is the absence of the Spirit that makes the gospel ministry so powerless. Learning, talent, eloquence, every natural or acquired endowment, may be possessed; but, without the presence of the Spirit of God, no heart will be touched, no sinner won to Christ. On the other hand, if they are connected with Christ, if the gifts of the Spirit are theirs, the poorest and most ignorant of His disciples will have a power that will tell upon hearts. God makes them channels for the outflowing of the highest influence in the universe.

Zeal for God moved the disciples to bear witness to the truth with mighty power. Should not this zeal fire our hearts with a determination to tell the story of redeeming love, of Christ and Him crucified? Is not the Spirit of God to come today, in answer to earnest, persevering prayer, and fill us with power for service? Why, then, is the church so weak and spiritless?

When the Holy Spirit controls the minds of our church members, there will be seen in our churches a much higher standard in speech, in ministry, in spirituality, than is now seen. The church members will be refreshed by the water of life, and the laborers, working under one Head, even Christ, will reveal their Master in spirit, in word, in deed, and will encourage one another to press forward in the grand, closing work in which we are engaged. There will be a healthy increase of unity and love, which will bear testimony to the world that God sent His Son to die for the redemption of sinners. Divine truth will be exalted; and as it shines forth as a lamp that burneth, we shall understand it more and still more clearly.—*Counsels for the Church,* p. 100.

August 24

2016

Unity Begets Strength

Behold, how good and how pleasant it is for brethren to dwell together in unity!
—*Psalm 133:1.*

Do we expect to meet our brethren and sisters in heaven? If we can live with them here in peace and harmony we could live with them there. But how could we live with them in heaven if we cannot live with them here without continued contention and strife? . . .

Our hard hearts need to be broken. We need to come together in perfect unity, and we need to realize that we are the purchase of the blood of Jesus Christ of Nazareth. Let each one say: "He gave His life for me, and He wants me, as I go through this world, to reveal the love that He revealed in giving Himself for me." Christ bore our sins in His own body on the cross, that God might be just and yet the justifier of those who believe in Him. There is life, eternal life, for all who will surrender to Christ.

Strive earnestly for unity. Pray for it, work for it. It will bring spiritual health, elevation of thought, nobility of character, heavenly-mindedness, enabling you to overcome selfishness and evil surmisings, and to be more than conquerors through Him that loved you and gave Himself for you. Crucify self; esteem others better than yourselves. Thus you will be brought into oneness with Christ. Before the heavenly universe, and before the church and the world, you will bear unmistakable evidence that you are God's sons and daughters. God will be glorified in the example that you set.

The world needs to see worked out before it the miracle that binds the hearts of God's people together in Christian love. It needs to see the Lord's people sitting together in heavenly places in Christ. Will you not give in your lives an evidence of what the truth of God can do for those who love and serve Him? God knows what you can be. He knows what divine grace can do for you if you will be partakers of the divine nature. . . .

Union is strength; division is weakness. When those who believe present truth are united, they exert a telling influence. Satan well understands this. Never was he more determined than now to make of none effect the truth of God by causing bitterness and dissension among the Lord's people.—*Counsels for the Church,* pp. 290, 291.

August 25

The Danger of Self-Confidence

And lest I should be exalted above measure by the abundance of the revelations, a thorn in the flesh was given to me, a messenger of Satan to buffet me, lest I be exalted above measure.
—2 Corinthians 12:7.

Self-confidence leads to neglect of watchfulness and of humble, penitential prayer. There are outward temptations to be shunned and inward foes and perplexities to be overcome, for Satan adapts his temptations to the different characters and temperaments of individuals.

The church of Christ is in constant peril. Satan is seeking to destroy the people of God, and one person's mind, one individual's judgment, is not sufficient to be trusted. Christ would have His followers brought together in church capacity, observing order, having rules and discipline, and all subject one to another, esteeming others better than themselves. Union and confidence are essential to the prosperity of the church. If all the members of the church feel at liberty to move independently of the others, taking their own peculiar course, how can the church be in any safety in the hour of danger and peril? The prosperity and very existence of a church depend upon the prompt, united action and mutual confidence of its members. When, at a critical time, one sounds the alarm of danger, there is need of prompt and active work, without stopping to question and canvass the whole subject from end to end, thus letting the enemy gain every advantage by delay, when united action might save many souls from perdition.

God wants His people to be united in the closest bonds of Christian fellowship; confidence in our fellow church members is essential to the prosperity of the church; union of action is important in a religious crisis. One imprudent step, one careless action, may plunge the church into difficulties and trials from which it may not recover for years. One member of the church filled with unbelief may give an advantage to the great foe that will affect the prosperity of the entire church, and many souls may be lost as the result. Jesus would have His followers subject one to another; then God can use them as instruments to save one another; for one may not discern the dangers which another's eye is quick to perceive; but if the undiscerning will in confidence obey the warning, they may be saved great perplexities and trials.—*Testimonies for the Church,* vol. 3, pp. 445, 446.

WARNINGS TO THE CHURCH

In the last days perilous times will come.
—2 Timothy 3:1.

Christ had foretold that deceivers would arise, through whose influence "iniquity" should "abound," and "the love of many" should "wax cold." (Matthew 24:12.) He had warned the disciples that the church would be in more danger from this evil than from the persecution of her enemies. Again and again Paul warned the believers against these false teachers. This peril, above all others, they must guard against; for by receiving false teachers, they would open the door to errors by which the enemy would dim the spiritual perceptions and shake the confidence of those newly come to the faith of the gospel. Christ was the standard by which they were to test the doctrines presented. All that was not in harmony with His teachings they were to reject. Christ crucified for sin, Christ risen from the dead, Christ ascended on high—this was the science of salvation that they were to learn and teach.

The warnings of the word of God regarding the perils surrounding the Christian church belong to us today. As in the days of the apostles some tried by tradition and philosophy to destroy faith in the Scriptures, so today, by the pleasing sentiments of higher criticism, evolution, spiritualism, theosophy, and pantheism, the enemy of righteousness is seeking to lead souls into forbidden paths. To many the Bible is as a lamp without oil, because they have turned their minds into channels of speculative belief that bring misunderstanding and confusion. The work of higher criticism, in dissecting, conjecturing, reconstructing, is destroying faith in the Bible as a divine revelation. It is robbing God's word of power to control, uplift, and inspire human lives. By spiritualism, multitudes are taught to believe that desire is the highest law, that license is liberty, and that man is accountable only to himself.

The followers of Christ will meet with the "enticing words" against which the apostle warned the Colossian believers. They will meet with spiritualistic interpretations of the Scriptures, but they are not to accept them. Their voices are to be heard in clear affirmation of the eternal truths of the Scriptures. Keeping their eyes fixed on Christ, they are to move steadily forward in the path marked out, discarding all ideas that are not in harmony with His teaching. The truth of God is to be the subject for their contemplation and meditation. They are to regard the Bible as the voice of God speaking directly to them. Thus they will find the wisdom which is divine.—*The Acts of the Apostles,* pp. 473–475.

2016

August 27

Set on a Hill

You are the light of the world. A city that is set on a hill cannot be hidden.
—*Matthew 5:14.*

During ages of spiritual darkness the church of God has been as a city set on a hill. From age to age, through successive generations, the pure doctrines of heaven have been unfolding within its borders. Enfeebled and defective as it may appear, the church is the one object upon which God bestows in a special sense His supreme regard. It is the theater of His grace, in which He delights to reveal His power to transform hearts.

"Whereunto," asked Christ, "shall we liken the kingdom of God? or with what comparison shall we compare it?" (Mark 4:30.) He could not employ the kingdoms of the world as a similitude. In society He found nothing with which to compare it. Earthly kingdoms rule by the ascendancy of physical power; but from Christ's kingdom every carnal weapon, every instrument of coercion, is banished. This kingdom is to uplift and ennoble humanity. God's church is the court of holy life, filled with varied gifts and endowed with the Holy Spirit. The members are to find their happiness in the happiness of those whom they help and bless.

Wonderful is the work which the Lord designs to accomplish through His church, that His name may be glorified. A picture of this work is given in Ezekiel's vision of the river of healing: "These waters issue out toward the east country, and go down into the desert, and go into the sea: which being brought forth into the sea, the waters shall be healed. And it shall come to pass, that everything that liveth, which moveth, whithersoever the rivers shall come, shall live: . . . and by the river upon the bank thereof, on this side and on that side, shall grow all trees for meat, whose leaf shall not fade, neither shall the fruit thereof be consumed: it shall bring forth new fruit according to his months." (Ezekiel 47:8–12.) . . .

Through the integrity of Joseph the life of that whole people was preserved. Through Daniel God saved the life of all the wise men of Babylon. And these deliverances are as object lessons; they illustrate the spiritual blessings offered to the world through connection with the God whom Joseph and Daniel worshiped. All in whose heart Christ abides, all who will show forth His love to the world, are workers together with God for the blessing of humanity. As they receive from the Saviour grace to impart to others, from their whole being flows forth the tide of spiritual life.—*The Acts of the Apostles,* pp. 12, 13.

The Church Can Hasten Jesus' Return

What manner of persons ought you to be in holy conduct and godliness, looking for and hastening the coming of the day of God?—2 Peter 3:11, 12.

Christ has given to the church a sacred charge. Every member should be a channel through which God can communicate to the world the treasures of His grace, the unsearchable riches of Christ. There is nothing that the Saviour desires so much as agents who will represent to the world His Spirit and His character. There is nothing that the world needs so much as the manifestation through humanity of the Saviour's love. All heaven is waiting for men and women through whom God can reveal the power of Christianity.

The church is God's agency for the proclamation of truth, empowered by Him to do a special work; and if she is loyal to Him, obedient to all His commandments, there will dwell within her the excellency of divine grace. If she will be true to her allegiance, if she will honor the Lord God of Israel, there is no power that can stand against her.

Zeal for God and His cause moved the disciples to bear witness to the gospel with mighty power. Should not a like zeal fire our hearts with a determination to tell the story of redeeming love, of Christ and Him crucified? It is the privilege of every Christian, not only to look for, but to hasten the coming of the Saviour.

If the church will put on the robe of Christ's righteousness, withdrawing from all allegiance with the world, there is before her the dawn of a bright and glorious day. God's promise to her will stand fast forever. He will make her an eternal excellency, a joy of many generations. Truth, passing by those who despise and reject it, will triumph. Although at times apparently retarded, its progress has never been checked. When the message of God meets with opposition, He gives it additional force, that it may exert greater influence. Endowed with divine energy, it will cut its way through the strongest barriers and triumph over every obstacle.

What sustained the Son of God during His life of toil and sacrifice? He saw the results of the travail of His soul and was satisfied. Looking into eternity, He beheld the happiness of those who through His humiliation had received pardon and everlasting life. His ear caught the shout of the redeemed. He heard the ranso[illegible]ones singing the song of Moses and the Lamb.—*The Acts of the Apostles,* [illegible]0, 601.

August 29

A Stormy Future

He exercises all the authority of the first beast in his presence, and causes the earth and those who dwell in it to worship the first beast, whose deadly wound was healed.—Revelation 13:12.

Zechariah's vision of Joshua and the Angel applies with peculiar force to the experience of God's people in the closing up of the great day of atonement. The remnant church will be brought into great trial and distress. Those who keep the commandments of God and the faith of Jesus will feel the ire of the dragon and his hosts. Satan numbers the world as his subjects, he has gained control of the apostate churches; but here is a little company that are resisting his supremacy. If he could blot them from the earth, his triumph would be complete. As he influenced the heathen nations to destroy Israel, so in the near future he will stir up the wicked powers of earth to destroy the people of God. All will be required to render obedience to human edicts in violation of the divine law. Those who will be true to God and to duty will be menaced, denounced, and proscribed. They will "be betrayed both by parents, and brethren, and kinsfolks, and friends."

Their only hope is in the mercy of God; their only defense will be prayer. As Joshua was pleading before the Angel, so the remnant church, with brokenness of heart and earnest faith, will plead for pardon and deliverance through Jesus their Advocate. They are fully conscious of the sinfulness of their lives, they see their weakness and unworthiness, and as they look upon themselves they are ready to despair. The tempter stands by to accuse them, as he stood by to resist Joshua. He points to their filthy garments, their defective characters. He presents their weakness and folly, their sins of ingratitude, their unlikeness to Christ, which has dishonored their Redeemer. He endeavors to affright the soul with the thought that their case is hopeless, that the stain of their defilement will never be washed away. He hopes to so destroy their faith that they will yield to his temptations, turn from their allegiance to God, and receive the mark of the beast.

Satan urges before God his accusations against them, declaring that they have by their sins forfeited the divine protection, and claiming the right to destroy them as transgressors. He pronounces them just as deserving as himself of exclusion from the favor of God. "Are these," he says, "the people who are to take my place in heaven and the place of the angels who united with me?"—*Testimonies for the Church,* vol. 5, pp. 472, 473.

Robes for the Remnant

Who are these arrayed in white robes, and where did they come from?
—Revelation 7:13.

The people of God have been in many respects very faulty. Satan has an accurate knowledge of the sins which he has tempted them to commit, and he presents these in the most exaggerated light, declaring: "Will God banish me and my angels from His presence, and yet reward those who have been guilty of the same sins? Thou canst not do this, O Lord, in justice. Thy throne will not stand in righteousness and judgment. Justice demands that sentence be pronounced against them."

But while the followers of Christ have sinned, they have not given themselves to the control of evil. They have put away their sins, and have sought the Lord in humility and contrition, and the divine Advocate pleads in their behalf. He who has been most abused by their ingratitude, who knows their sin, and also their repentance, declares: " 'The Lord rebuke thee, O Satan.' I gave My life for these souls. They are graven upon the palms of My hands." . . .

As the people of God afflict their souls before Him, pleading for purity of heart, the command is given, "Take away the filthy garments" from them, and the encouraging words are spoken, "Behold, I have caused thine iniquity to pass from thee, and I will clothe thee with change of raiment." The spotless robe of Christ's righteousness is placed upon the tried, tempted, yet faithful children of God. The despised remnant are clothed in glorious apparel, nevermore to be defiled by the corruptions of the world. Their names are retained in the Lamb's book of life, enrolled among the faithful of all ages. They have resisted the wiles of the deceiver; they have not been turned from their loyalty by the dragon's roar. Now they are eternally secure from the tempter's devices. Their sins are transferred to the originator of sin.

And the remnant are not only pardoned and accepted, but honored. "A fair miter" is set upon their heads. They are to be as kings and priests unto God. While Satan was urging his accusations and seeking to destroy this company, holy angels, unseen, were passing to and fro, placing upon them the seal of the living God. These are they that stand upon Mount Zion with the Lamb, having the Father's name written in their foreheads. They sing the new song before the throne, that song which no one can learn save the hundred and forty and four thousand, which were redeemed from the earth.
—*Testimonies for the Church,* vol. 5, pp. 474–476.

August 31

Advance as a Church United

Therefore, beloved, looking forward to these things, be diligent to be found by Him in peace, without spot and blameless.
—2 Peter 3:14.

The Lord desires to see the work of proclaiming the third angel's message carried forward with increasing efficiency. As He has worked in all ages to give victories to His people, so in this age He longs to carry to a triumphant fulfillment His purposes for His church. He bids His believing saints to advance unitedly, going from strength to greater strength, from faith to increased assurance and confidence in the truth and righteousness of His cause.

We are to stand firm as a rock to the principles of the Word of God, remembering that God is with us to give us strength to meet each new experience. Let us ever maintain in our lives the principles of righteousness, that we may go forward from strength to strength in the name of the Lord. We are to hold as very sacred the faith that has been substantiated by the instruction and approval of the Spirit of God from our earliest experience until the present time. We are to cherish as very precious the work that the Lord has been carrying forward through His commandment-keeping people, and which, through the power of His grace, will grow stronger and more efficient as time advances. The enemy is seeking to becloud the discernment of God's people, and to weaken their efficiency, but if they will labor as the Spirit of God shall direct, He will open doors of opportunity before them for the work of building up the old waste places. Their experience will be one of constant growth, until the Lord shall descend from heaven with power and great glory to set His seal of final triumph upon His faithful ones.

The work that lies before us is one that will put to the stretch every power of the human being. It will call for the exercise of strong faith and constant vigilance. At times the difficulties that we shall meet will be most disheartening. The very greatness of the task will appall us. And yet, with God's help, His servants will finally triumph.—*Selected Messages,* book 2, pp. 407, 408.

I have been deeply impressed by scenes that have recently passed before me in the night season. There seemed to be a great movement—a work of revival—going forward in many places. Our people were moving into line, responding to God's call.—*Selected Messages,* book 2, p. 402.

The Family of God

September 1

The Beginning of the Home

Then the Lord God took the man and put him in the garden of Eden to tend and keep it.
—*Genesis 2:15.*

The Eden home of our first parents was prepared for them by God Himself. When He had furnished it with everything that they could desire, He said: "Let Us make man in Our image, after Our likeness." . . .

The Lord was pleased with these last and noblest of all His creatures, and designed that they should be the perfect inhabitants of a perfect world. But it was not His purpose that any should live in solitude. He said: "It is not good that the man should be alone; I will make him an help meet for him."

God Himself gave Adam a companion. He provided "an help meet for him"—a helper corresponding to him—one who was fitted to be his companion, and who could be one with him in love and sympathy. Eve was created from a rib taken from the side of Adam, signifying that she was not to control him as the head, nor to be trampled under his feet as an inferior, but to stand by his side as an equal, to be loved and protected by him. A part of man, bone of his bone, and flesh of his flesh, she was his second self; showing the close union and the affectionate attachment that should exist in this relation. "For no man ever yet hated his own flesh; but nourisheth and cherisheth it." "Therefore shall a man leave his father and his mother, and shall cleave unto his wife: and they shall be one." . . .

Fathers and mothers who make God first in their households, who teach their children that the fear of the Lord is the beginning of wisdom, glorify God before angels and before mankind by presenting to the world a well-ordered, well-disciplined family—a family that love and obey God instead of rebelling against Him. Christ is not a stranger in their homes; His name is a household name, revered and glorified. Angels delight in a home where God reigns supreme and the children are taught to reverence religion, the Bible, and their Creator. Such families can claim the promise, "Them that honour Me I will honour." As from such a home the father goes forth to his daily duties, it is with a spirit softened and subdued by converse with God.—*The Adventist Home,* pp. 25, 27, 28.

A Little Heaven on Earth

We should live soberly, righteously, and godly in the present age.
—Titus 2:12.

We must let Christ into our hearts and homes if we would walk in the light. Home should be made all that the word implies. It should be a little heaven upon earth, a place where the affections are cultivated instead of being studiously repressed. Our happiness depends upon this cultivation of love, sympathy, and true courtesy to one another. The reason there are so many hardhearted men and women in our world is that true affection has been regarded as weakness and has been discouraged and repressed. The better part of the nature of persons of this class was perverted and dwarfed in childhood, and unless rays of divine light can melt away their coldness and hardhearted selfishness, the happiness of such is buried forever. If we would have tender hearts, such as Jesus had when He was upon the earth, and sanctified sympathy, such as the angels have for sinful mortals, we must cultivate the sympathies of childhood, which are simplicity itself. Then we shall be refined, elevated, and directed by heavenly principles.

A cultivated intellect is a great treasure; but without the softening influence of sympathy and sanctified love, it is not of the highest value. We should have words and deeds of tender consideration for others. We can manifest a thousand little attentions in friendly words and pleasant looks, which will be reflected upon us again. Thoughtless Christians manifest by their neglect of others that they are not in union with Christ. It is impossible to be in union with Christ and yet be unkind to others and forgetful of their rights. Many long intensely for friendly sympathy. God has given each of us an identity of our own, which cannot be merged in that of another; but our individual characteristics will be much less prominent if we are indeed Christ's and His will is ours. Our lives should be consecrated to the good and happiness of others, as was our Saviour's. We should be self-forgetful, ever looking out for opportunities, even in little things, to show gratitude for the favors we have received of others, and watching for opportunities to cheer others and lighten and relieve their sorrows and burdens by acts of tender kindness and little deeds of love. These thoughtful courtesies, that, commencing in our families, extend outside the family circle, help make up the sum of life's happiness; and the neglect of these little things makes up the sum of life's bitterness and sorrow.—*Testimonies for the Church,* vol. 3, pp. 539, 540.

September 3

The Family Circle

Therefore a man shall leave his father and mother and be joined to his wife, and they shall become one flesh.—Genesis 2:24.

There is a sacred circle around every family which should be preserved. No other one has any right in that sacred circle. The husband and wife should be all to each other. The wife should have no secrets to keep from her husband and let others know, and the husband should have no secrets to keep from his wife to relate to others. The heart of his wife should be the grave for the faults of the husband, and the heart of the husband the grave for his wife's faults. Never should either party indulge in a joke at the expense of the other's feelings. Never should either the husband or wife in sport or in any other manner complain of each other to others, for frequently indulging in this foolish and what may seem perfectly harmless joking will end in trial with each other and perhaps estrangement. I have been shown that there should be a sacred shield around every family.

The home circle should be regarded as a sacred place, a symbol of heaven, a mirror in which to reflect ourselves. Friends and acquaintances we may have, but in the home life they are not to meddle. A strong sense of proprietorship should be felt, giving a sense of ease, restfulness, trust.

Let those composing the family circle pray that God will sanctify their tongues, their ears, their eyes, and every member of their body. When brought into contact with evil, it is not necessary to be overcome of evil. Christ has made it possible for the character to be fragrant with good. . . .

How many dishonor Christ and misrepresent His character in the home circle! How many do not manifest patience, forbearance, forgiveness, and true love! Many have their likes and dislikes and feel at liberty to manifest their own perverse disposition rather than to reveal the will, the works, the character of Christ. The life of Jesus is full of kindness and love. Are we growing into His divine nature?

Let fathers and mothers make a solemn promise to God, whom they profess to love and obey, that by His grace they will not disagree between themselves, but will in their own life and temper manifest the spirit that they wish their children to cherish.—*The Adventist Home,* pp. 177, 178.

2016

TRUE JOY

In Your presence is fullness of joy.
—Psalm 16:11.

Let each give love rather than exact it. Cultivate that which is noblest in yourselves, and be quick to recognize the good qualities in each other. The consciousness of being appreciated is a wonderful stimulus and satisfaction. Sympathy and respect encourage the striving after excellence, and love itself increases as it stimulates to nobler aims.

Neither the husband nor the wife should merge his or her individuality in that of the other. Each has a personal relation to God. Of Him each is to ask, "What is right?" "What is wrong?" "How may I best fulfill life's purpose?" Let the wealth of your affection flow forth to Him who gave His life for you. Make Christ first and last and best in everything. As your love for Him becomes deeper and stronger, your love for each other will be purified and strengthened. . . .

Neither the husband nor the wife should attempt to exercise over the other an arbitrary control. Do not try to compel each other to yield to your wishes. You cannot do this and retain each other's love. Be kind, patient, and forbearing, considerate, and courteous. By the grace of God you can succeed in making each other happy, as in your marriage vow you promised to do.

But remember that happiness will not be found in shutting yourselves up to yourselves, satisfied to pour out all your affection upon each other. Seize upon every opportunity for contributing to the happiness of those around you. Remember that true joy can be found only in unselfish service.

Forbearance and unselfishness mark the words and acts of all who live the new life in Christ. As you seek to live His life, striving to conquer self and selfishness and to minister to the needs of others, you will gain victory after victory. Thus your influence will bless the world.

Men and women can reach God's ideal for them if they will take Christ as their helper. What human wisdom cannot do, His grace will accomplish for those who give themselves to Him in loving trust. His providence can unite hearts in bonds that are of heavenly origin. Love will not be a mere exchange of soft and flattering words. . . . Heart will be bound to heart in the golden bonds of a love that is enduring.—*The Ministry of Healing,* pp. 361, 362.

SEPTEMBER 5

THE ROLE OF THE CHRISTIAN HOME

Walk worthy of God who calls you into His own kingdom and glory.
—1 Thessalonians 2:12.

The restoration and uplifting of humanity begins in the home. The work of parents underlies every other. Society is composed of families, and is what the heads of families make it. Out of the heart are "the issues of life" (Proverbs 4:23); and the heart of the community, of the church, and of the nation is the household. The well-being of society, the success of the church, the prosperity of the nation, depend upon home influences.

The importance and the opportunities of the home life are illustrated in the life of Jesus. He who came from heaven to be our example and teacher spent thirty years as a member of the household at Nazareth. Concerning these years the Bible record is very brief. No mighty miracles attracted the attention of the multitude. No eager throngs followed His steps or listened to His words. Yet during all these years He was fulfilling His divine mission. He lived as one of us, sharing the home life, submitting to its discipline, performing its duties, bearing its burdens. In the sheltering care of a humble home, participating in the experiences of our common lot, He "increased in wisdom and stature, and in favor with God and man." (Luke 2:52.)

During all these secluded years His life flowed out in currents of sympathy and helpfulness. His unselfishness and patient endurance, His courage and faithfulness, His resistance of temptation, His unfailing peace and quiet joyfulness, were a constant inspiration. He brought a pure, sweet atmosphere into the home, and His life was as leaven working amidst the elements of society. None said that He had wrought a miracle; yet virtue—the healing, life-giving power of love—went out from Him to the tempted, the sick, and the disheartened. In an unobtrusive way, from His very childhood, He ministered to others, and because of this, when He began His public ministry, many heard Him gladly.

The Saviour's early years are more than an example to the youth. They are a lesson, and should be an encouragement, to every parent. . . . There is no more important field of effort than that committed to the founders and guardians of the home. No work entrusted to human beings involves greater or more far-reaching results than does the work of fathers and mothers.

It is by the youth and children of today that the future of society is to be determined, and what these youth and children shall be depends upon the home.—*The Ministry of Healing*, pp. 349–351.

SEPTEMBER 6

A LIGHT IN THE NEIGHBORHOOD

Let your light so shine before men, that they may see your good works and glorify your Father in heaven.
—Matthew 5:16.

We need more sunshiny parents and more sunshiny Christians. We are too much shut up within ourselves. Too often the kindly, encouraging word, the cheery smile, are withheld from our children and from the oppressed and discouraged.

Parents, upon you rests the responsibility of being light-bearers and light-givers. Shine as lights in the home, brightening the path that your children must travel. As you do this, your light will shine to those without.

From every Christian home a holy light should shine forth. Love should be revealed in action. It should flow out in all home relationships, showing itself in thoughtful kindness, in gentle, unselfish courtesy. There are homes where this principle is carried out—homes where God is worshiped and truest love reigns. From these homes morning and evening prayer ascends to God as sweet incense, and His mercies and blessings descend upon the suppliants like the morning dew.

The first work of Christians is to be united in the family. Then the work is to extend to their neighbors nigh and afar off. Those who have received light are to let the light shine forth in clear rays. Their words, fragrant with the love of Christ, are to be a savor of life unto life.

The more closely the members of a family are united in their work in the home, the more uplifting and helpful will be the influence that father and mother and sons and daughters will exert outside the home.

The happiness of families and churches depends upon home influences. Eternal interests depend upon the proper discharge of the duties of this life. The world is not so much in need of great minds as of good men and women who will be a blessing in their homes.

When religion is manifested in the home, its influence will be felt in the church and in the neighborhood. . . .

The truth lived at home makes itself felt in disinterested labor abroad. Those who live Christianity in the home will be a bright and shining light everywhere.—*The Adventist Home,* pp. 37–39.

September 7

Members of the Royal Family

For this reason I bow my knees to the Father of our Lord Jesus Christ, from whom the whole family in heaven and earth is named.—Ephesians 3:14, 15.

We are children of the Heavenly King, members of the royal family, heirs of God, and joint heirs with Christ. The mansions Jesus has gone to prepare are to receive only those who are true, who are pure, who love and obey His words. In the mansions above we shall meet to part no more. We shall know each other in our heavenly home. But if we would enjoy eternal bliss, we must cultivate religion in the home; for the home is to be the center of the purest and most elevated affection. Peace, harmony, affection, and happiness should be perseveringly cherished every day, until these precious things abide in the hearts of those who compose the family. The plant of love must be carefully nourished, else it will die. Every good principle must be cherished if we would have it thrive in the soul. That which Satan plants in the heart—envy, jealousy, evil surmising, evil speaking, impatience, prejudice, selfishness, covetousness, and vanity—must be uprooted. If these evil things are allowed to remain in the soul, they will bear fruit by which many shall be defiled. Oh, how many cultivate the poisonous plants, that kill out the precious fruits of love and defile the soul! Some of these who cherish evil, think they have a burden for souls. They make public profession of their love to God, and yet see no necessity for weeding the garden of the heart, for uprooting every unsightly, unholy weed, for letting the beams of the Sun of Righteousness shine into the soul temple. They do not know Jesus. They have no knowledge of what it is to be a practical Christian, that is, to be Christlike.

There is need of prayer, of genuine faith, of patient, untiring effort to war against every evil disposition, so that even our thoughts may be brought into subjection to Christ. That which will make the character lovely in the home is that which will make it lovely in the heavenly mansions. The measure of your Christianity is gauged by the character of your home life. The grace of Christ enables its possessors to make the home a happy place full of peace and rest. Unless you have the Spirit of Christ, you are none of His, and will never see the redeemed saints in His kingdom, who are to be one with Him in the heaven of bliss. God desires you to consecrate yourself wholly to Him, and represent His character in the home circle.—*Signs of the Times,* November 14, 1892.

Parents, Set the Right Example

Children, obey your parents in the Lord, for this is right.
—Ephesians 6:1.

The best way to educate children to respect their father and mother, is to give them the opportunity of seeing the father offering kindly attentions to the mother, and the mother rendering respect and reverence to the father. It is by beholding love in their parents, that children are led to obey the fifth commandment and to heed the injunction, "Children, obey your parents in the Lord: for this is right. Honor thy father and thy mother; which is the first commandment with promise; that it may be well with thee, and that thou mayest live long on the earth."

When children have unbelieving parents, and their commands contradict the requirements of Christ, then, painful though it may be, they must obey God and trust the consequences with Him. The Lord has expressly enjoined the duty upon children of honoring their father and their mother. As they have opportunity and ability, they are kindly to care for their parents. This commandment to children stands at the head of the last six precepts which show our duty to others. But while children are commanded to obey their parents, parents are also instructed to exercise their authority with wisdom. Paul writes, "And, ye fathers, provoke not your children to wrath: but bring them up in the nurture and admonition of the Lord." Great care should be exercised by parents lest they treat their children in such a way as to provoke obstinacy, disobedience, and rebellion. Parents often stir up the worst passions of the human heart, because of their lack of self-control. They correct them in a spirit of anger, and rather confirm them in their evil ways and defiant spirit, than influence them in the way of right. By their own arbitrary spirit they thrust their children under Satanic influences, instead of rescuing them from the snares of Satan by gentleness and love. How sad it is that many parents who profess to be Christians, are not converted! Christ does not abide in their hearts by faith. While professing to be followers of Jesus, they disgust their children, and, by their violent, unforgiving temper, make them averse to all religion. It is little wonder that the children become cold and rebellious toward their parents. And yet children are not excused for disobedience because of their parents' unsanctified ways.

O that every family professing to be devoted to God, were so in deed and in truth! Then would Christ be represented in the home-life, and parents and children would represent Him in the church, and what happiness would exist!—*Review and Herald*, November 15, 1892.

September 9

Make Christianity Attractive

Wives, likewise, be submissive to your own husbands, that even if some do not obey the word, they, without a word, may be won by the conduct of their wives.
—1 Peter 3:1.

When Christ is in the heart, He is brought into the family. The father and mother feel the importance of living in obedience to the Holy Spirit so that the heavenly angels, who minister to those who shall be heirs of salvation, will minister to them as teachers in the home, educating and training them for the work of teaching their children. In the home it is possible to have a little church which will honor and glorify the Redeemer.

Make the Christian life an attractive one. Speak of the country in which the followers of Christ are to make their home. As you do this, God will guide your children into all truth, filling them with a desire to fit themselves for the mansions which Christ has gone to prepare for those that love Him.

Parents are not to compel their children to have a form of religion, but they are to place eternal principles before them in an attractive light.

Parents are to make the religion of Christ attractive by their cheerfulness, their Christian courtesy, and their tender, compassionate sympathy; but they are to be firm in requiring respect and obedience. Right principles must be established in the mind of the child.

We need to present to the youth an inducement for right doing. Silver and gold is not sufficient for this. Let us reveal to them the love and mercy and grace of Christ, the preciousness of His word, and the joys of the overcomer. In efforts of this kind you will do a work that will last throughout eternity.

Some parents, although they profess to be religious, do not keep before their children the fact that God is to be served and obeyed, that convenience, pleasure, or inclination should not interfere with His claims upon them. "The fear of the Lord is the beginning of wisdom." This fact should be woven into the very life and character. The right conception of God through the knowledge of Christ, who died that we might be saved, should be impressed upon their minds.—*The Adventist Home,* pp. 323, 324.

Think Twice Before Marrying

Who can find a virtuous wife? For her worth is far above rubies.
—Proverbs 31:10.

Great care should be taken by Christian youth in the formation of friendships and in the choice of companions. Take heed, lest what you now think to be pure gold turns out to be base metal. Worldly associations tend to place obstructions in the way of your service to God, and many souls are ruined by unhappy unions, either business or matrimonial, with those who can never elevate or ennoble.

Weigh every sentiment, and watch every development of character in the one with whom you think to link your life destiny. The step you are about to take is one of the most important in your life, and should not be taken hastily. While you may love, do not love blindly.

Examine carefully to see if your married life would be happy or inharmonious and wretched. Let the questions be raised, Will this union help me heavenward? Will it increase my love for God? And will it enlarge my sphere of usefulness in this life? If these reflections present no drawback, then in the fear of God move forward.

Most men and women have acted in entering the marriage relation as though the only question for them to settle was whether they loved each other. But they should realize that a responsibility rests upon them in the marriage relation farther than this. They should consider whether their offspring will possess physical health and mental and moral strength. But few have moved with high motives and with elevated considerations which they could not lightly throw off—that society had claims upon them, that the weight of their family's influence would tell in the upward or downward scale.

The choice of a life companion should be such as best to secure physical, mental, and spiritual well-being for parents and for their children—such as will enable both parents and children to bless others and to honor their Creator.

Let a young man seek one to stand by his side who is fitted to bear her share of life's burdens, one whose influence will ennoble and refine him, and who will make him happy in her love.—*The Adventist Home,* pp. 44–46.

September 11

Like Parents, Like Children

Come, you children, listen to me; I will teach you the fear of the Lord.
—*Psalm 34:11.*

What the parents are, that, to a great extent, the children will be. The physical conditions of the parents, their dispositions and appetites, their mental and moral tendencies, are, to a greater or less degree, reproduced in their children.

The nobler the aims, the higher the mental and spiritual endowments, and the better developed the physical powers of the parents, the better will be the life equipment they give their children. In cultivating that which is best in themselves, parents are exerting an influence to mold society and to uplift future generations.

Fathers and mothers need to understand their responsibility. The world is full of snares for the feet of the young. Multitudes are attracted by a life of selfish and sensual pleasure. They cannot discern the hidden dangers or the fearful ending of the path that seems to them the way of happiness. Through the indulgence of appetite and passion, their energies are wasted, and millions are ruined for this world and for the world to come. Parents should remember that their children must encounter these temptations. Even before the birth of the child, the preparation should begin that will enable it to fight successfully the battle against evil.

Especially does responsibility rest upon the mother. She, by whose lifeblood the child is nourished and its physical frame built up, imparts to it also mental and spiritual influences that tend to the shaping of mind and character. It was Jochebed, the Hebrew mother, who, strong in faith, was "not afraid of the king's commandment" (Hebrews 11:23), of whom was born Moses, the deliverer of Israel. It was Hannah, the woman of prayer and self-sacrifice and heavenly inspiration, who gave birth to Samuel, the heaven-instructed child, the incorruptible judge, the founder of Israel's sacred schools. It was Elizabeth the kinswoman and kindred spirit of Mary of Nazareth, who was the mother of the Saviour's herald. . . .

The effect of prenatal influences is by many parents looked upon as a matter of little moment; but heaven does not so regard it. The message sent by an angel of God, and twice given in the most solemn manner [see Judges 13:7, 13, 14], shows it to be deserving of our most careful thought.—*The Ministry of Healing,* pp. 371, 372.

September 12

The Mother

Her children rise up and call her blessed; her husband also, and he praises her.
—Proverbs 31:28.

Happy are the parents whose lives are a true reflection of the divine, so that the promises and commands of God awaken in their children gratitude and reverence; the parents whose tenderness and justice and long-suffering interpret to the children the love and justice and long-suffering of God; and who, by teaching the children to love and trust and obey them, are teaching them to love and trust and obey their Father in heaven. Parents who impart to their children such a gift have endowed them with a treasure more precious than the wealth of all the ages—a treasure as enduring as eternity.

In the children committed to her care, every mother has a sacred charge from God. "Take this son, this daughter," He says; "train it for Me; give it a character polished after the similitude of a palace, that it may shine in the courts of the Lord forever."

The mother's work often seems to her an unimportant service. It is a work that is rarely appreciated. Others know little of her many cares and burdens. Her days are occupied with a round of little duties, all calling for patient effort, for self-control, for tact, wisdom, and self-sacrificing love; yet she cannot boast of what she has done as any great achievement. She has only kept things in the home running smoothly; often weary and perplexed, she has tried to speak kindly to the children, to keep them busy and happy, and to guide the little feet in the right path. She feels that she has accomplished nothing. But it is not so. Heavenly angels watch the care-worn mother, noting the burdens she carries day by day. Her name may not have been heard in the world, but it is written in the Lamb's book of life.

There is a God above, and the light and glory from His throne rests upon the faithful mother as she tries to educate her children to resist the influence of evil. No other work can equal hers in importance. She has not, like the artist, to paint a form of beauty upon canvas, nor, like the sculptor, to chisel it from marble. She has not, like the author, to embody a noble thought in words of power, nor, like the musician, to express a beautiful sentiment in melody. It is hers, with the help of God, to develop in a human soul the likeness of the divine.—*The Ministry of Healing,* pp. 375–378.

September 13

The Father

And you, fathers, do not provoke your children to wrath, but bring them up in the training and admonition of the Lord.—Ephesians 6:4.

The husband and father is the head of the household. The wife looks to him for love and sympathy, and for aid in the training of the children; and this is right. The children are his as well as hers, and he is equally interested in their welfare. The children look to their father for support and guidance; he needs to have a right conception of life and of the influences and associations that should surround his family; above all, he should be controlled by the love and fear of God and by the teaching of His word, that he may guide the feet of his children in the right way.

The father is the lawmaker of the household; and, like Abraham, he should make the law of God the rule of his home. God said of Abraham, "I know him, that he will command his children and his household." (Genesis 18:19.) There would be no sinful neglect to restrain evil, no weak, unwise, indulgent favoritism; no yielding of his conviction of duty to the claims of mistaken affection. Abraham would not only give right instruction, but he would maintain the authority of just and righteous laws. God has given rules for our guidance. Children should not be left to wander away from the safe path marked out in God's word, into ways leading to danger, which are open on every side. Kindly, but firmly, with persevering, prayerful effort, their wrong desires should be restrained, their inclinations denied.

The father should enforce in his family the sterner virtues—energy, integrity, honesty, patience, courage, diligence, and practical usefulness. And what he requires of his children he himself should practice, illustrating these virtues in his own manly bearing.

But, fathers, do not discourage your children. Combine affection with authority, kindness and sympathy with firm restraint. Give some of your leisure hours to your children; become acquainted with them; associate with them in their work and in their sports, and win their confidence. Cultivate friendship with them, especially with your sons. In this way you will be a strong influence for good. . . .

In a sense the father is the priest of the household, laying upon the family altar the morning and evening sacrifice. But the wife and children should unite in prayer and join in the song of praise.—*The Ministry of Healing*, pp. 390–392.

THE FAMILY AND DECISIVE BATTLES 2016

Daniel purposed in his heart that he would not defile himself with the portion of the king's delicacies, nor with the wine which he drank.—Daniel 1:8.

Parents, ask yourselves the solemn question, "Have we educated our children to yield to paternal authority, and thus trained them to obey God, to love Him, to hold His law as the supreme guide of conduct and life? Have we educated them to be missionaries for Christ? to go about doing good?" Believing parents, your children will have to fight decisive battles for the Lord in the day of conflict; and while they win victories for the Prince of Peace, they may be gaining triumphs for themselves. But if they have not been brought up in the fear of the Lord; if they have no knowledge of Christ, no connection with heaven, they will have no moral power, and they will yield to earthly potentates who have assumed to exalt themselves above the God of heaven in establishing a spurious sabbath to take the place of the Sabbath of Jehovah. The tender mercies of this power will be displayed in prison cells and dungeons. Already preparations are advancing, and movements are in progress, which will result in making an image to the beast. Events will be brought about in the earth's history that will fulfill the predictions of prophecy for these last days.

Decisions will be called for and made; backsliders will either return decidedly to their allegiance to God, or they will be enrolled in the ranks of the enemy: Satan will have control of all who finally refuse to be controlled by the law of God. He will inspire parents to war against their children, and children to war against their parents—to betray and deliver those of their own household to enemies. Coming events are casting their shadows upon our pathway. Fathers, mothers, I appeal to you to make most earnest efforts now for your children. Give them daily religious instruction. Teach them to love God, and to be true to the principles of right. With lofty, earnest faith, directed by the divine influence of the Holy Spirit, work, work now. Do not put it off one day, one hour. Teach your children that the heart must be trained to self-control and self-denial. The motives of the life must be in harmony with the law of God. Never be satisfied to have your children grow up apart from Christ. Never feel at ease while they are cold and indifferent. Cry to God day and night. Pray and work for the salvation of the souls of your children.—*Review and Herald,* April 23, 1889.

September 15

Parents, It's Up to You

Train up a child in the way he should go,
and when he is old he will not depart from it.
—Proverbs 22:6.

Parents, you carry responsibilities that no one can bear for you. As long as you live, you are accountable to God to keep His way. . . . Parents who make the word of God their guide, and who realize how much their children depend upon them for the characters they form, will set an example that it will be safe for their children to follow.

Fathers and mothers are responsible for the health, the constitution, the development of the character of their children. No one else should be left to see to this work. In becoming the parents of children, it devolves upon you to cooperate with the Lord in educating them in sound principles.

How sad it is that many parents have cast off their God-given responsibility to their children, and are willing that strangers should bear it for them! They are willing that others should labor for their children and relieve them of all burden in the matter. . . .

For some reason many parents dislike to give their children religious instruction. They leave them to pick up in Sabbath school the knowledge they should impart concerning their responsibility to God. Such parents need to understand that God desires them to educate, discipline, and train their children, ever keeping before them the fact that they are forming characters for the present and the future life.

Do not depend upon the teachers of the Sabbath school to do your work of training your children in the way they should go. The Sabbath school is a great blessing; it may help you in your work, but it can never take your place. God has given to all fathers and mothers the responsibility of bringing their children to Jesus, teaching them how to pray and believe in the word of God.

In the education of your children lay not the grand truths of the Bible to one side, supposing that the Sabbath school and the minister will do your neglected work. The Bible is not too sacred and sublime to be opened daily and studied diligently.—*The Adventist Home,* pp. 187, 189.

September 16

What Is "Family Religion"?

2016

And Jacob said to his household and to all who were with him, "Put away the foreign gods that are among you, purify yourselves, and change your garments."
—Genesis 35:2.

Family religion consists in bringing up the children in the nurture and admonition of the Lord. Every one in the family is to be nourished by the lessons of Christ, and the interest of each soul is to be strictly guarded, in order that Satan shall not deceive and allure away from Christ. This is the standard every family should aim to reach, and they should determine not to fail or to be discouraged. When parents are diligent and vigilant in their instruction, and train their children with an eye single to the glory of God, they cooperate with God, and God cooperates with them in the saving of the souls of the children for whom Christ has died.

Religious instruction means much more than ordinary instruction. It means that you are to pray with your children, teaching them how to approach Jesus and tell Him all their wants. It means that you are to show in your life that Jesus is everything to you, and that His love makes you patient, kind, forbearing, and yet firm in commanding your children after you, as did Abraham.

Just as you conduct yourself in your home life, you are registered in the books of heaven. Those who would become saints in heaven must first become saints in their own families. If fathers and mothers are true Christians in the family, they will be useful members of the church and be able to conduct affairs in the church and in society after the same manner in which they conduct their family concerns. Parents, let not your religion be simply a profession, but let it become a reality. . . .

In the home the foundation is laid for the prosperity of the church. The influences that rule in the home life are carried into the church life; therefore church duties should first begin in the home.

When we have good home religion, we will have excellent meeting religion. Hold the fort at home. Consecrate your family to God, and then speak and act at home as a Christian. Be kind and forbearing and patient at home, knowing that you are teachers.—*The Adventist Home,* pp. 317–319.

September 17

Home, the Base for Future Missionaries

I call to remembrance the genuine faith that is in you, which dwelt first in your grandmother Lois and your mother Eunice, and I am persuaded is in you also.
—2 Timothy 1:5.

The faithful performance of home duties has a reflex influence upon human beings. Our spiritual progress and perfection of Christian character in the home are carried into our missionary work abroad. Having on the whole armor of righteousness, we can fight as faithful soldiers of Christ. In the father's house the evidence is to be given of a preparedness for the work to be done abundantly in the church. With earnest, humble hearts the members of the family are to seek to know that Christ is abiding in the heart. Then they can go forth with the whole armor on, equipped for Christ's service. . . .

Self-denial practiced in the home fits us to work for others. The cultivation of our faculties to do what needs to be done to make the home what it should be—a symbol of the home in heaven—prepares us to work in a larger vineyard. The church needs all the cultivated spiritual force that can be obtained, especially to guard the youth, the younger members of the Lord's family. The truth lived at home makes itself felt in disinterested labor abroad. Those who show a Christian character in the home will be bright and shining lights everywhere. The education received in the home in showing a tender regard for each other enables us to know how to reach hearts that need to be taught the principles of true religion. . . .

Home duties should be performed with a realization that if they are done in the right spirit, they will give an experience that will enable us to work in spiritual lines in the most permanent and thorough manner. Oh, what might not a living Christian do in missionary lines by performing faithfully the daily duties, cheerfully lifting the cross, not neglecting that class of work that is not agreeable to the natural feelings. Missionaries for the Master are best prepared for work abroad in the Christian household, where God is feared, where God is loved, where God is worshiped, where faithfulness has become second nature, where haphazard, careless inattention to home duties is not permitted, where quiet communion with God is looked upon as essential to the faithful performance of daily duties.—*Manuscript 140,* 1897.

SEPTEMBER 18

HOMES WHERE ANGELS WILL LINGER

Do not forget to entertain strangers, for by so doing some have unwittingly entertained angels.
—Hebrews 13:2.

We can have the salvation of God in our families; but we must believe for it, live for it, and have a continual, abiding faith and trust in God. The restraint which God's Word imposes upon us is for our own interest. It increases the happiness of our families, and of all around us. It refines our taste, sanctifies our judgment, and brings peace of mind, and in the end, everlasting life. Ministering angels will linger in our dwellings, and with joy carry heavenward the tidings of our advance in the divine life, and the recording angel will make a cheerful, happy record.

The Spirit of Christ will be an abiding influence in the home life. If men and women will open their hearts to the heavenly influence of truth and love, these principles will flow forth again like streams in the desert, refreshing all and causing freshness to appear where now is barrenness and dearth.

The neglect of home religion, the neglect to train your children, is most displeasing to God. If one of your children were in the river, battling with the waves and in imminent danger of drowning, what a stir there would be! What efforts would be made, what prayers offered, what enthusiasm manifested, to save the human life! But here are your children out of Christ, their souls unsaved. Perhaps they are even rude and uncourteous, a reproach to the Adventist name. They are perishing without hope and without God in the world, and you are careless and unconcerned. . . .

Fathers and mothers, each morning and evening gather your children around you, and in humble supplication lift the heart to God for help. Your dear ones are exposed to temptation. Daily annoyances beset the path of young and old. Those who would live patient, loving, cheerful lives must pray. Only by receiving constant help from God can we gain the victory over self. . . .

By sincere, earnest prayer parents should make a hedge about their children. They should pray with full faith that God will abide with them and that holy angels will guard them and their children from Satan's cruel power.
—*Counsels for the Church,* pp. 151, 152.

September 19

True Love Is a Holy Principle

But I say to you, love your enemies, bless those who curse you, do good to those who hate you, and pray for those who spitefully use you and persecute you.
—*Matthew* 5:44.

Love is a precious gift, which we receive from Jesus. Pure and holy affection is not a feeling, but a principle. Those who are actuated by true love are neither unreasonable nor blind.

There is but little real, genuine, devoted, pure love. This precious article is very rare. Passion is termed love.

True love is a high and holy principle, altogether different in character from that love which is awakened by impulse, and which suddenly dies when severely tested.

Love is a plant of heavenly growth, and it must be fostered and nourished. Affectionate hearts, truthful, loving words, will make happy families and exert an elevating influence upon all who come within the sphere of their influence. . . .

While pure love will take God into all its plans, and will be in perfect harmony with the Spirit of God, passion will be headstrong, rash, unreasonable, defiant of all restraint, and will make the object of its choice an idol. In all the deportment of one who possesses true love, the grace of God will be shown. Modesty, simplicity, sincerity, morality, and religion will characterize every step toward an alliance in marriage. Those who are thus controlled will not be absorbed in each other's society, at a loss of interest in the prayer meeting and the religious service. Their fervor for the truth will not die on account of the neglect of the opportunities and privileges that God has graciously given to them.

That love which has no better foundation than mere sensual gratification will be headstrong, blind, and uncontrollable. Honor, truth, and every noble, elevated power of the mind are brought under the slavery of passions. Those who are bound in the chains of this infatuation are too often deaf to the voice of reason and conscience; neither argument nor entreaty can lead them to see the folly of their course.

True love is not a strong, fiery, impetuous passion. On the contrary, it is calm and deep in its nature. It looks beyond mere externals, and is attracted by qualities alone. It is wise and discriminating, and its devotion is real and abiding.—*The Adventist Home,* pp. 50, 51.

SEPTEMBER 20

THE POWER OF LOVE

My little children, let us not love in word or in tongue, but in deed and in truth.
—1 John 3:18.

Love's agencies have wonderful power, for they are divine. The soft answer that "turneth away wrath," the love that "suffereth long, and is kind," the charity that "covereth a multitude of sins"—would we learn the lesson, with what power for healing would our lives be gifted! How life would be transformed and the earth become a very likeness and foretaste of heaven!

These precious lessons may be so simply taught as to be understood even by little children. The heart of the child is tender and easily impressed; and when we who are older become "as little children," when we learn the simplicity and gentleness and tender love of the Saviour, we shall not find it difficult to touch the hearts of the little ones and teach them love's ministry of healing.

From a worldly point of view, money is power; but from the Christian standpoint, love is power. Intellectual and spiritual strength are involved in this principle. Pure love has special efficacy to do good, and can do nothing but good. It prevents discord and misery and brings the truest happiness. Wealth is often an influence to corrupt and destroy; force is strong to do hurt; but truth and goodness are the properties of pure love.

Home is to be the center of the purest and most elevated affection. Peace, harmony, affection, and happiness should be perseveringly cherished every day, until these precious things abide in the hearts of those who compose the family. The plant of love must be carefully nourished, else it will die. Every good principle must be cherished if we would have it thrive in the soul. That which Satan plants in the heart—envy, jealousy, evil surmising, evil speaking, impatience, prejudice, selfishness, covetousness, and vanity—must be uprooted. If these evil things are allowed to remain in the soul, they will bear fruit by which many shall be defiled. Oh, how many cultivate the poisonous plants that kill out the precious fruits of love and defile the soul!

In many families there is a great lack in expressing affection one for another. While there is no need of sentimentalism, there is need of expressing love and tenderness in a chaste, pure, dignified way.—*The Adventist Home*, pp. 195, 196, 198.

SEPTEMBER 21

THE HONOR DUE PARENTS

Honor your father and your mother, that your days may be long upon the land that the LORD your God is giving you.—Exodus 20:12.

This is the first commandment with promise. It is binding upon childhood and youth, upon the middle-aged and the aged. There is no period in life when children are excused from honoring their parents. This solemn obligation is binding upon every son and daughter and is one of the conditions to their prolonging their lives upon the land which the Lord will give the faithful. This is not a subject unworthy of notice, but a matter of vital importance. The promise is upon condition of obedience. If you obey, you shall live long in the land which the Lord your God gives you. If you disobey, you shall not prolong your life in that land.

Parents are entitled to a degree of love and respect which is due to no other person. God Himself, who has placed upon them a responsibility for the souls committed to their charge, has ordained that during the earlier years of life parents shall stand in the place of God to their children. And any who reject the rightful authority of their parents are rejecting the authority of God. The fifth commandment requires children not only to yield respect, submission, and obedience to their parents, but also to give them love and tenderness, to lighten their cares, to guard their reputation, and to succor and comfort them in old age.

God cannot prosper those who go directly contrary to the plainest duty specified in His word, the duty of children to their parents. . . . If they disrespect and dishonor their earthly parents, they will not respect and love their Creator.

When children have unbelieving parents, and their commands contradict the requirements of Christ, then, painful though it may be, they must obey God and trust the consequences with Him. . . .

Bring all the rays of sunshine, of love, and of affection into the home circle. Your father and mother will appreciate these little attentions you can give. Your efforts to lighten the burdens, and to repress every word of fretfulness and ingratitude, show that you are not a thoughtless child, and that you do appreciate the care and love that has been bestowed upon you in the years of your helpless infancy and childhood.

Children, it is necessary that your mothers love you, or else you would be very unhappy. And is it not also right that children love their parents?—*The Adventist Home,* pp. 292, 293, 295.

Home Missions

I was hungry and you gave Me food; I was thirsty and you gave Me drink; I was a stranger and you took Me in.—Matthew 25:35.

The mission of the home extends beyond its own members. The Christian home is to be an object lesson, illustrating the excellence of the true principles of life. Such an illustration will be a power for good in the world. Far more powerful than any sermon that can be preached is the influence of a true home upon human hearts and lives. . . .

There are many others to whom we might make our homes a blessing. Our social entertainments should not be governed by the dictates of worldly custom, but by the Spirit of Christ and the teaching of His word. The Israelites, in all their festivities, included the poor, the stranger, and the Levite, who was both the assistant of the priest in the sanctuary, and a religious teacher and missionary. These were regarded as the guests of the people, to share their hospitality on all occasions of social and religious rejoicing, and to be tenderly cared for in sickness or in need. It is such as these whom we should make welcome to our homes. How much such a welcome might do to cheer and encourage the missionary nurse or the teacher, the care-burdened, hard-working mother, or the feeble and aged, so often without a home, and struggling with poverty and many discouragements.

"When thou makest a dinner or a supper," Christ says, "call not thy friends, nor thy brethren, neither thy kinsmen, nor thy rich neighbors; lest they also bid thee again, and a recompense be made thee. But when thou makest a feast, call the poor, the maimed, the lame, the blind: and thou shalt be blessed; for they cannot recompense thee: for thou shalt be recompensed at the resurrection of the just." (Luke 14:12–14.)

These are guests whom it will lay on you no great burden to receive. You will not need to provide for them elaborate or expensive entertainment. You will need to make no effort at display. The warmth of a genial welcome, a place at your fireside, a seat at your home table, the privilege of sharing the blessing of the hour of prayer, would to many of these be like a glimpse of heaven.

Our sympathies are to overflow the boundaries of self and the enclosure of family walls. There are precious opportunities for those who will make their homes a blessing to others. Social influence is a wonderful power.—*The Ministry of Healing*, pp. 352–354.

September 23 2016

A Sympathetic Hand

Everyone helped his neighbor, and said to his brother, "Be of good courage!"
—Isaiah 41:6.

Forbearance and unselfishness mark the words and acts of all who live the new life in Christ. As you seek to live His life, striving to conquer self and selfishness and to minister to the needs of others, you will gain victory after victory. Thus your influence will bless the world. . . .

Our homes should be a place of refuge for the tempted youth. Many there are who stand at the parting of the ways. Every influence, every impression, is determining the choice that shapes their destiny both here and hereafter. Evil invites them. Its resorts are made bright and attractive. They have a welcome for every comer. All about us are youth who have no home, and many whose homes have no helpful, uplifting power, and the youth drift into evil. They are going down to ruin within the very shadow of our own doors.

These youth need a hand stretched out to them in sympathy. Kind words simply spoken, little attentions simply bestowed, will sweep away the clouds of temptation which gather over the soul. The true expression of heaven-born sympathy has power to open the door of hearts that need the fragrance of Christlike words, and the simple, delicate touch of the spirit of Christ's love. If we would show an interest in the youth, invite them to our homes, and surround them with cheering, helpful influences, there are many who would gladly turn their steps into the upward path.

Our time here is short. We can pass through this world but once; as we pass along, let us make the most of life. The work to which we are called does not require wealth or social position or great ability. It requires a kindly, self-sacrificing spirit and a steadfast purpose. A lamp, however small, if kept steadily burning, may be the means of lighting many other lamps. Our sphere of influence may seem narrow, our ability small, our opportunities few, our acquirements limited; yet wonderful possibilities are ours through a faithful use of the opportunities of our own homes. If we will open our hearts and homes to the divine principles of life we shall become channels for currents of life-giving power. From our homes will flow streams of healing, bringing life and beauty and fruitfulness where now are barrenness and dearth.—*The Ministry of Healing*, pp. 362, 354, 355.

September 24

Refinement in the Home

Behold, I have refined you, but not as silver;
I have tested you in the furnace of affliction.
—Isaiah 48:10.

There is great need of the cultivation of true refinement in the home. This is a powerful witness in favor of the truth. In whomsoever they may appear, vulgarity of language and of demeanor indicate a vitiated heart. Truth of heavenly origin never degrades the receiver, never makes a person coarse or rough. Truth is softening and refining in its influence. When received into the heart, it makes the youth respectful and polite. Christian politeness is received only under the working of the Holy Spirit. It does not consist in affectation or artificial polish, in bowing and simpering. This is the class of politeness possessed by those of the world, but they are destitute of true Christian politeness. True polish, true politeness, is obtained only from a practical knowledge of the gospel of Christ. True politeness, true courtesy, is a kindness shown to all, high or low, rich or poor.

The essence of true politeness is consideration for others. The essential, enduring education is that which broadens the sympathies and encourages universal kindliness. That so-called culture which does not make the youth deferential toward their parents, appreciative of their excellences, forbearing toward their defects, and helpful to their necessities; which does not make them considerate and tender, generous and helpful toward the young, the old, and the unfortunate, and courteous toward all is a failure.

Christian courtesy is the golden clasp which unites the members of the family in bonds of love, becoming closer and stronger every day.

The most valuable rules for social and family relationships are to be found in the Bible. There is not only the best and purest standard of morality but the most valuable code of politeness. Our Saviour's Sermon on the Mount contains instruction of priceless worth to old and young. It should be often read in the family circle and its precious teachings exemplified in the daily life. The golden rule, "Whatsoever ye would that men should do to you, do ye even so to them," as well as the apostolic injunction, "In honour preferring one another," should be made the law of the family. Those who cherish the spirit of Christ will manifest politeness at home, a spirit of benevolence even in little things.—*The Adventist Home,* pp. 422, 423.

September 25

Family Worship

Be anxious for nothing, but in everything by prayer and supplication, with thanksgiving, let your requests be made known to God.—Philippians 4:6.

In every family there should be a fixed time for morning and evening worship. How appropriate it is for parents to gather their children about them before the fast is broken, to thank the heavenly Father for His protection during the night, and to ask Him for His help and guidance and watchcare during the day! How fitting, also, when evening comes, for parents and children to gather once more before Him and thank Him for the blessings of the day that is past!

The father, or, in his absence, the mother, should conduct the worship, selecting a portion of Scripture that is interesting and easily understood. The service should be short. When a long chapter is read and a long prayer offered, the service is made wearisome, and at its close a sense of relief is felt. God is dishonored when the hour of worship is made dry and irksome, when it is so tedious, so lacking in interest, that the children dread it.

Fathers and mothers, make the hour of worship intensely interesting. There is no reason why this hour should not be the most pleasant and enjoyable of the day. A little thought given to preparation for it will enable you to make it full of interest and profit. From time to time let the service be varied. Questions may be asked on the portion of Scripture read, and a few earnest, timely remarks may be made. A song of praise may be sung. The prayer offered should be short and pointed. In simple, earnest words let the one who leads in prayer praise God for His goodness and ask Him for help. As circumstances permit, let the children join in the reading and the prayer. . . .

Each morning consecrate yourselves and your children to God for that day. Make no calculation for months or years; these are not yours. One brief day is given you. As if it were your last on earth, work during its hours for the Master. Lay all your plans before God, to be carried out or given up, as His providence shall indicate. Accept His plans instead of your own, even though their acceptance requires the abandonment of cherished projects. Thus the life will be molded more and more after the divine example; "and the peace of God, which passeth all understanding, shall keep your hearts and minds through Christ Jesus." (Philippians 4:7.)—*Testimonies for the Church,* vol. 7, pp. 43, 44.

2016

Family Recreation

It is good and fitting for one to eat and drink, and to enjoy the good of all his labor in which he toils under the sun all the days of his life which God gives him: for it is his heritage.
—Ecclesiastes 5:18.

There is a distinction between recreation and amusement. Recreation, when true to its name, re-creation, tends to strengthen and build up. Calling us aside from our ordinary cares and occupations, it affords refreshment for mind and body and thus enables us to return with new vigor to the earnest work of life.

Amusement, on the other hand, is sought for the sake of pleasure and is often carried to excess; it absorbs the energies that are required for useful work and thus proves a hindrance to life's true success. . . .

Let us never lose sight of the fact that Jesus is a wellspring of joy. He does not delight in the misery of human beings, but loves to see them happy.

Christians have many sources of happiness at their command, and they may tell with unerring accuracy what pleasures are lawful and right. They may enjoy such recreations as will not dissipate the mind or debase the soul, such as will not disappoint and leave a sad after-influence to destroy self-respect or bar the way to usefulness. If they can take Jesus with them and maintain a prayerful spirit, they are perfectly safe.

Any amusement in which you can engage asking the blessing of God upon it in faith will not be dangerous. But any amusement which disqualifies you for secret prayer, for devotion at the altar of prayer, or for taking part in the prayer meeting is not safe, but dangerous.

We are of that class who believe that it is our privilege every day of our lives to glorify God upon the earth, that we are not to live in this world merely for our own amusement, merely to please ourselves. We are here to benefit humanity and to be a blessing to society; and if we let our minds run in that low channel that many who are seeking only vanity and folly permit their minds to run in, how can we be a benefit to our race and generation? How can we be a blessing to society around us? We cannot innocently indulge in any amusement which will unfit us for the more faithful discharge of ordinary duties.—*The Adventist Home,* pp. 512, 513.

September 27

Appeal to Unsaved Family Members

Now then, we are ambassadors for Christ, as though God were pleading through us: we implore you on Christ's behalf, be reconciled to God.—2 Corinthians 5:20.

[Part of a letter to Ellen White's twin sister, Elizabeth Bangs:] Don't you believe on Jesus, Lizzie? Do you not believe He is your Saviour—that He has evidenced His love for you in giving His own precious life that you might be saved? All that is required of you is to take Jesus as your own precious Saviour. I pray most earnestly that the Lord Jesus shall reveal Himself to you and to Reuben [Lizzie's husband]. Your life in this world is not one of pleasure but of pain; and if you will not doubt Jesus but believe that He died to save you, if you will come to Him just as you are, and give yourself to Jesus and grasp His promises by living faith, He will be to you all that you can desire.

To everyone inquiring, "What must I do to be saved?" I answer, Believe on the Lord Jesus Christ. Do not doubt for a moment but that He wants to save you just as you are. He says to the Jews, "Ye will not come unto Me that ye might have life." Let not this be said of Reuben and you, and your helper in your household. Jesus wants to save you, to give you peace and rest and assurance while you live, and eternal life in His kingdom at last. No one will be compelled to be saved. The Lord Jesus forces the will of none. He says to all, Choose ye this day whom ye will serve. The mind and heart given to Jesus Christ will find rest in His love. . . .

Then you, my dear sister, Reuben, and your attendant, have reason to hope in His mercy and to believe on Jesus Christ, that He can save you. Why? Because you are guiltless? No; because you are sinners, and Jesus says, "I came not to call the righteous but sinners to repentance." When the devil whispers to you, There is no hope, tell him you know there is, for "God so loved the world that he gave his only begotten Son that whosoever believeth in him should not perish, but have everlasting life." What more could God do for you, more than He has done, to make you love Him? Lizzie, believe, simply believe that Jesus means just what He says. Take Him at His word and hang your helpless soul on Jesus Christ.

The hands that were nailed to the cross for you are stretched out to save you. . . . Will you give yourself in trusting faith to Jesus? I long to take you in my arms and lay you on the bosom of Jesus Christ.

You must accept of Jesus. He longs to give you His peace and the light of His countenance. Lizzie, my heart longs to see you trusting in Jesus, for He can give you His grace to bear all your acute sufferings. He loves you. He wants to save you.—*Letter 61,* 1891.

2016

September 28

Introduce Jesus to Neighbors

Philip found Nathanael and said to him, "We have found Him of whom Moses in the law, and also the prophets, wrote."—John 1:45.

With the calling of John and Andrew and Simon, of Philip and Nathanael, began the foundation of the Christian church. John directed two of his disciples to Christ. Then one of these, Andrew, found his brother, and called him to the Saviour. Philip was then called, and he went in search of Nathanael. These examples should teach us the importance of personal effort, of making direct appeals to our kindred, friends, and neighbors. There are those who for a lifetime have professed to be acquainted with Christ, yet who have never made a personal effort to bring even one soul to the Saviour. They leave all the work for the minister. He may be well qualified for his calling, but he cannot do that which God has left for the members of the church.

There are many who need the ministration of loving Christian hearts. Many have gone down to ruin who might have been saved if their neighbors, common men and women, had put forth personal effort for them. Many are waiting to be personally addressed. In the very family, the neighborhood, the town, where we live, there is work for us to do as missionaries for Christ. If we are Christians, this work will be our delight. No sooner are we converted than there is born within us a desire to make known to others what a precious friend we have found in Jesus. The saving and sanctifying truth cannot be shut up in our hearts.

All who are consecrated to God will be channels of light. God makes them His agents to communicate to others the riches of His grace. His promise is, "I will make them and the places round about My hill a blessing; and I will cause the shower to come down in his season; there shall be showers of blessing." (Ezekiel 34:26.)

Philip said to Nathanael, "Come and see." He did not ask him to accept another's testimony, but to behold Christ for himself. Now that Jesus has ascended to heaven, His disciples are His representatives among humanity, and one of the most effective ways of winning souls to Him is in exemplifying His character in our daily life. Our influence upon others depends not so much upon what we say as upon what we are. People may combat and defy our logic, they may resist our appeals; but a life of disinterested love is an argument they cannot gainsay. A consistent life, characterized by the meekness of Christ, is a power in the world.—*The Desire of Ages*, pp. 141, 142.

September 29

The Influence of Jesus in the Home

As He who called you is holy, you also be holy in all your conduct.
—1 Peter 1:15.

The truth as it is in Jesus does much for the receivers, and not only for them, but for all who are brought within the sphere of their influence. The truly converted souls are illuminated from on high, and Christ is in them "a well of water springing up into everlasting life." Their words, their motives, their actions, may be misinterpreted and falsified; but they do not mind it because they have greater interests at stake. They do not consider present convenience; they are not ambitious for display; they do not crave the praise of others. Their hope is in heaven, and they keep straight on, with their eyes fixed on Jesus. They do right because it is right, and because only those who do right will have an entrance into the kingdom of God. They are kind and humble, and thoughtful of others' happiness. They never say, "Am I my brother's keeper?" but they love their neighbor as themselves. Their manner is not harsh and dictatorial, like that of the godless; but they reflect light from heaven upon others. They are true, bold soldiers of the cross of Christ, holding forth the word of life. As they gain in influence, prejudice against them dies away, their piety is acknowledged, and their Bible principles are respected.

Thus it is with all who are truly converted. They bear precious fruit, and in so doing walk as Christ walked, talk as He talked, work as He worked, and the truth as it is in Jesus, through them, makes an impression in their homes, in their neighborhoods, and in the church. They are building characters for eternity, while working out their own salvation with fear and trembling. They are exemplifying before the world the valuable principles of truth, showing what the truth will do for the life and character of the genuine believer. They are unconsciously acting their part in the sublime work of Christ in the redemption of the world, a work which, in its character and influence, is far-reaching, undermining the foundation of false religion and false science. . . .

The Lord wants you and your family to be Christians in every sense of the word and to show in your characters the sanctifying power of the truth. If you had formed such characters, your works would stand the test of the judgment; should the fires of the last day kindle upon your works as they now are, they would prove to be only hay, wood, and stubble. Do not think this severe; it is true. Self has been mingled with all your labors. Will you come up to the high standard?—*Testimonies for the Church,* vol. 5, pp. 569, 570.

September 30

The Home's Only Safeguard

For not the hearers of the law are just in the sight of God, but the doers of the law will be justified.—Romans 2:13.

Those who bear the last message of mercy to the world should feel it their duty to instruct parents in regard to home religion. The great reformatory movement must begin in presenting to fathers and mothers and children the principles of the law of God. As the claims of the law are presented, and men and women are convicted of their duty to render obedience, show them the responsibility of their decision, not only for themselves but for their children. Show that obedience to God's word is our only safeguard against the evils that are sweeping the world to destruction. Parents are giving to their children an example either of obedience or of transgression. By their example and teaching, the eternal destiny of their households will in most cases be decided. In the future life the children will be what their parents have made them.

If parents could be led to trace the results of their action, and could see how by their example and teaching they perpetuate and increase the power of sin or the power of righteousness, a change would certainly be made. Many would break the spell of tradition and custom.

Let ministers urge this matter upon their congregations. Press home upon the consciences of parents the conviction of their solemn duties, so long neglected. This will break up the spirit of pharisaism and resistance to the truth as nothing else can. Religion in the home is our great hope and makes the prospect bright for the conversion of the whole family to the truth of God. . . .

Our life must be hid with Christ in God. We must know Christ personally. Then only can we rightly represent Him to the world. Let the prayer constantly ascend: "Lord, teach me how to do as Jesus would do were He in my place." Wherever we are we must let our light shine forth to the glory of God in good works. This is the great, important interest of our life. . . .

Carry forward the work of God firmly and strongly, but in the meekness of Christ and as quietly as possible. Let no human boasting be heard. Let no sign of self-sufficiency be made. Let it be seen that God has called us to handle sacred trusts; preach the word, be diligent, earnest, and fervent.—*Testimonies for the Church*, vol. 6, pp. 119, 121, 122.

Jesus, Our High Priest

OCTOBER 1

THE CENTRAL PILLAR OF ADVENTISM

How long will the vision be, concerning the daily sacrifices and the transgression of desolation, the giving of both the sanctuary and the host to be trampled underfoot?—Daniel 8:13.

The scripture which above all others had been both the foundation and the central pillar of the advent faith was the declaration: "Unto two thousand and three hundred days; then shall the sanctuary be cleansed." (Daniel 8:14.) These had been familiar words to all believers in the Lord's soon coming. By the lips of thousands was this prophecy repeated as the watchword of their faith. All felt that upon the events therein foretold depended their brightest expectations and most cherished hopes. These prophetic days had been shown to terminate in the autumn of 1844. In common with the rest of the Christian world, Adventists then held that the earth, or some portion of it, was the sanctuary. They understood that the cleansing of the sanctuary was the purification of the earth by the fires of the last great day, and that this would take place at the second advent. Hence the conclusion that Christ would return to the earth in 1844.

But the appointed time had passed, and the Lord had not appeared. The believers knew that God's word could not fail; their interpretation of the prophecy must be at fault; but where was the mistake? Many rashly cut the knot of difficulty by denying that the 2300 days ended in 1844. No reason could be given for this except that Christ had not come at the time they expected Him. They argued that if the prophetic days had ended in 1844, Christ would then have returned to cleanse the sanctuary by the purification of the earth by fire; and that since He had not come, the days could not have ended. . . .

But God had led His people in the great advent movement; His power and glory had attended the work, and He would not permit it to end in darkness and disappointment, to be reproached as a false and fanatical excitement. He would not leave His word involved in doubt and uncertainty. . . .

They found in the Bible a full explanation of the subject of the sanctuary, its nature, location, and services; the testimony of the sacred writers being so clear and ample as to place the matter beyond all question.—*The Great Controversy,* pp. 409–411.

October 2

The Correct Understanding of the Heavenly Sanctuary

But Christ came as High Priest of the good things to come, with the greater and more perfect tabernacle not made with hands, that is, not of this creation.
—*Hebrews 9:11.*

The correct understanding of the ministration in the heavenly sanctuary is the foundation of our faith.—*Evangelism,* p. 221.

The earthly sanctuary was built by Moses according to the pattern shown him in the mount. It was "a figure for the time then present, in which were offered both gifts and sacrifices;" its two holy places were "patterns of things in the heavens;" Christ, our great High Priest, is "a minister of the sanctuary, and of the true tabernacle, which the Lord pitched, and not man." (Hebrews 9:9, 23; 8:2.) As in vision the apostle John was granted a view of the temple of God in heaven, he beheld there "seven lamps of fire burning before the throne." . . . Here the prophet was permitted to behold the first apartment of the sanctuary in heaven; and he saw there the "seven lamps of fire" and the "golden altar" represented by the golden candlestick and the altar of incense in the sanctuary on earth. Again, "the temple of God was opened" (Revelation 11:19), and he looked within the inner veil, upon the holy of holies. Here he beheld "the ark of His testament" (Revelation 11:19), represented by the sacred chest constructed by Moses to contain the law of God. . . .

John says that he saw the sanctuary in heaven. That sanctuary, in which Jesus ministers in our behalf, is the great original, of which the sanctuary built by Moses was a copy.

The heavenly temple, the abiding place of the King of kings, where "thousand thousands ministered unto Him, and ten thousand times ten thousand stood before Him" (Daniel 7:10), that temple filled with the glory of the eternal throne, where seraphim, its shining guardians, veil their faces in adoration—no earthly structure could represent its vastness and its glory. Yet important truths concerning the heavenly sanctuary and the great work there carried forward for our redemption were to be taught by the earthly sanctuary and its services.

After His ascension, our Saviour was to begin His work as our High Priest. Says Paul, "Christ is not entered into the holy places made with hands, which are the figures of the true; but into heaven itself, now to appear in the presence of God for us." (Hebrews 9:24.)—*Patriarchs and Prophets,* pp. 356, 357.

October 3

In the Holy of Holies

But this Man, after He had offered one sacrifice for sins forever, sat down at the right hand of God.—Hebrews 10:12.

The subject of the sanctuary was the key which unlocked the mystery of the disappointment of 1844. It opened to view a complete system of truth, connected and harmonious, showing that God's hand had directed the great advent movement and revealing present duty as it brought to light the position and work of His people. As the disciples of Jesus after the terrible night of their anguish and disappointment were "glad when they saw the Lord," so did those now rejoice who had looked in faith for His second coming. They had expected Him to appear in glory to give reward to His servants. As their hopes were disappointed, they had lost sight of Jesus, and with Mary at the sepulcher they cried: "They have taken away my Lord, and I know not where they have laid Him." Now in the holy of holies they again beheld Him, their compassionate High Priest, soon to appear as their king and deliverer. Light from the sanctuary illumined the past, the present, and the future. They knew that God had led them by His unerring providence. Though, like the first disciples, they themselves had failed to understand the message which they bore, yet it had been in every respect correct. In proclaiming it they had fulfilled the purpose of God, and their labor had not been in vain in the Lord. Begotten "again unto a lively hope," they rejoiced "with joy unspeakable and full of glory."

Both the prophecy of Daniel 8:14, "Unto two thousand and three hundred days; then shall the sanctuary be cleansed," and the first angel's message, "Fear God, and give glory to Him; for the hour of His judgment is come," pointed to Christ's ministration in the most holy place, to the investigative judgment, and not to the coming of Christ for the redemption of His people and the destruction of the wicked. The mistake had not been in the reckoning of the prophetic periods, but in the event to take place at the end of the 2300 days. Through this error the believers had suffered disappointment, yet all that was foretold by the prophecy, and all that they had any Scripture warrant to expect, had been accomplished. At the very time when they were lamenting the failure of their hopes, the event had taken place which was foretold by the message, and which must be fulfilled before the Lord could appear to give reward to His servants.—*The Great Controversy*, pp. 423, 424.

A Figure of the Heavenly

Then indeed, even the first covenant had ordinances of divine service and the earthly sanctuary.—Hebrews 9:1.

I was also shown a sanctuary upon the earth containing two apartments. It resembled the one in heaven, and I was told that it was a figure of the heavenly. The furniture of the first apartment of the earthly sanctuary was like that in the first apartment of the heavenly. The veil was lifted, and I looked into the holy of holies and saw that the furniture was the same as in the most holy place of the heavenly sanctuary. The priest ministered in both apartments of the earthly. He went daily into the first apartment, but entered the most holy only once a year, to cleanse it from the sins which had been conveyed there. I saw that Jesus ministered in both apartments of the heavenly sanctuary. The priests entered into the earthly with the blood of an animal as an offering for sin. Christ entered into the heavenly sanctuary by the offering of His own blood. The earthly priests were removed by death; therefore they could not continue long; but Jesus was a priest forever. Through the sacrifices and offerings brought to the earthly sanctuary, the children of Israel were to lay hold of the merits of a Saviour to come. And in the wisdom of God the particulars of this work were given us that we might, by looking to them, understand the work of Jesus in the heavenly sanctuary.

As Jesus died on Calvary, He cried, "It is finished," and the veil of the temple was rent in twain, from the top to the bottom. This was to show that the services of the earthly sanctuary were forever finished, and that God would no more meet with the priests in their earthly temple, to accept their sacrifices. The blood of Jesus was then shed, which was to be offered by Himself in the heavenly sanctuary. As the priest entered the most holy once a year to cleanse the earthly sanctuary, so Jesus entered the most holy of the heavenly, at the end of the 2300 days of Daniel 8, in 1844, to make a final atonement for all who could be benefited by His mediation, and thus to cleanse the sanctuary. . . .

Above the place where Jesus stood, before the ark, was exceedingly bright glory that I could not look upon; it appeared like the throne of God. As the incense ascended to the Father, the excellent glory came from the throne to Jesus, and from Him it was shed upon those whose prayers had come up like sweet incense.—*Early Writings*, pp. 252–253, 252.

October 5

The Sanctuary and Judgment Must Be Clearly Understood

Let us hold fast the confession of our hope without wavering, for He who promised is faithful.—Hebrews 10:23.

Sad is the record which angels bear to heaven. Intelligent beings, professed followers of Christ, are absorbed in the acquirement of worldly possessions or the enjoyment of earthly pleasures. . . . But few are the moments devoted to prayer, to the searching of the Scriptures, to humiliation of soul and confession of sin.

Satan invents unnumbered schemes to occupy our minds, that they may not dwell upon the very work with which we ought to be best acquainted. The archdeceiver hates the great truths that bring to view an atoning sacrifice and an all-powerful mediator. He knows that with him everything depends on his diverting minds from Jesus and His truth.

Those who would share the benefits of the Saviour's mediation should permit nothing to interfere with their duty to perfect holiness in the fear of God. The precious hours, instead of being given to pleasure, to display, or to gain seeking, should be devoted to an earnest, prayerful study of the word of truth. The subject of the sanctuary and the investigative judgment should be clearly understood by the people of God. All need a knowledge for themselves of the position and work of their great High Priest. Otherwise it will be impossible for them to exercise the faith which is essential at this time or to occupy the position which God designs them to fill. Every individual has a soul to save or to lose. Each has a case pending at the bar of God. Each must meet the great Judge face to face. How important, then, that every mind contemplate often the solemn scene when the judgment shall sit and the books shall be opened, when, with Daniel, every individual must stand in his lot, at the end of the days.

All who have received the light upon these subjects are to bear testimony of the great truths which God has committed to them. The sanctuary in heaven is the very center of Christ's work in our behalf. It concerns every soul living upon the earth. It opens to view the plan of redemption, bringing us down to the very close of time and revealing the triumphant issue of the contest between righteousness and sin. It is of the utmost importance that all should thoroughly investigate these subjects and be able to give an answer to everyone that asketh them a reason of the hope that is in them.—*The Great Controversy,* pp. 487–489.

Christ's Intercession Essential

We have such a High Priest, who is seated at the right hand of the throne of the Majesty in the heavens, a Minister of the the sanctuary and of the true tabernacle which the Lord erected, and not man.—Hebrews 8:1, 2.

The intercession of Christ in our behalf in the sanctuary above is as essential to the plan of salvation as was His death upon the cross. By His death He began that work which after His resurrection He ascended to complete in heaven. We must by faith enter within the veil, "whither the forerunner is for us entered." (Hebrews 6:20.) There the light from the cross of Calvary is reflected. There we may gain a clearer insight into the mysteries of redemption. The salvation of humanity is accomplished at an infinite expense to heaven; the sacrifice made is equal to the broadest demands of the broken law of God. Jesus has opened the way to the Father's throne, and through His mediation the sincere desire of all who come to Him in faith may be presented before God.

"He that covereth his sins shall not prosper: but whoso confesseth and forsaketh them shall have mercy." (Proverbs 28:13.) If those who hide and excuse their faults could see how Satan exults over them, how he taunts Christ and holy angels with their course, they would make haste to confess their sins and to put them away. Through defects in the character, Satan works to gain control of the whole mind, and he knows that if these defects are cherished, he will succeed. Therefore he is constantly seeking to deceive the followers of Christ with his fatal sophistry that it is impossible for them to overcome. But Jesus pleads in their behalf His wounded hands, His bruised body; and He declares to all who would follow Him: "My grace is sufficient for thee." (2 Corinthians 12:9.) "Take My yoke upon you, and learn of Me; for I am meek and lowly in heart: and ye shall find rest unto your souls. For My yoke is easy, and My burden is light." (Matthew 11:29, 30.) Let none, then, regard their defects as incurable. God will give faith and grace to overcome them.

We are now living in the great day of atonement. In the typical service, while the high priest was making the atonement for Israel, all were required to afflict their souls by repentance of sin and humiliation before the Lord, lest they be cut off from among the people. In like manner, all who would have their names retained in the book of life should now, in the few remaining days of their probation, afflict their souls before God by sorrow for sin and true repentance.—*The Great Controversy,* pp. 489, 490.

October 7

Two Sanctuaries

Moses was divinely instructed when he was about to make the tabernacle. For He said, "See that you make all things according to the pattern shown you on the mountain."—Hebrews 8:5.

This is the only sanctuary that ever existed on the earth, of which the Bible gives any information. This was declared by Paul to be the sanctuary of the first covenant. But has the new covenant no sanctuary?

Turning again to the book of Hebrews, the seekers for truth found that the existence of a second, or new-covenant sanctuary, was implied in the words of Paul already quoted: "Then verily the first covenant had also ordinances of divine service, and a worldly sanctuary." And the use of the word "also" intimates that Paul has before made mention of this sanctuary. Turning back to the beginning of the previous chapter, they read: "Now of the things which we have spoken this is the sum: We have such an High Priest, who is set on the right hand of the throne of the Majesty in the heavens; a Minister of the sanctuary, and of the true tabernacle, which the Lord pitched, and not man." (Hebrews 8:1, 2.)

Here is revealed the sanctuary of the new covenant. The sanctuary of the first covenant was pitched by man, built by Moses; this is pitched by the Lord, not by man. In that sanctuary the earthly priests performed their service; in this, Christ, our great High Priest, ministers at God's right hand. One sanctuary was on earth, the other is in heaven.

Further, the tabernacle built by Moses was made after a pattern. The Lord directed him: "According to all that I show thee, after the pattern of the tabernacle, and the pattern of all the instruments thereof, even so shall ye make it." And again the charge was given, "Look that thou make them after their pattern, which was showed thee in the mount." (Exodus 25: 9, 40.) And Paul says that the first tabernacle "was a figure for the time then present, in which were offered both gifts and sacrifices;" that its holy places were "patterns of things in the heavens;" that the priests who offered gifts according to the law served "unto the example and shadow of heavenly things," and that "Christ is not entered into the holy places made with hands, which are the figures of the true; but into heaven itself, now to appear in the presence of God for us." (Hebrews 9:9, 23; 8:5; 9:24.)—*The Great Controversy,* pp. 412, 413.

2016

THE MEANING OF THE SANCTUARY SERVICES

For every high priest is appointed to offer both gifts and sacrifices. Therefore it is necessary that this One also have something to offer.—Hebrews 8:3.

After His ascension, our Saviour was to begin His work as our High Priest. Says Paul, "Christ is not entered into the holy places made with hands, which are the figures of the true; but into heaven itself, now to appear in the presence of God for us." (Hebrews 9:24.) As Christ's ministration was to consist of two great divisions, each occupying a period of time and having a distinctive place in the heavenly sanctuary, so the typical ministration consisted of two divisions, the daily and the yearly service, and to each a department of the tabernacle was devoted.

As Christ at His ascension appeared in the presence of God to plead His blood in behalf of penitent believers, so the priest in the daily ministration sprinkled the blood of the sacrifice in the holy place in the sinner's behalf.

The blood of Christ, while it was to release the repentant sinner from the condemnation of the law, was not to cancel the sin; it would stand on record in the sanctuary until the final atonement; so in the type the blood of the sin offering removed the sin from the penitent, but it rested in the sanctuary until the Day of Atonement.

In the great day of final award, the dead are to be "judged out of those things which were written in the books, according to their works." (Revelation 20:12.) Then by virtue of the atoning blood of Christ, the sins of all the truly penitent will be blotted from the books of heaven. Thus the sanctuary will be freed, or cleansed, from the record of sin. In the type, this great work of atonement, or blotting out of sins, was represented by the services of the Day of Atonement—the cleansing of the earthly sanctuary, which was accomplished by the removal, by virtue of the blood of the sin offering, of the sins by which it had been polluted.

As in the final atonement the sins of the truly penitent are to be blotted from the records of heaven, no more to be remembered or come into mind, so in the type they were borne away into the wilderness, forever separated from the congregation.

Since Satan is the originator of sin, the direct instigator of all the sins that caused the death of the Son of God, justice demands that Satan shall suffer the final punishment.—*Patriarchs and Prophets*, pp. 357, 358.

OCTOBER 9

ACCESS TO GOD

For Christ has not entered the holy places made with hands, which are copies of the true, but into heaven itself, now to appear in the presence of God for us.
—*Hebrews 9:24.*

In the courts above, Christ is pleading for His church—pleading for those for whom He has paid the redemption price of His blood. Centuries, ages, can never lessen the efficacy of His atoning sacrifice. . . .

The sin of Adam and Eve caused a fearful separation between God and humanity. And Christ steps in between fallen sinners and God, and says to them: "You may yet come to the Father; there is a plan devised through which God can be reconciled to humanity, and humanity to God; through a mediator you can approach God." And now He stands to mediate for you. He is the great High Priest who is pleading in your behalf; and you are to come and present your case to the Father through Jesus Christ. Thus you can find access to God.

Christ Jesus is represented as continually standing at the altar, momentarily offering up the sacrifice for the sins of the world. He is a minister of the true tabernacle which the Lord pitched and not man. The typical shadows of the Jewish tabernacle no longer possess any virtue. A daily and yearly typical atonement is no longer to be made, but the atoning sacrifice through a mediator is essential because of the constant commission of sin. Jesus is officiating in the presence of God, offering up His shed blood, as it had been a lamb slain. . . .

The religious services, the prayers, the praise, the penitent confession of sin, ascend from true believers as incense to the heavenly sanctuary: but passing through the corrupt channels of humanity, they are so defiled that unless purified by blood, they can never be of value with God. . . . All incense from earthly tabernacles must be moist with the cleansing drops of the blood of Christ. He holds before the Father the censer of His own merits, in which there is no taint of earthly corruption. He gathers into this censer the prayers, the praise, and the confessions of His people, and with these He puts His own spotless righteousness. Then, perfumed with the merits of Christ's propitiation, the incense comes up before God wholly and entirely acceptable. . . .

O, that all may see that everything in obedience, in penitence, in praise and thanksgiving must be placed upon the glowing fire of the righteousness of Christ.—*God's Amazing Grace,* pp. 153, 154.

2016

THE TRUE MEDIATOR

Let us therefore come boldly to the throne of grace, that we may obtain mercy and find grace to help in time of need.
—*Hebrews 4:16.*

In the mediatorial work of Christ, the love of God was revealed in its perfection to mortals and angels.

He stands to mediate for you. He is the great High Priest who is pleading in your behalf; and you are to come and present your case to the Father through Jesus Christ. Thus you can find access to God; and though you sin, your case is not hopeless. "If any man sin, we have an advocate with the Father, Jesus Christ the righteous." (1 John 2:1.)

Christ is your Redeemer; He will take no advantage of your humiliating confessions. If you have sin of a private character, confess it to Christ, who is the only mediator between God and man.

He presents us to the Father clothed in the white raiment of His own character. He pleads before God in our behalf, saying: I have taken the sinner's place. Look not upon this wayward child, but look on Me. Does Satan plead loudly against our souls, . . . claiming us as his prey, the blood of Christ pleads with greater power.

The work of Christ in the sanctuary above, presenting His own blood each moment before the mercy seat, as He makes intercession for us, should have its full impression upon the heart, that we may realize the worth of each moment. Jesus ever liveth to make intercession for us; but one moment carelessly spent can never be recovered.

Think of Jesus. He is in His holy place, not in a state of solitude, but surrounded by ten thousand times ten thousand of heavenly angels who wait to do His bidding. And He bids them go and work for the weakest saints who put their trust in God. High and low, rich and poor, have the same help provided.

Consider this great fact that Christ ceases not to engage in His solemn work in the heavenly sanctuary, and if you wear Christ's yoke, if you lift Christ's burden, you will be engaged in a work of like character with that of your living Head.—*The Faith I Live By*, p. 205.

October 11

The Work in the First Apartment

Now when these things had been thus prepared, the priests always went into the first part of the tabernacle, performing the services.—Hebrews 9:6.

Important truths concerning the atonement are taught by the typical service. A substitute was accepted in the sinner's stead; but the sin was not canceled by the blood of the victim. A means was thus provided by which it was transferred to the sanctuary. By the offering of blood the sinners acknowledged the authority of the law, confessed their guilt in transgression, and expressed their desire for pardon through faith in a Redeemer to come; but they were not yet entirely released from the condemnation of the law. On the Day of Atonement the high priest, having taken an offering from the congregation, went into the most holy place with the blood of this offering, and sprinkled it upon the mercy seat, directly over the law, to make satisfaction for its claims. Then, in his character of mediator, he took the sins upon himself and bore them from the sanctuary. Placing his hands upon the head of the scapegoat, he confessed over him all these sins, thus in figure transferring them from himself to the goat. The goat then bore them away, and they were regarded as forever separated from the people.

Such was the service performed "unto the example and shadow of heavenly things." And what was done in type in the ministration of the earthly sanctuary is done in reality in the ministration of the heavenly sanctuary. After His ascension our Saviour began His work as our high priest. Says Paul: "Christ is not entered into the holy places made with hands, which are the figures of the true; but into heaven itself, now to appear in the presence of God for us." (Hebrews 9:24.)

The ministration of the priest throughout the year in the first apartment of the sanctuary, "within the veil" which formed the door and separated the holy place from the outer court, represents the work of ministration upon which Christ entered at His ascension. It was the work of the priest in the daily ministration to present before God the blood of the sin offering, also the incense which ascended with the prayers of Israel. So did Christ plead His blood before the Father in behalf of sinners, and present before Him also, with the precious fragrance of His own righteousness, the prayers of penitent believers. Such was the work of ministration in the first apartment of the sanctuary in heaven.—*The Great Controversy*, pp. 420, 421.

The Work in the Second Apartment

But into the second part the high priest went alone once a year, not without blood, which he offered for himself and for the people's sins committed in ignorance.
—Hebrews 9:7.

For eighteen centuries this work of ministration continued in the first apartment of the sanctuary. The blood of Christ, pleaded in behalf of penitent believers, secured their pardon and acceptance with the Father, yet their sins still remained upon the books of record. As in the typical service there was a work of atonement at the close of the year, so before Christ's work for our redemption is completed there is a work of atonement for the removal of sin from the sanctuary. This is the service which began when the 2300 days ended. At that time, as foretold by Daniel the prophet, our High Priest entered the most holy, to perform the last division of His solemn work—to cleanse the sanctuary.

As anciently the sins of the people were by faith placed upon the sin offering and through its blood transferred, in figure, to the earthly sanctuary, so in the new covenant the sins of the repentant are by faith placed upon Christ and transferred, in fact, to the heavenly sanctuary. And as the typical cleansing of the earthly was accomplished by the removal of the sins by which it had been polluted, so the actual cleansing of the heavenly is to be accomplished by the removal, or blotting out, of the sins which are there recorded. But before this can be accomplished, there must be an examination of the books of record to determine who, through repentance of sin and faith in Christ, are entitled to the benefits of His atonement. The cleansing of the sanctuary therefore involves a work of investigation—a work of judgment. This work must be performed prior to the coming of Christ to redeem His people; for when He comes, His reward is with Him to give to every man according to his works. (Revelation 22:12.)

Thus those who followed in the light of the prophetic word saw that, instead of coming to the earth at the termination of the 2300 days in 1844, Christ then entered the most holy place of the heavenly sanctuary to perform the closing work of atonement preparatory to His coming.

It was seen, also, that while the sin offering pointed to Christ as a sacrifice, and the high priest represented Christ as a mediator, the scapegoat typified Satan, the author of sin, upon whom the sins of the truly penitent will finally be placed.—*The Great Controversy,* pp. 421, 422.

October 13

The Union of Justice and Mercy

Behind the second veil, the part of the tabernacle which is called the Holiest of All, which had the golden censer and the ark of the covenant.—Hebrews 9:3, 4.

Thus those who were studying the subject found indisputable proof of the existence of a sanctuary in heaven. Moses made the earthly sanctuary after a pattern which was shown him. Paul teaches that that pattern was the true sanctuary which is in heaven. And John testifies that he saw it in heaven.

In the temple in heaven, the dwelling place of God, His throne is established in righteousness and judgment. In the most holy place is His law, the great rule of right by which all mankind are tested. The ark that enshrines the tables of the law is covered with the mercy seat, before which Christ pleads His blood in the sinner's behalf. Thus is represented the union of justice and mercy in the plan of human redemption. This union infinite wisdom alone could devise and infinite power accomplish; it is a union that fills all heaven with wonder and adoration. The cherubim of the earthly sanctuary, looking reverently down upon the mercy seat, represent the interest with which the heavenly host contemplate the work of redemption. This is the mystery of mercy into which angels desire to look—that God can be just while He justifies the repenting sinner and renews His relationship with the fallen race; that Christ could stoop to raise unnumbered multitudes from the abyss of ruin and clothe them with the spotless garments of His own righteousness to unite with angels who have never fallen and to dwell forever in the presence of God.

The work of Christ as our intercessor is presented in that beautiful prophecy of Zechariah concerning Him "whose name is the Branch." Says the prophet: "He shall build the temple of the Lord; and He shall bear the glory, and shall sit and rule upon His [the Father's] throne; and He shall be a priest upon His throne: and the counsel of peace shall be between Them both." (Zechariah 6:12, 13.)

"He shall build the temple of the Lord." By His sacrifice and mediation Christ is both the foundation and the builder of the church of God. The apostle Paul points to Him as "the chief Cornerstone; in whom all the building fitly framed together groweth into an holy temple in the Lord." (Ephesians 2:20, 21.)—*The Great Controversy*, pp. 415, 416.

Behold, the Bridegroom Cometh

Watch therefore, for you know neither the day nor the hour in which the Son of Man is coming.—Matthew 25:13.

The proclamation, "Behold, the Bridegroom cometh," in the summer of 1844, led thousands to expect the immediate advent of the Lord. At the appointed time the Bridegroom came, not to the earth, as the people expected, but to the Ancient of Days in heaven, to the marriage, the reception of His kingdom. "They that were ready went in with Him to the marriage: and the door was shut." They were not to be present in person at the marriage; for it takes place in heaven, while they are upon the earth. The followers of Christ are to "wait for their Lord, when He will *return from* the wedding." (Luke 12:36.) But they are to understand His work, and to follow Him by faith as He goes in before God. It is in this sense that they are said to go in to the marriage.

In the parable it was those that had oil in their vessels with their lamps that went in to the marriage. Those who, with a knowledge of the truth from the Scriptures, had also the Spirit and grace of God, and who, in the night of their bitter trial, had patiently waited, searching the Bible for clearer light—these saw the truth concerning the sanctuary in heaven and the Saviour's change in ministration, and by faith they followed Him in His work in the sanctuary above. And all who through the testimony of the Scriptures accept the same truths, following Christ by faith as He enters in before God to perform the last work of mediation, and at its close to receive His kingdom—all these are represented as going in to the marriage.

In the parable of Matthew 22 the same figure of the marriage is introduced, and the investigative judgment is clearly represented as taking place before the marriage. Previous to the wedding the king comes in to see the guests, to see if all are attired in the wedding garment, the spotless robe of character washed and made white in the blood of the Lamb. (Matthew 22:11; Revelation 7:14.) The one who is found wanting is cast out, but all who upon examination are seen to have the wedding garment on are accepted of God and accounted worthy of a share in His kingdom and a seat upon His throne. This work of examination of character, of determining who are prepared for the kingdom of God, is that of the investigative judgment, the closing work in the sanctuary above.—*The Great Controversy,* pp. 427, 428.

October 15

A Period of Trial

Then I took the little book out of the angel's hand and ate it, and it was as sweet as honey in my mouth. But when I had eaten it, my stomach became bitter.
—Revelation 10:10.

The condition of the unbelieving Jews illustrates the condition of the careless and unbelieving among professed Christians, who are willingly ignorant of the work of our merciful High Priest. In the typical service, when the high priest entered the most holy place, all Israel were required to gather about the sanctuary and in the most solemn manner humble their souls before God, that they might receive the pardon of their sins and not be cut off from the congregation. How much more essential in this antitypical Day of Atonement that we understand the work of our High Priest and know what duties are required of us.

People cannot with impunity reject the warning which God in mercy sends them. A message was sent from heaven to the world in Noah's day, and their salvation depended upon the manner in which they treated that message. Because they rejected the warning, the Spirit of God was withdrawn from the sinful race, and they perished in the waters of the Flood. . . .

But Christ still intercedes in humanity's behalf, and light will be given to those who seek it. Though this was not at first understood by Adventists, it was afterward made plain as the Scriptures which define their true position began to open before them.

The passing of the time in 1844 was followed by a period of great trial to those who still held the advent faith. Their only relief, so far as ascertaining their true position was concerned, was the light which directed their minds to the sanctuary above. Some renounced their faith in their former reckoning of the prophetic periods and ascribed to human or satanic agencies the powerful influence of the Holy Spirit which had attended the advent movement. Another class firmly held that the Lord had led them in their past experience; and as they waited and watched and prayed to know the will of God they saw that their great High Priest had entered upon another work of ministration, and, following Him by faith, they were led to see also the closing work of the church. They had a clearer understanding of the first and second angels' messages, and were prepared to receive and give to the world the solemn warning of the third angel of Revelation 14.—*The Great Controversy,* pp. 430–432.

2016

BEFORE THE ANCIENT OF DAYS

Behold, One like the Son of Man, coming with the clouds of heaven! He came to the Ancient of Days, and they brought Him near before Him.—Daniel 7:13.

Thus was presented to the prophet's vision the great and solemn day when the characters and the lives of all should pass in review before the Judge of all the earth, and to every one should be rendered "according to his works." The Ancient of Days is God the Father. . . . It is He, the source of all being, and the fountain of all law, that is to preside in the judgment. And holy angels as ministers and witnesses, in number "ten thousand times ten thousand, and thousands of thousands," attend this great tribunal. . . .

He [Christ] comes to the Ancient of Days in heaven to receive dominion and glory and a kingdom, which will be given Him at the close of His work as a mediator. It is this coming, and not His second advent to the earth, that was foretold in prophecy to take place at the termination of the 2300 days in 1844. Attended by heavenly angels, our great High Priest enters the holy of holies and there appears in the presence of God to engage in the last acts of His ministration in behalf of man—to perform the work of investigative judgment and to make an atonement for all who are shown to be entitled to its benefits. . . .

Thus those who followed in the light of the prophetic word saw that, instead of coming to the earth at the termination of the 2300 days in 1844, Christ then entered the most holy place of the heavenly sanctuary to perform the closing work of atonement preparatory to His coming.

It was seen, also, that while the sin offering pointed to Christ as a sacrifice, and the high priest represented Christ as a mediator, the scapegoat typified Satan, the author of sin, upon whom the sins of the truly penitent will finally be placed. When the high priest, by virtue of the blood of the sin offering, removed the sins from the sanctuary, he placed them upon the scapegoat. When Christ, by virtue of His own blood, removes the sins of His people from the heavenly sanctuary at the close of His ministration, He will place them upon Satan, who, in the execution of the judgment, must bear the final penalty. The scapegoat was sent away into a land not inhabited, never to come again into the congregation of Israel. So will Satan be forever banished from the presence of God and His people, and he will be blotted from existence in the final destruction of sin and sinners.—*The Great Controversy*, pp. 479, 480, 422.

OCTOBER 17 2016

THE STANDARD OF JUDGMENT

So speak and so do as those who will be judged by the law of liberty.
—James 2:12.

Every individual's work passes in review before God and is registered for faithfulness or unfaithfulness. Opposite each name in the books of heaven is entered with terrible exactness every wrong word, every selfish act, every unfulfilled duty, and every secret sin, with every artful dissembling. Heaven-sent warnings or reproofs neglected, wasted moments, unimproved opportunities, the influence exerted for good or for evil, with its far-reaching results, all are chronicled by the recording angel.

The law of God is the standard by which the characters and the lives of all will be tested in the judgment. Says the wise man: "Fear God, and keep His commandments: for this is the whole duty of man. For God shall bring every work into judgment." (Ecclesiastes 12:13, 14.) The apostle James admonishes his fellow Christians: "So speak ye, and so do, as they that shall be judged by the law of liberty." (James 2:12.)

Those who in the judgment are "accounted worthy" will have a part in the resurrection of the just. Jesus said: "They which shall be accounted worthy to obtain that world, and the resurrection from the dead, . . . are equal unto the angels; and are the children of God, being the children of the resurrection." (Luke 20:35, 36.) And again He declares that "they that have done good" shall come forth "unto the resurrection of life." (John 5:29.) The righteous dead will not be raised until after the judgment at which they are accounted worthy of "the resurrection of life." Hence they will not be present in person at the tribunal when their records are examined and their cases decided.

Jesus will appear as their advocate, to plead in their behalf before God. "If any man sin, we have an advocate with the Father, Jesus Christ the righteous." (1 John 2:1.) "For Christ is not entered into the holy places made with hands, which are the figures of the true; but into heaven itself, now to appear in the presence of God for us." "Wherefore He is able also to save them to the uttermost that come unto God by Him, seeing He ever liveth to make intercession for them." (Hebrews 9:24; 7:25.)—*The Great Controversy,* p. 482.

The Books of Record in Heaven

The court was seated, and the books were opened.
—Daniel 7:10.

In the typical service only those who had come before God with confession and repentance, and whose sins, through the blood of the sin offering, were transferred to the sanctuary, had a part in the service of the Day of Atonement. So in the great day of final atonement and investigative judgment the only cases considered are those of the professed people of God. The judgment of the wicked is a distinct and separate work, and takes place at a later period. "Judgment must begin at the house of God: and if it first begin at us, what shall the end be of them that obey not the gospel?" (1 Peter 4:17.)

The books of record in heaven, in which the names and the deeds of all are registered, are to determine the decisions of the judgment. Says the prophet Daniel: "The judgment was set, and the books were opened." The revelator, describing the same scene, adds: "Another book was opened, which is the book of life: and the dead were judged out of those things which were written in the books, according to their works." (Revelation 20:12.)

The book of life contains the names of all who have ever entered the service of God. Jesus bade His disciples: "Rejoice, because your names are written in heaven." (Luke 10:20.) Paul speaks of his faithful fellow workers, "whose names are in the book of life." (Philippians 4:3.) Daniel, looking down to "a time of trouble, such as never was," declares that God's people shall be delivered, "everyone that shall be found written in the book." And the revelator says that those only shall enter the city of God whose names "are written in the Lamb's book of life." (Daniel 12:1; Revelation 21:27.)

"A book of remembrance" is written before God, in which are recorded the good deeds of "them that feared the Lord, and that thought upon His name." (Malachi 3:16.) Their words of faith, their acts of love, are registered in heaven. Nehemiah refers to this when he says: "Remember me, O my God, . . . and wipe not out my good deeds that I have done for the house of my God." (Nehemiah 13:14.) In the book of God's remembrance every deed of righteousness is immortalized. There every temptation resisted, every evil overcome, every word of tender pity expressed, is faithfully chronicled. And every act of sacrifice, every suffering and sorrow endured for Christ's sake, is recorded.—*The Great Controversy,* pp. 480, 481.

OCTOBER 19

PARDONED

I will pardon all their iniquities by which they have sinned.
—Jeremiah 33:8.

As the books of record are opened in the judgment, the lives of all who have believed on Jesus come in review before God. Beginning with those who first lived upon the earth, our Advocate presents the cases of each successive generation, and closes with the living. Every name is mentioned, every case closely investigated. Names are accepted, names rejected. When any have sins remaining upon the books of record, unrepented of and unforgiven, their names will be blotted out of the book of life, and the record of their good deeds will be erased from the book of God's remembrance. The Lord declared to Moses: "Whosoever hath sinned against Me, him will I blot out of My book." (Exodus 32:33.) And says the prophet Ezekiel: "When the righteous turneth away from his righteousness, and committeth iniquity, . . . all his righteousness that he hath done shall not be mentioned." (Ezekiel 18:24.)

All who have truly repented of sin, and by faith claimed the blood of Christ as their atoning sacrifice, have had pardon entered against their names in the books of heaven; as they have become partakers of the righteousness of Christ, and their characters are found to be in harmony with the law of God, their sins will be blotted out, and they themselves will be accounted worthy of eternal life. The Lord declares, by the prophet Isaiah: "I, even I, am He that blotteth out thy transgressions for Mine own sake, and will not remember thy sins." (Isaiah 43:25.) Said Jesus: "He that overcometh, the same shall be clothed in white raiment; and I will not blot out his name out of the book of life, but I will confess his name before My Father, and before His angels." "Whosoever therefore shall confess Me before men, him will I confess also before My Father which is in heaven. But whosoever shall deny Me before men, him will I also deny before My Father which is in heaven." (Revelation 3:5; Matthew 10:32, 33.)

The deepest interest manifested among people in the decisions of earthly tribunals but faintly represents the interest evinced in the heavenly courts when the names entered in the book of life come up in review before the Judge of all the earth. The divine Intercessor presents the plea that all who have overcome through faith in His blood be forgiven their transgressions, that they be restored to their Eden home, and crowned as joint heirs with Himself to "the first dominion." (Micah 4:8.)—*The Great Controversy,* pp. 483, 484.

The Giving of Rewards

For the Son of Man will come in the glory of His Father with His angels, and then He will reward each according to his works.—Matthew 16:27.

Jesus does not excuse their sins, but shows their penitence and faith, and, claiming for them forgiveness, He lifts His wounded hands before the Father and the holy angels, saying: I know them by name. I have graven them on the palms of My hands. . . .

The work of the investigative judgment and the blotting out of sins is to be accomplished before the second advent of the Lord. Since the dead are to be judged out of the things written in the books, it is impossible that the sins of mortals should be blotted out until after the judgment at which their cases are to be investigated. But the apostle Peter distinctly states that the sins of believers will be blotted out "when the times of refreshing shall come from the presence of the Lord; and He shall send Jesus Christ." (Acts 3:19, 20.) When the investigative judgment closes, Christ will come, and His reward will be with Him to give to every man as his work shall be.

In the typical service the high priest, having made the atonement for Israel, came forth and blessed the congregation. So Christ, at the close of His work as mediator, will appear, "without sin unto salvation" (Hebrews 9:28), to bless His waiting people with eternal life. As the priest, in removing the sins from the sanctuary, confessed them upon the head of the scapegoat, so Christ will place all these sins upon Satan, the originator and instigator of sin. The scapegoat, bearing the sins of Israel, was sent away "unto a land not inhabited" (Leviticus 16:22); so Satan, bearing the guilt of all the sins which he has caused God's people to commit, will be for a thousand years confined to the earth, which will then be desolate, without inhabitant, and he will at last suffer the full penalty of sin in the fires that shall destroy all the wicked. Thus the great plan of redemption will reach its accomplishment in the final eradication of sin and the deliverance of all who have been willing to renounce evil.

At the time appointed for the judgment—the close of the 2300 days, in 1844—began the work of investigation and blotting out of sins. All who have ever taken upon themselves the name of Christ must pass its searching scrutiny. Both the living and the dead are to be judged "out of those things which were written in the books, according to their works."—*The Great Controversy,* pp. 484–486.

October 21

End of Jesus' Work as Priest and Mediator

But without faith it is impossible to please Him, for he who comes to God must believe that He is, and that He is a rewarder of those who diligently seek Him.
—Hebrews 11:6.

But the people were not yet ready to meet their Lord. There was still a work of preparation to be accomplished for them. Light was to be given, directing their minds to the temple of God in heaven; and as they should by faith follow their High Priest in His ministration there, new duties would be revealed. Another message of warning and instruction was to be given to the church.

Says the prophet: "Who may abide the day of His coming? and who shall stand when He appeareth? for He is like a refiner's fire, and like fullers' soap: and He shall sit as a refiner and purifier of silver: and He shall purify the sons of Levi, and purge them as gold and silver, that they may offer unto the Lord an offering in righteousness." (Malachi 3:2, 3.) Those who are living upon the earth when the intercession of Christ shall cease in the sanctuary above are to stand in the sight of a holy God without a mediator. Their robes must be spotless, their characters must be purified from sin by the blood of sprinkling. Through the grace of God and their own diligent effort they must be conquerors in the battle with evil. While the investigative judgment is going forward in heaven, while the sins of penitent believers are being removed from the sanctuary, there is to be a special work of purification, of putting away of sin, among God's people upon earth. This work is more clearly presented in the messages of Revelation 14.

When this work shall have been accomplished, the followers of Christ will be ready for His appearing. "Then shall the offering of Judah and Jerusalem be pleasant unto the Lord, as in the days of old, and as in former years." (Malachi 3:4.) Then the church which our Lord at His coming is to receive to Himself will be a "glorious church, not having spot, or wrinkle, or any such thing." (Ephesians 5:27.) Then she will look "forth as the morning, fair as the moon, clear as the sun, and terrible as an army with banners." (Song of Solomon 6:10.)

Besides the coming of the Lord to His temple, Malachi also foretells His second advent, His coming for the execution of the judgment. (Malachi 3:5.)—*The Great Controversy,* pp. 424, 425.

Words of Approval

Well done, good and faithful servant; . . . Enter into the joy of your lord. —*Matthew 25:23.*

All who have been born into the heavenly family are in a special sense the brothers and sisters of our Lord. The love of Christ binds together the members of His family, and wherever that love is made manifest there the divine relationship is revealed. "Everyone that loveth is born of God, and knoweth God." (1 John 4:7.)

Those whom Christ commends in the judgment may have known little of theology, but they have cherished His principles. Through the influence of the divine Spirit they have been a blessing to those about them. Even among the heathen are those who have cherished the spirit of kindness; before the words of life had fallen upon their ears, they have befriended the missionaries, even ministering to them at the peril of their own lives. Among the heathen are those who worship God ignorantly, those to whom the light is never brought by human instrumentality, yet they will not perish. Though ignorant of the written law of God, they have heard His voice speaking to them in nature, and have done the things that the law required. Their works are evidence that the Holy Spirit has touched their hearts, and they are recognized as the children of God.

How surprised and gladdened will be the lowly among the nations, and among the heathen, to hear from the lips of the Saviour, "Inasmuch as ye have done it unto one of the least of these My brethren, ye have done it unto Me"! How glad will be the heart of Infinite Love as His followers look up with surprise and joy at His words of approval!

But not to any class is Christ's love restricted. He identifies Himself with every child of humanity. That we might become members of the heavenly family, He became a member of the earthly family. He is the Son of man, and thus a brother to every son and daughter of Adam. His followers are not to feel themselves detached from the perishing world around them. They are a part of the great web of humanity; and Heaven looks upon them as kin to sinners as well as to saints. The fallen, the erring, and the sinful, Christ's love embraces; and every deed of kindness done to uplift a fallen soul, every act of mercy, is accepted as done to Him.—*The Desire of Ages,* p. 638.

October 23

Rescue Souls Before Jesus Ends His Ministry

Go out into the highways and hedges, and compel them to come in, that my house may be filled.
—Luke 14:23.

It is no small thing to be a Christian and to be owned and approved of God. The Lord has shown me some who profess the present truth, whose lives do not correspond with their profession. They have the standard of piety altogether too low, and they come far short of Bible holiness. Some engage in vain and unbecoming conversation, and others give way to the risings of self. We must not expect to please ourselves, live and act like the world, have its pleasures, and enjoy the company of those who are of the world, and reign with Christ in glory.

We must be partakers of Christ's sufferings here if we would share in His glory hereafter. If we seek our own interest, how we can best please ourselves, instead of seeking to please God and advance His precious, suffering cause, we shall dishonor God and the holy cause we profess to love. We have but a little space of time left in which to work for God. Nothing should be too dear to sacrifice for the salvation of the scattered and torn flock of Jesus. Those who make a covenant with God by sacrifice now will soon be gathered home to share a rich reward and possess the new kingdom forever and ever.

Oh, let us live wholly for the Lord and show by a well-ordered life and godly conversation that we have been with Jesus and are His meek and lowly followers. We must work while the day lasts, for when the dark night of trouble and anguish comes, it will be too late to work for God. Jesus is in His holy temple and will now accept our sacrifices, our prayers, and our confessions of faults and sins and will pardon all the transgressions of Israel, that they may be blotted out before He leaves the sanctuary. When Jesus leaves the sanctuary, then they who are holy and righteous will be holy and righteous still; for all their sins will then be blotted out, and they will be sealed with the seal of the living God. But those that are unjust and filthy will be unjust and filthy still; for then there will be no Priest in the sanctuary to offer their sacrifices, their confessions, and their prayers before the Father's throne. Therefore what is done to rescue souls from the coming storm of wrath must be done before Jesus leaves the most holy place of the heavenly sanctuary.—*Early Writings*, pp. 47, 48.

2016

The Close of Probation

In the days of the sounding of the seventh angel, when he is about to sound, the mystery of God would be finished, as He declared to His servants the prophets.
—Revelation 10:7.

There is earnest warfare before all who would subdue the evil tendencies that strive for the mastery. The work of preparation is an individual work. We are not saved in groups. The purity and devotion of one will not offset the want of these qualities in another. Though all nations are to pass in judgment before God, yet He will examine the case of each individual with as close and searching scrutiny as if there were not another being upon the earth. Everyone must be tested and found without spot or wrinkle or any such thing.

Solemn are the scenes connected with the closing work of the atonement. Momentous are the interests involved therein. The judgment is now passing in the sanctuary above. For many years this work has been in progress. Soon—none know how soon—it will pass to the cases of the living. In the awful presence of God our lives are to come up in review. At this time above all others it behooves every soul to heed the Saviour's admonition: "Watch and pray: for ye know not when the time is." (Mark 13:33.) "If therefore thou shalt not watch, I will come on thee as a thief, and thou shalt not know what hour I will come upon thee." (Revelation 3:3.)

When the work of the investigative judgment closes, the destiny of all will have been decided for life or death. Probation is ended a short time before the appearing of the Lord in the clouds of heaven. Christ in the Revelation, looking forward to that time, declares: "He that is unjust, let him be unjust still: and he which is filthy, let him be filthy still: and he that is righteous let him be righteous still: and he that is holy, let him be holy still. And, behold, I come quickly; and My reward is with Me, to give every man according as his work shall be." (Revelation 22:11, 12.)

The righteous and the wicked will still be living upon the earth in their mortal state—they will be planting and building, eating and drinking, all unconscious that the final, irrevocable decision has been pronounced in the sanctuary above. Before the Flood, after Noah entered the ark, God shut him in and shut the ungodly out; but for seven days the people, knowing not that their doom was fixed, continued their careless, pleasure-loving life and mocked the warnings of impending judgment. "So," says the Saviour, "shall also the coming of the Son of man be." (Matthew 24:39.)—*The Great Controversy,* pp. 490, 491.

October 25

Satan Fell Like Lightning

I saw Satan fall like lightning from heaven.
—Luke 10:18.

With a great show of prudence the rabbis had warned the people against receiving the new doctrines taught by this new teacher [Jesus]; for His theories and practices were contrary to the teachings of the fathers. The people gave credence to what the priests and Pharisees taught, in place of seeking to understand the word of God for themselves. They honored the priests and rulers instead of honoring God, and rejected the truth that they might keep their own traditions. Many had been impressed and almost persuaded; but they did not act upon their convictions, and were not reckoned on the side of Christ. Satan presented his temptations, until the light appeared as darkness. Thus many rejected the truth that would have proved the saving of the soul.

The True Witness says, "Behold, I stand at the door, and knock." (Revelation 3:20.) Every warning, reproof, and entreaty in the word of God or through His messengers is a knock at the door of the heart. It is the voice of Jesus asking for entrance. With every knock unheeded, the disposition to open becomes weaker. The impressions of the Holy Spirit if disregarded today, will not be as strong tomorrow. The heart becomes less impressible, and lapses into a perilous unconsciousness of the shortness of life, and of the great eternity beyond. Our condemnation in the judgment will not result from the fact that we have been in error, but from the fact that we have neglected heaven-sent opportunities for learning what is truth.

Like the apostles, the seventy [see Luke 10:1] had received supernatural endowments as a seal of their mission. When their work was completed, they returned with joy, saying, "Lord, even the devils are subject unto us through Thy name." Jesus answered, "I beheld Satan as lightning fall from heaven."

The scenes of the past and the future were presented to the mind of Jesus. He beheld Lucifer as he was first cast out from the heavenly places. He looked forward to the scenes of His own agony, when before all the worlds the character of the deceiver should be unveiled. . . .

Beyond the cross of Calvary, with its agony and shame, Jesus looked forward to the great final day, when the prince of the power of the air will meet his destruction in the earth so long marred by his rebellion. Jesus beheld the work of evil forever ended, and the peace of God filling heaven and earth.
—*The Desire of Ages,* pp. 489, 490.

October 26

Jesus' Pleasure in His People

The blameless in their ways are His delight.
—Proverbs 11:20.

He who dwells in the heavenly sanctuary judges righteously. His pleasure is more in His people, struggling with temptation in a world of sin, than in the host of angels that surround His throne.

In this speck of a world the whole heavenly universe manifests the greatest interest, for Christ has paid an infinite price for the souls of its inhabitants. The world's Redeemer has bound earth to heaven by ties of intelligence, for the redeemed of the Lord are here. Heavenly beings still visit the earth as in the days when they walked and talked with Abraham and with Moses. Amid the busy activity of our great cities, amid the multitudes that crowd the thoroughfares and fill the marts of trade where from morning till evening the people act as if business and sport and pleasure were all there is to life, where there are so few to contemplate unseen realities—even here heaven has still its watchers and its holy ones. There are invisible agencies observing every word and deed of human beings. In every assembly for business or pleasure, in every gathering for worship, there are more listeners than can be seen with the natural sight. Sometimes the heavenly intelligences draw aside the curtain which hides the unseen world that our thoughts may be withdrawn from the hurry and rush of life to consider that there are unseen witnesses to all we do or say.

We need to understand better than we do the mission of the angel visitants. It would be well to consider that in all our work we have the cooperation and care of heavenly beings. Invisible armies of light and power attend the meek and lowly ones who believe and claim the promises of God. Cherubim and seraphim and angels that excel in strength—ten thousand times ten thousand and thousands of thousands—stand at His right hand, "all ministering spirits, sent forth to minister for them who shall be heirs of salvation." (Hebrews 1:14.)

By these angel messengers a faithful record is kept of the words and deeds of the children of humanity. Every act of cruelty or injustice toward God's people, all they are caused to suffer through the power of evil workers, is registered in heaven.—*Christ's Object Lessons,* pp. 176, 177.

October 27

From the Earthly to the Heavenly Temple

The veil of the temple was torn in two from top to bottom.
—Matthew 27:51.

By virtue of His death and resurrection He [Jesus] became the minister of the "true tabernacle, which the Lord pitched, and not man." (Hebrews 8:2.) Human beings reared the Jewish tabernacle; mere mortals builded the Jewish temple; but the sanctuary above, of which the earthly was a type, was built by no human architect. "Behold the Man whose name is The Branch; . . . He shall build the temple of the Lord; and He shall bear the glory, and shall sit and rule upon His throne; and He shall be a priest upon His throne." (Zechariah 6:12, 13.)

The sacrificial service that had pointed to Christ passed away; but the eyes of humanity were turned to the true sacrifice for the sins of the world. The earthly priesthood ceased; but we look to Jesus, the minister of the new covenant, and "to the blood of sprinkling, that speaketh better things than that of Abel." "The way into the holiest of all was not yet made manifest, while as the first tabernacle was yet standing: . . . but Christ being come an high priest of good things to come, by a greater and more perfect tabernacle, not made with hands, . . . by His own blood He entered in once into the holy place, having obtained eternal redemption for us." (Hebrews 12:24; 9:8–12.)

"Wherefore He is able also to save them to the uttermost that come unto God by Him, seeing He ever liveth to make intercession for them." (Hebrews 7:25.) Though the ministration was to be removed from the earthly to the heavenly temple; though the sanctuary and our great high priest would be invisible to human sight, yet the disciples were to suffer no loss thereby. They would realize no break in their communion, and no diminution of power because of the Saviour's absence. While Jesus ministers in the sanctuary above, He is still by His Spirit the minister of the church on earth. He is withdrawn from the eye of sense, but His parting promise is fulfilled, "Lo, I am with you alway, even unto the end of the world." (Matthew 28:20.) While He delegates His power to inferior ministers, His energizing presence is still with His church.

"Seeing then that we have a great high priest, . . . Jesus, the Son of God, let us hold fast our profession. . . . Let us therefore come boldly unto the throne of grace, that we may obtain mercy, and find grace to help in time of need." (Hebrews 4:14–16.)—*The Desire of Ages,* pp. 165, 166.

2016

October 28

Working With Our High Priest

Seeing then that we have a great High Priest who has passed through the heavens, Jesus the Son of God, let us hold fast our confession.
—Hebrews 4:14.

We are to fit ourselves with the self-same spirit that was in Christ Jesus. Christ is working for us; will we work for Christ in His lines? Children, cultivate patience and faith and hope. May the Lord increase our joy of faith in this ever-living Intercessor. Try to let no day pass in which you fail to realize your accountability to God through the sacrifice of His only begotten Son. Jesus does not receive glory from any one who is an accuser of the brethren. Let not a day pass that we are not healing and restoring old wounds. Cultivate love, and let no words of evil surmising escape our lips. Close this door quickly, and keep it closed; open the door where Christ presides, and keep it open, because we know the value of Christ's sacrifice and His unchangeable love. Drink in the ever-refreshing waters of life from the wells of Lebanon, but refuse the murky waters from the valley—the dark, suspicious feelings. There is much truthfulness in the cause, but shall we spoil our fragrance of spirit because others clothe themselves with bitterness? God forbid. There is not one tithe of the imaginings of evil that is worth the time we give to consider it and repeat it. Cut away from our speech all severity; talk sweetly; and hold our confidence in Jesus firmly.

We have an ever-living Advocate who is making intercession for us. Then let us become advocates in principle in behalf of those who err. "And having an high priest over the house of God [here is His intercession in our behalf]; let us draw near with a true heart in full assurance of faith, having our hearts sprinkled from an evil conscience; and our bodies washed with pure water. Let us hold fast the profession of our faith without wavering." He is a "faithful high priest in things pertaining to God." (Hebrews 10:22, 23; 2:17.)

Then as He is working for us, let us work just as earnestly and interestedly to promote union with one another. Christ prayed that we might be of that same nature and oneness as that existing between Himself and His Father. Try in everything we do to secure confidence and love one for another, and thus we will answer the prayer of Christ Jesus. . . . Keep close on the side of Christ, and think of the rich encouragement He has given us, that we may in our turn give to others.—*Lift Him Up*, p. 321.

October 29

Jesus Does Not Forget His Church

Therefore, holy brethren, partakers of the heavenly calling, consider the Apostle and High Priest of our confession, Christ Jesus. —*Hebrews 3:1.*

Our crucified Lord is pleading for us in the presence of the Father at the throne of grace. His atoning sacrifice we may plead for our pardon, our justification, and our sanctification. The Lamb slain is our only hope. Our faith looks up to Him, grasps Him as the One who can save to the uttermost, and the fragrance of the all-sufficient offering is accepted of the Father. Unto Christ is committed all power in heaven and in earth, and all things are possible to him that believeth. Christ's glory is concerned in our success. He has a common interest in all humanity. He is our sympathizing Saviour. . . .

Let us remember that our great High Priest is pleading before the mercy seat in behalf of His ransomed people. He ever liveth to make intercession for us. "If any man sin, we have an advocate with the Father, Jesus Christ the righteous."

The blood of Jesus is pleading with power and efficacy for those who are backslidden, for those who are rebellious, for those who sin against great light and love. Satan stands at our right hand to accuse us, and our Advocate stands at God's right hand to plead for us. He has never lost a case that has been committed to Him. We may trust in our Advocate; for He pleads His own merits in our behalf. Hear His prayer before His betrayal and trial. Listen to His prayer for us; for He had us in remembrance.

He will not forget His church in the world of temptation. He looks upon His tried and suffering people, and prays for them. . . . Yes, He beholds His people in this world, which is a persecuting world, and all seared and marred with the curse, and [He] knows that they need all the divine resources of His sympathy and His love. Our Forerunner hath for us entered within the veil, and yet by the golden chain of love and truth, He is linked with His people in closest sympathy.

He is making intercession for the most lowly, the most oppressed and suffering, for the most tried and tempted ones. With upraised hands He pleads, "I have graven thee upon the palms of my hands." God loves to hear, and responds to the pleadings of His Son.—*Seventh-day Adventist Bible Commentary,* vol. 7, p. 948.

Jesus, a Righteous Judge

Therefore, in all things He had to be made like His brethren, that He might be a merciful and faithful High Priest in things pertaining to God, to make propitiation for the sins of the people.—Hebrews 2:17.

Jesus clothed His divinity with humanity in order that He might reach humanity. The apostle says, "Forasmuch then as the children are partakers of flesh and blood, He also Himself likewise took part of the same. . . . For verily He took not on Him the nature of angels; but He took on Him the seed of Abraham. Wherefore in all things it behooved Him to be made like unto His brethren, that He might be a merciful and faithful High Priest in things pertaining to God, to make reconciliation for the sins of the people. For in that He Himself hath suffered being tempted, He is able to succor them that are tempted." Jesus is the only one that has ever walked in the flesh who is able to judge righteously. Looking at outward acts, people may condemn and root up that which they think to be tares; but they may greatly mistake. Both ministers and laity should be Bible students, and understand how to act in regard to the erring. They are not to move rashly, to be actuated by prejudices or partiality, to be ready with an unfeeling heart, to uproot one and tear down another; for this is most solemn work. In criticising and condemning their brethren and sisters, the accusers wound and bruise the souls for whom Christ has died. Christ has purchased them with His own precious blood; and although others, judging from outward appearances, pronounce sentence against them, their judgment in the courts of heaven is more favorable than that of their accusers. Before any of you speak against other believers, or act decidedly to cut them off from church fellowship, follow the injunction of the apostle: "Examine yourselves, whether ye be in the faith; prove your own selves. Know ye not your own selves, how that Jesus Christ is in you, except ye be reprobates?"

Let those who would dispose of their brethren and sisters, look well to the character of their own thoughts, their motives, their impulses, purposes, and deeds. . . . If upon careful, prayerful examination of ourselves, we discover that we are not able to bear the test of human investigation, then how shall we endure the test of the eyes of God, if we set ourselves up as judges of others?

Before judging others, our first work is to watch and pray, to institute a warfare against the evils of our own hearts through the grace of Christ.
—*Review and Herald*, January 3, 1893.

A Perfect Atonement

If anyone sins, we have an Advocate with the Father, Jesus Christ the righteous.—1 John 2:1.

Jesus is our Advocate, our High Priest, our Intercessor. Our position is like that of the Israelites on the Day of Atonement. When the high priest entered the most holy place, representing the place where our High Priest is now pleading, and sprinkled the atoning blood upon the mercy seat, no propitiatory sacrifices were offered without. While the priest was interceding with God, every heart was to be bowed in contrition, pleading for the pardon of transgression.

Type met antitype in the death of Christ, the Lamb slain for the sins of the world. Our great High Priest has made the only sacrifice that is of any value in our salvation. When He offered Himself on the cross, a perfect atonement was made for the sins of the people. We are now standing in the outer court, waiting and looking for that blessed hope, the glorious appearing of our Lord and Saviour Jesus Christ. No sacrifices are to be offered without, for the great High Priest is performing His work in the most holy place. In His intercession as our advocate, Christ needs no one's virtue, no one's intercession. He is the only sin-bearer, the only sin-offering. Prayer and confession are to be offered only to Him who has entered once for all into the most holy place. He will save to the uttermost all who come to Him in faith. He ever liveth to make intercession for us. . . .

Christ represented the Father to the world, and He represents before God the chosen ones in whom He has restored the moral image of God. They are His heritage. To them He says, "He that hath seen Me hath seen the Father." No man "knoweth the Son, but the Father; neither knoweth any man the Father, but the Son, and he to whomsoever the Son will reveal Him." No priest, no religionist, can reveal the Father to any son or daughter of Adam. We have only one Advocate, one Intercessor, who is able to pardon transgression. Shall not our hearts swell with gratitude to Him who gave Jesus to be the propitiation for our sins? Think deeply upon the love that the Father has manifested in our behalf, the love that He has expressed for us. We can not measure this love; for measurement there is none. Can we measure infinity? We can only point to Calvary, to the Lamb slain from the foundation of the world.—*Signs of the Times,* June 28, 1899.

The Great Controversy

The Origin of Sin Is Unexplainable

War broke out in heaven: Michael and his angels fought with the dragon; and the dragon and his angels fought.—Revelation 12:7.

To many minds the origin of sin and the reason for its existence are a source of great perplexity. They see the work of evil, with its terrible results of woe and desolation, and they question how all this can exist under the sovereignty of One who is infinite in wisdom, in power, and in love. Here is a mystery of which they find no explanation. And in their uncertainty and doubt they are blinded to truths plainly revealed in God's word and essential to salvation. There are those who, in their inquiries concerning the existence of sin, endeavor to search into that which God has never revealed; hence they find no solution of their difficulties; and such as are actuated by a disposition to doubt and cavil seize upon this as an excuse for rejecting the words of Holy Writ. Others, however, fail of a satisfactory understanding of the great problem of evil, from the fact that tradition and misinterpretation have obscured the teaching of the Bible concerning the character of God, the nature of His government, and the principles of His dealing with sin.

It is impossible to explain the origin of sin so as to give a reason for its existence. Yet enough may be understood concerning both the origin and the final disposition of sin to make fully manifest the justice and benevolence of God in all His dealings with evil. Nothing is more plainly taught in Scripture than that God was in no wise responsible for the entrance of sin; that there was no arbitrary withdrawal of divine grace, no deficiency in the divine government, that gave occasion for the uprising of rebellion. Sin is an intruder, for whose presence no reason can be given. It is mysterious, unaccountable; to excuse it is to defend it. Could excuse for it be found, or cause be shown for its existence, it would cease to be sin. Our only definition of sin is that given in the word of God; it is "the transgression of the law;" it is the outworking of a principle at war with the great law of love which is the foundation of the divine government. . . .

God desires from all His creatures the service of love—homage that springs from an intelligent appreciation of His character. He takes no pleasure in a forced allegiance, and to all He grants freedom of will, that they may render Him voluntary service.—*The Great Controversy,* pp. 492, 493.

SELFISHNESS, THE ROOT OF SIN

I will ascend above the heights of the clouds, I will be like the Most High.
—*Isaiah 14:14.*

But there was one that chose to pervert this freedom [of will]. Sin originated with him who, next to Christ, had been most honored of God and who stood highest in power and glory among the inhabitants of heaven. Before his fall, Lucifer was first of the covering cherubs, holy and undefiled. "Thus saith the Lord God; Thou sealest up the sum, full of wisdom, and perfect in beauty. Thou hast been in Eden the garden of God; every precious stone was thy covering. . . . Thou art the anointed cherub that covereth; and I have set thee so: thou wast upon the holy mountain of God; thou hast walked up and down in the midst of the stones of fire. Thou wast perfect in thy ways from the day that thou wast created, till iniquity was found in thee." (Ezekiel 28:12–15.)

Lucifer might have remained in favor with God, beloved and honored by all the angelic host, exercising his noble powers to bless others and to glorify his Maker. But, says the prophet, "Thine heart was lifted up because of thy beauty, thou hast corrupted thy wisdom by reason of thy brightness." (Verse 17.) Little by little, Lucifer came to indulge a desire for self-exaltation. . . . Instead of seeking to make God supreme in the affections and allegiance of His creatures, it was Lucifer's endeavor to win their service and homage to himself. And coveting the honor which the infinite Father had bestowed upon His Son, this prince of angels aspired to power which it was the prerogative of Christ alone to wield.

All heaven had rejoiced to reflect the Creator's glory and to show forth His praise. And while God was thus honored, all had been peace and gladness. But a note of discord now marred the celestial harmonies. The service and exaltation of self, contrary to the Creator's plan, awakened forebodings of evil in minds to whom God's glory was supreme. The heavenly councils pleaded with Lucifer. The Son of God presented before him the greatness, the goodness, and the justice of the Creator, and the sacred, unchanging nature of His law. God Himself had established the order of heaven; and in departing from it, Lucifer would dishonor his Maker, and bring ruin upon himself. But the warning, given in infinite love and mercy, only aroused a spirit of resistance. Lucifer allowed jealousy of Christ to prevail, and he became the more determined.—*The Great Controversy,* pp. 493–495.

Lucifer Ejected

So the great dragon was cast out, that serpent of old, called the Devil and Satan, who deceives the whole world; he was cast to the earth, and his angels were cast out with him.—Revelation 12:9.

All the heavenly host were summoned to appear before the Father, to have each case determined. Satan unblushingly made known his dissatisfaction that Christ should be preferred before him. He stood up proudly and urged that he should be equal with God, and should be taken into conference with the Father and understand His purposes. God informed Satan that to His Son alone He would reveal His secret purposes, and He required all the family in heaven, even Satan, to yield Him implicit, unquestioned obedience; but that he (Satan) had proved himself unworthy [of] a place in heaven. Then Satan exultingly pointed to his sympathizers, comprising nearly one half of all the angels, and exclaimed, These are with me! Will you expel these also, and make such a void in Heaven? He then declared that he was prepared to resist the authority of Christ and to defend his place in Heaven by force of might, strength against strength.

Good angels wept to hear the words of Satan, and his exulting boasts. God declared that the rebellious should remain in Heaven no longer. Their high and happy state had been held upon condition of obedience to the law which God had given to govern the high order of intelligences. But no provision had been made to save those who should venture to transgress His law. Satan grew bold in his rebellion, and expressed his contempt of the Creator's law. This Satan could not bear. He claimed that angels needed no law but should be left free to follow their own will, which would ever guide them right; that law was a restriction of their liberty, and that to abolish law was one great object of his standing as he did. The condition of the angels he thought needed improvement. Not so the mind of God, who had made laws and exalted them equal to Himself. The happiness of the angelic host consisted in their perfect obedience to law. All had their special work assigned them; and until Satan rebelled, there had been perfect order and harmonious action in Heaven. . . .

The Father consulted Jesus in regard to at once carrying out their purpose to make human beings to inhabit the earth. He would place them upon probation to test their loyalty, before they could be rendered eternally secure. —*The Spirit of Prophecy,* vol. 1, pp. 22, 23.

November 4

Hostilities

They overcame him by the blood of the Lamb and by the word of their testimony, and they did not love their lives to the death.—Revelation 12:11.

"I will put enmity between thee and the woman, and between thy seed and her seed; it shall bruise thy head, and thou shalt bruise His heel." (Genesis 3:15.) The divine sentence pronounced against Satan after the fall of Adam and Eve was also a prophecy, embracing all the ages to the close of time and foreshadowing the great conflict to engage all the races of mankind who should live upon the earth.

God declares: "I will put enmity." This enmity is not naturally entertained. When our first parents transgressed the divine law, their nature became evil, and they were in harmony, and not at variance, with Satan. There exists naturally no enmity between sinful humanity and the originator of sin. Both became evil through apostasy. Apostates are never at rest, except as they obtain sympathy and support by inducing others to follow their example. For this reason fallen angels and wicked human beings unite in desperate companionship. Had not God specially interposed, Satan and mankind would have entered into an alliance against Heaven; and instead of cherishing enmity against Satan, the whole human family would have been united in opposition to God.

Satan tempted Adam and Eve to sin, as he had caused angels to rebel, that he might thus secure cooperation in his warfare against Heaven. There was no dissension between himself and the fallen angels as regards their hatred of Christ; while on all other points there was discord, they were firmly united in opposing the authority of the Ruler of the universe. But when Satan heard the declaration that enmity should exist between himself and the woman, and between his seed and her seed, he knew that his efforts to deprave human nature would be interrupted; that by some means mankind was to be enabled to resist his power.

Satan's enmity against the human race is kindled because, through Christ, they are the objects of God's love and mercy. He desires to thwart the divine plan for our redemption, to cast dishonor upon God, by defacing and defiling His handiwork; he would cause grief in heaven and fill the earth with woe and desolation. And he points to all this evil as the result of God's work in creating mankind.—*The Great Controversy,* pp. 505, 506.

NOVEMBER 5

IMPLANTED GRACE

Therefore submit to God. Resist the devil and he will flee from you.
—James 4:7.

It is the grace that Christ implants in the soul which creates in us enmity against Satan. Without this converting grace and renewing power, we would continue the captive of Satan, servants ever ready to do his bidding. But the new principle in the soul creates conflict where hitherto had been peace. The power which Christ imparts enables us to resist the tyrant and usurper. Whoever is seen to abhor sin instead of loving it, whoever resists and conquers those passions that have held sway within, displays the operation of a principle wholly from above.

The antagonism that exists between the spirit of Christ and the spirit of Satan was most strikingly displayed in the world's reception of Jesus. It was not so much because He appeared without worldly wealth, pomp, or grandeur that the Jews were led to reject Him. They saw that He possessed power which would more than compensate for the lack of these outward advantages. But the purity and holiness of Christ called forth against Him the hatred of the ungodly. His life of self-denial and sinless devotion was a perpetual reproof to a proud, sensual people. It was this that evoked enmity against the Son of God. Satan and evil angels joined with evil human beings. All the energies of apostasy conspired against the Champion of truth.

The same enmity is manifested toward Christ's followers as was manifested toward their Master. Whoever sees the repulsive character of sin, and in strength from above resists temptation, will assuredly arouse the wrath of Satan and his subjects. Hatred of the pure principles of truth, and reproach and persecution of its advocates, will exist as long as sin and sinners remain. The followers of Christ and the servants of Satan cannot harmonize. The offense of the cross has not ceased. "All that will live godly in Christ Jesus shall suffer persecution." (2 Timothy 3:12.) . . .

As Satan endeavored to cast reproach upon God, so do his agents seek to malign God's people. The spirit which put Christ to death moves the wicked to destroy His followers. All this is foreshadowed in that first prophecy: "I will put enmity between thee and the woman, and between thy seed and her seed." And this will continue to the close of time.—*The Great Controversy*, pp. 506, 507.

November 6

No Sinful Act Without Consent

Whoever abides in Him does not sin.
—1 John 3:6.

All who are not decided followers of Christ are servants of Satan. In the unregenerate heart there is love of sin and a disposition to cherish and excuse it. In the renewed heart there is hatred of sin and determined resistance against it. When Christians choose the society of the ungodly and unbelieving, they expose themselves to temptation. Satan conceals himself from view and stealthily draws his deceptive covering over their eyes. . . .

While Satan is constantly seeking to blind their minds to the fact, let Christians never forget that they "wrestle not against flesh and blood, but against principalities, against powers, against the rulers of the darkness of this world, against wicked spirits in high places." (Ephesians 6:12, margin.) The inspired warning is sounding down the centuries to our time: "Be sober, be vigilant; because your adversary the devil, as a roaring lion, walketh about, seeking whom he may devour." (1 Peter 5:8.) "Put on the whole armor of God, that ye may be able to stand against the wiles of the devil." (Ephesians 6:11.)

From the days of Adam to our own time, our great enemy has been exercising his power to oppress and destroy. He is now preparing for his last campaign against the church. All who seek to follow Jesus will be brought into conflict with this relentless foe. The more nearly the Christian imitates the divine Pattern, the more surely will he make himself a mark for the attacks of Satan. All who are actively engaged in the cause of God, seeking to unveil the deceptions of the evil one and to present Christ before the people, will be able to join in the testimony of Paul, in which he speaks of serving the Lord with all humility of mind, with many tears and temptations.

Satan assailed Christ with his fiercest and most subtle temptations, but he was repulsed in every conflict. Those battles were fought in our behalf; those victories make it possible for us to conquer. Christ will give strength to all who seek it. None without their own consent can be overcome by Satan. The tempter has no power to control the will or to force the soul to sin. He may distress, but he cannot contaminate. He can cause agony, but not defilement. The fact that Christ has conquered should inspire His followers with courage to fight manfully the battle against sin and Satan.—*The Great Controversy*, pp. 508, 510.

November 7

Vindication of God's Character

Father, the hour has come. Glorify Your Son, that Your Son also may glorify You.—John 17:1.

But the plan of redemption had a yet broader and deeper purpose than the salvation of humanity. It was not for this alone that Christ came to the earth; it was not merely that the inhabitants of this little world might regard the law of God as it should be regarded; but it was to vindicate the character of God before the universe. To this result of His great sacrifice—its influence upon the intelligences of other worlds, as well as upon man—the Saviour looked forward when just before His crucifixion He said: "Now is the judgment of this world: now shall the prince of this world be cast out. And I, if I be lifted up from the earth, will draw all unto Me." (John 12:31, 32.) The act of Christ in dying for the salvation of mankind would not only make heaven accessible to men and women, but before all the universe it would justify God and His Son in their dealing with the rebellion of Satan. It would establish the perpetuity of the law of God and would reveal the nature and the results of sin.

From the first the great controversy had been upon the law of God. Satan had sought to prove that God was unjust, that His law was faulty, and that the good of the universe required it to be changed. In attacking the law he aimed to overthrow the authority of its Author. In the controversy it was to be shown whether the divine statutes were defective and subject to change, or perfect and immutable.

When Satan was thrust out of heaven, he determined to make the earth his kingdom. When he tempted and overcame Adam and Eve, he thought that he had gained possession of this world; "because," said he, "they have chosen me as their ruler." He claimed that it was impossible that forgiveness should be granted to the sinner, and therefore the fallen race were his rightful subjects, and the world was his. But God gave His own dear Son—one equal with Himself—to bear the penalty of transgression, and thus He provided a way by which they might be restored to His favor, and brought back to their Eden home. Christ undertook to redeem mankind and to rescue the world from the grasp of Satan. The great controversy begun in heaven was to be decided in the very world, on the very same field, that Satan claimed as his.—*Patriarchs and Prophets,* pp. 68, 69.

November 8

Satan's Claim

All this authority I will give you, and their glory; for this has been delivered to me, and I give it to whomever I wish.—Luke 4:6.

When Jesus was led into the wilderness to be tempted, He was led by the Spirit of God. He did not invite temptation. He went to the wilderness to be alone, to contemplate His mission and work. By fasting and prayer He was to brace Himself for the bloodstained path He must travel. But Satan knew that the Saviour had gone into the wilderness, and he thought this the best time to approach Him.

Mighty issues for the world were at stake in the conflict between the Prince of light and the leader of the kingdom of darkness. After tempting Adam and Eve to sin, Satan claimed the earth as his, and styled himself the prince of this world. Having conformed to his own nature the father and mother of our race, he thought to establish here his empire. He declared that mankind had chosen him as their sovereign. Through his control of them, he held dominion over the world. Christ had come to disprove Satan's claim. As the Son of man, Christ would stand loyal to God. Thus it would be shown that Satan had not gained complete control of the human race, and that his claim to the world was false. All who desired deliverance from his power would be set free. The dominion that Adam had lost through sin would be recovered.

Since the announcement to the serpent in Eden, "I will put enmity between thee and the woman, and between thy seed and her seed" (Genesis 3:15), Satan had known that he did not hold absolute sway over the world. There was seen in humanity the working of a power that withstood his dominion. With intense interest he watched the sacrifices offered by Adam and his sons. In these ceremonies he discerned a symbol of communion between earth and heaven. He set himself to intercept this communion. He misrepresented God, and misinterpreted the rites that pointed to the Saviour. People were led to fear God as one who delighted in their destruction. The sacrifices that should have revealed His love were offered only to appease His wrath. Satan excited people's evil passions, in order to fasten his rule upon them. When God's written word was given, Satan studied the prophecies of the Saviour's advent. From generation to generation he worked to blind the people to these prophecies, that they might reject Christ at His coming.—*The Desire of Ages*, pp. 114, 115.

November 9

A Perpetual Safeguard

Affliction will not rise up a second time.
—*Nahum 1:9.*

Satan's rebellion was to be a lesson to the universe through all coming ages, a perpetual testimony to the nature and terrible results of sin. The working out of Satan's rule, its effects upon both men and angels, would show what must be the fruit of setting aside the divine authority. It would testify that with the existence of God's government and His law is bound up the well-being of all the creatures He has made. Thus the history of this terrible experiment of rebellion was to be a perpetual safeguard to all holy intelligences, to prevent them from being deceived as to the nature of transgression, to save them from committing sin and suffering its punishments.

To the very close of the controversy in heaven the great usurper continued to justify himself. When it was announced that with all his sympathizers he must be expelled from the abodes of bliss, then the rebel leader boldly avowed his contempt for the Creator's law. He reiterated his claim that angels needed no control, but should be left to follow their own will, which would ever guide them right. He denounced the divine statutes as a restriction of their liberty and declared that it was his purpose to secure the abolition of law; that, freed from this restraint, the hosts of heaven might enter upon a more exalted, more glorious state of existence.

With one accord, Satan and his host threw the blame of their rebellion wholly upon Christ, declaring that if they had not been reproved, they would never have rebelled. Thus stubborn and defiant in their disloyalty, seeking vainly to overthrow the government of God, yet blasphemously claiming to be themselves the innocent victims of oppressive power, the archrebel and all his sympathizers were at last banished from heaven.

The same spirit that prompted rebellion in heaven still inspires rebellion on earth. Satan has continued with human beings the same policy which he pursued with the angels. His spirit now reigns in the children of disobedience. Like him they seek to break down the restraints of the law of God and promise liberty through transgression of its precepts. Reproof of sin still arouses the spirit of hatred and resistance. When God's messages of warning are brought home to the conscience, Satan leads people to justify themselves and to seek the sympathy of others in their course of sin.—*The Great Controversy,* pp. 499, 500.

SATAN'S PLAN OF ATTACK

And the dragon was enraged with the woman, and he went to make war with the rest of her offspring, who keep the commandments of God and have the testimony of Jesus Christ.
—Revelation 12:17.

Through the two great errors, the immortality of the soul and Sunday sacredness, Satan will bring the people under his deceptions. While the former lays the foundation of spiritualism, the latter creates a bond of sympathy with Rome. The Protestants of the United States will be foremost in stretching their hands across the gulf to grasp the hand of spiritualism; they will reach over the abyss to clasp hands with the Roman power; and under the influence of this threefold union, this country will follow in the steps of Rome in trampling on the rights of conscience.

As spiritualism more closely imitates the nominal Christianity of the day, it has greater power to deceive and ensnare. Satan himself is converted, after the modern order of things. He will appear in the character of an angel of light. Through the agency of spiritualism, miracles will be wrought, the sick will be healed, and many undeniable wonders will be performed. And as the spirits will profess faith in the Bible, and manifest respect for the institutions of the church, their work will be accepted as a manifestation of divine power.

The line of distinction between professed Christians and the ungodly is now hardly distinguishable. Church members love what the world loves and are ready to join with them, and Satan determines to unite them in one body and thus strengthen his cause by sweeping all into the ranks of spiritualism. Papists, who boast of miracles as a certain sign of the true church, will be readily deceived by this wonder-working power; and Protestants, having cast away the shield of truth, will also be deluded. Papists, Protestants, and worldlings will alike accept the form of godliness without the power, and they will see in this union a grand movement for the conversion of the world and the ushering in of the long-expected millennium.

Through spiritualism, Satan appears as a benefactor of the race, healing the diseases of the people, and professing to present a new and more exalted system of religious faith; but at the same time he works as a destroyer.—*The Great Controversy,* pp. 588, 589.

November 11, 2016

Satan Is a Destroyer

Woe to the inhabitants of the earth and the sea! For the devil has come down to you, having great wrath, because he knows that he has a short time.
—*Revelation 12:12.*

Satan delights in war, for it excites the worst passions of the soul and then sweeps into eternity its victims steeped in vice and blood. It is his object to incite the nations to war against one another, for he can thus divert the minds of the people from the work of preparation to stand in the day of God.

Satan works through the elements also to garner his harvest of unprepared souls. He has studied the secrets of the laboratories of nature, and he uses all his power to control the elements as far as God allows. When he was suffered to afflict Job, how quickly flocks and herds, servants, houses, children, were swept away, one trouble succeeding another as in a moment. It is God that shields His creatures and hedges them in from the power of the destroyer. But the Christian world have shown contempt for the law of Jehovah; and the Lord will do just what He has declared that He would—He will withdraw His blessings from the earth and remove His protecting care from those who are rebelling against His law and teaching and forcing others to do the same. Satan has control of all whom God does not especially guard. He will favor and prosper some in order to further his own designs, and he will bring trouble upon others and lead men to believe that it is God who is afflicting them.

While appearing to the children of humanity as a great physician who can heal all their maladies, he will bring disease and disaster, until populous cities are reduced to ruin and desolation. Even now he is at work. In accidents and calamities by sea and by land, in great conflagrations, in fierce tornadoes and terrific hailstorms, in tempests, floods, cyclones, tidal waves, and earthquakes, in every place and in a thousand forms, Satan is exercising his power. He sweeps away the ripening harvest, and famine and distress follow. He imparts to the air a deadly taint, and thousands perish by the pestilence. These visitations are to become more and more frequent and disastrous. Destruction will be upon both man and beast. "The earth mourneth and fadeth away," "the haughty people . . . do languish. The earth also is defiled under the inhabitants thereof; because they have transgressed the laws, changed the ordinance, broken the everlasting covenant." (Isaiah 24:4, 5.)—*The Great Controversy,* pp. 589, 590.

NOVEMBER 12

THE PUSH FOR A SUNDAY LAW

He causes all, both small and great, rich and poor, free and slave, to receive a mark on their right hand or on their foreheads.
—Revelation 13:16.

While Satan seeks to destroy those who honor God's law, he will cause them to be accused as lawbreakers, as people who are dishonoring God and bringing judgments upon the world. . . .

Those who honor the Bible Sabbath will be denounced as enemies of law and order, as breaking down the moral restraints of society, causing anarchy and corruption, and calling down the judgments of God upon the earth. Their conscientious scruples will be pronounced obstinacy, stubbornness, and contempt of authority. They will be accused of disaffection toward the government. Ministers who deny the obligation of the divine law will present from the pulpit the duty of yielding obedience to the civil authorities as ordained of God. In legislative halls and courts of justice, commandment keepers will be misrepresented and condemned. A false coloring will be given to their words; the worst construction will be put upon their motives.

As the Protestant churches reject the clear, Scriptural arguments in defense of God's law, they will long to silence those whose faith they cannot overthrow by the Bible. Though they blind their own eyes to the fact, they are now adopting a course which will lead to the persecution of those who conscientiously refuse to do what the rest of the Christian world are doing, and acknowledge the claims of the papal sabbath.

The dignitaries of church and state will unite to bribe, persuade, or compel all classes to honor the Sunday. The lack of divine authority will be supplied by oppressive enactments. Political corruption is destroying love of justice and regard for truth; and even in free America, rulers and legislators, in order to secure public favor, will yield to the popular demand for a law enforcing Sunday observance. Liberty of conscience, which has cost so great a sacrifice, will no longer be respected. In the soon-coming conflict we shall see exemplified the prophet's words: "The dragon was wroth with the woman, and went to make war with the remnant of her seed, which keep the commandments of God, and have the testimony of Jesus Christ." (Revelation 12:17.)—*The Great Controversy,* pp. 591, 592.

November 13

The Crowning Act of Deception

For false christs and false prophets will rise and show great signs and wonders to deceive, if possible, even the elect.
—Matthew 24:24.

Fearful sights of a supernatural character will soon be revealed in the heavens, in token of the power of miracle-working demons. The spirits of devils will go forth to the kings of the earth and to the whole world, to fasten them in deception, and urge them on to unite with Satan in his last struggle against the government of heaven. By these agencies, rulers and subjects will be alike deceived. Persons will arise pretending to be Christ Himself, and claiming the title and worship which belong to the world's Redeemer. They will perform wonderful miracles of healing and will profess to have revelations from heaven contradicting the testimony of the Scriptures.

As the crowning act in the great drama of deception, Satan himself will personate Christ. The church has long professed to look to the Saviour's advent as the consummation of her hopes. Now the great deceiver will make it appear that Christ has come. In different parts of the earth, Satan will manifest himself among the people as a majestic being of dazzling brightness, resembling the description of the Son of God given by John in the Revelation. (Revelation 1:13–15.) The glory that surrounds him is unsurpassed by anything that mortal eyes have yet beheld. The shout of triumph rings out upon the air: "Christ has come! Christ has come!" The people prostrate themselves in adoration before him, while he lifts up his hands and pronounces a blessing upon them, as Christ blessed His disciples when He was upon the earth. His voice is soft and subdued, yet full of melody. In gentle, compassionate tones he presents some of the same gracious, heavenly truths which the Saviour uttered; he heals the diseases of the people, and then, in his assumed character of Christ, he claims to have changed the Sabbath to Sunday, and commands all to hallow the day which he has blessed. He declares that those who persist in keeping holy the seventh day are blaspheming his name by refusing to listen to his angels sent to them with light and truth. This is the strong, almost overmastering delusion. Like the Samaritans who were deceived by Simon Magus, the multitudes, from the least to the greatest, give heed to these sorceries, saying: This is "the great power of God." (Acts 8:10.)—*The Great Controversy,* pp. 624, 625.

NOVEMBER 14

GOD'S PEOPLE NOT DECEIVED

Therefore if they say to you, "Look, He is in the desert!" do not go out; or "Look, He is in the inner rooms!" do not believe it.—Matthew 24:26.

But the people of God will not be misled. The teachings of this false christ are not in accordance with the Scriptures. His blessing is pronounced upon the worshipers of the beast and his image, the very class upon whom the Bible declares that God's unmingled wrath shall be poured out.

And, furthermore, Satan is not permitted to counterfeit the manner of Christ's advent. The Saviour has warned His people against deception upon this point, and has clearly foretold the manner of His second coming. . . . "For as the lightning cometh out of the east, and shineth even unto the west; so shall also the coming of the Son of man be." (Matthew 24:24–27, 31.) This coming there is no possibility of counterfeiting. It will be universally known—witnessed by the whole world.

Only those who have been diligent students of the Scriptures and who have received the love of the truth will be shielded from the powerful delusion that takes the world captive. By the Bible testimony these will detect the deceiver in his disguise. To all the testing time will come. By the sifting of temptation the genuine Christian will be revealed. Are the people of God now so firmly established upon His word that they would not yield to the evidence of their senses? Would they, in such a crisis, cling to the Bible and the Bible only? Satan will, if possible, prevent them from obtaining a preparation to stand in that day. He will so arrange affairs as to hedge up their way, entangle them with earthly treasures, cause them to carry a heavy, wearisome burden, that their hearts may be overcharged with the cares of this life and the day of trial may come upon them as a thief.

As the decree issued by the various rulers of Christendom against commandment keepers shall withdraw the protection of government and abandon them to those who desire their destruction, the people of God will flee from the cities and villages and associate together in companies, dwelling in the most desolate and solitary places. Many will find refuge in the strongholds of the mountains. Like the Christians of the Piedmont valleys, they will make the high places of the earth their sanctuaries and will thank God for "the munitions of rocks." (Isaiah 33:16.) But many of all nations and of all classes, high and low, rich and poor, black and white, will be cast into the most unjust and cruel bondage.—*The Great Controversy,* pp. 625, 626.

November 15

Troublers of the People

Then it happened, when Ahab saw Elijah, that Ahab said to him, "Is that you, O troubler of Israel?"—1 Kings 18:17.

Those who honor the law of God have been accused of bringing judgments upon the world, and they will be regarded as the cause of the fearful convulsions of nature and the strife and bloodshed among people that are filling the earth with woe. The power attending the last warning has enraged the wicked; their anger is kindled against all who have received the message, and Satan will excite to still greater intensity the spirit of hatred and persecution.

When God's presence was finally withdrawn from the Jewish nation, priests and people knew it not. Though under the control of Satan, and swayed by the most horrible and malignant passions, they still regarded themselves as the chosen of God. The ministration in the temple continued; sacrifices were offered upon its polluted altars, and daily the divine blessing was invoked upon a people guilty of the blood of God's dear Son and seeking to slay His ministers and apostles. So when the irrevocable decision of the sanctuary has been pronounced and the destiny of the world has been forever fixed, the inhabitants of the earth will know it not. The forms of religion will be continued by a people from whom the Spirit of God has been finally withdrawn; and the satanic zeal with which the prince of evil will inspire them for the accomplishment of his malignant designs, will bear the semblance of zeal for God.

As the Sabbath has become the special point of controversy throughout Christendom, and religious and secular authorities have combined to enforce the observance of the Sunday, the persistent refusal of a small minority to yield to the popular demand will make them objects of universal execration. It will be urged that the few who stand in opposition to an institution of the church and a law of the state ought not to be tolerated; that it is better for them to suffer than for whole nations to be thrown into confusion and lawlessness. . . . This argument will appear conclusive; and a decree will finally be issued against those who hallow the Sabbath of the fourth commandment, denouncing them as deserving of the severest punishment and giving the people liberty, after a certain time, to put them to death. Romanism in the Old World and apostate Protestantism in the New will pursue a similar course toward those who honor all the divine precepts.—*The Great Controversy,* pp. 614–616.

NOVEMBER 16

THE GOSPEL COMMISSION

Go therefore and make disciples of all the nations.
—*Matthew 28:19.*

The events of Christ's life, His death and resurrection, the prophecies pointing to these events, the mysteries of the plan of salvation, the power of Jesus for the remission of sins—to all these things they [His disciples] had been witnesses, and they were to make them known to the world. They were to proclaim the gospel of peace and salvation through repentance and the power of the Saviour.

Before ascending to heaven, Christ gave His disciples their commission. He told them that they were to be the executors of the will in which He bequeathed to the world the treasures of eternal life. You have been witnesses of My life of sacrifice in behalf of the world, He said to them. You have seen My labors for Israel. And although My people would not come to Me that they might have life, although priests and rulers have done unto Me as they listed, although they have rejected Me, they shall have still another opportunity of accepting the Son of God. You have seen that all who come to Me confessing their sins, I freely receive. Him that cometh to Me I will in no wise cast out. To you, My disciples, I commit this message of mercy. It is to be given to both Jews and Gentiles—to Israel, first, and then to all nations, tongues, and peoples. All who believe are to be gathered into one church.

The gospel commission is the great missionary charter of Christ's kingdom. The disciples were to work earnestly for souls, giving to all the invitation of mercy. They were not to wait for the people to come to them; they were to go to the people with their message.

The disciples were to carry their work forward in Christ's name. Their every word and act was to fasten attention on His name, as possessing that vital power by which sinners may be saved. Their faith was to center in Him who is the source of mercy and power. In His name they were to present their petitions to the Father, and they would receive answer. They were to baptize in the name of the Father, the Son, and the Holy Spirit. Christ's name was to be their watchword, their badge of distinction, their bond of union, the authority for their course of action, and the source of their success. Nothing was to be recognized in His kingdom that did not bear His name and superscription.—*The Acts of the Apostles,* pp. 27, 28.

November 17

Truth Will Conquer the World

As You, Father, are in Me, and I in You; that they also may be one in Us, that the world may believe that You sent Me.
—John 17:21.

After the descent of the Holy Spirit, the disciples were so filled with love for Him and for those for whom He died, that hearts were melted by the words they spoke and the prayers they offered. They spoke in the power of the Spirit; and under the influence of that power, thousands were converted.

As Christ's representatives the apostles were to make a decided impression on the world. The fact that they were humble men would not diminish their influence, but increase it; for the minds of their hearers would be carried from them to the Saviour, who, though unseen, was still working with them. The wonderful teaching of the apostles, their words of courage and trust, would assure all that it was not in their own power that they worked, but in the power of Christ. Humbling themselves, they would declare that He whom the Jews had crucified was the Prince of life, the Son of the living God, and that in His name they did the works that He had done.

In His parting conversation with His disciples on the night before the crucifixion the Saviour made no reference to the suffering that He had endured and must yet endure. He did not speak of the humiliation that was before Him, but sought to bring to their minds that which would strengthen their faith, leading them to look forward to the joys that await the overcomer. He rejoiced in the consciousness that He could and would do more for His followers than He had promised; that from Him would flow forth love and compassion, cleansing the soul temple, and making sinners like Him in character; that His truth, armed with the power of the Spirit, would go forth conquering and to conquer.

"These things I have spoken unto you," He said, "that in Me ye might have peace. In the world ye shall have tribulation: but be of good cheer; I have overcome the world." (John 16:33.) Christ did not fail, neither was He discouraged; and the disciples were to show a faith of the same enduring nature. They were to work as He had worked, depending on Him for strength. Though their way would be obstructed by apparent impossibilities, yet by His grace they were to go forward, despairing of nothing and hoping for everything.—*The Acts of the Apostles*, pp. 22, 23.

Help From the Holy Spirit

John truly baptized with water, but you shall be baptized with the Holy Spirit not many days from now.—Acts 1:5.

Christ's sacrifice in our behalf was full and complete. The condition of the atonement had been fulfilled. The work for which He had come to this world had been accomplished. He had won the kingdom. He had wrested it from Satan and had become heir of all things. . . .

Just before leaving His disciples, Christ once more plainly stated the nature of His kingdom. He recalled to their remembrance things He had previously told them regarding it. He declared that it was not His purpose to establish in this world a temporal kingdom. He was not appointed to reign as an earthly monarch on David's throne. When the disciples asked Him, "Lord, wilt Thou at this time restore again the kingdom to Israel?" He answered, "It is not for you to know the times or the seasons, which the Father hath put in His own power." (Acts 1:6, 7.) It was not necessary for them to see farther into the future than the revelations He had made enabled them to see. Their work was to proclaim the gospel message.

Christ's visible presence was about to be withdrawn from the disciples, but a new endowment of power was to be theirs. The Holy Spirit was to be given them in its fullness, sealing them for their work. "Behold," the Saviour said, "I send the promise of My Father upon you: but tarry ye in the city of Jerusalem, until ye be endued with power from on high." (Luke 24:49.) . . . "Ye shall receive power, after that the Holy Ghost is come upon you: and ye shall be witnesses unto Me both in Jerusalem, and in all Judea, and in Samaria, and unto the uttermost part of the earth." (Acts 1:8.)

The Saviour knew that no argument, however logical, would melt hard hearts or break through the crust of worldliness and selfishness. He knew that His disciples must receive the heavenly endowment; that the gospel would be effective only as it was proclaimed by hearts made warm and lips made eloquent by a living knowledge of Him who is the way, the truth, and the life. The work committed to the disciples would require great efficiency; for the tide of evil ran deep and strong against them. A vigilant, determined leader was in command of the forces of darkness, and the followers of Christ could battle for the right only through the help that God, by His Spirit, would give them.—*The Acts of the Apostles,* pp. 29–31.

November 19

The Power of the Latter Rain

Let us know, let us pursue the knowledge of the Lord. His going forth is established as the morning; He will come to us like the rain, like the latter and former rain to the earth.—*Hosea 6:3.*

And today God is still using His church to make known His purpose in the earth. Today the heralds of the cross are going from city to city, and from land to land, preparing the way for the second advent of Christ. The standard of God's law is being exalted. The Spirit of the Almighty is moving upon people's hearts, and those who respond to its influence become witnesses for God and His truth. In many places consecrated men and women may be seen communicating to others the light that has made plain to them the way of salvation through Christ. And as they continue to let their light shine, as did those who were baptized with the Spirit on the Day of Pentecost, they receive more and still more of the Spirit's power. Thus the earth is to be lightened with the glory of God. . . .

It is true that in the time of the end, when God's work in the earth is closing, the earnest efforts put forth by consecrated believers under the guidance of the Holy Spirit are to be accompanied by special tokens of divine favor. Under the figure of the early and the latter rain, that falls in Eastern lands at seedtime and harvest, the Hebrew prophets foretold the bestowal of spiritual grace in extraordinary measure upon God's church. The outpouring of the Spirit in the days of the apostles was the beginning of the early, or former, rain, and glorious was the result. To the end of time the presence of the Spirit is to abide with the true church.

But near the close of earth's harvest, a special bestowal of spiritual grace is promised to prepare the church for the coming of the Son of man. This outpouring of the Spirit is likened to the falling of the latter rain; and it is for this added power that Christians are to send their petitions to the Lord of the harvest "in the time of the latter rain." In response, "the Lord shall make bright clouds, and give them showers of rain." "He will cause to come down . . . the rain, the former rain, and the latter rain," (Zechariah 10:1; Joel 2:23.)

But unless the members of God's church today have a living connection with the Source of all spiritual growth, they will not be ready for the time of reaping. Unless they keep their lamps trimmed and burning, they will fail of receiving added grace in times of special need.

Those only who are constantly receiving fresh supplies of grace, will have power proportionate to their daily need and their ability to use that power.
—*The Acts of the Apostles,* pp. 53–55.

NOVEMBER 20

COME OUT OF BABYLON

Come out of her, my people, lest you share in her sins, and lest you receive of her plagues.—Revelation 18:4.

I saw angels hurrying to and fro in heaven, descending to the earth, and again ascending to heaven, preparing for the fulfillment of some important event. Then I saw another mighty angel commissioned to descend to the earth, to unite his voice with the third angel, and give power and force to his message. Great power and glory were imparted to the angel, and as he descended, the earth was lightened with his glory. The light which attended this angel penetrated everywhere, as he cried mightily, with a strong voice, "Babylon the great is fallen, is fallen, and is become the habitation of devils, and the hold of every foul spirit, and a cage of every unclean and hateful bird." The message of the fall of Babylon, as given by the second angel, is repeated, with the additional mention of the corruptions which have been entering the churches since 1844. The work of this angel comes in at the right time to join in the last great work of the third angel's message as it swells to a loud cry. And the people of God are thus prepared to stand in the hour of temptation, which they are soon to meet. I saw a great light resting upon them, and they united to fearlessly proclaim the third angel's message.

Angels were sent to aid the mighty angel from heaven, and I heard voices which seemed to sound everywhere, "Come out of her, My people, that ye be not partakers of her sins, and that ye receive not of her plagues. For her sins have reached unto heaven, and God hath remembered her iniquities." This message seemed to be an addition to the third message, joining it as the midnight cry joined the second angel's message in 1844. The glory of God rested upon the patient, waiting saints, and they fearlessly gave the last solemn warning, proclaiming the fall of Babylon and calling upon God's people to come out of her that they might escape her fearful doom.

The light that was shed upon the waiting ones penetrated everywhere, and those in the churches who had any light, who had not heard and rejected the three messages, obeyed the call and left the fallen churches. Many had come to years of accountability since these messages had been given, and the light shone upon them, and they were privileged to choose life or death. Some chose life and took their stand with those who were looking for their Lord and keeping all His commandments.—*Early Writings,* pp. 277, 278.

November 21

God's Answer to Satan's Charges

If anyone worships the beast and his image, and receives his mark on his forehead or on his hand, he himself shall also drink of the wine of the wrath of God.
—Revelation 14:9, 10.

How is the world treating the law of God? Everywhere people are working against the divine precepts. In their desire to evade the cross bearing attendant on obedience, even the churches are taking sides with the great apostate in claiming that the law of God has been changed or abrogated. Many in their blindness boast of wonderful progress and enlightenment; but the heavenly watchers see the earth filled with corruption and violence. Because of sin the atmosphere of our world has become as the atmosphere of a pesthouse.

A great work is to be accomplished in setting before the world the saving truths of the gospel. This is the means ordained by God to stem the tide of moral corruption. This is His means of restoring His moral image in humanity. It is His remedy for universal disorganization. It is the power that draws people together in unity. To present these truths is the work of the third angel's message. The Lord designs that the presentation of this message shall be the highest, greatest work carried on in the world at this time.

Satan is constantly urging mankind to accept his principles. Thus he seeks to counterwork the work of God. He is constantly representing the chosen people of God as a deluded people. He is an accuser of the brethren, and his accusing power he is constantly using against those who work righteousness. The Lord desires through His people to answer Satan's charges by showing the result of obedience to right principles.

All the light of the past, all the light which shines in the present and reaches forth into the future, as revealed in the word of God, is for every soul who will receive it. The glory of this light, which is the very glory of the character of Christ, is to be manifested in the individual Christian, in the family, in the church, in the ministry of the word, and in every institution established by God's people. All these the Lord designs shall be symbols of what can be done for the world. They are to be types of the saving power of the truths of the gospel. They are agencies in the fulfillment of God's great purpose for the human race.—*Testimonies for the Church,* vol. 6, pp. 10, 11.

NOVEMBER 22

2016

BABYLON'S SINS LAID OPEN

Therefore behold, the days are coming that I will bring judgment on the carved images of Babylon; her whole land shall be ashamed.—Jeremiah 51:47.

Thus the message of the third angel will be proclaimed. As the time comes for it to be given with greatest power, the Lord will work through humble instruments, leading the minds of those who consecrate themselves to His service. The laborers will be qualified rather by the unction of His Spirit than by the training of literary institutions. People of faith and prayer will be constrained to go forth with holy zeal, declaring the words which God gives them. The sins of Babylon will be laid open. The fearful results of enforcing the observances of the church by civil authority, the inroads of spiritualism, the stealthy but rapid progress of the papal power—all will be unmasked. By these solemn warnings the people will be stirred. Thousands upon thousands will listen who have never heard words like these. In amazement they hear the testimony that Babylon is the church, fallen because of her errors and sins, because of her rejection of the truth sent to her from heaven. As the people go to their former teachers with the eager inquiry, Are these things so? the ministers present fables, prophesy smooth things, to soothe their fears and quiet the awakened conscience. But since many refuse to be satisfied with mere human authority and demand a plain "Thus saith the Lord," the popular ministry, like the Pharisees of old, filled with anger as their authority is questioned, will denounce the message as of Satan and stir up the sin-loving multitudes to revile and persecute those who proclaim it.

As the controversy extends into new fields and the minds of the people are called to God's downtrodden law, Satan is astir. The power attending the message will only madden those who oppose it. The clergy will put forth almost superhuman efforts to shut away the light lest it should shine upon their flocks. By every means at their command they will endeavor to suppress the discussion of these vital questions. The church appeals to the strong arm of civil power, and, in this work, papists and Protestants unite. As the movement for Sunday enforcement becomes more bold and decided, the law will be invoked against commandment keepers. They will be threatened with fines and imprisonment, and some will be offered positions of influence, and other rewards and advantages, as inducements to renounce their faith. But their steadfast answer is: "Show us from the word of God our error."—*The Great Controversy,* pp. 606, 607.

November 23 

Statesmen Won to Truth

You will be brought before governors and kings for My sake, as a testimony to them and to the Gentiles.—Matthew 10:18.

As the opposition rises to a fiercer height, the servants of God are again perplexed; for it seems to them that they have brought the crisis. But conscience and the word of God assure them that their course is right; and although the trials continue, they are strengthened to bear them. The contest grows closer and sharper, but their faith and courage rise with the emergency. Their testimony is: "We dare not tamper with God's word, dividing his holy law; calling one portion essential and another non-essential, to gain the favor of the world. The Lord whom we serve is able to deliver us. Christ has conquered the powers of earth; and shall we be afraid of a world already conquered?"

Persecution in its varied forms is the development of a principle which will exist as long as Satan exists and Christianity has vital power. No man can serve God without enlisting against himself the opposition of the hosts of darkness. Evil angels will assail him, alarmed that his influence is taking the prey from their hands. Evil men, rebuked by his example, will unite with them in seeking to separate him from God by alluring temptations. When these do not succeed, then a compelling power is employed to force the conscience.

But as long as Jesus remains as intercessor in the sanctuary above, the restraining influence of the Holy Spirit is felt by rulers and people. It still controls to some extent the laws of the land. Were it not for these laws, the condition of the world would be much worse than it now is. While many of our rulers are active agents of Satan, God also has His agents among the leaders of the nation. The enemy moves upon his servants to propose measures that would greatly impede the work of God; but statesmen who fear the Lord are influenced by holy angels to oppose such propositions with unanswerable arguments. Thus a few people will hold in check a powerful current of evil. The opposition of the enemies of truth will be restrained that the third message may do its work. When the final warning shall be given, it will arrest the attention of these leaders through whom the Lord is now working, and some of them will accept it, and will stand with the people of God through the time of trouble.—*The Great Controversy,* pp. 610, 611.

November 24

Know Why You Believe What You Believe

I saw three unclean spirits like frogs coming out of the mouth of the dragon, out of the mouth of the beast, and out of the mouth of the false prophet. For they are the spirits of demons.—Revelation 16:13, 14.

I saw that the saints must have a thorough understanding of present truth, which they will be obliged to maintain from the Scriptures. They must understand the state of the dead; for the spirits of devils will yet appear to them, professing to be beloved relatives or friends, who will declare to them unscriptural doctrines. They will do all in their power to excite sympathy and will work miracles before them to confirm what they declare. The people of God must be prepared to withstand these spirits with the Bible truth that the dead know not anything, and that they who thus appear are the spirits of devils.

We must examine well the foundation of our hope; for we shall have to give a reason for it from the Scriptures. This delusion will spread, and we shall have to contend with it face to face; and unless we are prepared for it, we shall be ensnared and overcome. But if we do what we can on our part to be ready for the conflict that is just before us, God will do His part, and His all-powerful arm will protect us. He would sooner send every angel out of glory to make a hedge about faithful souls, than have them deceived and led away by the lying wonders of Satan.

I saw the rapidity with which this delusion was spreading. A train of cars was shown me, going with the speed of lightning. The angel bade me look carefully. I fixed my eyes upon the train. It seemed that the whole world was on board. Then he showed me the conductor, a fair, stately person, whom all the passengers looked up to and reverenced. I was perplexed and asked my attending angel who it was. He said, "It is Satan. He is the conductor, in the form of an angel of light. He has taken the world captive. They are given over to strong delusions, to believe a lie that they may be damned. His agent, the highest in order next to him, is the engineer, and others of his agents are employed in different offices as he may need them, and they are all going with lightning speed to perdition."

I asked the angel if there were none left. He bade me look in the opposite direction, and I saw a little company traveling a narrow pathway. All seemed to be firmly united by the truth.—*Early Writings*, pp. 262, 263.

November 25

The Close of Probation

Therefore, since we are receiving a kingdom which cannot be shaken, let us have grace, by which we may serve God acceptably with reverence and godly fear.—Hebrews 12:28.

When Jesus ceases to plead for mankind, the cases of all are forever decided. This is the time of reckoning with His servants. To those who have neglected the preparation of purity and holiness, which fits them to be waiting ones to welcome their Lord, the sun sets in gloom and darkness, and rises not again. Probation closes; Christ's intercessions cease in heaven. This time finally comes suddenly upon all, and those who have neglected to purify their souls by obeying the truth are found sleeping. They became weary of waiting and watching; they became indifferent in regard to the coming of their Master. They longed not for His appearing, and thought there was no need of such continued, persevering watching. They had been disappointed in their expectations and might be again. They concluded that there was time enough yet to arouse. They would be sure not to lose the opportunity of securing an earthly treasure. It would be safe to get all of this world they could. And in securing this object, they lost all anxiety and interest in the appearing of the Master. They became indifferent and careless, as though His coming were yet in the distance. But while their interest was buried up in their worldly gains, the work closed in the heavenly sanctuary, and they were unprepared.

If such had only known that the work of Christ in the heavenly sanctuary would close so soon, how differently would they have conducted themselves, how earnestly would they have watched! The Master, anticipating all this, gives them timely warning in the command to watch. He distinctly states the suddenness of His coming. He does not measure the time, lest we shall neglect a momentary preparation, and in our indolence look ahead to the time when we think He will come, and defer the preparation. "Watch ye therefore: for ye know not." Yet this foretold uncertainty, and suddenness at last, fails to rouse us from stupidity to earnest wakefulness, and to quicken our watchfulness for our expected Master. Those not found waiting and watching are finally surprised in their unfaithfulness. The Master comes, and instead of their being ready to open unto Him immediately, they are locked in worldly slumber, and are lost at last.

A company was presented before me in contrast to the one described. They were waiting and watching. Their eyes were directed heavenward, and the words of their Master were upon their lips: "What I say unto you I say unto all, Watch."—*Testimonies for the Church,* vol. 2, pp. 191, 192.

THE TIME OF JACOB'S TROUBLE

2016

Then Jacob was left alone; and a Man wrestled with him until the breaking of day.—Genesis 32:24.

As Satan influenced Esau to march against Jacob, so he will stir up the wicked to destroy God's people in the time of trouble. And as he accused Jacob, he will urge his accusations against the people of God. He numbers the world as his subjects; but the little company who keep the commandments of God are resisting his supremacy. If he could blot them from the earth, his triumph would be complete. He sees that holy angels are guarding them, and he infers that their sins have been pardoned; but he does not know that their cases have been decided in the sanctuary above. He has an accurate knowledge of the sins which he has tempted them to commit, and he presents these before God in the most exaggerated light, representing this people to be just as deserving as himself of exclusion from the favor of God. He declares that the Lord cannot in justice forgive their sins and yet destroy him and his angels. He claims them as his prey and demands that they be given into his hands to destroy.

As Satan accuses the people of God on account of their sins, the Lord permits him to try them to the uttermost. Their confidence in God, their faith and firmness, will be severely tested. As they review the past, their hopes sink; for in their whole lives they can see little good. They are fully conscious of their weakness and unworthiness. Satan endeavors to terrify them with the thought that their cases are hopeless, that the stain of their defilement will never be washed away. He hopes so to destroy their faith that they will yield to his temptations and turn from their allegiance to God.

Though God's people will be surrounded by enemies who are bent upon their destruction, yet the anguish which they suffer is not a dread of persecution for the truth's sake; they fear that every sin has not been repented of, and that through some fault in themselves they will fail to realize the fulfillment of the Saviour's promise: I "will keep thee from the hour of temptation, which shall come upon all the world." (Revelation 3:10.) If they . . . should . . . prove unworthy, and lose their lives because of their own defects of character, then God's holy name would be reproached. . . .

Though suffering the keenest anxiety, terror, and distress, they do not cease their intercessions. They lay hold of the strength of God as Jacob laid hold of the Angel; and the language of their souls is: "I will not let Thee go, except Thou bless me."—*The Great Controversy,* pp. 618–620.

NOVEMBER 27

GOD IS OUR DEFENSE

At that time Michael shall stand up, the great prince who stands watch over the sons of your people; and there shall be a time of trouble.—Daniel 12:1.

When this time of trouble comes, every case is decided; there is no longer probation, no longer mercy for the impenitent. The seal of the living God is upon His people. This small remnant, unable to defend themselves in the deadly conflict with the powers of earth that are marshaled by the dragon host, make God their defense. The decree has been passed by the highest earthly authority that they shall worship the beast and receive his mark under pain of persecution and death. May God help His people now, for what can they then do in such a fearful conflict without His assistance!

Courage, fortitude, faith, and implicit trust in God's power to save do not come in a moment. These heavenly graces are acquired by the experience of years. By a life of holy endeavor and firm adherence to the right the children of God were sealing their destiny. Beset with temptations without number, they knew they must resist firmly or be conquered. They felt that they had a great work to do, and at any hour they might be called to lay off their armor; and should they come to the close of life with their work undone, it would be an eternal loss. They eagerly accepted the light from heaven, as did the first disciples from the lips of Jesus. When those early Christians were exiled to mountains and deserts, when left in dungeons to die with hunger, cold, and torture, when martyrdom seemed the only way out of their distress, they rejoiced that they were counted worthy to suffer for Christ, who was crucified for them. Their worthy example will be a comfort and encouragement to the people of God who will be brought into the time of trouble such as never was.

Not all who profess to keep the Sabbath will be sealed. There are many even among those who teach the truth to others who will not receive the seal of God in their foreheads. They had the light of truth, they knew their Master's will, they understood every point of our faith, but they had not corresponding works. These who were so familiar with prophecy and the treasures of divine wisdom should have acted their faith. They should have commanded their households after them, that by a well-ordered family they might present to the world the influence of the truth upon the human heart. . . .

In this life we must meet fiery trials and make costly sacrifices, but the peace of Christ is the reward.—*Testimonies for the Church,* vol. 5, pp. 213–215.

November 28

Prayers Will Be Answered

How long, O Lord, holy and true, until You judge and avenge our blood on those who dwell on the earth?
—*Revelation 6:10.*

The day of God is right upon us. The world has converted the church. Both are in harmony, and are acting on a short-sighted policy. Protestants will work upon the rulers of the land to make laws to restore the lost ascendancy of the man of sin, who sits in the temple of God, showing himself that he is God. Roman Catholic principles will be taken under the care and protection of the state. This national apostasy will speedily be followed by national ruin. The protest of Bible truth will be no longer tolerated by those who have not made the law of God their rule of life. Then will the voice be heard from the graves of martyrs, represented by the souls that John saw slain for the word of God and the testimony of Jesus Christ which they held; then the prayer will ascend from every true child of God, "It is time for thee, Lord, to work: for they have made void thy law." . . .

From time to time the Lord has made known His manner of working. He is mindful of what is passing upon the earth; and when a crisis has come, He has revealed Himself, and has interposed to hinder the working of Satan's plans. He has often permitted matters with nations, with families, and with individuals, to come to a crisis, that His interference might become marked. Then He has let the fact be known that there was a God in Israel who would sustain and vindicate His people. When the defiance of the law of Jehovah shall be almost universal, when His people shall be pressed in affliction by their fellow mortals, God will interpose. The fervent prayers of His people will be answered; for He loves to have His people seek Him with all their heart, and depend upon Him as their deliverer. He will be sought unto to do these things for His people, and He will arise as the protector and avenger of His people. The promise is, "Shall not God avenge His own elect, which cry day and night unto Him? . . . I tell you that He will avenge them speedily." . . .

Their united prayers should ascend to heaven for the Lord to arise, and put an end to the violence and abuse which are practiced in our world. More prayer and less talk is what God desires, and it would make His people a tower of strength.—*Review and Herald,* June 15, 1897.

November 29

Under the Lord's Banner

The Spirit and the bride say, "Come!" And let him who hears say, "Come!" And let him who thirsts come. Whoever desires, let him take the water of life freely.
—Revelation 22:17.

As representatives for Christ we have no time to lose. Our efforts are not to be confined to a few places where the light has become so abundant that it is not appreciated. The gospel message is to be proclaimed to all nations and kindreds and tongues and peoples.

In vision I saw two armies in terrible conflict. One army was led by banners bearing the world's insignia; the other was led by the bloodstained banner of Prince Immanuel. Standard after standard was left to trail in the dust as company after company from the Lord's army joined the foe and tribe after tribe from the ranks of the enemy united with the commandment-keeping people of God. An angel flying in the midst of heaven put the standard of Immanuel into many hands, while a mighty general cried out with a loud voice: "Come into line. Let those who are loyal to the commandments of God and the testimony of Christ now take their position. Come out from among them, and be ye separate, and touch not the unclean, and I will receive you, and will be a Father unto you, and ye shall be My sons and daughters. Let all who will come up to the help of the Lord, to the help of the Lord against the mighty."

The battle raged. Victory alternated from side to side. Now the soldiers of the cross gave way, "as when a standardbearer fainteth." (Isaiah 10:18.) But their apparent retreat was but to gain a more advantageous position. Shouts of joy were heard. A song of praise to God went up, and angel voices united in the song, as Christ's soldiers planted His banner on the walls of fortresses till then held by the enemy. The Captain of our salvation was ordering the battle and sending support to His soldiers. His power was mightily displayed, encouraging them to press the battle to the gates. He taught them terrible things in righteousness as He led them on step by step, conquering and to conquer.

At last the victory was gained. The army following the banner with the inscription, "The commandments of God, and the faith of Jesus," was gloriously triumphant. The soldiers of Christ were close beside the gates of the city, and with joy the city received her King. The kingdom of peace and joy and everlasting righteousness was established.—*Testimonies for the Church,* vol. 8, pp. 40–42.

November 30

Victory in the Great Controversy

They shall see His face, and His name shall be on their foreheads.
—Revelation 22:4.

But even here Christians may have the joy of communion with Christ; they may have the light of His love, the perpetual comfort of His presence. Every step in life may bring us closer to Jesus, may give us a deeper experience of His love, and may bring us one step nearer to the blessed home of peace. . . .

We cannot but look forward to new perplexities in the coming conflict, but we may look on what is past as well as on what is to come, and say, "Hitherto hath the Lord helped us." "As thy days, so shall thy strength be." (1 Samuel 7:12; Deuteronomy 33:25.) The trial will not exceed the strength that shall be given us to bear it. Then let us take up our work just where we find it, believing that whatever may come, strength proportionate to the trial will be given.

And by and by the gates of heaven will be thrown open to admit God's children, and from the lips of the King of glory the benediction will fall on their ears like richest music, "Come, ye blessed of My Father, inherit the kingdom prepared for you from the foundation of the world." (Matthew 25:34.)

Then the redeemed will be welcomed to the home that Jesus is preparing for them. There their companions will not be the vile of earth, liars, idolaters, the impure, and unbelieving; but they will associate with those who have overcome Satan and through divine grace have formed perfect characters. Every sinful tendency, every imperfection, that afflicts them here has been removed by the blood of Christ, and the excellence and brightness of His glory, far exceeding the brightness of the sun, is imparted to them. And the moral beauty, the perfection of His character, shines through them, in worth far exceeding this outward splendor. They are without fault before the great white throne, sharing the dignity and the privileges of the angels.

In view of the glorious inheritance that may be his, "what shall a man give in exchange for his soul?" (Matthew 16:26.) He may be poor, yet he possesses in himself a wealth and dignity that the world could never bestow. The soul redeemed and cleansed from sin, with all its noble powers dedicated to the service of God, is of surpassing worth; and there is joy in heaven in the presence of God and the holy angels over one soul redeemed, a joy that is expressed in songs of holy triumph.—*Steps to Christ,* pp. 125, 126.

The Beginning of Eternity

December 1

Christ Could Have Come Before This

Lord, will You at this time restore the kingdom to Israel?
—Acts 1:6.

If all who had labored unitedly in the work in 1844, had received the third angel's message and proclaimed it in the power of the Holy Spirit, the Lord would have wrought mightily with their efforts. A flood of light would have been shed upon the world. Years ago the inhabitants of the earth would have been warned, the closing work completed, and Christ would have come for the redemption of His people.

It was not the will of God that Israel should wander forty years in the wilderness; He desired to lead them directly to the land of Canaan and establish them there, a holy, happy people. But "they could not enter in because of unbelief." (Hebrews 3:19.) Because of their backsliding and apostasy they perished in the desert, and others were raised up to enter the Promised Land. In like manner, it was not the will of God that the coming of Christ should be so long delayed and His people should remain so many years in this world of sin and sorrow. But unbelief separated them from God. As they refused to do the work which He had appointed them, others were raised up to proclaim the message. In mercy to the world, Jesus delays His coming, that sinners may have an opportunity to hear the warning and find in Him a shelter before the wrath of God shall be poured out.

Now as in former ages, the presentation of a truth that reproves the sins and errors of the times will excite opposition. "Everyone that doeth evil hateth the light, neither cometh to the light, lest his deeds should be reproved." (John 3:20.) As people see that they cannot maintain their position by the Scriptures, many determine to maintain it at all hazards, and with a malicious spirit they assail the character and motives of those who stand in defense of unpopular truth. It is the same policy which has been pursued in all ages. Elijah was declared to be a troubler in Israel, Jeremiah a traitor, Paul a polluter of the temple. From that day to this, those who would be loyal to truth have been denounced as seditious, heretical, or schismatic.

In view of this, what is the duty of the messenger of truth? . . . Has God given light to His servants in this generation? Then they should let it shine forth to the world.—*The Great Controversy,* pp. 458, 459.

December 2

God's Jewels

I will spare them as a man spares his own son who serves him.
—Malachi 3:17.

The eye of God, looking down the ages, was fixed upon the crisis which His people are to meet, when earthly powers shall be arrayed against them. Like the captive exile, they will be in fear of death by starvation or by violence. But the Holy One who divided the Red Sea before Israel, will manifest His mighty power and turn their captivity. "They shall be Mine, saith the Lord of hosts, in that day when I make up My jewels; and I will spare them, as a man spareth his own son that serveth him." (Malachi 3:17.) If the blood of Christ's faithful witnesses were shed at this time, it would not, like the blood of the martyrs, be as seed sown to yield a harvest for God. Their fidelity would not be a testimony to convince others of the truth; for the obdurate heart has beaten back the waves of mercy until they return no more. If the righteous were now left to fall a prey to their enemies, it would be a triumph for the prince of darkness. . . .

When the protection of human laws shall be withdrawn from those who honor the law of God, there will be, in different lands, a simultaneous movement for their destruction. As the time appointed in the decree draws near, the people will conspire to root out the hated sect. It will be determined to strike in one night a decisive blow, which shall utterly silence the voice of dissent and reproof.

The people of God—some in prison cells, some hidden in solitary retreats in the forests and the mountains—still plead for divine protection, while in every quarter companies of armed men, urged on by hosts of evil angels, are preparing for the work of death. It is now, in the hour of utmost extremity, that the God of Israel will interpose for the deliverance of His chosen. . . .

With shouts of triumph, jeering, and imprecation, throngs of evil men are about to rush upon their prey, when, lo, a dense blackness, deeper than the darkness of the night, falls upon the earth. Then a rainbow, shining with the glory from the throne of God, spans the heavens and seems to encircle each praying company. The angry multitudes are suddenly arrested. Their mocking cries die away. The objects of their murderous rage are forgotten. With fearful forebodings they gaze upon the symbol of God's covenant and long to be shielded from its overpowering brightness.—*The Great Controversy,* pp. 634–636.

DECEMBER 3

THE SHOUT OF VICTORY

Behold, this is our God; we have waited for Him, and He will save us.
—Isaiah 25:9.

By the people of God a voice, clear and melodious, is heard, saying, "Look up," and lifting their eyes to the heavens, they behold the bow of promise. The black, angry clouds that covered the firmament are parted, and like Stephen they look up steadfastly into heaven and see the glory of God and the Son of man seated upon His throne. In His divine form they discern the marks of His humiliation; and from His lips they hear the request presented before His Father and the holy angels: "I will that they also, whom Thou hast given Me, be with Me where I am." (John 17:24.) Again a voice, musical and triumphant, is heard, saying: "They come! they come! holy, harmless, and undefiled. They have kept the word of My patience; they shall walk among the angels;" and the pale, quivering lips of those who have held fast their faith utter a shout of victory.

It is at midnight that God manifests His power for the deliverance of His people. The sun appears, shining in its strength. Signs and wonders follow in quick succession. The wicked look with terror and amazement upon the scene, while the righteous behold with solemn joy the tokens of their deliverance. Everything in nature seems turned out of its course. The streams cease to flow. Dark, heavy clouds come up and clash against each other. In the midst of the angry heavens is one clear space of indescribable glory, whence comes the voice of God like the sound of many waters, saying: "It is done." (Revelation 16:17.)

That voice shakes the heavens and the earth. There is a mighty earthquake, "such as was not since men were upon the earth, so mighty an earthquake, and so great." (Verses 17, 18.) The firmament appears to open and shut. The glory from the throne of God seems flashing through. The mountains shake like a reed in the wind, and ragged rocks are scattered on every side. There is a roar as of a coming tempest. The sea is lashed into fury. There is heard the shriek of a hurricane like the voice of demons upon a mission of destruction. The whole earth heaves and swells like the waves of the sea. Its surface is breaking up. Its very foundations seem to be giving way. Mountain chains are sinking. Inhabited islands disappear. The seaports that have become like Sodom for wickedness are swallowed up by the angry waters.—*The Great Controversy,* pp. 636, 637.

TWO SPECIAL RESURRECTIONS

Blessed are the dead who die in the Lord from now on.
—Revelation 14:13.

Babylon the great has come in remembrance before God, "to give unto her the cup of the wine of the fierceness of His wrath." Great hailstones, every one "about the weight of a talent," are doing their work of destruction. (Revelation 16:19, 21.) The proudest cities of the earth are laid low. The lordly palaces, upon which the world's great men have lavished their wealth in order to glorify themselves, are crumbling to ruin before their eyes. Prison walls are rent asunder, and God's people, who have been held in bondage for their faith, are set free.

Graves are opened, and "many of them that sleep in the dust of the earth . . . awake, some to everlasting life, and some to shame and everlasting contempt." (Daniel 12:2.) All who have died in the faith of the third angel's message come forth from the tomb glorified, to hear God's covenant of peace with those who have kept His law. "They also which pierced Him" (Revelation 1:7), those that mocked and derided Christ's dying agonies, and the most violent opposers of His truth and His people, are raised to behold Him in His glory and to see the honor placed upon the loyal and obedient.

Thick clouds still cover the sky; yet the sun now and then breaks through, appearing like the avenging eye of Jehovah. Fierce lightnings leap from the heavens, enveloping the earth in a sheet of flame. Above the terrific roar of thunder, voices, mysterious and awful, declare the doom of the wicked. The words spoken are not comprehended by all; but they are distinctly understood by the false teachers. Those who a little before were so reckless, so boastful and defiant, so exultant in their cruelty to God's commandment-keeping people, are now overwhelmed with consternation and shuddering in fear. Their wails are heard above the sound of the elements. Demons acknowledge the deity of Christ and tremble before His power, while people are supplicating for mercy and groveling in abject terror.

Said the prophets of old, as they beheld in holy vision the day of God: "Howl ye; for the day of the Lord is at hand; it shall come as a destruction from the Almighty." (Isaiah 13:6.) "Enter into the rock, and hide thee in the dust, for fear of the Lord, and for the glory of His majesty." (Isaiah 2:10.)
—*The Great Controversy,* pp. 637, 638.

DECEMBER 5

SECURE AT LAST

And that You should reward Your servants the prophets and the saints, and those who fear Your name, small and great.—Revelation 11:18.

Through a rift in the clouds there beams a star whose brilliancy is increased fourfold in contrast with the darkness. It speaks hope and joy to the faithful, but severity and wrath to the transgressors of God's law. Those who have sacrificed all for Christ are now secure, hidden as in the secret of the Lord's pavilion. They have been tested, and before the world and the despisers of truth they have evinced their fidelity to Him who died for them. A marvelous change has come over those who have held fast their integrity in the very face of death. They have been suddenly delivered from the dark and terrible tyranny of human beings transformed to demons. Their faces, so lately pale, anxious, and haggard, are now aglow with wonder, faith, and love. Their voices rise in triumphant song: "God is our refuge and strength, a very present help in trouble. Therefore will not we fear, though the earth be removed, and though the mountains be carried into the midst of the sea; though the waters thereof roar and be troubled, though the mountains shake with the swelling thereof." (Psalm 46:1–3.) . . .

The voice of God is heard from heaven, declaring the day and hour of Jesus' coming, and delivering the everlasting covenant to His people. Like peals of loudest thunder His words roll through the earth. The Israel of God stand listening, with their eyes fixed upward. Their countenances are lighted up with His glory, and shine as did the face of Moses when he came down from Sinai. The wicked cannot look upon them. And when the blessing is pronounced on those who have honored God by keeping His Sabbath holy, there is a mighty shout of victory.

Soon there appears in the east a small black cloud, about half the size of a man's hand. It is the cloud which surrounds the Saviour and which seems in the distance to be shrouded in darkness. The people of God know this to be the sign of the Son of man. In solemn silence they gaze upon it as it draws nearer the earth, becoming lighter and more glorious, until it is a great white cloud, its base a glory like consuming fire, and above it the rainbow of the covenant. Jesus rides forth as a mighty conqueror. Not now a "Man of Sorrows," to drink the bitter cup of shame and woe, He comes, victor in heaven and earth, to judge the living and the dead.—*The Great Controversy*, pp. 638–641.

December 6

God's Grace Is Sufficient

2016

God resists the proud, but gives grace to the humble.
—*James 4:6.*

The firmament seems filled with radiant forms—"ten thousand times ten thousand, and thousands of thousands." No human pen can portray the scene; no mortal mind is adequate to conceive its splendor. "His glory covered the heavens, and the earth was full of His praise. And His brightness was as the light." (Habakkuk 3:3, 4.) As the living cloud comes still nearer, every eye beholds the Prince of life. No crown of thorns now mars that sacred head; but a diadem of glory rests on His holy brow. His countenance outshines the dazzling brightness of the noonday sun. "And He hath on His vesture and on His thigh a name written, *King of kings, and Lord of lords.*" (Revelation 19:16.)

Before His presence "all faces are turned into paleness;" upon the rejecters of God's mercy falls the terror of eternal despair. "The heart melteth, and the knees smite together, . . . and the faces of them all gather blackness." (Jeremiah 30:6; Nahum 2:10.) The righteous cry with trembling: "Who shall be able to stand?" The angels' song is hushed, and there is a period of awful silence. Then the voice of Jesus is heard, saying: "My grace is sufficient for you." The faces of the righteous are lighted up, and joy fills every heart. And the angels strike a note higher and sing again as they draw still nearer to the earth.

The King of kings descends upon the cloud, wrapped in flaming fire. The heavens are rolled together as a scroll, the earth trembles before Him, and every mountain and island is moved out of its place. "Our God shall come, and shall not keep silence: a fire shall devour before Him, and it shall be very tempestuous round about Him. He shall call to the heavens from above, and to the earth, that He may judge His people." (Psalm 50:3, 4.) . . .

The derisive jests have ceased. Lying lips are hushed into silence. The clash of arms, the tumult of battle, "with confused noise, and garments rolled in blood" (Isaiah 9:5), is stilled. Nought now is heard but the voice of prayer and the sound of weeping and lamentation. The cry bursts forth from lips so lately scoffing: "The great day of His wrath is come; and who shall be able to stand?" The wicked pray to be buried beneath the rocks of the mountains rather than meet the face of Him whom they have despised and rejected. —*The Great Controversy,* pp. 641, 642.

DECEMBER 7 2016

THE SPECIAL RESURRECTION OF THE LOST

Hereafter you will see the Son of Man sitting at the right hand of the Power, and coming on the clouds of heaven.
—Matthew 26:64.

That voice which penetrates the ear of the dead, they know. How often have its plaintive, tender tones called them to repentance. How often has it been heard in the touching entreaties of a friend, a brother, a Redeemer. To the rejecters of His grace no other could be so full of condemnation, so burdened with denunciation, as that voice which has so long pleaded: "Turn ye, turn ye from your evil ways; for why will ye die?" (Ezekiel 33:11.) . . . That voice awakens memories which they would fain blot out—warnings despised, invitations refused, privileges slighted.

There are those who mocked Christ in His humiliation. With thrilling power come to their minds the Sufferer's words, when, adjured by the high priest, He solemnly declared: "Hereafter shall ye see the Son of man sitting on the right hand of power, and coming in the clouds of heaven." (Matthew 26:64.) Now they behold Him in His glory, and they are yet to see Him sitting on the right hand of power.

Those who derided His claim to be the Son of God are speechless now. There is the haughty Herod who jeered at His royal title and bade the mocking soldiers crown Him king. There are the very men who with impious hands placed upon His form the purple robe, upon His sacred brow the thorny crown, and in His unresisting hand the mimic scepter, and bowed before Him in blasphemous mockery. The men who smote and spit upon the Prince of life now turn from His piercing gaze and seek to flee from the overpowering glory of His presence. Those who drove the nails through His hands and feet, the soldier who pierced His side, behold these marks with terror and remorse.

With awful distinctness do priests and rulers recall the events of Calvary. With shuddering horror they remember how, wagging their heads in satanic exultation, they exclaimed: "He saved others; Himself He cannot save. If He be the King of Israel, let Him now come down from the cross, and we will believe Him. He trusted in God; let Him deliver Him now, if He will have Him." (Matthew 27:42, 43.)—*The Great Controversy,* pp. 642, 643.

December 8

The Destiny of the False Shepherds

Wail, shepherds, and cry! Roll about in the ashes, you leaders of the flock! For the days of your slaughter and your dispersions are fulfilled. —*Jeremiah 25:34.*

The minister who has sacrificed truth to gain human favor now discerns the character and influence of his teachings. It is apparent that the omniscient eye was following him as he stood in the desk, as he walked the streets, as he mingled with others in the various scenes of life. Every emotion of the soul, every line written, every word uttered, every act that led people to rest in a refuge of falsehood, has been scattering seed; and now, in the wretched, lost souls around him, he beholds the harvest. . . .

Ministers and people see that they have not sustained the right relation to God. They see that they have rebelled against the Author of all just and righteous law. The setting aside of the divine precepts gave rise to thousands of springs of evil, discord, hatred, iniquity, until the earth became one vast field of strife, one sink of corruption. This is the view that now appears to those who rejected truth and chose to cherish error. No language can express the longing which the disobedient and disloyal feel for that which they have lost forever—eternal life. Those whom the world has worshiped for their talents and eloquence now see these things in their true light. They realize what they have forfeited by transgression, and they fall at the feet of those whose fidelity they have despised and derided, and confess that God has loved them.

The people see that they have been deluded. They accuse one another of having led them to destruction; but all unite in heaping their bitterest condemnation upon the ministers. Unfaithful pastors have prophesied smooth things; they have led their hearers to make void the law of God and to persecute those who would keep it holy. Now, in their despair, these teachers confess before the world their work of deception. The multitudes are filled with fury. "We are lost!" they cry, "and you are the cause of our ruin;" and they turn upon the false shepherds. The very ones that once admired them most will pronounce the most dreadful curses upon them. The very hands that once crowned them with laurels will be raised for their destruction. The swords which were to slay God's people are now employed to destroy their enemies. Everywhere there is strife and bloodshed.—*The Great Controversy*, pp. 654–656.

December 9 2016

The Resurrection of the Righteous

For the Lord Himself will descend from heaven with a shout, with the voice of an archangel, and with the trumpet of God. And the dead in Christ will rise first.—1 Thessalonians 4:16.

Those who would have destroyed Christ and His faithful people now witness the glory which rests upon them. . . .

Amid the reeling of the earth, the flash of lightning, and the roar of thunder, the voice of the Son of God calls forth the sleeping saints. He looks upon the graves of the righteous, then, raising His hands to heaven, He cries: "Awake, awake, awake, ye that sleep in the dust, and arise!" Throughout the length and breadth of the earth the dead shall hear that voice, and they that hear shall live. And the whole earth shall ring with the tread of the exceeding great army of every nation, kindred, tongue, and people. From the prison house of death they come, clothed with immortal glory, crying: "O death, where is thy sting? O grave, where is thy victory?" (1 Corinthians 15:55.) And the living righteous and the risen saints unite their voices in a long, glad shout of victory.

All come forth from their graves the same in stature as when they entered the tomb. Adam, who stands among the risen throng, is of lofty height and majestic form, in stature but little below the Son of God. He presents a marked contrast to the people of later generations; in this one respect is shown the great degeneracy of the race. But all arise with the freshness and vigor of eternal youth. In the beginning, mankind was created in the likeness of God, not only in character, but in form and feature. Sin defaced and almost obliterated the divine image; but Christ came to restore that which had been lost. He will change our vile bodies and fashion them like unto His glorious body. The mortal, corruptible form, devoid of comeliness, once polluted with sin, becomes perfect, beautiful, and immortal. All blemishes and deformities are left in the grave. Restored to the tree of life in the long-lost Eden, the redeemed will "grow up" (Malachi 4:2) to the full stature of the race in its primeval glory. The last lingering traces of the curse of sin will be removed, and Christ's faithful ones will appear in "the beauty of the Lord our God," in mind and soul and body reflecting the perfect image of their Lord. Oh, wonderful redemption! long talked of, long hoped for, contemplated with eager anticipation, but never fully understood.—*The Great Controversy*, pp. 644, 645.

December 10

2016

The Translation of the Righteous Living

We who are alive and remain shall be caught up together with them in the clouds to meet the Lord in the air.
—1 Thessalonians 4:17.

The living righteous are changed "in a moment, in the twinkling of an eye." At the voice of God they were glorified; now they are made immortal and with the risen saints are caught up to meet their Lord in the air. Angels "gather together His elect from the four winds, from one end of heaven to the other." Little children are borne by holy angels to their mothers' arms. Friends long separated by death are united, nevermore to part, and with songs of gladness ascend together to the City of God.

On each side of the cloudy chariot are wings, and beneath it are living wheels; and as the chariot rolls upward, the wheels cry, "Holy," and the wings, as they move, cry, "Holy," and the retinue of angels cry, "Holy, holy, holy, Lord God Almighty." And the redeemed shout, "Alleluia!" as the chariot moves onward toward the New Jerusalem.

Before entering the City of God, the Saviour bestows upon His followers the emblems of victory and invests them with the insignia of their royal state. The glittering ranks are drawn up in the form of a hollow square about their King, whose form rises in majesty high above saint and angel, whose countenance beams upon them full of benignant love. Throughout the unnumbered host of the redeemed every glance is fixed upon Him, every eye beholds His glory whose "visage was so marred more than any man, and His form more than the sons of men." Upon the heads of the overcomers, Jesus with His own right hand places the crown of glory. For each there is a crown, bearing his own "new name" (Revelation 2:17), and the inscription, "Holiness to the Lord." In every hand are placed the victor's palm and the shining harp. Then, as the commanding angels strike the note, every hand sweeps the harp strings with skillful touch, awaking sweet music in rich, melodious strains. Rapture unutterable thrills every heart, and each voice is raised in grateful praise: "Unto Him that loved us, and washed us from our sins in His own blood, and hath made us kings and priests unto God and His Father; to Him be glory and dominion for ever and ever." (Revelation 1:5, 6.)—*The Great Controversy*, pp. 645, 646.

December 11, 2016

The Restoration of Adam

So all the days that Adam lived were nine hundred and thirty years; and he died.—Genesis 5:5.

As the ransomed ones are welcomed to the City of God, there rings out upon the air an exultant cry of adoration. The two Adams are about to meet. The Son of God is standing with outstretched arms to receive the father of our race—the being whom He created, who sinned against his Maker, and for whose sin the marks of the crucifixion are borne upon the Saviour's form. As Adam discerns the prints of the cruel nails, he does not fall upon the bosom of his Lord, but in humiliation casts himself at His feet, crying: "Worthy, worthy is the Lamb that was slain!" Tenderly the Saviour lifts him up and bids him look once more upon the Eden home from which he has so long been exiled.

After his expulsion from Eden, Adam's life on earth was filled with sorrow. Every dying leaf, every victim of sacrifice, every blight upon the fair face of nature, every stain upon mankind's purity, was a fresh reminder of his sin. Terrible was the agony of remorse as he beheld iniquity abounding, and, in answer to his warnings, met the reproaches cast upon himself as the cause of sin. With patient humility he bore, for nearly a thousand years, the penalty of transgression. Faithfully did he repent of his sin and trust in the merits of the promised Saviour, and he died in the hope of a resurrection. The Son of God redeemed humanity's failure and fall; and now, through the work of the atonement, Adam is reinstated in his first dominion.

Transported with joy, he beholds the trees that were once his delight—the very trees whose fruit he himself had gathered in the days of his innocence and joy. He sees the vines that his own hands have trained, the very flowers that he once loved to care for. His mind grasps the reality of the scene; he comprehends that this is indeed Eden restored, more lovely now than when he was banished from it. The Saviour leads him to the tree of life and plucks the glorious fruit and bids him eat. He looks about him and beholds a multitude of his family redeemed, standing in the Paradise of God. Then he casts his glittering crown at the feet of Jesus and, falling upon His breast, embraces the Redeemer. He touches the golden harp, and the vaults of heaven echo the triumphant song: "Worthy, worthy, worthy is the Lamb that was slain, and lives again!" The family of Adam take up the strain and cast their crowns at the Saviour's feet as they bow before Him in adoration.—*The Great Controversy,* pp. 647, 648.

DECEMBER 12

THE 144,000

Then I looked, and behold, a Lamb standing on Mount Zion, and with Him one hundred and forty-four thousand, having His Father's name written on their foreheads.—Revelation 14:1.

Upon the crystal sea before the throne, that sea of glass as it were mingled with fire—so resplendent is it with the glory of God—are gathered the company that have "gotten the victory over the beast, and over his image, and over his mark, and over the number of his name." With the Lamb upon Mount Zion, "having the harps of God," they stand, the hundred and forty and four thousand that were redeemed from among men; and there is heard, as the sound of many waters, and as the sound of a great thunder, "the voice of harpers harping with their harps." And they sing "a new song" before the throne, a song which no one can learn save the hundred and forty and four thousand. It is the song of Moses and the Lamb—a song of deliverance. None but the hundred and forty-four thousand can learn that song; for it is the song of their experience—an experience such as no other company have ever had. "These are they which follow the Lamb whithersoever He goeth." These, having been translated from the earth, from among the living, are counted as "the first fruits unto God and to the Lamb." (Revelation 15:2, 3; 14:1–5.) "These are they which came out of great tribulation;" they have passed through the time of trouble such as never was since there was a nation; they have endured the anguish of the time of Jacob's trouble; they have stood without an intercessor through the final outpouring of God's judgments. But they have been delivered, for they have "washed their robes, and made them white in the blood of the Lamb." "In their mouth was found no guile: for they are without fault" before God. "Therefore are they before the throne of God, and serve Him day and night in His temple: and He that sitteth on the throne shall dwell among them." They have seen the earth wasted with famine and pestilence, the sun having power to scorch the inhabitants with great heat, and they themselves have endured suffering, hunger, and thirst. But "they shall hunger no more, neither thirst any more; neither shall the sun light on them, nor any heat. For the Lamb which is in the midst of the throne shall feed them, and shall lead them unto living fountains of waters: and God shall wipe away all tears from their eyes." (Revelation 7:14–17.) . . .

By their own painful experience they learned the evil of sin, its power, its guilt, its woe; and they look upon it with abhorrence.—*The Great Controversy,* pp. 648–650.

December 13

The Joy of the Heirs of God

Great and marvelous are Your works, Lord God Almighty! Just and true are Your ways, O King of the saints!—Revelation 15:3.

The heirs of God have come from garrets, from hovels, from dungeons, from scaffolds, from mountains, from deserts, from the caves of the earth, from the caverns of the sea. On earth they were "destitute, afflicted, tormented." Millions went down to the grave loaded with infamy because they steadfastly refused to yield to the deceptive claims of Satan. By human tribunals they were adjudged the vilest of criminals. But now "God is judge Himself." (Psalm 50:6.) Now the decisions of earth are reversed. "The rebuke of His people shall He take away." (Isaiah 25:8.) "They shall call them, The holy people, The redeemed of the Lord." He hath appointed "to give unto them beauty for ashes, the oil of joy for mourning, the garment of praise for the spirit of heaviness." (Isaiah 62:12; 61:3.) They are no longer feeble, afflicted, scattered, and oppressed. Henceforth they are to be ever with the Lord. They stand before the throne clad in richer robes than the most honored of the earth have ever worn. They are crowned with diadems more glorious than were ever placed upon the brow of earthly monarchs. The days of pain and weeping are forever ended. The King of glory has wiped the tears from all faces; every cause of grief has been removed. Amid the waving of palm branches they pour forth a song of praise, clear, sweet, and harmonious; every voice takes up the strain, until the anthem swells through the vaults of heaven: "Salvation to our God which sitteth upon the throne, and unto the Lamb." And all the inhabitants of heaven respond in the ascription: "Amen: Blessing, and glory, and wisdom, and thanksgiving, and honor, and power, and might, be unto our God for ever and ever." (Revelation 7:10, 12.)

In this life we can only begin to understand the wonderful theme of redemption. With our finite comprehension we may consider most earnestly the shame and the glory, the life and the death, the justice and the mercy, that meet in the cross; yet with the utmost stretch of our mental powers we fail to grasp its full significance. The length and the breadth, the depth and the height, of redeeming love are but dimly comprehended.—*The Great Controversy,* pp. 650, 651.

December 14

A Study That Lasts Through Eternity

And this is eternal life, that they may know You, the only true God, and Jesus Christ whom You have sent.—John 17:3.

The plan of redemption will not be fully understood, even when the ransomed see as they are seen and know as they are known; but through the eternal ages new truth will continually unfold to the wondering and delighted mind. Though the griefs and pains and temptations of earth are ended and the cause removed, the people of God will ever have a distinct, intelligent knowledge of what their salvation has cost.

The cross of Christ will be the science and the song of the redeemed through all eternity. In Christ glorified they will behold Christ crucified. Never will it be forgotten that He whose power created and upheld the unnumbered worlds through the vast realms of space, the Beloved of God, the Majesty of heaven, He whom cherub and shining seraph delighted to adore—humbled Himself to uplift fallen humanity; that He bore the guilt and shame of sin, and the hiding of His Father's face, till the woes of a lost world broke His heart and crushed out His life on Calvary's cross. That the Maker of all worlds, the Arbiter of all destinies, should lay aside His glory and humiliate Himself from love to mankind will ever excite the wonder and adoration of the universe. As the nations of the saved look upon their Redeemer and behold the eternal glory of the Father shining in His countenance; as they behold His throne, which is from everlasting to everlasting, and know that His kingdom is to have no end, they break forth in rapturous song: "Worthy, worthy is the Lamb that was slain, and hath redeemed us to God by His own most precious blood!"

The mystery of the cross explains all other mysteries. In the light that streams from Calvary the attributes of God which had filled us with fear and awe appear beautiful and attractive. Mercy, tenderness, and parental love are seen to blend with holiness, justice, and power. While we behold the majesty of His throne, high and lifted up, we see His character in its gracious manifestations, and comprehend, as never before, the significance of that endearing title, "Our Father."

It will be seen that He who is infinite in wisdom could devise no plan for our salvation except the sacrifice of His Son. . . . The result of the Saviour's conflict with the powers of darkness is joy to the redeemed, redounding to the glory of God throughout eternity.—*The Great Controversy,* pp. 651, 652.

December 15

Angel Interventions Revealed

Are they not all ministering spirits sent forth to minister for those who will inherit salvation?
—*Hebrews 1:14.*

Then will be opened before us the course of the great conflict that had its birth before time began, and that ends only when time shall cease. The history of the inception of sin; of fatal falsehood in its crooked working; of truth that, swerving not from its own straight lines, has met and conquered error—all will be made manifest. The veil that interposes between the visible and the invisible world will be drawn aside, and wonderful things will be revealed.

Not until the providences of God are seen in the light of eternity shall we understand what we owe to the care and interposition of His angels. Celestial beings have taken an active part in human affairs. They have appeared in garments that shone as the lightning; they have come as men, in the garb of wayfarers. They have accepted the hospitalities of human homes; they have acted as guides to benighted travelers. They have thwarted the spoiler's purpose and turned aside the stroke of the destroyer.

Though the rulers of this world know it not, yet often in their councils angels have been spokesmen. Human eyes have looked upon them. Human ears have listened to their appeals. In the council hall and the court of justice, heavenly messengers have pleaded the cause of the persecuted and oppressed. They have defeated purposes and arrested evils that would have brought wrong and suffering to God's children. To the students in the heavenly school, all this will be unfolded.

Every redeemed one will understand the ministry of angels in his own life. The angel who was his guardian from his earliest moment; the angel who watched his steps, and covered his head in the day of peril; the angel who was with him in the valley of the shadow of death, who marked his resting place, who was the first to greet him in the resurrection morning—what will it be to hold converse with him, and to learn the history of divine interposition in the individual life, of heavenly cooperation in every work for humanity!

All the perplexities of life's experience will then be made plain. Where to us have appeared only confusion and disappointment, broken purposes and thwarted plans, will be seen a grand, overruling, victorious purpose, a divine harmony.—*Education,* pp. 304, 305.

Satan's Imprisonment

He laid hold of the dragon, that serpent of old, who is the Devil and Satan, and bound him for a thousand years.—Revelation 20:2.

The revelator foretells the banishment of Satan and the condition of chaos and desolation to which the earth is to be reduced, and he declares that this condition will exist for a thousand years. After presenting the scenes of the Lord's second coming and the destruction of the wicked, the prophecy continues: "I saw an angel come down from heaven, having the key of the bottomless pit and a great chain in his hand. And he laid hold on the dragon, that old serpent, which is the devil, and Satan, and bound him a thousand years, and cast him into the bottomless pit, and shut him up, and set a seal upon him, that he should deceive the nations no more, till the thousand years should be fulfilled: and after that he must be loosed a little season." (Revelation 20:1–3.)

That the expression "bottomless pit" represents the earth in a state of confusion and darkness is evident from other scriptures. . . .

Here is to be the home of Satan with his evil angels for a thousand years. Limited to the earth, he will not have access to other worlds to tempt and annoy those who have never fallen. It is in this sense that he is bound: there are none remaining, upon whom he can exercise his power. He is wholly cut off from the work of deception and ruin which for so many centuries has been his sole delight. . . .

For six thousand years, Satan's work of rebellion has "made the earth to tremble." He had "made the world as a wilderness, and destroyed the cities thereof." And he "opened not the house of his prisoners." For six thousand years his prison house has received God's people, and he would have held them captive forever; but Christ had broken his bonds and set the prisoners free. . . .

For a thousand years, Satan will wander to and fro in the desolate earth to behold the results of his rebellion against the law of God. During this time his sufferings are intense. Since his fall his life of unceasing activity has banished reflection; but he is now deprived of his power and left to contemplate the part which he has acted since first he rebelled against the government of heaven, and to look forward with trembling and terror to the dreadful future.—*The Great Controversy,* pp. 658–660.

December 17, 2016

Work of the Redeemed During the Millennium

And I saw thrones, and they sat on them, and judgment was committed to them.—Revelation 20:4.

To God's people the captivity of Satan will bring gladness and rejoicing. Says the prophet: "It shall come to pass in the day that Jehovah shall give thee rest from thy sorrow, and from thy trouble." (Isaiah 14:3, R.V.) . . .

During the thousand years between the first and the second resurrection the judgment of the wicked takes place. The apostle Paul points to this judgment as an event that follows the second advent. "Judge nothing before the time, until the Lord come, who both will bring to light the hidden things of darkness, and will make manifest the counsels of the hearts." (1 Corinthians 4:5.) Daniel declares that when the Ancient of Days came, "judgment was given to the saints of the Most High." (Daniel 7:22.) At this time the righteous reign as kings and priests unto God. John in the Revelation says: "I saw thrones, and they sat upon them, and judgment was given unto them." "They shall be priests of God and of Christ, and shall reign with Him a thousand years." (Revelation 20:4, 6.) It is at this time that, as foretold by Paul, "the saints shall judge the world." (1 Corinthians 6:2.) In union with Christ they judge the wicked, comparing their acts with the statute book, the Bible, and deciding every case according to the deeds done in the body. Then the portion which the wicked must suffer is meted out, according to their works; and it is recorded against their names in the book of death.

Satan also and evil angels are judged by Christ and His people. Says Paul: "Know ye not that we shall judge angels?" (Verse 3.) And Jude declares that "the angels which kept not their first estate, but left their own habitation, He hath reserved in everlasting chains under darkness unto the judgment of the great day." (Jude 6.)

At the close of the thousand years the second resurrection will take place. Then the wicked will be raised from the dead and appear before God for the execution of "the judgment written." Thus the revelator, after describing the resurrection of the righteous, says: "The rest of the dead lived not again until the thousand years were finished." (Revelation 20:5.) And Isaiah declares, concerning the wicked: "They shall be gathered together, as prisoners are gathered in the pit, and shall be shut up in the prison, and *after many days shall they be visited.*" (Isaiah 24:22.)—*The Great Controversy,* pp. 660, 661.

The Ranks of the Redeemed

Then I saw a great white throne and Him who sat on it,
from whose face the earth and the heaven fled away.
—*Revelation 20:11.*

At the close of the thousand years, Christ again returns to the earth. He is accompanied by the host of the redeemed and attended by a retinue of angels. As He descends in terrific majesty He bids the wicked dead arise to receive their doom. They come forth, a mighty host, numberless as the sands of the sea. What a contrast to those who were raised at the first resurrection! The righteous were clothed with immortal youth and beauty. The wicked bear the traces of disease and death. . . .

As the New Jerusalem, in its dazzling splendor, comes down out of heaven, it rests upon the place purified and made ready to receive it, and Christ, with His people and the angels, enters the Holy City. . . .

Now Christ again appears to the view of His enemies. Far above the city, upon a foundation of burnished gold, is a throne, high and lifted up. Upon this throne sits the Son of God, and around Him are the subjects of His kingdom. The power and majesty of Christ no language can describe, no pen portray. The glory of the Eternal Father is enshrouding His Son. The brightness of His presence fills the City of God, and flows out beyond the gates, flooding the whole earth with its radiance.

Nearest the throne are those who were once zealous in the cause of Satan, but who, plucked as brands from the burning, have followed their Saviour with deep, intense devotion. Next are those who perfected Christian characters in the midst of falsehood and infidelity, those who honored the law of God when the Christian world declared it void, and the millions, of all ages, who were martyred for their faith. And beyond is the "great multitude, which no man could number, of all nations, and kindreds, and people, and tongues, . . . before the throne, and before the Lamb, clothed with white robes, and palms in their hands." (Revelation 7:9.) Their warfare is ended, their victory won. They have run the race and reached the prize. The palm branch in their hands is a symbol of their triumph, the white robe an emblem of the spotless righteousness of Christ which now is theirs.—*The Great Controversy,* pp. 662, 663, 665.

December 19,

The Cleansing of the Earth

The devil, who deceived them, was cast into the lake of fire and brimstone where the beast and the false prophet are.—Revelation 20:10.

To our merciful God the act of punishment is a strange act. "As I live, saith the Lord God, I have no pleasure in the death of the wicked; but that the wicked turn from his way and live." Ezekiel 33:11. . . . While He does not delight in vengeance, He will execute judgment upon the transgressors of His law.—*Patriarchs and Prophets,* p. 628.

Fire comes down from God out of heaven. The earth is broken up. The weapons concealed in its depths are drawn forth. Devouring flames burst from every yawning chasm. The very rocks are on fire. The day has come that shall burn as an oven. The elements melt with fervent heat, the earth also, and the works that are therein are burned up. (Malachi 4:1; 2 Peter 3:10.) The earth's surface seems one molten mass—a vast, seething lake of fire. It is the time of the judgment and perdition of ungodly men. . . .

The wicked receive their recompense in the earth. (Proverbs 11:31.) They "shall be stubble: and the day that cometh shall burn them up, saith the Lord of hosts." (Malachi 4:1.) Some are destroyed as in a moment, while others suffer many days. All are punished "according to their deeds." The sins of the righteous having been transferred to Satan, he is made to suffer not only for his own rebellion, but for all the sins which he has caused God's people to commit. His punishment is to be far greater than that of those whom he has deceived. After all have perished who fell by his deceptions, he is still to live and suffer on. In the cleansing flames the wicked are at last destroyed, root and branch—Satan the root, his followers the branches. The full penalty of the law has been visited; the demands of justice have been met; and heaven and earth, beholding, declare the righteousness of Jehovah.

Satan's work of ruin is forever ended. For six thousand years he has wrought his will, filling the earth with woe and causing grief throughout the universe. The whole creation has groaned and travailed together in pain. Now God's creatures are forever delivered from his presence and temptations. . . .

While the earth was wrapped in the fire of destruction, the righteous abode safely in the Holy City. Upon those that had part in the first resurrection, the second death has no power. While God is to the wicked a consuming fire, He is to His people both a sun and a shield. (Revelation 20:6; Psalm 84:11.)—*The Great Controversy,* pp. 672, 673.

Eden Restored

Now I saw a new heaven and a new earth, for the first heaven and the first earth had passed away.
—Revelation 21:1.

The garden of Eden remained upon the earth long after man had become an outcast from its pleasant paths. The fallen race were long permitted to gaze upon the home of innocence, their entrance barred only by the watching angels. At the cherubim-guarded gate of Paradise the divine glory was revealed. Hither came Adam and his sons to worship God. Here they renewed their vows of obedience to that law the transgression of which had banished them from Eden. When the tide of iniquity overspread the world, and the wickedness of men and women determined their destruction by a flood of waters, the hand that had planted Eden withdrew it from the earth. But in the final restitution, when there shall be "a new heaven and a new earth" (Revelation 21:1), it is to be restored more gloriously adorned than at the beginning.

Then they that have kept God's commandments shall breathe in immortal vigor beneath the tree of life; and through unending ages the inhabitants of sinless worlds shall behold, in that garden of delight, a sample of the perfect work of God's creation, untouched by the curse of sin—a sample of what the whole earth would have become, had mankind but fulfilled the Creator's glorious plan. . . .

Pain cannot exist in the atmosphere of heaven. In the home of the redeemed there will be no tears, no funeral trains, no badges of mourning. "The inhabitant shall not say, I am sick: the people that dwell therein shall be forgiven their iniquity" (Isaiah 33:24). One rich tide of happiness will flow and deepen as eternity rolls on.

The time has come to which God's people have looked with longing since the flaming sword barred the first pair from Eden, the time for the "redemption of the purchased possession" (Ephesians 1:14). The earth originally given to mankind as their kingdom, betrayed by them into the hands of Satan, and so long held by the mighty foe, has been brought back by the great plan of redemption. All that was lost by sin has been restored. . . . God's original purpose in the creation of the earth is fulfilled as it is made the eternal abode of the redeemed.—*God's Amazing Grace,* pp. 360, 361.

December 21

Mansions for the Redeemed

In My Father's house are many mansions; if it were not so, I would have told you.—John 14:2.

Christ, by His sacrifice paying the penalty of sin, would not only redeem mankind, but recover the dominion which they had forfeited. All that was lost by the first Adam will be restored by the second. The prophet says, "O Tower of the flock, the stronghold of the daughter of Zion, to thee shall it come, even the first dominion." And Paul points forward to the "redemption of the purchased possession." God created the earth to be the abode of holy, happy beings. That purpose will be fulfilled when, renewed by the power of God, and freed from sin and sorrow, it shall become the eternal home of the redeemed.

A fear of making the future inheritance seem too material has led many to spiritualize away the very truths which lead us to look upon it as our home. Christ assured His disciples that He went to prepare mansions for them in the Father's house. Those who accept the teachings of God's Word will not be wholly ignorant concerning the heavenly abode. And yet "eye hath not seen, nor ear heard, neither have entered into the heart of man, the things which God hath prepared for them that love Him." Human language is inadequate to describe the reward of the righteous. It will be known only to those who behold it. No finite mind can comprehend the glory of the paradise of God.

In the Bible the inheritance of the saved is called a country. There the heavenly Shepherd leads His flock to fountains of living waters. The tree of life yields its fruit every month, and the leaves of the tree are for the service of the nations. There are ever-flowing streams, clear as crystal, and beside them waving trees cast their shadows upon the paths prepared for the ransomed of the Lord. There the wide-spreading plains swell into hills of beauty, and the mountains of God rear their lofty summits. On those peaceful plains, beside those living streams, God's people, so long pilgrims and wanderers, shall find a home. . . .

All the paternal love which has come down from generation to generation through the channel of human hearts, all the springs of tenderness which have opened in the souls of men and women, are but as a tiny rill to the boundless ocean, when compared with the infinite, exhaustless love of God.—*Review and Herald,* October 22, 1908.

A View of Other Worlds

He made the Pleiades and Orion; He turns the shadow of death into morning.—Amos 5:8.

Heaven is a good place. I long to be there and behold my lovely Jesus, who gave His life for me, and be changed into His glorious image. Oh, for language to express the glory of the bright world to come! I thirst for the living streams that make glad the city of our God.

The Lord has given me a view of other worlds. Wings were given me, and an angel attended me from the city to a place that was bright and glorious. The grass of the place was living green, and the birds there warbled a sweet song. The inhabitants of the place were of all sizes; they were noble, majestic, and lovely. They bore the express image of Jesus, and their countenances beamed with holy joy, expressive of the freedom and happiness of the place. I asked one of them why they were so much more lovely than those on the earth. The reply was, "We have lived in strict obedience to the commandments of God, and have not fallen by disobedience, like those on the earth." Then I saw two trees, one looked much like the tree of life in the city. The fruit of both looked beautiful, but of one they could not eat. They had power to eat of both, but were forbidden to eat of one. Then my attending angel said to me, "None in this place have tasted of the forbidden tree; but if they should eat, they would fall."

Then I was taken to a world which had seven moons. There I saw good old Enoch, who had been translated. On his right arm he bore a glorious palm, and on each leaf was written "Victory." Around his head was a dazzling white wreath, and leaves on the wreath, and in the middle of each leaf was written "Purity," and around the wreath were stones of various colors, that shone brighter than the stars, and cast a reflection upon the letters and magnified them. On the back part of his head was a bow that confined the wreath, and upon the bow was written "Holiness." Above the wreath was a lovely crown that shone brighter than the sun. I asked him if this was the place he was taken to from the earth. He said, "It is not; the city is my home, and I have come to visit this place." He moved about the place as if perfectly at home. I begged of my attending angel to let me remain in that place. I could not bear the thought of coming back to this dark world again. Then the angel said, "You must go back, and if you are faithful, you, with the 144,000, shall have the privilege of visiting all the worlds and viewing the handiwork of God."—*Early Writings*, pp. 39, 40.

December 23 2016

Heaven-Granted Opportunities

Open the gates, that the righteous nation which keeps the truth may enter in.—Isaiah 26:2.

There we shall know even as also we are known. There the loves and sympathies that God has planted in the soul will find truest and sweetest exercise. The pure communion with holy beings, the harmonious social life with the blessed angels and with the faithful ones of all ages, the sacred fellowship that binds together "the whole family in heaven and earth"—all are among the experiences of the hereafter.

There will be music there, and song, such music and song as, save in the visions of God, no mortal ear has heard or mind conceived. . . .

There every power will be developed, every capability increased. The grandest enterprises will be carried forward, the loftiest aspirations will be reached, the highest ambitions realized. And still there will arise new heights to surmount, new wonders to admire, new truths to comprehend, fresh objects to call forth the powers of body and mind and soul.

All the treasures of the universe will be open to the study of God's children. With unutterable delight we shall enter into the joy and the wisdom of unfallen beings. We shall share the treasures gained through ages upon ages spent in contemplation of God's handiwork. And the years of eternity, as they roll, will continue to bring more glorious revelations. "Exceeding abundantly above all that we ask or think" (Ephesians 3:20) will be, forever and forever, the impartation of the gifts of God.

"His servants shall serve Him." (Revelation 22:3.) The life on earth is the beginning of the life in heaven; education on earth is an initiation into the principles of heaven; the lifework here is a training for the lifework there. What we now are, in character and holy service, is the sure foreshadowing of what we shall be. . . .

In the plan of redemption there are heights and depths that eternity itself can never exhaust, marvels into which the angels desire to look. The redeemed only, of all created beings, have in their own experience known the actual conflict with sin; they have wrought with Christ, and, as even the angels could not do, have entered into the fellowship of His sufferings; will they have no testimony as to the science of redemption—nothing that will be of worth to unfallen beings?—*Education,* pp. 306–308.

December 24

Beyond the Power of Evil

Eye has not seen, nor ear heard, nor have entered into the heart of man the things which God has prepared for those who love Him.
—1 Corinthians 2:9.

Heaven is a school; its field of study, the universe; its teacher, the Infinite One. A branch of this school was established in Eden; and, the plan of redemption accomplished, education will again be taken up in the Eden school. . . .

Between the school established in Eden at the beginning and the school of the hereafter there lies the whole compass of this world's history—the history of human transgression and suffering, of divine sacrifice, and of victory over death and sin. Not all the conditions of that first school of Eden will be found in the school of the future life. No tree of knowledge of good and evil will afford opportunity for temptation. No tempter is there, no possibility of wrong. Every character has withstood the testing of evil, and none are longer susceptible to its power.

"To him that overcometh," Christ says, "will I give to eat of the tree of life, which is in the midst of the Paradise of God." (Revelation 2:7.) The giving of the tree of life in Eden was conditional, and it was finally withdrawn. But the gifts of the future life are absolute and eternal. . . .

There, when the veil that darkens our vision shall be removed, and our eyes shall behold that world of beauty of which we now catch glimpses through the microscope; when we look on the glories of the heavens, now scanned afar through the telescope; when, the blight of sin removed, the whole earth shall appear in "the beauty of the Lord our God," what a field will be open to our study! There the students of science may read the records of creation and discern no reminders of the law of evil. They may listen to the music of nature's voices and detect no note of wailing or undertone of sorrow. In all created things they may trace one handwriting—in the vast universe behold "God's name writ large," and not in earth or sea or sky one sign of ill remaining.

There shall be nothing to "hurt nor destroy in all My holy mountain, saith the Lord." (Isaiah 65:25.) There humanity will be restored to its lost kingship, and the lower order of beings will again recognize its sway; the fierce will become gentle, and the timid trustful.—*Education,* pp. 301–304.

, 2016

THE CROWN OF LIFE

Be faithful until death, and I will give you the crown of life.
—Revelation 2:10.

It is the waiting ones who are to be crowned with glory, honor, and immortality. You need not talk to me of the honors of the world, or the praise of its great ones. They are all vanity. Let but the finger of God touch them, and they would soon go back to dust again. I want honor that is lasting, honor that is immortal, honor that will never perish; a crown that is richer than any crown that ever decked the brow of a monarch.—*Review and Herald,* August 17, 1869.

I saw a very great number of angels bring from the city glorious crowns—a crown for every saint, with his or her name written thereon. As Jesus called for the crowns, angels presented them to Him, and with His own right hand, the lovely Jesus placed the crowns on the heads of the saints. In the same manner the angels brought the harps, and Jesus presented them also to the saints. The commanding angels first struck the note, and then every voice was raised in grateful, happy praise, and every hand skillfully swept over the strings of the harp, sending forth melodious music in rich and perfect strains. . . .

Within the city there was everything to feast the eye. Rich glory they beheld everywhere. Then Jesus looked upon His redeemed saints; their countenances were radiant with glory; and as He fixed His loving eyes upon them, He said, with His rich, musical voice, "I behold the travail of My soul, and am satisfied. This rich glory is yours to enjoy eternally. Your sorrows are ended. There shall be no more death, neither sorrow nor crying, neither shall there be any more pain." . . .

I then saw Jesus leading His people to the tree of life. . . . Upon the tree of life was most beautiful fruit, of which the saints could partake freely. In the city was a most glorious throne, from which proceeded a pure river of water of life, clear as crystal. On each side of this river was the tree of life, and on the banks of the river were other beautiful trees bearing fruit. . . .

Language is altogether too feeble to attempt a description of heaven. As the scene rises before me, I am lost in amazement. Carried away with the surpassing splendor and excellent glory, I lay down the pen, and exclaim, "Oh, what love! what wondrous love!" The most exalted language fails to describe the glory of heaven or the matchless depths of a Saviour's love.—*Early Writings,* pp. 288, 289.

2016

Red Borders

He who overcomes shall not be hurt by the second death.
—*Revelation 2:11.*

With Jesus at our head, we all descended from the city down to this earth, on a great and mighty mountain, which could not bear Jesus up, and it parted asunder, and there was a mighty plain. Then we looked up and saw the great city, with twelve foundations, and twelve gates, three on each side, and an angel at each gate. We all cried out: "The city, the great city, it's coming, it's coming down from God out of heaven," and it came and settled on the place where we stood. Then we began to look at the glorious things outside of the city. There I saw most beautiful houses, that had the appearance of silver, supported by four pillars set with pearls, most glorious to behold, which were to be inhabited by the saints, and in which was a golden shelf. I saw many of the saints go into the houses, take off their glittering crowns and lay them on the shelf, then go out into the field by the houses to do something with the earth; not as we have to do with the earth here; no, no. A glorious light shone all about their heads, and they were continually offering praise to God.

And I saw another field full of all kinds of flowers, and as I plucked them, I cried out: "They will never fade." Next I saw a field of tall grass, most glorious to behold; it was living green, and had a reflection of silver and gold, as it waved proudly to the glory of King Jesus. Then we entered a field full of all kinds of beasts—the lion, the lamb, the leopard, and the wolf, all together in perfect union. We passed through the midst of them, and they followed on peaceably after. Then we entered a wood, not like the dark woods we have here; no, no; but light, and all over glorious; the branches of the trees waved to and fro, and we all cried out: "We will dwell safely in the wilderness and sleep in the woods." We passed through the woods, for we were on our way to Mount Zion.

As we were traveling along, we met a company who were also gazing at the glories of the place. I noticed red as a border on their garments; their crowns were brilliant; their robes were pure white. As we greeted them, I asked Jesus who they were. He said they were martyrs that had been slain for Him. With them was an innumerable company of little ones; they had a hem of red on their garments also.—*Testimonies for the Church,* vol. 1, pp. 67–69.

December 27, 2016

Sharing Jesus' Glory

Father, I desire that they also whom You gave Me may be with Me where I am, that they may behold My glory which You have given Me.
—John 17:24.

The resurrection and ascension of our Lord is a sure evidence of the triumph of the saints of God over death and the grave, and a pledge that heaven is open to those who wash their robes of character and make them white in the blood of the Lamb. Jesus ascended to the Father as a representative of the human race, and God will bring those who reflect His image to behold and share with Him His glory.

There are homes for the pilgrims of earth. There are robes for the righteous, with crowns of glory and palms of victory. All that has perplexed us in the providences of God will in the world to come be made plain. The things hard to be understood will then find explanation. The mysteries of grace will unfold before us. Where our finite minds discovered only confusion and broken promises, we shall see the most perfect and beautiful harmony. We shall know that infinite love ordered the experiences that seemed most trying. As we realize the tender care of Him who makes all things work together for our good, we shall rejoice with joy unspeakable and full of glory. . . .

We are still amidst the shadows and turmoil of earthly activities. Let us consider most earnestly the blessed hereafter. Let our faith pierce through every cloud of darkness and behold Him who died for the sins of the world. He has opened the gates of paradise to all who receive and believe on Him. To them He gives power to become the sons and daughters of God. Let the afflictions which pain us so grievously become instructive lessons, teaching us to press forward toward the mark of the prize of our high calling in Christ. Let us be encouraged by the thought that the Lord is soon to come. Let this hope gladden our hearts. "Yet a little while, and He that shall come will come, and will not tarry." (Hebrews 10:37.) Blessed are those servants who, when their Lord comes, shall be found watching.

We are homeward bound. He who loved us so much as to die for us hath builded for us a city. The New Jerusalem is our place of rest. There will be no sadness in the city of God. No wail of sorrow, no dirge of crushed hopes and buried affections, will evermore be heard.—*Testimonies for the Church,* vol. 9, pp. 286, 287.

December 28

Songs to Be Sung

They sang as it were a new song before the throne, before the four living creatures, and the elders.
—Revelation 14:3.

He that is to come says, "Behold, I come quickly; and My reward is with Me, to give every man according as his work shall be." Every good deed done by the people of God as the fruit of their faith, will have its corresponding reward. As one star differeth from another star in glory, so will believers have their different spheres assigned them in the future life. . . .

And the next scene is recorded, "After these things . . . I heard as it were the voice of a great multitude, and as the voice of many waters, and as the voice of mighty thunderings, saying, Alleluia: for the Lord God Omnipotent reigneth." They sing the song of Moses and the song of the Lamb.

We must keep close to our great Leader, or we shall become bewildered, and lose sight of the Providence which presides over the church and the world, and over each individual. There will be profound mysteries in the divine dealings. We may lose the footsteps of God and follow our own bewilderment, and say, Thy judgments are not known; but if the heart is loyal to God everything will be made plain.

There is a day just about to burst upon us when God's mysteries will be seen, and all His ways vindicated; when justice, mercy, and love will be the attributes of His throne. When the earthly warfare is accomplished, and the saints are all gathered home, our first theme will be the song of Moses, the servant of God. The second theme will be the song of the Lamb, the song of grace and redemption. This song will be louder, loftier, and in sublimer strains, echoing and re-echoing through the heavenly courts. Thus the song of God's providence is sung, connecting the varying dispensations; for all is now seen without a veil between the legal, the prophetical, and the gospel. The church history upon the earth and the church redeemed in heaven all center around the cross of Calvary. This is the theme, this is the song—Christ all and in all—in anthems of praise resounding through heaven from thousands and ten thousand times ten thousand and an innumerable company of the redeemed host. All unite in this song of Moses and of the Lamb. It is a new song, for it was never before sung in heaven.—*Testimonies to Ministers,* pp. 428, 429, 432, 433.

December 29

Visions of Glory

Hold fast what you have, that no one may take your crown.
—Revelation 3:11.

If the church will put on the robe of Christ's righteousness, withdrawing from all allegiance with the world, there is before her the dawn of a bright and glorious day. God's promise to her will stand fast forever. He will make her an eternal excellency, a joy of many generations. Truth, passing by those who despise and reject it, will triumph. Although at times apparently retarded, its progress has never been checked. When the message of God meets with opposition, He gives it additional force, that it may exert greater influence. Endowed with divine energy, it will cut its way through the strongest barriers and triumph over every obstacle.

What sustained the Son of God during His life of toil and sacrifice? He saw the results of the travail of His soul and was satisfied. Looking into eternity, He beheld the happiness of those who through His humiliation had received pardon and everlasting life. His ear caught the shout of the redeemed. He heard the ransomed ones singing the song of Moses and the Lamb.

We may have a vision of the future, the blessedness of heaven. In the Bible are revealed visions of the future glory, scenes pictured by the hand of God, and these are dear to His church. By faith we may stand on the threshold of the eternal city, and hear the gracious welcome given to those who in this life cooperate with Christ, regarding it as an honor to suffer for His sake. As the words are spoken, "Come, ye blessed of My Father," they cast their crowns at the feet of the Redeemer, exclaiming, "Worthy is the Lamb that was slain to receive power, and riches, and wisdom, and strength, and honor, and glory, and blessing. . . . Honor, and glory, and power, be unto Him that sitteth upon the throne, and unto the Lamb for ever and ever." (Matthew 25:34; Revelation 5:12, 13.)

There the redeemed greet those who led them to the Saviour, and all unite in praising Him who died that human beings might have the life that measures with the life of God. The conflict is over. Tribulation and strife are at an end. Songs of victory fill all heaven as the ransomed ones take up the joyful strain, Worthy, worthy is the Lamb that was slain, and lives again, a triumphant conqueror.—*The Acts of the Apostles,* pp. 601, 602.

December 30

Heaven Begins in the Soul

You shall love the Lord *your God with all your heart, with all your soul, and with all your mind.—Matthew 22:37.*

Heaven begins in the soul, and as heavenly-mindedness increases, Christ is more and more appreciated, and finally becomes the Chiefest among ten thousand, the One altogether lovely. But as Satan is allowed to control the mind, his attributes become a part of the character of the one whom he controls, and sinners exercise themselves unto more and more ungodliness.

If we would see heaven, we must have heaven below. We must have a heaven to go to heaven in. We must have heaven in our families, through Christ continually approaching unto God. Christ is the great center of attraction, and the child of God hid in Christ, meets with God, and is lost in the divine being. Prayer is the life of the soul; it is feeding on Christ; it is turning our faces fully toward the Sun of Righteousness. As we turn our faces toward Him, He turns His face toward us. He longs to give us divine grace; and as we draw nigh to God with full assurance of faith, our spiritual conceptions are quickened. We do not then walk in blindness, bemoaning our spiritual barrenness; for by diligent, prayerful searching of the word of God, we apply His rich promises unto our souls. Angels draw close to our side, and the enemy with his manifold devices is driven back.

Prayer is the strength of the soul, and yet this exercise has been sadly neglected. By simple, earnest, contrite prayer, heavenly mindedness is greatly increased. No other means of grace can be substituted and healthiness of the soul be preserved. Prayer brings the soul into immediate contact with the wellspring of life, and strengthens the spiritual sinew and muscle of our religious experience; for we live by faith, seeing Him who is invisible. Neglect the exercise of prayer, or engage in prayer spasmodically, now and then, as it is deemed convenient, and you lose your connection with God. The Christian life becomes dry, and the spiritual faculties have no vitality. The religious experience lacks health and vigor. There is a growing tendency to substitute human writings and sayings for the word of God. . . .

It is the grace of God alone which can vitalize and refresh the soul. The precious sure word of prophecy reveals to those who are searchers for truth, the riches of the grace of Christ.—*Signs of the Times,* July 31, 1893.

2016

December 31

The Controversy Ended

The grace of our Lord Jesus Christ be with you all. Amen.
—Revelation 22:21.

The people of God are privileged to hold open communion with the Father and the Son. . . .

All the treasures of the universe will be open to the study of God's redeemed. Unfettered by mortality, they wing their tireless flight to worlds afar—worlds that thrilled with sorrow at the spectacle of human woe and rang with songs of gladness at the tidings of a ransomed soul. With unutterable delight the children of earth enter into the joy and the wisdom of unfallen beings. They share the treasures of knowledge and understanding gained through ages upon ages in contemplation of God's handiwork. With undimmed vision they gaze upon the glory of creation—suns and stars and systems, all in their appointed order circling the throne of Deity. Upon all things, from the least to the greatest, the Creator's name is written, and in all are the riches of His power displayed.

And the years of eternity, as they roll, will bring richer and still more glorious revelations of God and of Christ. As knowledge is progressive, so will love, reverence, and happiness increase. The more people learn of God, the greater will be their admiration of His character. As Jesus opens before them the riches of redemption and the amazing achievements in the great controversy with Satan, the hearts of the ransomed thrill with more fervent devotion, and with more rapturous joy they sweep the harps of gold; and ten thousand times ten thousand and thousands of thousands of voices unite to swell the mighty chorus of praise.

"And every creature which is in heaven, and on the earth, and under the earth, and such as are in the sea, and all that are in them, heard I saying, Blessing, and honor, and glory, and power, be unto Him that sitteth upon the throne, and unto the Lamb for ever and ever." (Revelation 5:13.)

The great controversy is ended. Sin and sinners are no more. The entire universe is clean. One pulse of harmony and gladness beats through the vast creation. From Him who created all, flow life and light and gladness, throughout the realms of illimitable space. From the minutest atom to the greatest world, all things, animate and inanimate, in their unshadowed beauty and perfect joy, declare that God is love.—*The Great Controversy,* pp. 676–678.